TRUST THE TRUTH

**A Symposium on the
Twentieth Anniversary of the
Encyclical *Humanae Vitae***

TRUST THE TRUTH

A Symposium on the
Twentieth Anniversary of the
Encyclical *Humanae Vitae*

Russell E. Smith
Editor

Sponsored by
The Roman Atheneum Foundation
and
The Aquinas Institute

On the Campus of
Princeton University

THE POPE JOHN CENTER

Nihil Obstat: Reverend James A. O'Donohoe, J.C.D.

Imprimatur: His Eminence   Date: August 21, 1991
            Bernard Cardinal Law

HQ
766.3
.S97
1988

The Nihil Obstat and Imprimatur are a declaration that a book or pamphlet is considered to be free from doctrinal or moral error. It is not implied that those who have granted the Nihil Obstat and Imprimatur agree with the contents, opinions or statements expressed.

Copyright 1991
by
The Pope John XXIII Medical-Moral
Research and Education Center
Braintree, Massachusetts 02184

Library of Congress Cataloging-in-Publication Data

Symposium on the Twentieth Anniversary of Encyclical Humanae
    Vitae (1988 : Princeton University)
    Trust the Truth : A Symposium on the Twentieth Anniversary
of the Encyclical Humanae Vitae / [Russell E. Smith, editor].
        p. 384   cm. xxiv
        ISBN 0-935372-30-X
        1. Birth control—Religious aspects—Catholic Church—
    Congresses.   2. Contraception—Religious aspects—Catholic
    Church—Congresses. Church. Pope (1963–1978 : Paul VI). Hu-
    manae vitae—Congresses. I. Smith, Russell E. (Russell Edward)
    II. Pope John XXIII Medical-Moral Research and Education
    Center. III. Title.
    HQ766.3.S97   1988
    241'.66—dc20   91–20331
                                                              CIP

Contents

The campus of Princeton University was the setting for a scholarly celebration of the twentieth anniversary of Pope Paul VI's encyclical *Humanae vitae*. The symposium took place from August 7 to 12, 1988. The organizers of the symposium, the Roman Atheneum Foundation* and the Aquinas Institute, took this occasion to review the Church's teaching on contraception from the perspective of many disciplines. The twenty-six speakers are experts in the fields of theology, philosophy, medicine, law, human behavior and communication.

The text of the proceedings includes introductory remarks by Fathers Charles B. Weiser and William H. Stetson of the Aquinas Institute and the Roman Atheneum Foundation, respectively. Edouard Cardinal Gagnon's preface is adapted from his sermon at the Solemn Mass which opened the symposium. The twenty-three chapters which follow compose the body of the week-long gathering. The postscript of these proceedings is provided by Joseph Cardinal Ratzinger. It is an address given during the nine hundredth anniversary celebration of the founding of the University of Bologna. It is included because of its relevance to this symposium's theme.

A special word of thanks goes to James. A. Kearns, Esq., for his indefatigable assistance in tracking down the not infrequently elusive manuscripts and overseeing the legal aspects of this project.

The Pope John Center is honored to publish these proceedings. In this volume one finds a comprehensive, inter-disciplinary study of the morality of contraception. In this way, we hope to provide a cogent *apologia* of the Church's teaching. In short, from the many lines of thought which converge on what the Church teaches regarding the inseparability of the unitive and procreative aspects of the conjugal act, we hope many readers will be enabled to trust the truth.

Father Russell E. Smith, S.T.D.
Editor

Feast of St. Patrick, 1991
Boston

---

*At the time the symposium was held, the legal name of the Roman Atheneum Foundation was the "Roman Academic Center Foundation."

Part One
The Reverend Charles B. Weiser
Past Director, The Aquinas Institute

The escutcheon of Princeton University is orange, because the people who founded the University were proud of being Orangemen and the descendants of Orangemen: they were a group of Congregationalist ministers who had become Presbyterian. They wanted to establish a place where people would be trained not just for ministry, as in some other institutions (such as one by the Charles River in Cambridge, Massachusetts, that will go unmentioned), but to go out into the world with the best of human knowledge and with the best of reflection on Christian truth. An openness to religious life marks the history of Princeton University down to today. When the chairman of the Board of Trustees introduced the new President of Princeton, who happens to be Jewish, he bothered to remark that one of the strengths of this man was that he was devout. The University supports chaplaincies more strongly than any other university of which I am aware, including Catholic universities. The Dean of the Chapel reports immediately to the President of the University and sits on the core committee group of the University. It is a place where the language that you will find in these proceedings is not strange. This, after all, is the place where Jacques Maritain taught, and I cannot think of the discussion contained in these pages without thinking of Paul Ramsey, a professor at Princeton who died a few months before the symposium was held. A non-Catholic, he was nonetheless a man who respected the language that we Roman Catholics use and who insisted that we not deny that language. He sometimes kept us very honest in a way that we might otherwise not have been.

It is also worth noting that Princeton is the northernmost of the Southern schools. If Christian charity is no longer so central to the vision of the University as it may once have been, a legacy of courtesy, at least, remains. Everyone from the University who was involved in the details of conducting the symposium was interested, courteous, and approachable. This is typical: I often saw the President of the University helping people to find their way around the campus, who had no idea who he was. In the 18 years that I was at Princeton, the number of times that I encountered rudeness could be counted on one hand.

So it is that Princeton was a place where it made sense to hold a scholarly symposium marking the twentieth anniversary of the issuance of the Encyclical *Humanae vitae:* the language has been used here before; the people are interested in the intellectual enterprise; religion is not something that has been shunted off to the side in the way that it has been in so many other places, although it is no longer so central as it once was.

The Aquinas Institute was established by the Catholic faculty at Princeton. The first two Catholic members of the faculty, Professors McCabe and Taylor, wanted the Catholic students at Princeton to be well cared for. They hired the first Catholic chaplain, a Dominican, out of their own pockets and saw to his support; the University provided the chaplain with a place to stay. When the second chaplain arrived, who was also the first Director of the Aquinas Institute, he was another Dominican who held a doctorate from Oxford. He wanted a place where there would be found both chaplaincy activity and intellectual vitality. There is now a tradition of that combination at this chaplaincy, where there are typically student priests or priests on sabbatical who are provided with room and board so that they can pursue their intellectual interests. Over a quarter of the underclassmen at Princeton are Roman Catholic, and this chaplaincy provides them with a wide variety of services; it is an integral part of the religious life of the campus, and it is a lively part of the community life on campus. In fact, in some years it has been the largest student organization at Princeton. Thus, co-sponsoring a symposium like this one is in line with what the chaplaincy is all about.

I have always been something of a traditional clergyman and wanted to be sure that the students knew what the Church teaches and that they understood it as well as they could at the point of life where they were and with the background that they had. However, during the three years prior to the symposium I had two former students come to me, each of whom had had a conversation with me while at Princeton, and each of whom was angry with me. One was an alumnus who was dying of AIDS, who remembered a conversation that we had, although I did not remember it so well as he did. He did not fault me for not telling him what the Church taught, or why, but he did fault me for the lack of vigor with which I presented it. The other was a woman who had been involved in the life of the chaplaincy, and again with whom I had had a conversation, and who likewise had left that conversation knowing what the Church taught, and why. Now, as a result of venereal disease, she is barren. She was angry with me, not because of my lack of clarity in that conversation, but because of my lack of fire.

I think, therefore, that the discussion which you will find in these proceedings is a valuable one to have occurred in a place where young people wrestle with their identities, and where adults think carefully and argue rigorously, at least most of the time. In these pages you will find the teaching of the Church presented with fire and vigor, and I hope that the University at which the symposium took place caught a bit of this conversation.

Part Two
The Very Reverend William H. Stetson
President, The Roman Atheneum Foundation

The Roman Atheneum Foundation was established to support from the United States the programs and work of the Roman Academic Center of the Holy Cross, now the Roman Atheneum of the Holy Cross. One way of accomplishing this goal is to offer in the United States programs such as this symposium marking the twentieth anniversary of the issuance of the Encyclical *Humanae vitae*. Programs such as these reflect the academic excellence of the Atheneum, a center for higher studies in ecclesiastical sciences comprising the faculties of Theology and Philosophy, as well as the Rome section of the faculty of Canon Law of the University of Navarre in Spain.

The Roman Atheneum is the fulfillment of one of the dreams of the founder of the Prelature of the Holy Cross and Opus Dei, the Venerable Josemaría Escrivá de Balaguer. Monsignor Escrivá did not live to see this dream fulfilled. The realization of the project of the Roman Atheneum fell to Monsignor Alvaro del Portillo, the longtime collaborator of Monsignor Escrivá and his successor as the head of Opus Dei.

There is an element of history which I had the good fortune to experience first-hand in connection with these centers of ecclesiastical studies. In the spring of 1959 I was present at a gathering in Rome when Monsignor Escrivá mentioned for the first time his desire of founding such institutions. He told us that in the fall of that year, 1959, a faculty of Canon Law would start at the University of Navarre, which he had founded in 1951. A few days later, he asked me if I would like to take part in this new undertaking as a member of the faculty. I gladly accepted his invitation, and was there for five years as a professor of Canon Law.

One of Monsignor Escrivá's oft-repeated expressions was, "Dream, and you will fall short." The growth of the ecclesiastical faculties at the University of Navarre over 25 years prepared the way for the Roman Atheneum and, by extension, for its associated Foundation here in the United States and this symposium. God does indeed work miracles, but he counts on our hard work, our cooperation, and the passage of time.

I recall another conversation that I had with Monsignor Escrivá at that time, which has a direct bearing on this symposium. He spoke to me about the importance of what is commonly referred to as the "natural law", as a foundation for the study of both civil and canon law and, in general, about the importance of a reasoned approach to ethical and legal studies in order to achieve the widest possible consensus on the truth about man. In its orientation and in the variety of the backgrounds of its participants, this symposium is fully in accord with this vision of Monsignor Escrivá. The initial prospectus for the symposium said that the conference would "aim to reflect the confidence expressed by Paul VI and John Paul II that moral truth on human sexuality is not only accessible to man, but has the inherent power to attract him at the level of his own nature; that the truth not only can speak to man, but can do so convincingly, showing itself to be ultimately for his own benefit."

The dreams of the founder of Opus Dei were always to provide a more effective service to the Church and her teaching, and to man and his human dignity. It has been a source of great joy for me to have seen these dreams become more and more a reality, not only in Rome and in Spain and in many other parts of the world, but also during the symposium in Princeton.

The task of all of us who took part in the symposium was to work together for the defense of the truth about man, human sexuality, marriage, and the family, and to prepare ourselves to teach this truth in all of its human and reasoned intelligibility, with greater conviction on our own part, and with greater effectiveness in our presentation of it to others. It is my hope that the proceedings of the symposium will serve not only as a reminder to those of us who were there of the work that we did, but also as a resource for the many others who were not present, in order that they, too, might reap the abundant fruits of what transpired during those days.

Special thanks are due to Bishop John Reiss, the bishop of the Diocese of Trenton, for giving his blessing to the idea of the symposium when it was first proposed to him. Thanks are due as well to Father Charles Weiser, the immediate past Director of The Aquinas Institute at Princeton, and to Father Vincent Keane, the current Director, for their generous cooperation and support.

July 15, 1988

Prot. no. 221.964

Dear Bishop Reiss,

The Holy Father was pleased to learn of the Symposium on the Twentieth Anniversary of the Encyclical *Humane vitae* which will be held at Princeton University, and he has asked me to convey the assurance of his pastoral interest and prayerful good wishes.

On numerous occasions, His Holiness has reaffirmed and more fully elaborated the truths contained in this famous document of his beloved predecessor. Recently to the participants in the Fourth International Conference for the Family of Europe and of Africa, he described the Encyclical as "a teaching which belongs to the permanent patrimony of the Church's moral doctrine. The uninterrupted continuity with which the Church has taught it derives from her responsibility for the true good of the human person, of the human person of the spouses, first of all, for conjugal love is their most precious good" (March 14, 1988).

At a time when the Church feels called to make extraordinary efforts to defend the dignity and truth of conjugal love, the Holy Father willingly offers his encouragement and support to the participants in this Symposium. He is confident that they will derive from it greater understanding and fresh enthusiasm so as to continue their individual and collective efforts on behalf of life and love, in the service of the truth.

Upon all those taking part in the Symposium and upon their loved ones, His Holiness invokes grace and peace in our Lord Jesus Christ and cordially imparts to them his Apostolic Blessing.

With personal good wishes, I remain

Sincerely yours in Christ,

Agostino Card. Casaroli

Secretary of State

The Most Reverend John C. Reiss
Bishop of Trenton
Chancery Office
701 Lawrenceville Rd.
P.O. Box 5309
Trenton, NJ 08638

His Eminence, Edouard Cardinal Gagnon
President, Pontifical Council for the Family

This volume presents the proceedings of the symposium, "Trust the Truth," sponsored by The Roman Atheneum Foundation and The Aquinas Institute at Princeton University in the summer of 1988, to commemorate the twentieth anniversary of the Encyclical *Humanae vitae*. It seems to me especially fitting that the first full day of the symposium was held on August 8th, the feast of Saint Dominic. The Latin text for the Opening Prayer in the Mass for this feast could be translated, "Lord, let the merits and the teaching of Saint Dominic be a help for us; we rely on his help because he was an outstanding preacher of your truth." Saint Dominic is a great model for us, and is a powerful intercessor in obtaining for us the graces of enlightenment and courage, which are necessary not only to find the truth, but also to present it simply and with conviction.

If we reflect upon the life of Saint Dominic, we find that what brought him to his own search for the truth, and to the special vocation for himself and the members of the family of preachers that he founded, was, first, his love for the children of God and, second, his realization of how the ignorance of God's revealed truth leads people to moral disorder in their personal lives and in their relationships with others. He was a canon in his diocese, as well as a teacher with impressive academic credentials.

At the same time, he was a man of kindness, of prayer, and of virtue, so that people came to him for spiritual guidance, and told him what they thought about the condition of the world in which they lived. This prompted him to leave his comfortable ecclesiastical and academic situation, in order to become an itinerant preacher. From a position of economic security and social standing, he became one of the poor. The order that he founded was one of the mendicant orders, whose members lived only on the alms of others.

His preaching was often greeted with ridicule, derision, and even open hostility, because what he preached was disturbing: he told people that they were not living according to God's plan. He preached this disturbing message because his love of God convinced him that God's will and commands were acts of love on the part of God, who has made us and who knows better than we do what will bring us happiness and what will help us to find our own perfection.

We often worry about what is going wrong in our society today, about the immorality that is rampant and seems to be growing; we worry when we see the confusion of ideas that exists. But we must remember that when Christ sent his Apostles to evangelize, the situation was no better than ours is today, as the writings of Saint Paul so amply attest. So also, when Saint Dominic started his movement of preaching and of teaching the Gospel to the people of his time, the poor and the humble as well as the learned, the situation was hardly better than it is now.

The destiny of Christianity is to renew the work of evangelization in every generation. The problem for us who have been raised in strong Catholic communities is that we have been led to believe that the truth is transmitted almost automatically from one generation to the other. When our parents went to school they learned to transmit the truth to their children through the institution of the family. I have taught theology for 30 years, and I have never met a better theologian than my mother, because when my mother went to school, everything that she learned in the domain of faith or of culture was taught to her so that she would transmit it to her children. When I went to school, on the other hand, while we had all kinds of organizations in the parish, and good schools run by religious brothers, I was never once told that what I was learning I had to transmit to my children. I learned that from my mother. What we were told by the educators in our generation in effect was, "Send us your children; we will educate them; we will teach them the faith, and culture, and how to live decent and productive lives." We were not told that we ourselves had the responsibility of transmitting this truth.

This is one of the reasons why we have come to the present situation. The schools became so large and so impersonal that they could no longer do what they had done when I was a student. They could no longer substitute for the parents, but they continued to insist on trying to do so. This is one of the causes of the "generation gap" and of the demise of the family. Others have tried to take over the responsibility of the family. Thus, we have a very difficult task before us: to make families conscious again of their responsibility, to make them aware that parents who love their children are the best teachers, even if they are not so learned as others. Even the most ignorant of parents are better educators of their children than anybody else, because they love them.

It is difficult to make this understood today. Whenever I speak about the responsibilities and the mission of the family, the first reaction that I often get is that the family is not equipped for this task. In his Apostolic Exhortation, *Familiaris consortio*, however, the Holy Father teaches us that the family is equipped with more than what any academic credential can confer; the sacrament of Matrimony gives the family a special mission and ability to transmit the faith and social virtues.

Why could Saint Dominic give himself so completely to the teaching of the truth? Why did he understand that it is only by accepting the truth that people can find the way to happiness and the way to temporal and eternal salvation? When we examine the life of Saint Dominic, we see that, in order to be able to find the truth and to transmit it, three conditions are necessary. The first requirement is purity of heart. Only if we ask for the grace of God to free us of sin can we find the truth. Saint Thomas Aquinas taught this very often in his writings on the intellectual life. If we are not pure of heart, we do not care for the things of God, we do not understand that the most important thing is the glory of God, and that the glory of God alone should be the motive for the life of all his children.

Whenever I go to a parish to confer Confirmation, I try to meet with the children beforehand, and I explain to them the Sacrament of Confirmation, starting with the last conversation of Jesus with his Apostles on Holy Thursday, when he told them, "If you love me, you will keep my words, and if you keep my words, my Father also will love you. My Father and I will come and will give you the Holy Spirit, who will console you for my absence, for my leaving you, because he will live in you. He will be your teacher; he will be your consoler; he will be your advocate." I ask the children if they know some of these words of Jesus, which he said that we must keep, and all too often I receive only one answer, "You must love." I then ask if Jesus did not first say, "Our Father, who art in heaven, hallowed be thy name; thy kingdom come; thy will be done"? Usually the children answer that this is a prayer called the "Our Father," but they do not recognize them as the words of Jesus. All the rest is useless, however, and cannot be understood, if we do not start by saying, "Our Father, thy kingdom come; thy will be done."

We can arrive at looking at things from that point of view only if our hearts are pure, only if our God is the true God, and not pleasure, power, or intellectual pride. This is the first condition to finding the truth and transmitting it. If we understand who God is, and why he sent his Son, then we understand that Christ died for our sins. We must be pure in order to understand the God who cared so much for us that he would he send his Son to die for our redemption, for the reparation of our sins. There is no way to understand who God is, and what the plan of God is, unless we worry about sin, unless we detest sin, unless we try to get sin out of our lives, with humility and counting on the grace of God.

This is one of the characteristics of the life of Saint Dominic. People came to him because, in a period of great corruption, even—and maybe mostly—among the leaders in the Church, he was pure. This attracted people to him. Because of the purity of his heart, they knew that he was faithful to God and could communicate to them the real knowledge of God.

xxii

The second condition that made Saint Dominic able to preach the truth was his readiness to become poor, his readiness to free himself from everything that would limit his freedom to see and to teach the truth. Being poor in the material sense, however, is just one aspect of true poverty. It is even more difficult to be poor in the spiritual sense, to be free from our love for prestige, from our concern for our reputation. Much of the dissent from *Humanae vitae* was founded, not on genuine theological reasoning, but on personal pride on the part of many people and their incapacity to recognize their mistake and to accept the truth as it was taught by the Holy Father. If Saint Dominic had not abandoned everything that he had, his position of prestige, his hometown, and his friends, to go and preach the Gospel, he would not have been the great apostle that he was, one of those who transformed society at that time, much like his contemporary, Saint Francis. God does not ask from us the same material or visible detachment, but if we want to be faithful to the truth and to be convincing in transmitting the truth, we also must accept a spiritual poverty like that of Saint Dominic.

The third condition for Saint Dominic's effectiveness was his humility in knowing that he could not do it alone, that he needed others to work with him, that he did not have a monopoly on the truth. He went and found others who also loved God and who knew that happiness is found in the word of God. In order to bring happiness to the people who were suffering from all sides, they had to be united and to give an example of unity in their faith and in their teaching. Humility such as this is also one of the vital necessities if we are to find the truth.

Because Saint Dominic insisted on these three qualities—his purity of heart, which manifested his love for God; his poverty, which meant that he was ready to leave everything to follow the path that God traced out for him; and his humility, which led him to look for collaborators—the family that he founded would eventually give us Saint Thomas Aquinas, one of the great gifts of God to his Church. Because Saint Dominic understood that pastoral work, true love for people, must start with teaching them the truth, he gave his disciples the desire to know and to teach the truth, which provoked the vocation of such men as Saint Thomas Aquinas.

Some years ago Josef Pieper wrote a book, *The Silence of Saint Thomas*, in which he explained how the virtues that we have found in Saint Dominic are to found also in Saint Thomas. I have taught the *Summa theologica* for more than 20 years, and I have always been astonished at the humility of Saint Thomas. He did his best to show that others had taught the same things before him. Even when he dealt with the objections of others, he did so with respect, trying to understand what they were saying. His love for the truth made him considerate of others.

What a contrast to what we have seen in the years following the Second Vatican Council! I remained in Rome between the last two sessions of the Council, to work on the conciliar documents. Whenever I had a few hours, I would go to one or another of the pontifical universities and listen to the teachers who were then in vogue. I calculated that in a class period of 45 minutes, it was not uncommon for some of these teachers to spend 40 minutes in saying that everything that had been taught before was wrong, that it was now they who had the truth. I have observed this phenomenon afterwards, too. I have heard it said by some that all of the books written before the Council should be burnt, as if they thought that the Council would have been possible without the theological literature that had been produced up to that time. This lack of humility on the part of so many in presenting the doctrine of Vatican II, instead of showing how Vatican II was really presenting the traditional doctrine of the Church, was the reason why many people abandoned the Church or founded movements which are now having difficulty in finding their way back into the mainstream of the Church.

Purity of heart, poverty of spirit, and humility are all required if we are to find the truth, to adhere to the truth, and to be able to change our minds when the Church teaches us in a clear way. Let us ask Saint Dominic to help us to grow in those virtues, not so much that we may obtain the truth for ourselves, but so that by transmitting it we may bring back to God many of his children.

Princeton, August 8, 1988
Feast of St. Dominic

Chapter 1

KEYNOTE ADDRESS
HUMANAE VITAE: GOING "BACK TO THE FUTURE"

Bernard N. Nathanson

To me, the Encyclical *Humanae vitae* by Pope Paul VI is curiously and eerily prophetic, with its emphasis on the two meanings of the conjugal act, the unitive and the procreative; its absolute proscription on the act of abortion; its prediction of the grave consequences of the methods for artificial birth control, such as infidelity and a general decline in morality; and its warning that such technology is a dangerous weapon when placed in the hands of public authorities who take no heed of moral exigencies. It cautions physicians and medical personnel to practice their profession by faith and right reason. Finally, and this is very important with respect to men and women of science, there is this cautionary: do not allow the morality of your peoples to be degraded; do not permit that, by legal means, practices contrary to the natural and divine law be introduced.

I am struck by the parallels between *Humanae vitae* and another document, written 2500 years ago by a man named Hippocrates, which reads in part:

> I swear . . . that according to my ability and judgment I will keep this oath and this stipulation. . . . I will follow that system of regimen which according to my ability and judgment I consider to the benefit of my patients and abstain from whatever is deleterious and mischievous. I will give no deadly medicine to anyone if asked, nor suggest any such counsel. In like manner, I will not give to a woman a recipe to produce abortion.

I took this oath, as my father did before me, on the quadrangle at McGill University. I took it in June, 1949; my father took it in 1919. Several years ago, I was asked to attend the commencement exercises of the graduating class of a medical school in New York City. My father had been given the oath to read to the students, and found that it had been "sanitized": there was no mention of "deadly medicine" and the cautionary about abortion had been stricken.

As a practicing obstetrician and gynecologist, I am going to take you "back to the future" in obstetrics and gynecology. Let me begin by referring to the 1968 edition of the *Yearbook of Obstetrics and Gynecology,* an annual compilation of articles in those fields drawn from the medical literature all over the world. In the *Yearbook* for 1968, the same year in which *Humanae vitae* was issued, we find, among the other articles that are summarized, a great number of articles on deaths from birth control pills, a number of articles on new ovulating agents, and so on. In the beginning of the *Yearbook,* however, we find the stirrings of what has become a pell-mell ride down a long, slimy slope. In the summary of the presidential address, we read:

Physicians must understand that a woman who seeks abortion is doing so because pregnancy places her in an untenable social, economic, or psychological position. He must encourage the expansion of public and private and facilities to provide contraceptive advice for sexually active females, and the physician must become a leader in the campaign to modernize our outmoded abortion laws.

Such are the first, embryonic stirrings of what we have now, which Richard Cohen has described as the "administrative massacre" of 20 million lives over the past 15 years.

As you may know, I was, in fact, a founder of the National Abortion Rights Action League in 1968. In 1970, I became Director of the Center for Reproductive and Sexual Health, the largest abortion clinic in the world, where in my tenure we did 60,000 abortions, 120 a day for two years. In 1973 I became Chief of the Obstetrical Service of St. Luke's Hospital in New York City, which is part of the Columbia University College of Physicians and Surgeons, and I began carrying on research there in fetology. Over the next several years, I changed my mind on the subject of abortion, to such an extent that in 1979 I published a book called *Aborting America* in which I took a clearly pro-life stand.

In the ten years since I have had a crystallization of my views on abortion, I have heard a great many exegeses on the philosophy of the pro-life position, and I am confident that the theologians and philosophers will continue to articulate this position with eloquence and erudition. For my own part, however, I have found the core content of the pro-life position articulated in a way that most closely corresponds to my own position by Joan Andrews, the woman who is renowned for her heroism in the face of the abominable treatment that she received at the hands of the judicial and penal systems of the state of Florida. There is a volume of her letters published, called *You Reject Them, You Reject Me,* and in one of those letters she says:

The closer we are to the preborn children, the more faithful we are, and the more identically aligned with them we become. This is our aim and goal: to wipe out

3

the line of distinction between the preborn and their born friends, becoming ourselves discriminated against. Good! This is necessary. Why should we be treated any differently? The rougher it gets for us, the more we can rejoice that we are succeeding. No longer are we being treated so much as the privileged born, but as the discriminated against preborn. We must become aligned with them completely and totally, or else the double standard separating the preborn from the rest of humanity will never be eliminated. I don't want to be treated any differently than my brother or sister; you reject them, you reject me.

We do not expect justice in the courts. Furthermore, we do not seek it for ourselves when it is being denied our beloved preborn brothers and sisters. Thus I plead a case for complete and total vulnerability in court by refusing self-defense and all legal argumentation for self-protection. We should in truth tell the court that we as defenders and friends of the preborn expect no justice and no compassion as the true defendants, the preborn children, received none and were killed without due process on the day of the rescue attempt. We only stand here in their stead, being substitute defendants by a compelling and a painful logic. They died for the crimes of being preborn and unwanted. We expect no justice from a judicial system which allows that, which decrees such savagery, and from a government which sets its seal of approval upon it. If it is a crime punishable by death to be unwanted, maybe it should be a crime punishable by death to love the unwanted and to act to protect them.

As the result of an Operation Rescue at a Florida abortion clinic, Joan was convicted in 1985 of third-degree burglary, of resisting arrest, and of the destruction of equipment. In September, 1986, she was sentenced by Judge Anderson in a Pensacola courtroom to five years in solitary confinement at the Broward Correctional Institution, a maximum-security prison in Florida outside of Fort Lauderdale. Judge Anderson, several hours later on that same day, and in that same courtroom, sentenced two men who had been accomplices to first-degree murder to four years of imprisonment each, with possibility of parole in two years. While in solitary confinement in the Broward Correctional Institution, she rejected any measure of comfort, security, health, or sustenance from that prison system, which she said served this savage machine. She slept on concrete floors without a blanket; she took only the barest minimum of food; she even rejected the false eye that the prison gave her—she had had an eye removed for cancer in 1980—and smashed it. She was not allowed to attend Mass, even though she is a devout Roman Catholic.

Nat Hentoff, a columnist in the *Village Voice*, recently took note of her plight and wrote a column in *The Washington Post*, dated July 16, 1988, in which he observed the following:

> As punishment, Joan Andrews has spent much of her prison term so far in solitary confinement. She is a practicing Catholic, but she is not allowed to leave her cell to attend Mass. A priest, however, is permitted to visit her and offer Communion. An official of the Florida Department of Correction explained that permission to go to Mass has been denied because of her "disciplinary status," but added that she is "allowed to pray." The State of Florida is not without mercy. . . . Recently, I spoke to Charles Oberly, Attorney General of the State of Delaware, where Andrews had been incarcerated for several months, being transferred from Florida to be near her family. First, Oberly made a point of identifying himself as pro-choice. Oberly then went on to say that, as a long-time prosecutor, he believed that the original sentence given to Andrews was "absurd." "She is not a bomber," he said. "Since the sentencing," he added, "Florida has been trying to break her; for instance, solitary confinement for months at a time, and probably unconstitutional denial of her right to go to Mass. She is no danger to the system: she won't escape; she won't hurt anyone. In Delaware, we don't treat our most hardened criminals that way." Yet a Florida official said of her,

"she is going to play by our rules, or else." Joan Andrews has not yet been broken by the State of Florida. Her tentative release date is not until October, 1991. So, the State of Florida still has time to show its mettle.

It is unquestionable that the unitive and procreative aspects of marriage were dealt a sundering blow by the advent of oral contraception and artificial means of birth control. Ultimately, of course, abortion was the final stroke. I want to take that cleavage a little further down the road, if you will. To begin with, the unitive aspects of marriage were being assaulted by a variety of forces: social chaos, in the form of loosened divorce laws, pornography, the sexual revolution, the generally affluent society, television, and alluring sexual images in promotion of commercial products, the increasingly intrusive role of government in family life, the predictable onslaught of drugs and other anodynes acting to provide some analgesia for the wounded spirit of our time.

But there is another cleavage, one that has taken place in the procreative side of that former unity, a cleavage in the act of procreativity. Abortion has become institutionalized: this is the fifteenth year of *Roe;* we have had 20 million victims; whole generations of medical students, nurses, and other health care providers have grown up with abortion taken as much for granted as penicillin. It will be extremely difficult to rip abortion out of the fabric of our society. But with that institutionalization, the bioengineers were emboldened to split off the act of procreativity from the results of procreativity. In other words, "Who needs you anyway? We need only your organs."

As a result, we now have *in vitro* fertilization and its array of corollary, death-dealing beneficences, such as selective feticide. In *in vitro* fertilization, there are more human beings created in the test tube than are actually needed. For every *in vitro* fertilization the desideratum is to have at least four human beings, zygotes, embryos, implanted into the uterus, because the calculation is that probably two or three will not "take." In point of fact, in some instances, all four take, and the mother, or woman bearing the pregnancy, then comes to the doctor and says, "Doctor, I

6

wanted to be pregnant, but four! No! What do we do now?"
"Well," he says, "selective feticide, of course."

Before there is ever an social or biological engineering there has to be verbal engineering. We call it "selective feticide"; it is a wonderful euphemism. What it means in essence is: put the woman in front of the ultrasound machine, locate each pregnancy under this real-time ultrasound, take a long spinal needle attached to a 10 cc. syringe, pierce the heart, under ultrasound, of each of these unwanted embryos, and either wiggle the needle around and destroy the heart, or inject some air or potassium solution into the heart, and you have "selective feticide".

We also now have the "cryo-preservation" of embryos and a flourishing business now in embryo "banks"—frozen embryos. You know that such things exist. What you may not know is that there is an enormous amount of research going on in "flash freezing". The lead article in the May, 1988 issue of the journal *Fertility and Sterility* is entitled, "Modern Trends: Cryo-Preservation of Embryos and Ova," and it describes new methods of flash-freezing human beings. There are no laws or regulations in this technology, save in Sweden and several states in Australia. These practice of *in vitro* fertilization, cryopreservation, flash-freezing, and all the rest are absolutely unregulated by law in this country.

There is now the franchising of these *in vitro* operations; they are being franchised out like McDonald's. There are probably no fewer than a hundred of them in this country now. This is a very profitable operation, much more profitable, by the way, than abortion. The typical charge is $6,000 per cycle. This means that if a woman presents herself for *in vitro* fertilization, then for that one month during which she will be stimulated with various drugs to ovulate, the ova will be recovered under ultrasound, they will be placed in the test tube with the father's semen, and then the embryos, the human beings, will be implanted into the uterus at the appropriate time. Usually it takes four, five, or six cycles for success. For one patient, therefore, there is a business of approximately $35,000. It is spreading like wildfire; it is one of the most profitable franchising operations in the world today, and it is totally unregulated. Even a McDonald's has an inspector coming in from the Food and Health Department to see if the operation is acceptable.

In order to carry out *in vitro* fertilization, what the doctor must do is to paralyze the whole reproductive rhythm of the woman. For example, her hormones cannot be surging around, producing ovulation when the doctor is not prepared for it and when conditions are not exactly right endocrinologically. So what is now done is to use what are called "GNRH agonists," a whole new class of drugs, undreamt of even five years ago, which are given to paralyze the harmonious rhythms of the female reproductive organs. The system paralyzed, the doctor can administer to the woman those drugs which will make her ovulate on schedule and with the appropriate number of eggs at the appropriate time to be recovered easily. You will hear more about these drugs; they have other, more sinister, applications which I will not go into now, but I can assure you that this is a dangerous class of chemicals.

Other chemicals have been produced in this whole grisly quadrille, such as anti-progesterone agents which are used for, among other things, both contraception and abortion. There are techniques now for perfusing the excised uterus: the hysterectomy specimen is taken out of the woman, if it is a healthy organ, placed in a preparation and cannulated—tubes are placed in its arteries and veins—and the uterus can be kept alive and flourishing so that embryos from the in vitro operation can be placed in it and allowed to grow. "We do not need you, you see, we need only your organs."

The man in Italy who is doing this work, Carlo Bulletti, has told me that in Italy this work is going on; there is some discussion about its morality, but it is being carried forward. In the United States, he said, we are too "backward" to do this kind of thing. Not for long.

There are other agents of cleavage: surrogate motherhood, exemplified by the unfortunate case of "Baby M," which the news media have chronicled in typically tasteless fashion. Fortunately, a number of states have now moved to regulate and even to ban this practice on a commercial basis. There is a new method of sex selection of the baby, which is very reliable but also very costly. Even though, theoretically, fetal research has been banned in this country since 1980, work has been going on at Loma

Linda University on fetal organ transplant from anencephalic babies, which is still going on today. Fetal tissue research has been going on for at least 15 years, funded by large corporations and foundations, using the bodies of aborted babies. The babies are aborted by prostaglandins, so as to keep them whole and even alive; they are then split open, and the pancreas is extracted, grouped up and mixed into a solution where it can be injected into adult diabetics for their treatment.

The area of organ and tissue transplants is something inconceivable in its dimensions and its potentialities. Today, its focus is limited to vital organs, such as the pancreas, or the research being done in England on transplanting fetal brain cells for the treatment of Parkinson's disease and Alzheimer's disease. But tomorrow, it will be directed to the replacement of non-vital organs. I recently wrote an article for Liberty Report entitled, "Obscene Harvest," in which I proposed the following scenario:

> Next year, along about Christmas, you may receive a catalogue of gift suggestions from Hana Biologics, or any one of a dozen or so other companies that undoubtedly will have sprung up within the next twelve months, which will read something like this: "Do you have someone dear to you—child, parent, sibling, life-long friend—who is afflicted with a serious or fatal disease? For this Christmas, why not consider the ultimate gift, the gift of life. By filling out the attached coupon, you can now order the necessary amount of fetal tissue or the appropriate fetal organ, and we will ship it to you by return mail, in a perfectly preserved state, for the tissue or the organ. All you need to do is to take the material to a qualified surgeon (and a list of suggested surgeons is included in our catalogue and will be available to you for a small additional charge) for transplantation into the affected loved one.
>
> Below is a partial list of our prices:
>
> Fetal brain tissue, $1,000 an ounce;
> Fetal whole brain, $5,000;

9

Fetal pancreatic tissue, $500 an ounce;
Fetal kidney tissue, $300 an ounce;
Fetal heart, $1,000.

We accept VISA, Master-Card, and American Express. You
can also order by phone through our toll-free number.

You may consider that scenario to be pure science fiction,
but I can assure you that ten years ago *in vitro* fertilization was
also considered pure science fiction, as was abortion, at least in
the way that it is being practiced now. In the world of tomorrow,
such advertisements will not even be restricted to vital organs;
they will offer fetal gonads for failing sexual prowess, or a transplant of fetal skin as a cure for baldness. An entire book on the
subject, *The Fetus as Transplant Donor,* has been written by Peter McCullough. The ultimate goal is nothing less than somatic
immortality on this planet.

Now there is talk that the Ethics Advisory Board, a governmental institution mercifully defunct since 1980, is about to be
resuscitated in order to lend the governmental *imprimatur* to
fetal tissue research. From McCullough's book, we learn what
kind of research has been done on fetuses in the past. For example, eight human fetal heads obtained by abdominal hysterotomy
at twelve to seventeen weeks of gestation were perfused through
the internal carotid arteries. Fragments of pancreatic tissue were
obtained from seven fetuses ranging from nine to twenty weeks
of gestation within one to two minutes following hysterotomy for
abortion. These fetuses were alive when this work was done.

There is no need of a reminder of the inglorious history of
medical research. It is appalling what has been done in the name
of scientific investigation, such as the Nazi experiments at Dachau in which naked Jewish prisoners were lowered into tanks of
ice water and readings were taken of their temperature until they
died. Recently, these data have tried to make their way back into
publications in this country, and there is great controversy in the
scientific community as to whether data achieved through such
means should ever be allowed into scientific journals. There is a
school of thought which promotes this. You are probably familiar
with the experiments carried out at Willowbrook on Staten Island

on mentally retarded children in the 1950's. From 1952 on, for a period of almost eight years, every mentally retarded child admitted to that institution, about 1500 altogether, was given an injection of live hepatitis virus vaccine to study the evolution of the disease.

The worst instance of all was the Tuskegee experiments. From 1932 until 1972, under the auspices of the U.S. Public Health Service, 400 black men in the area of Tuskegee, Alabama, were identified as having syphilis and were followed periodically by tests and investigations, but were given no treatment. This went on for forty years. These experiments appeared from time to time in the medical journals, and in the last few years the experiments came under the auspices of the Centers for Disease Control in Atlanta. Those black men were denied treatment for syphilis, even though penicillin came into use in 1945; for the next 27 years they were given only blood tests and no treatment, to see the natural evolution of the disease, from which most of them died. I can attest that dying from tertiary syphilis is horrible; it makes AIDS look mild by comparison.

These are some of the glorious annals of medical research which the Ethics Advisory Board is now contemplating reviving. The logic is clear: at Dachau, the Jews; at Willowbrook, the mentally retarded; in Tuskegee, the blacks. All of them were defenseless, mute victims. Why not the unborn next? It follows logically, inexorably, inevitably.

There is also genetic engineering going on, including the patenting of new animal forms. The Judiciary Committee of the U.S. House of Representatives has just approved the patenting of new forms of animal life; the U.S. Patent Office has recently declared that a mouse that has been genetically altered for use in cancer research is to be defined as a "composition of matter, and a product of human ingenuity," and therefore can be patented. The first such patent was issued to two researchers at Harvard Medical School. At present, new human forms are not allowed to be patented, according to the House Judiciary Committee; but I would wager that in the twenty-first century it may be a very different matter. We will have animal genes placed into humans, to create a "sub-race" designed to do the menial tasks; we will have massive engineering of intelligence genes pushed into other human beings to create a "super race" of philosophers and kings. And so it goes, the relentless cleavage between procreativity and humanity.

I recall that when I was a medical student at McGill, and I went into the physiology laboratory one day in my second year, there was a dog which had been operated upon to show us what happens when the gastric juices are stimulated. This dog had a hole in his throat, called an esophageal fistula. When he would go to eat, he would swallow the food, having a wonderful time. The food would go down his esophagus through the hole, so that nothing he ate would ever get to his stomach. That dog was having a wonderful time, eating bowls and bowls of meat, all the while slowly starving to death. That is precisely what is happening in this society today. We are physically, and in every other way, enjoying ourselves, and all the while spiritually starving to death.

We have, then, the systematic, cold-blooded manipulation of the human body, the treatment of human procreativity and its products as a commodity. This decimates the human spirit, defiles our divinity, denies the soul, and reduces us, at least all of us who fail to resist, to the status of laboratory rats. If we cooperate, if we fail to resist, that is exactly what we deserve. Those who are not morally deaf must resist; we are obligated to do so, in adherence to a higher order. I am reminded of the story of when Thoreau was jailed for failing to pay his poll tax, the moneys from which were being used to support by Fugitive Slave Act. While he was in prison he was visited by Ralph Waldo Emerson, who looked at Thoreau and said, "What are you doing in there?" Thoreau replied, "What are you doing out there?"

This attitude shows itself not only in the way that human life is dealt with in its origins, but also in the way that it is dealt with at its conclusion: in euthanasia. Dr. Daniel Callaghan, the bioethicist at the Hastings Center, has written a new book called *Setting Limits,* in which he proposes that no one over the age of 75 be given any life-saving treatment; it is a waste of money and facilities, he says. In return, we will take those over the age of 75 and put them in comfortable, government-supported nursing homes. This comes from one of the most respected bioethicists in the country. My father, who is 94 years old, once said to me, "If I ever get seriously ill, promise me one thing. Don't let a bioethicist in my room!'"

The progression of events in our courts is disheartening. First, there was allowed the denial of extraordinary means for the dying, which is reasonable. But then there was permitted the denial of medications for the dying, and of extraordinary means for the comatose (now euphemistically referred to as "persistent vegetative state"). There quickly followed the authorized withdrawal of food and water from the comatose. What is next, the denial of shelter? Shall we put the comatose out on the fire escape in January because it is wasteful to heat them? Shall we refuse them the human touch? Shall we stop turning them so that they do not get bed sores?

Euthanasia has now come to include infanticide in the delivery rooms and in the nurseries. I refer you to the explosive article by Duff and Campbell, "Moral and Ethical Dilemmas in the Special Care Nursery," in the *New England Journal of Medicine* in 1972, one year before Roe. Both neonatologists working in the special care nursery at Yale-New Haven Hospital, they confessed in that article that, of 299 deaths that had occurred in that nursery from 1970 to 1972, fully 43 of them, or almost 25 percent, had resulted from the intentional withdrawal of all supports from defective or deformed babies. This is how far we have traveled in twenty years.

Science moves, not at a constant velocity, but at an accelerating pace. Let me give you an example. When I was a medical student in 1949, viability was defined as 32 weeks. By 1973, the year of *Roe,* it was defined as 28 weeks, an advance of four weeks in 24 years. By 1985, it was defined as 24 weeks, another advance of four weeks, in only six years. At this rate, therefore, it is reasonably certain that by 1994 viability will begin at 16 weeks, and by the turn of the century there will be no such concept: every human being will be viable from the moment that he or she is conceived.

Faced, therefore, not only with the progression of events thus far, but also with the accelerating pace at which they are moving, it is imperative that we come to grips with questions such as the following: First, because we are capable of doing something technologically, ought we to do it? Second, is a new ethic required for this new biology? Must we continue to invent an elastic, "one size fits all" morality, to cover each new, debasing advance in technology? Third, are we a unique and different species, possessing a touch of divinity, or are we nothing more than laboratory rats, to be manipulated, rearranged, and discarded at the whim of an increasingly powerful, vocal, and ruthless oligarchy of technocrats?

Martin Luther King once said:

> Science investigates; religion interprets. Science gives man knowledge, which is power; religion gives man wisdom, which is control. Science deals mainly with facts; religion deals mainly with values. The two are not rivals; they are complementary. Science keeps religion from sinking into the valley of crippling irrationalism and paralyzing obscurantism. Religion prevents science from falling into the marsh of absolute materialism and moral nihilism.

I have painted for you a rather bleak picture, but I am heartened by another thought expressed by Dr. King, whom I revere: "Love is the most durable power in the world. This creative force, so beautifully exemplified in the life of Christ, is the most potent instrument available in mankind's endless quest for peace and justice." As for myself, I am constantly aware of the timeless quality of *Humanae vitae,* and I am simultaneously provoked and stimulated by the observation of Thomas Jefferson, of all people, who two hundred years ago said this: "The question before the human race is whether the God of nature shall govern the world by His own laws, or whether innovators and kings shall rule it by fictitious miracles. In the latter lies only chaos and the death of the species; in the former, salvation."

Chapter 2

HUMANAE VITAE AND RESPECT FOR THE DIGNITY OF THE HUMAN PERSON

The Most Reverend Austin B. Vaughan

This is the first time that I have been asked to talk about *Humanae vitae* in 15, maybe 19, years. I gave a fair number of talks and took part in several debates between 1968 and 1969. When the encyclical was issued at the end of July, 1968, I was the newly elected President of the Catholic Theological Society and the newly-elected Vice President at that time was Father Charles Curran. So we had an interesting year in that regard, but the topic faded after that. Father Richard McCormick wrote an article in *America* in July, 1978, on the tenth anniversary of *Humanae vitae,* and in effect he said that it was a dead issue: nobody paid any attention to it anymore; even though it stayed on the books, we no longer had to be much concerned about it. A year later, on the first anniversary of the death of Pope Paul VI, Pope John Paul II spoke abut it for the first time in his pontificate. Since that time, it has been a growing issue, a growing reality.

I have been asked to speak on the topic, "*Humanae vitae* and Respect for the Dignity of the Human Person." What I would like to do is to make some comments on the encyclical itself and then offer some remarks on the dignity of the human person as I think it has been, and still is, affected by the encyclical.

First, it is obvious to us now that Pope Paul VI was prophetic in this document. He indicated in the document itself, in paragraph 18, that the Church had to be prepared to be countercultural. He used the Biblical term, a "sign of contradiction." This is what the Church had to be prepared to be. What he may not have realized when he issued the encyclical was that, with his teaching, he himself would be a sign of contradiction to much of the Church as well. It was not simply those outside the Church who were going to raise problems or difficulties. Most of the episcopal conferences did not clearly and strongly support him. To be sure, the episcopal conferences of Scotland and Ireland did support him, but that does not represent a vast majority of the population in the world. From many of the other episcopal conferences there was practically no response at all. Many seemed to dull the message in one way or another.

The French episcopal conference made reference to the principle of the lesser of two evils, which left the implication that it could be applied to practicing birth control. The Belgians in a short message laid all of their emphasis on the rights of a person who has an erroneous conscience. The Dutch indicated that it was not determining or definitive. In what was probably the worst of the statements, the Scandinavians spoke out strongly against abortion but said nothing about contraception at all. To some extent this is understandable, since they were in countries where abortion was so much of a problem that birth control looked like a minor issue in comparison; that came through clearly in their document. The Austrians emphasized that contraception was not a mortal sin; I am not sure where they got that doctrine, but that is in effect what they put forward. In a document that certainly was influenced, if not written, by Karl Rahner, the German bishops indicated that this was a matter where there was a lot of room for discussion and dispute. The Mexicans and Indonesians raised problems. The Canadian bishops laid all of their emphasis on freedom of conscience. All of those were conveying the impression, certainly, that it was not something absolutely clear, and had to be binding.

It took great strength for Pope Paul to issue this document, because it went against the overwhelming majority of the papal population commission that replied to him. Some of the things that I will say at first might seem to be a bit critical, but I myself believe that Paul VI was a saint. I pray to him. I heard Cardinal Madeiros once say that he thought the day would come when he would be described as "Paul the Great." I doubt that this is going to happen, but I have no question about his own goodness, and about his own courage and strength in this matter. But there was no clear-cut, strong response from Rome to the ambiguities of the episcopal conferences. So far as I know, something might have been done secretly or privately, in letters, but, if it was, it did not show. The only changes that were clearly seen over the years were a switch in the position of the Mexican bishops, some five or six years later, a kind of a crackdown on the Indonesian bishops, and a subsequent document from the Canadian bishops that in a sense replaced the original one that had laid the great emphasis on conscience. But otherwise there was very little to be seen.

I went to the world synod of bishops in 1969 as an advisor to Cardinal Cooke, who was a papal appointee. The subject for that extraordinary synod was "The Primacy in Collegiality," basically the relationship between Rome and local bishops. It has to be remarkable, and not an accident, that in September, 1969, only a little over a year after the encyclical that there was no mention of birth control, except for one mention in an intervention by an Indonesian cardinal. Then it disappeared again. It is obvious to me that a decision had been made, on whatever level, to concentrate on avoiding a repetition of the problems and difficulties that had arisen over *Humanae vitae*. To make sure that the communications were clearer in the future, much was done to establish ground rules on the world synod of bishops and on communications from Rome to the bishops, but nothing at all was done with regard to *Humanae vitae*.

To my knowledge there was no clear-cut response to the teaching being done in Catholic colleges and universities, including universities in Rome, that opposed the encyclical. Certainly in the best known of the moral theology faculties in Rome, two of the professors continued to teach, in the years subsequent to *Humanae vitae,* that it was not binding, and in effect they were teaching that it was erroneous. That went on for a long time.

The fact it was still being taught in Roman universities led to an allegation here in our own country that it was permissible to introduce sterilization into Catholic hospitals. I was a member of a board that the bishops had appointed on updating Catholic health directives in the early and middle 1970's. Sterilizations were done in some instances in the early 1970's; they were advocated in some others. Ultimately there was an appeal by the American bishops to Rome for a clarification on whether or not it was permissible to perform sterilizations in Catholic hospitals. The argument had been proposed that since the teaching on birth control was disputed, and since it was a matter that was thereby a doubtful opinion, the principle of probability could be used to allow the performance of sterilizations.

They received a clarification in 1975, in a document from the Congregation for the Doctrine of the Faith. This document clearly stated that no kind of moral probability could be attributed to a position that directly contradicted current teaching of the Church. It is interesting that it took two years for this document to reach American bishops from the United States Catholic Conference. When it finally came out in 1977, it came out with the document on material cooperation in sterilization in hospitals that in effect would have opened the door to just such sterilizations. That latter document ultimately had to be withdrawn and was replaced by another one three years later.

I mention this as an indication that, even though the statement itself is clear enough and has been clear enough from the beginning, not only was it not welcomed to any great extent, but in fact many ways were found to ignore it in practice. So far as I can see, no strong action was taken from the episcopal leadership with regard to that.

A third point that I wish to make is that the prophetic character of the encyclical is clearer now that it was in 1968. In some of the early debates, I found that the part of the encyclical that was most difficult to defend was paragraph 17, which deals with the grave consequences of artificial birth control. The grave consequences that Pope Paul VI predicted were three: first, he foresaw that contraception would lead more and more to sexual license and general immorality; second, he predicted that it would lead to the demeaning of women; and third, he said that it would lead to increased governmental interference with people's practices with regard to marital fertility. He could foresee that if an individual couple could decide that they had good reasons to prevent having children, then governments would consider themselves justified in deciding that, for the common good, they would do the same thing.

In 1968, I found it very difficult to defend these predictions. I was on a Canadian television program, taped at St. Michael's College in Toronto, with members of the faculty and their wives. It was supposed to be a five-person panel, but it ended up as four-versus-one panel, which I got accustomed to in those times. On that program, the strongest objections came from the wives of faculty members, who ridiculed the notion that the practice of contraception would demean women. They said that the enforcement of the regulations involved in the rhythm method to a large extent confined people to expressing love at times when they were not inclined to, and that this was much more demeaning for women. They resented having rules like this imposed on them by aged celibates like Pope Paul VI and myself. It was an expression of the anger and annoyance that was there at that time. Now, that would be the easiest part of this encyclical to defend; no difficulty at all.

As regards sexual license, Daniel Callahan wrote an article for the *National Catholic Reporter* in the fall of 1968, just after he had come back from a trip to Sweden. He was appalled by what he had seen, with sexual devices of all kinds being sold; anything was available. He said that he had reached the conclusion that on that one point, that is, the risk that contraception would lead to sexual license, the Pope was probably right. He thought that the Pope was wrong in the rest of the encyclical, but that point he was willing to concede.

I can personally attest to the way in which contraception leads to the demeaning of women. I live in a poor neighborhood, a neighborhood that is generally considered a "slum" area. It is a neighborhood that has many, many single-parent women now, who live below the poverty line, who often live in degradation or on the verge of it, who are the leftovers of liaisons with men who have felt no responsibility for them at all, and no responsibility for their children who have drifted off. Newburgh is not unique in that; you can knock on any door in our urban society today and find people who are not below the poverty level, but who find themselves left deserted, abandoned, or cast off in one way or another. Almost inevitably the ones that have suffered the most in that have been women. Russell Baker, the columnist with *The New York Times,* wrote an article about seven or eight years ago that was humorous, but not totally humorous. He said that people like to know who won the wars; he asked who won the sexual revolution, and answered that sometimes we do not know, but in this case there was no doubt: "the boys won it." He said that this was because the women got stuck with all of the undesirable consequences of the sexual revolution. Paul VI predicted this in 1968, and people laughed at him. Nobody would laugh at him now.

As for government interference: we have lived through a period of enforced sterilization in a state in India, a time when the Chinese government has tried to enforce abortions. Much closer to home, we have lived with the much more horrendous consequences of *Roe v. Wade,* which has justified and legalized abortion on a vast scale in our own country, making it acceptable, although not desirable, in the minds of many people.

It is now much easier to defend the encyclical in its predictions of the consequences of contraception, since we are living with the disasters that have come from desacralizing sex. This is really what this encyclical is all about.

A fourth point that I would like to make is a personal opinion: I think that the encyclical is basically still not accepted on any level in Church life. There is, relatively speaking, no clear teaching on birth control or purity in Catholic high schools or colleges. I do not say that there is none at all, but in terms of a clear, certain, and forceful teaching, it is done by at most a few out of the many.

To my knowledge, there is no insistence on uniform direction in the confessional in any diocese in our own country. I mentioned that to the bishops in our last meeting; there cannot be any bishop in our country who is not aware that, for almost twenty years, people have been able to get different answers on one side of the church and the other. On one side they will be told that they cannot practice birth control; on the other they will be told to follow their conscience. That continues; it goes on without any strong effort, possibly no effort at all, to change it.

We live with a continued approval, although a little less in recent years, of teachers who clearly dissent from the encyclical. Father Curran continued to teach in a pontifical faculty in the university owned by the Church, owned by the bishops in our own country, for nineteen years after the encyclical was issued, and when he was removed it was by an action from Rome, not by an action from our own country. Daniel Maguire is not only still teaching at Marquette University, but also put together the pro-abortion advertisement in *The New York Times* in 1984, which has succeeded in getting two nuns dismissed from their order or they quit. But the man who wrote the advertisement is still there; I think that if we are open to some allegation of unfairness with regard to dealing with people, it would be in this case.

Our own bishops' conference throughout those years had frequently made use of dissenting theologians. In fact, I was a member of the Administrative Board as the Chairman of the Human Values Committee, about seven or eight years ago, when one of the committees started to put together a paper on sexuality and the priesthood. The man who was the chairman of the administrative committee read out the list of five theological advisors that they had, four men and a woman. All five of them, I pointed out, dissented from *Humanae vitae*. I objected to that; we had a debate; a motion by a bishop that there be added to the committee a few people who support the encyclical barely won. The executive secretary for the committee was instructed to ask me for a number of names of theologians who would be acceptable for that. I gave him ten names and told him I could give him ten more. Eventually, he put two people who were pro-encyclical on it, but neither was from the list of ten that I had submitted.

I mention that not as an indication of malice, but as an indication that this has never become a major issue or a matter of great importance, and is not at the present time. If it is so, it has been true universally in our own country. I am as guilty as anybody; I have not pushed hard on it. Right up to the present, it is not an issue that we are prepared to push. Yet, if it is true, and if it is central—and I think that in terms of understanding human sexuality it is central, and not a peripheral matter at all—then we are not being true to the Faith if we do not push it. We are not prepared to push it in a society that goes in the opposite direction.

The encyclical strongly reaffirmed a number of basic principles that are seriously questioned in our own day, which I would like just to mention; none of these are new to you. Let me list ten, although I think there are at least thirty of them in this encyclical.

First, it clearly reaffirms the existence of absolute moral principles. There are many moralists in our own day, in our own country, who admit absolutes only with regard to moral abstractions. They claim that in any individual case one must consider all of the circumstances and one may well come up with different solutions. I even found this introduced as a justifying reason by the theologian who was the advisor for the pastoral letter of the bishops of the United States on "The Challenge of Peace." He gave that reason as an explanation on why it was permissible to say that something was a principle to be upheld but that the applications were prudential judgements to be left up to the individual. In effect, he was saying that every individual case, on anything, involves a prudential judgement that may wind up deviating from general principle that is there. Pope Paul VI is clear on this: artificial contraception is always against God's will, is always wrong, even when it seems to solve human problems.

A second point in the encyclical is that the physical is an intregal part of the human make-up and of its own nature. As a consequence, it has to be respected. You are aware that one of the arguments that some of the dissenters used was that the encyclical was wrapped up in what they called "biologism," that is, not allowing enough importance to the act of the mind and the will, to the intentions of the individual. Yet we accept it as basic that good intentions cannot change the nature of a physical organism. It is a real question that we must face in our own day of what things we can indeed change in the use or make-up of the physical body of human beings, but we have to do that without undermining God's plans as they are expressed in the nature of things. The encyclical is a clear rejection of a kind of dualism whereby we could make the human body and every part of it whatever we would like it to be. Otherwise, so long as one's intentions are good, then whatever use one makes of the human body is permissible. That really is too much of an idealism, casting off the reality of the material as God has made it, as he intends it to be.

A third point that is basic in this encyclical is that our lives are supposed to be ruled by God's Providence. The ultimate answer to a situation in which obedience to God's law makes serious demands on people, which could be avoided by ignoring his command, is that God's way is always the best way, even when it seems stupid to us at the time. In terms of salvation history, our faith is fundamentally tied up with the crucifixion, with something that on the day on which it happened seemed absolutely stupid to the people, which seemed to be a disaster. Three days later the Apostles could see it as a blessing, but they did not see it that way when it happened. We believe that this is a pattern for our lives. It does not mean that any of us, except maybe a few, should pray to be martyrs. Most of us are better off praying to survive. But at times survival means accepting the hard things that God proposes to us, and accepting them not merely as things to be endured, but insofar as we can, accepting them as ultimately the wisest, even though they do not look that way in the beginning, even though they may seem to be foolish.

That has a lot of application in the lives of other people. How else do you justify a woman living as the spouse of a husband who has deserted her, who has abandoned her with her children, when she very easily could enter into a union with someone who would care for her and care for them? The only basis for it has to be a faith, and a faith that in this sense is blind: not that we do not know what God is asking, but, we do not know why. We may find out in this life; we may not find out until the next life.

That says a lot about the life of an invalid. We live in a period now when there is more and more pressure on people in our society to get out of the way if they are not productive. In his address yesterday, Dr. Nathanson mentioned David Callahan's proposal that we start to move 75-year old people off the scene. I suspect that he may start to think a bit differently when he passes 70. It has a lot to do with the significance of the life of a disabled child. We live in an age in which selective infanticide is already in some instances a reality; a kind of quiet reality, but it is there. Ordinarily God does not want us to look for the hard way to do things, but when he thrusts a hard way upon us, his way is best. This encyclical is based completely on that notion, that if it is God's law, then it has to be the best way.

I do not think that collectively we have accepted that. There are many good people in the Church who will accept something out of obedience: "That is the way that I am told that I have to do it, and I will grit my teeth and do it." That is different from accepting God's way as the best way, even at times when it seems to hurt a good deal.

A fourth point in the encyclical is that the Holy Spirit speaks through the Church, and especially through Peter. This means that we need his guidance and we need his discernment. The Holy Spirit tells us as much as we need to know at a given time. Even if we will come to modify our belief in the light of new knowledge, his teaching is still normative for us when it is given, and with the force with which it is given. That is always true; it was of this encyclical. When I was a seminarian, there would be brought up the fact that the Church had gradually come to accept the modified notion of evolution. When Darwin first put forward his idea of the way in which the universe had come into existence, it was condemned in a council in Cologne. As time went on, theologians and philosophers were able to separate out some of the physical aspects of evolution from a completely mechanistic interpretation of the universe, so as to be able to say that God could have worked in different ways. One of the ways in which he could have worked would have been evolution, so long as one maintained the uniqueness of man and the creation of man's soul by God.

When that kind of a matter would come up in those years, people would say that the decision made in Cologne had been mistaken. But what had been decided in Cologne was the right thing: it was necessary to reject mechanism, because it was wrong then and it always would be wrong. As questions are gradually separated out, something that no longer comes under that heading can be accepted. To do that, however, we need the guidance of the Holy Spirit.

The teaching on birth control is not exactly like that; it will not change. I am sure of that now; I was sure of it in the beginning. I do not believe that there was a definition in 1968, because there was a lack of a clear intention on the part of Paul VI to define. Archbishop Lambruschini, in the press conference that he gave then, said that this remains reformable, changeable. Paul VI never clearly indicated that this was to be the final word. But I thought at the time that it was impossible that Paul VI would ever retract this. When a reporter asked me about it, I said it would be easier for Pope Paul to resign than to retract this kind of a statement. The supportive evidence has become stronger as time goes by; all of the evidence in support of the truth and validity of this teaching is stronger now than it was in 1968; there is no possibility of a change on this.

A fifth point is that natural law is fully understood only in the light of Christs' revelation. Back in the 1960's, Karl Rahner made a remark that had great deal of truth in it and was profound in its own way. He said that we cannot have a valid and a true anthropology without Christology. He said that we cannot really know what human beings are, and are intended to be, in this life without relating them to Christ, because Christ has purified our notions of what a human being is, has raised them up, has elevated them. That is true with regard to many things that we know from natural law. Our old ethics books used to try to prove the indissolubility of marriage from natural reasons. It always seemed to me that the reasoning was never completely conclusive; it seemed to come up short in a case in which an innocent party had been badly hurt in the marriage, and in which dissolubility would open a way to curing that for the future, to let the innocent party enter into a union with somebody else. The only basis for accepting that must be God's Revelation, God's assurance

25

that, even though it looks bad and even harmful from a human point of view, ultimately in his plan this is what he is asking of us.

Only about six months before the encyclical, Father Richard McCormick had, unfortunately for him, reversed his position on birth control. Writing in *Theological Studies* for December, 1967, Father McCormick said that he had decided that birth control was permissible, following the position taken by Father Fuchs. When the encyclical came out, Father McCormick adhered to his position, rejecting the encyclical because, in his view, this was a matter of natural law and the Pope had proposed no new reasons in the natural law context for condemning contraception: all of the natural law arguments that had been given before had appeared to Father McCormick to be insufficient, and thus were, for him, still insufficient. As a consequence, he saw no reason to accept this teaching.

What Paul VI had inserted was his own act of discernment with the providential guidance of the Holy Spirit, which makes all the difference in the world. Ecclesiologically and as a point of moral methodology, the basic difference between the two sides on *Humanae vitae* was whether or not things were to stand completely and totally on the basis of arguments of natural reason, or whether or not the God-given authority of the Pope added something to that—not in terms of changing the argument, but in terms of Divine Providence providing guidance on discerning what was to be true.

At the same time, Gregory Baum posed another kind of difficulty, that was more to the point, namely, that the Church had no power to define matters of natural law, but had teaching authority only in what directly dealt with Revelation. In that view, natural law is not directly a part of Christian Revelation, so that the Church was outside the realm of its teaching authority, and had no right to speak here at all. I think the answer to that is easy enough to see: all of this is a part of the plan of salvation through Christ. The whole of the world and everything that is in it must be related to Christ. He is the center of the universe, and the things that are there by nature may be elevated, or may be modified to some extent, but they cannot be eliminated by Christ's Revelation; we can always learn more about them.

A sixth point that is absolutely essential and central to this document is its emphasis on the sacredness of human sexuality. The main theological point of this encyclical is not about birth or conception; it is about the nature of human sexuality. It cannot be true to itself unless the openness to human life and the openness to human love are both preserved. That is what it says, and the use of human sexuality has to be governed and guided by that.

Strangely enough, I think that, Father Curran saw this as soon as the encyclical came out and even sometime before. Two days before the encyclical was issued, he was quoted in the newspapers denouncing the encyclical that was coming. Evidently, the contents of the encyclical had been leaked to *Time* Magazine, which had gone to him for a reaction. He was quoted as objecting especially on the grounds that it seemed to rule out masturbation. Not that masturbation itself was the main issue, but the principle that underlay it was a main issue for him. Ultimately, his teaching is based on the notion that human sexuality is instrumental: it is something that can be used for the particular benefit of a given individual or of some others. On that basis, anything that appears as beneficial, to a particular individual or to somebody else, or to society at large, is legitimate, at least in the circumstances where that can be established. On that basis, it would be wrong ever to say masturbation was always wrong, if it were useful, for example, either to obtain semen for a fertility test or as a means to release tension.

He saw, correctly I think, that this was a crucial point. This is the reason, which many people did not see at the time, why acceptance of birth control leads logically to the acceptance of homosexuality, to the acceptance of divorce, or for that matter polygamy in a society where it fit, and even to the acceptance of abortion. This is because it makes sexuality wholly instrumental: it is there to serve the purposes of the individuals involved, and if a particular way of acting seems to serve those purposes, then there is no reason not to allow it. Fundamentally what *Humanae vitae* says is that there are aspects of human sexuality that are not subject to human whim or to human choice; that there are aspects of human sexuality in the way in which it was created by God that are so sacred that they cannot be ignored or brushed aside.

The acceptance of contraception, at least among Catholics, opened the way to the sexual revolution. This was not apparent to many people. I knew good people, including priests, who at that time were arguing in favor of contraception for married couples with problems. The argument that if there is enough trouble, then contraception is allowed, leads inevitably to simply trying to judge whose trouble is enough trouble. I have seen some statements recently by one of the dissenting theologians to the effect that, in hindsight, the conservative theologians had seen this more clearly than the dissenters, who did not realize in the beginning how far it would carry them. But they kept moving with it; the acceptance of selective homosexuality, and even of selective infanticide, was not present in the beginning but has developed in the intervening time.

A seventh point is the need for grace in order to live according to God's law. We are not fully redeemed. Some temptations are very hard to handle, but God's grace enables us to do things that are beyond our powers. This means that it is vitally important for people to ask for grace and prayer, and to use the means that God has given us to gain that grace. That is obvious, I suppose, in the spirituality of the past, but it has almost disappeared now because we no longer lay emphasis on the importance of resisting temptations, and of being able to overcome them.

An eighth point that the encyclical brings out, especially for educators, is the importance of the virtues of purity and chastity. The Pope appeals to educators to make a special effort to train young people in this. I think that there have been very few efforts made along those lines in the last twenty years; they are almost non-existent. This has come about largely through a de-emphasis on the importance of purity.

A ninth point that the encyclical brings out is the very close ties between marriage, married love, sex, children and family. In the intervening years the use of sex has been separated from the other four, which leaves us with a distorted view of human sexuality. It also leaves us with a lot of practical problems: teenage pregnancy; people living together with no thought of getting married; the acceptance of homosexuality; and a great deal of confusion on the role of women.

28

Finally, the last of the points that I want to make is that, in a very beautiful passage that has not been cited much, the encyclical points out that God is the author of human life, and that the human beings who are involved, the parents, are instruments. If that principle had been accepted, there would be no legal abortion. If it were seen that God is the one who really owns this new life, who is mainly responsible for it, then it would be seen that neither the mother, the father, nor anybody else has any right to decree that a child should be killed.

We believe as a matter of faith, which we learned in the catechism, that every human soul is created by God; the body is formed by the parents. The only thing we know God to have created, since he brought the whole universe into existence at the very beginning, is the soul of every human being. The reason why it takes a creative act on God's part to bring a human soul into existence is because every single one of them is unique and distinct. There has never been another person exactly like this child: never anybody with this mind, with this heart, with this will, with this mission in life, with this destiny. That is true of even the frailest, the poorest, the weakest of human beings. Every one of them is a soul created by God, and is intended to be a part of the whole of the plan of human destiny.

Certainly with the children who have lived to birth, it is easy enough to see this. Anybody who has been a chaplain in a hospital is aware of the impact that children who were badly deformed or who suffered a great deal have had on doctors, on nurses, on parents, on all of the people who came in contact with them. Often they have profoundly changed the lives of others. The one patient who had the greatest impact that I have ever seen in a hospital was a little girl five years old, dying of a very virulent form of cancer, who had even her skull misshaped, and who lived with great pain that the hospital could not relieve to any great extent. But she lived with great patience, and gave everybody there an image and a picture of what a human being, even a tiny human being, was and could be, far beyond what any number of sermons could have accomplished. There has never been any life that was unwanted by God.

Let me conclude with some remarks on the original topic, "Christian Respect for the Dignity of the Human Person," as applied to different people. First, with regard to a married couple, the encyclical stresses the sacred nature of human love, and of the origin of human life. Neither can rightly be made the subject of human whim or of scientific processes that are divorced from what God had intended. If they are, then the man and the woman who are involved are abused, and so is the child who is conceived. The notion of the dignity both of the parents and of the child is enormously important.

The "Baby M" case is an example. The "Baby M" case, it seems to me, may have been an instance of God's Providence, too. On the day on which the document on bioethics came out from Rome, the newspapers in my area sharply criticized it as antiquarian, ridiculous, foolish. They had quotes from learned, moderate, Catholic theologians who thought the same thing. Strangely enough, an editorial in *The New York Times* criticized the Vatican for interfering. Three weeks later, the *Times* had an editorial that said this was a serious document which had to be given a great deal of consideration. The editorial did not agree with the Vatican document completely, especially with the part in which the Vatican was trying to tell governments what to do. What had changed it in the intervening time was the "Baby M" case, in which the reporters had begun to look at things through the eyes of the mother, and had found this whole thing to be a horror. Suddenly the Vatican did not look so foolish. It is an indication that the dignity of human persons, of parents and of children, is very much involved.

As I mentioned before, I live in a neighborhood where there are a lot of single mothers in poverty. There are also a lot of women who were discarded without children. All of that is a loss of dignity of immense proportion that has come out of this. It is also a loss of dignity to find on television stations advertisements for condoms that are directed at women as well as at men, in order to avoid AIDS.

God has taught us, and we know it, that we are different from animals: human breeding is not just breeding; human coupling is not just coupling; it is intended by God to involve love, to involve the formation of a family, to involve keeping people together. The values of married life are more apparent now than they were twenty years ago. I do not mean that everybody accepts them, but it is a lot easier to speak in favor of them now, than it was when we were at the beginning of the brave new age. The brave new age has collapsed.

The encyclical represents respect for the dignity of the unborn child. The pragmatic approach of contraception has led to the acceptance of the non-personhood of unborn children. It has led to the use of abortion as a means of contraception, on the grounds that conception as well as sexual relations are merely instrumental: if the newly conceived child interferes with what will be useful to a woman, to her family, to her career, then better to get rid of it. The difficulty there is that somebody else's rights have been violently violated.

The encyclical and what happened as a consequence of it has had an impact on the dignity of the human person of theologians. Catholic theology in the last twenty years has been relatively sterile. There is nothing that has been produced that is going to last through the ages. The severance of ties with the Magisterium has been a major factor in that. None of the dissenters, to my knowledge, has made a major contribution that will survive the newspaper accounts of their dissent. None of them has put anything in the books that is going to last, apart from the argument over dissent itself.

Magisterial teaching supplies the security for our own research. What Chesterton once said of the ordinary faithful can also be applied to theologians. When people maintained that the Church's doctrinal teaching was hemming them in too much, keeping them from intellectual freedom, he used the image of a group of children playing on top of a high mountain; if there was nothing around them, they would huddle together, in the middle of it, afraid of falling off; if a fence were built around them, they could play to their hears' content, because they would no longer be afraid of falling off. The acceptance of the fundamental teaching of the Magisterium has always played that kind of a role. The dignity of the Catholic theologian demands a tie with the Magisterium.

It also has an effect on the Christian dignity of bishops. Doctrinal ties with Rome have been weakened. There has not been any explicit rejection, and I do not think that such a thing is likely to happen on the part of anybody at all, but there has been some resentment of decisions made in Rome. It was obvious in the reactions of the episcopal conferences to *Humanae vitae,* trying to minimize the damage by not emphasizing what had been taught. It has been obvious from the reaction of some bishops in some countries that they consider the Roman reaction to the ordination of women to be wrong and harmful, when actually Rome was simply re-asserting what is essential in this matter. There was a similar reaction in our own country to a decision from Rome on the material that can rightly be used for Mass, that is, what is really bread.

What this does is to leave local teaching much less secure, and to leave it much less full and fruitful. The bishop is less a bishop if his union with Peter has become less. The Pope said that, almost explicitly, in his talk to the American bishops in Los Angeles, namely, that the notion of the primacy is absolutely important if communion is to mean what it is supposed to mean, and among bishops as well.

This encyclical is important to the human dignity of scientists. What they are creating are new Frankensteins. We are no longer in the realm of horror movies; this is for real, and it is happening right now. There is no question that people who are carrying out the processes of genetic manipulation are much less human than God intended them to be.

It has had an impact on the human dignity of doctors and nurses. We have witnessed the disappearance of the Hippocratic Oath, and what that has done to the medical profession. I heard Father William Smith make an interesting observation on that back about a year ago. He was talking about Our Lady of Guadalupe, how the appearance of Our Lady to Juan Diego in 1531 had brought about the conversion of eight million indians in the period of the next years and had wiped out human sacrifice. The witch doctors used to kill twenty thousand people a year up to that time; it disappeared when the population became Catholic. He went on to point out that in our own country we have moved into the age of witch doctors. The Aztec society was advanced in many respects, yet they had witch doctors. We, too, live in a very advanced society now, where a million and a half babies are killed every year. Father Smith pointed out that what distinguished true doctors from witch doctors in the past had been the

Hippocratic Oath, the assurance that the doctor would be safe-guarding and protecting human life at all time. If that goes, we are back into an advanced yet barbaric society.

This encyclical has a great deal to do with the human dignity of priests. One of the consequences of the widespread refusal to accept the encyclical has been that the teaching on contraception in the confessional has become almost non-existent, or at least shy, on the part of priests. What has happened as a result of the vagueness in theology that has followed it, has been vagueness in the pulpit. It is rare now to hear a doctrinal sermon, because the priest giving the sermon cannot be sure that some member of the congregation will not tell him that he heard precisely the opposite last week in a Catholic institution. The result is sermons that are bland and safe, that do not give much of the reality of doctrine at all. This in turn leaves the man who is giving such sermons feeling much less useful, much less needed, with much less to give in his own life. I am not sure that this is totally divorced from the problem of priestly vocations that we have had in more recent times. It certainly leaves the priest with no sense of urgency in his own vocation.

At the end of the encyclical, Pope Paul speaks about educators. We live in a period where there is almost no teaching on birth control. There is very little teaching on purity. There is little stress on the importance of salvation and of efforts toward it. I think that one of the consequences of this has been far fewer vocations to the teaching communities. Even those who have joined teaching communities are, for the most part, no longer teaching. While the number of sisters that we had in our diocese two years ago was half the number we had in 1962, the number we had who were teaching was one quarter what it had been in 1962. I think that part of the reason is not only there is no longer a sense of urgency, but there is no longer even any sense of worth.

This encyclical has had an impact on the dignity of the human person for lawyers and for public officials. A while back I wrote to a newspaper because I was so annoyed at what to me has been almost a complete corruption of the party to which I have belonged since I was a child, and to which everybody in my home neighborhood belonged. Nobody runs for statewide and national office now on the Democratic ticket and stays pro-life. Not in New York at any rate; it does not happen at all. That has not led to a conversion to the Republicans for me. Mario Cuomo was one of the founders of the Catholic Lawyers Guild in Brooklyn. When he ran for governor, he said that nobody had fought harder for abortions for poor women that he did. The two Assembly persons in my district are practicing Catholics; they vote for Medicaid funding for abortion every time; because it is the Cuomo party line, they go along with it. This time in going for the national nomination for the presidency, two of the seven Democratic candidates had once been pro-life, Gephardt and Jackson, but neither of them was after they had come through the campaign. That is a corrupting influence on the people who are involved: they have surrendered something that has been vital in their own principles for the sake of gain. We have let them do it, and in the course of doing that we may let them move along on the road toward hell. I am not sure that the Lord may not call some of the rest of us to account for not having stopped them from moving in that direction.

The corruption of the dignity of the human person has taken place among the general public. We now live in a society in which most of us ignore the killing of unborn babies that goes on a gigantic scale along side of us. We do not approve of it, and we would never do it, but we get used to it. It has been going on for so long, and it does not interfere with our meals; we are still earning the same salary; the society has not collapsed; things seem to be going along okay. So we get used to it; we go along with it. But what that has done has been to corrupt us, as accepting it, as becoming a part of it, as no longer sensitive to what is there.

I would like to suggest that we read the encyclical again. I read it just the end of last week. It is a lot easier to take twenty years later, than it was then. It is a lot easier to understand and even to see what is there. To me, it is a reminder of how close God is to us, especially in hard moments.

Finally, if at times I seem to have stressed problems and difficulties, let me say that I believe in the fundamental message of the Crucifixion: that God uses our mistakes and our failures, and even the tragedies that we're involved in, to save us and to bless

34

us. I believe that in his own way he has already started to use, in a visible way, some of the difficulties and the hardships that have come with this encyclical to bring us to eternal salvation and to bring us to a richer understanding of this message.

Chapter 3

THE PERSONALISM OF JOHN PAUL II AS THE BASIS OF HIS APPROACH TO THE TEACHING OF *HUMANAE VITAE*

John F. Crosby

In his address of September 17, 1983, The Holy Father said that "it is not sufficient that it [the encyclical, *Humanae vitae*] be faithfully and fully proposed . . .". This seems at first glance surprising, for it is, as everyone knows, relatively rare for a Catholic pastor or teacher, or for that matter even the Bishops' Conference

Published in *Anthropotes: Rivista di Studi sulla Persona e la Famiglia,* Istituto Giovanni Paolo II, anno V, n. 1; Maggio 1989; pp. 47–69. Reprinted here with permission.

of a country, to present the teachings of the encyclical "faithfully and fully". Those who do present it fully usually give evidence thereby of their faithfulness to the entire magisterium of the Church. And yet the Holy Father said that this is not enough; it is indispensable, of course, but not enough. His sentence continues: "but it also is necessary to devote oneself to demonstrating its deepest reasons"[2]. No-one in the Church has done more than John Paul himself to advance this work of finding "the deepest reasons" for the moral teachings of the Church concerning man and woman; indeed, one of the most precious legacies of his pontificate will surely be his own profound and original reflection on the foundations of these teachings[3]. But long before he was elected Pope and while he was still only Karol Wojtyla, he was already doing original philosophical and theological work which is very rich in what it says and implies about "the deepest reasons" for the teachings of the Church on marriage, parenthood, chastity[4]. In the present paper I want to draw on all these sources, and to offer a brief introduction to those philosophical themes in the thought of the Pope which form the basis of his preferred way of presenting the teachings of the encyclical, *Humanae vitae*. But I do not aim at developing completely his arguments for these teachings; my primary concern is with the philosophical foundations on which John Paul attempts to build his arguments.

Where does the Holy Father look for the reasons which underlie the moral teachings of the Church? Does he look right away to the will of God? Does he say that God has forbidden the use of artificial contraception, and that we ought to obey God whenever He exercises His authority? Not at all; though his reflection is theological, and refers repeatedly to God, he does not appeal to any divine prohibition. Or if one insists on saying that God prohibits artificial contraception, the Holy Father will ask in turn, But why does God prohibit it? And his answer is that it is opposed to "the truth about man", as he likes to say, and that this is in a sense a deeper answer to the question. There is a truth about who we are, about our bodies, our masculinity and femininity, and above all, about our personhood, and about our creaturehood; it is this truth, and ultimately the God who is Truth, but not any legislative will of God, which is the ultimate basis for the norms for responsible procreation as enunciated in *Humanae vitae*. If someone does not accept these norms, his problem is usually not in the first place with the norms, but with his whole philosophy and theology of human nature; he has to begin with rethinking his philosophy and theology if he is ever going to see the reasonableness of the norms. This is why Karol Wojtyla said in 1978: "It seems that we can consider as the deepest level of this event [the struggle surrounding the encyclical] the controversy and the struggle over man, over the value and meaning of human existence . . ."[5]

The Holy Father develops this idea by saying (in *Familiaris consortio,* n. 32, among many other places) that the person who takes contraception for granted, and sees in it a morally harmless way of avoiding conception, does not just have a slightly different understanding of human nature from the Christian one, but a fundamentally different one. He holds that to the acceptance of artificial contraception there corresponds one vision of the human person, and to the rejection of it there corresponds an entirely different vision of the person. The norms taught in the encyclical, then, do not just concern the marital practice of spouses in their child-bearing years; they raise the whole question of the truth about man and woman and about the human person. If the Holy Father goes to a lot of trouble to explain these norms, it is not because he is onesidedly obsessed with them, but because he is aware of this vaster truth about man on which they depend, and because he feels keenly his calling to proclaim this truth in its integrity.

We are about to discuss this truth as the Holy Father sees it. But first we need to get acquainted with one other idea of his about its importance; he thinks that it is *pastorally* of the utmost importance to trace the norms of *Humanae vitae* back to the truth about man and woman. He thinks that we need this truth, not just in order to *understand* the norms of the encyclical, but also in order to *live* in accordance with them. In other words, it is not just theologians but also spouses who need to know the "truth about man" which underlies the prohibition of contraception[6]. And the reason is this: without any insight into this underlying truth, the norm seems to be outside of us, and is felt to be an imposition, or at least a burden. But in seeing how the norm grows out of the truth about man, and how we *live in the truth* of our being by acting according to the norm, it is internalized, made our own, and thus ceases to be a burden even when it requires considerable sacrifice of us. In his major philosophical treatise John Paul reflects on this process of internalization, and says: "The tension arising between the objective order of norms and the inner freedom of the person is relieved by truth, by the conviction of the truthfulness of good. But it is, on the contrary, intensified and not relieved by external pressures, by the power of injunction and compulsion"[7]. Hence the supreme pastoral importance of bringing out in a convincing way the truthfulness of the moral norms taught by the Church. The human person is so made for the truth, that he can live it only if he understands it. This of course does not mean that a Catholic is excused from a norm which he does not yet fully understand; it just means that the faithful owe it to themselves as persons to do everything they can to develop their understanding of the norms of the Church, and that the Church owes it to the faithful to do everything she can to build up their understanding of what she teaches. And I might add that she owes this to them, in the view of John Paul, not just because their understanding of the norms facilitates their compliance with the norms, but in the first place because she takes them seriously as persons by leading them beyond a blind obedience and by educating them to a rational obedience, an *obsequium rationabile,* as St. Paul calls it.

One can see how congenial to the mind of John Paul the motto of our conference on *Humanae vitae* is: Trust the Truth. In other words: trust the truth about man and woman; it can win, as nothing else can win, the allegiance of spouses. Do not teach the norms of conjugal morality apart from the anthropological truth which grounds them; be confident in the power of truth to do what the norms, taken in isolation, are impotent to do, and impotent even if they are supported by compulsion, namely to enter into the heart and appeal to our freedom.

But enough of introduction. We want now to get acquainted with this so compelling "truth about man" and to understand why John Paul deserves to be called a kind of prophet of this truth. Though we will study the "truth about man" with a view to understanding better the teaching of *Humanae vitae,* we do not, I repeat, claim to develop a complete argument for this teaching; we are primarily concerned with presenting the anthropological vision of the Holy Father on the basis of which one could then (in another article) develop his preferred arguments for the central teaching of the encyclical. We limit ourselves in this way because we are well aware that even after the Christian vision of the human person has been secured there remain various difficulties which one has to deal with in trying to draw the right ethical conclusions about the regulation of births. But this in no way calls into question the supreme importance of the anthropological foundation of the ethical analysis; without this foundation the ethical analysis is doomed to failure.

It is natural to begin by asking what *the* most important single element is in the "adequate anthropology" of the Holy Father, as he also calls his attempt to formulate the "truth about man". This most important single element, and most fundamental element, is not difficult to find; it is this, that each human being is a person. This is why I have chosen in my title to speak of his "personalism" rather than of his anthropology. We do not have to hear John Paul talk for long before we realize that he is fascinated with, and in awe of, the personhood of man.

We begin by speaking of his distinctive way of approaching the study of the person. Though this will indirectly introduce us to his vision of the human person, it is only in the second and third section that we will speak directly of it.

1. THE BEING OF THE PERSON AS REVEALED IN THE "SUBJECTIVITY" OF THE PERSON

In analyzing the structure of the person John Paul goes beyond the philosophical tradition which he inherits in a remarkable way: he makes much of the conscious experience which the person has of himself. This tradition had defined the person, to quote the classical formula of Boethius, as an "individual substance of rational nature", but it did not, it precisely did not express itself in terms of self-presence, subjectivity, inter-subjectivity, interiority, solitude, communion. Now John Paul, while of course entirely affirming the substantiality and the rationality of the person, does speak, indeed makes a point of speaking, and takes a particular delight in speaking, in just these "subjective" terms. Thus he commonly discusses the nature of the person in terms of *interiority* and of *inwardness* (just as *Gaudium et spes* does in para. 14). This is nothing other than the belonging of the person to himself (of which we shall speak directly below) *as it is experienced from within by the person.* Here is another example. In his extraordinarily profound meditation on the first three chapters of Genesis he observes that the account of the creation of man in ch. 2 is more subjective than the "priestly" account found in ch. 1, by which he means that only in ch. 2 do we read of such things as the *solitude* of man before the creation of woman, and of the *experience of shame,* both of its absence and then, after the fall, of its presence. This subjective approach fascinates John Paul, who marvels at the fact that it is found in so archaic a text as Genesis 2. He centers his meditation mainly around this second and more subjective account of creation.

One has to understand correctly this interest of the Holy Father in personal subjectivity. He does not think that his is departing from the *being* of the person, and studying instead only *psychological experiences* in the person; even less does he think that there is nothing more to the being of the person than such experiences. He knows well that the person has a being and a structure as person whether he is consciously present to himself or not. *But he thinks that in the conscious self-presence of the person we have a uniquely intimate access to the being of the person.* When, for example, John Paul studies the human person through the experience of sexual shame, he gives not just a psychological but a deeply personalist reading of this experience, which he explicitly calls a metaphysical reading of it[8].

We could say that there are for John Paul two extremes to be avoided in our understanding of consciousness and being in the human person. We must not reduce the being of the person to consciousness, as if the person were real as person only in conscious self-presence. But we must also not separate being from consciousness in the person, as if the deeper, more metaphysical being of the person in no way communicated with the conscious self-presence of the person and lay entirely outside of consciousness. The Pope thinks that this deeper being of the person is actualized in conscious self-presence, and is thus reflected in conscious self-presence, and this far more than had been generally recognized in pre-modern thought, and he thinks that this self-presence should be used more as a source for the deepening of our image of the human person[9].

And why should it be used more? What is to be gained by supplementing the older, more objective approach with this more subjective approach? In a very important but neglected little essay entitled, "Subjectivity and the Irreducible in Man"[10], which is surely one of his boldest philosophical statements, he claims that the objective approach, left to itself, runs the danger of losing what is distinctive of man as person. He goes so far as to claim that the whole Aristotelian metaphysics runs the risk of "reducing man to the world", of failing to do justice to the proprium of man, to what makes him a person. He says that there is a *cosmological* focus of the Aristotelian tradition which needs to be completed by a more *personalist* focus, which is characterized by studying man not only in terms of substance, potentiality, and the like, but also of self-presence and self-donation, and thereby studying him in all his concreteness and specificity. And he thinks that as a matter of historical fact the recourse to subjectivity in the last few centuries has enabled many thinkers to achieve a more adequate vision of man as person, and to achieve it without any least concession to subjectivism[11].

Here we can say a word about the "phenomenology" of the Pope. I find that very many people would like to understand just what it is in his thought which gets called phenomenological; they are not sure what this term means, but are intrigued at its being applied to the thought of a Pope. Well, one answer, not an exhaustive answer, but part of the answer, is that phenomenological philosophy has cultivated the study of personal subjectivity, and that the method and even many of the results of this philosophy can serve to enrich the Christian personalism towards which John Paul is working.

Now his interest in the subjectivity of the person show itself in his way of explaining the teaching of *Humanae vitae*. He starts from the self-donation which is enacted in the sexual union of spouses. In what follows we will have much to say about this self-donation, but already now we can see that spousal self-donation is by its very nature something consciously lived through; spouses could not possibly perform this self-donation without being aware of it; they are necessarily present to themselves as donating themselves to each other. John Paul proceeds to argue as follows: "The act of contraception introduces a substantial limitation within this reciprocal giving and expresses an objective refusal to give to the other all the good of femininity and masculinity"[12]. He often expands this thought by saying that as a result of resorting to contraception the self-donation of each spouse inevitably gets eroded by the attitude of selfishly using the other for one's own gratification. This almost implies that the disorder involved in contraception cannot remain entirely unknown to contracepting spouses, but that they can find it in their own self-experience if only they look deeply enough. For if self-donation is by its very nature something consciously lived through, then, one would think, self-donation compromised by selfishness cannot remain completely outside of the consciousness of the spouses.

Notice that other ways of explaining the teaching of *Humanae vitae* are not as "subjective" as the one which is so congenial to John Paul and to his personalism. If for instance one starts from the anti-life character of contraception, or if one starts from the impiety of contraception (as John Paul himself often does), then one starts from facts which may or may not be experienced by contracepting spouses; they are not essentially embedded in our self-experience in the same way as compromised self-donation is.

In his important paper of 1978, "La visione antropologica dell' *Humanae vitae*"[13], Karol Wojtyla carried out an extremely careful textual comparison of *Humanae vitae* with the chapter on Christian marriage in *Gaudium et spes,* and came to the conclusion that the latter text deals with the wrong of contraception in primarily objective terms, whereas the encyclical deals with it in more subjective terms. His main point is that in speaking of the inseparability of the unitive and procreative "meanings" of the marital act, the encyclical speaks of the act as consciously performed and experienced by the spouses. Karol Wojtyla saw in this more subjective approach a significant "progress" of the encyclical over the conciliar text.

But of course this subjective approach of John Paul is not to be confused with subjectivism (any more than the subjective emphasis of the encyclical could be confused with a concession to subjectivism). John Paul does not mean that contraceptive intercourse simply weakens the experience of self-donation; he means that it compromises the *reality* of self-donation, and that it is this deformed reality which can be experienced. Nor does he mean that there is a merely empirical connection between contraception and compromised self-donation; he means that there is an intrinsically necessary connection between them, that there is an inexorable personalist logic whereby the one leads to the other. Nor finally does he mean that if spouses using contraception should not be able to find in their self-experience anything in the way of sexual selfishness, then they are free of this selfishness and are not guilty of any moral disorder; he means that in their intercourse there is an *"objective refusal* to give to the other all the good of masculinity and femininity"* (my italics) and hence an objective moral disorder. In order to grasp the breadth and balance of John Paul's thought one has to dwell on the fact that in the very passage where he probes the *subjectivity* of the contracepting spouses, he speaks of the *objectivity* of their refusal[14].

John Paul thinks that the more subjective approach to the teachings of the encyclical, besides being deeply congenial to his own mind, is also pastorally indispensable, that it is exactly the approach required by our age.

[The author of the encyclical] was undoubtedly aware of that particular sensibility of modern man which refers to the subjectivity of his acting and his experience. The development in modern philosophy of the anthropological subject corresponds to this sensibility. It follows from our analysis that this sensibility does not lead man to the position of pure subjectivism. *On the contrary, by grasping the objective moral order in being conscious of himself as subject, he is enabled to understand in a more mature way the authenticity, the reasonableness, the beauty of this order* [my italics].

Perhaps it is precisely then that we achieve what St. Thomas wanted to express when he spoke of the "participatione legis aeternae in rationali creatura"[15].

We get a glimpse here of the boldness with which John Paul attempts to unite *vetera* and *nova,* to unite the traditional and the modern.

So far we have simply spoken of the subjective approach for which John Paul has such a great affinity, and though this has introduced us to his personalism and to his understanding of the relation between being and consciousness in the human person, we must now make the attempt, if we are going to throw new light on the teaching of *Humanae vitae,* to speak more directly about his vision of the human person.

2. THE PARADOXICAL STRUCTURE OF THE HUMAN PERSON

When talking of man as person, John Paul often quotes a line from *Gaudium et spes;* indeed, there is I think no other conciliar text which he quotes as much as this one. In para. 24 the Council fathers say "that man, though he is the only creature on earth which God willed for its own sake, cannot fully find himself except through a sincere gift of himself". The Holy Father is taken with the paradoxical structure which is here ascribed to the human person: each human person is so much a being of his own that he can only be willed for his own sake, and yet he is not so much a being of his own as to be able to live for himself and be happy in the solitude of his own being, he has instead to make a gift of himself to another in order to gain that being of his own which belongs to him as person. The Pope thinks that much of the "truth about man" is epitomized in this conciliar expression of this paradoxical structure. Let us see what he has to say about each of the two terms of the paradox; let us hear him first on the selfhood of the human person, and then on the need which the human person has for communion with others.

a. *Persona est sui iuris et alteri incommunicabilis.* Freely rendered, a person is a being who belongs to himself and who is not a part or property of anything else. Each person is so much a being of his own, is so strongly gathered into himself and anchored in himself, that he resists being incorporated into any totality in which he would be a mere part, serving only to build up the totality; he is rather a totality of his own, a world for himself. The thought can be expressed in the famous terms of Kant: each person is an end in himself and is never to be treated, whether by himself or by another, as an instrumental means for realizing some result[16].

As one sees in this Kantian formulation, this basic truth about the person gives rise to a basic moral norm; the selfhood of the person gives rise to the norm directing us to respect persons in this far-reaching "being of their own" which they have as person, and to abstain from all using, owning, absorbing of persons. This norm, which for John Paul is *the* first principle of morality—he calls it the "personalist principle"—is so strong as to hold even for God. In his early work, *Love and Responsibility,* he says, "This principle has a universal validity. Nobody can use a person as a means towards an end, no human being, not even God the Creator. . . . if God intends to direct man towards certain goals, he allows him to . . . know those goals, so that he may make them his own and strive towards them independently"[17]. This is why the passage in the Pastoral Constitution, 24, which John Paul so loves to quote, speaks of man being willed by God *for his [man's] own sake.* The Holy Father means that God is simply recognizing the personhood of man by willing him, and also ruling him, for his own sake. He often says that we, when we respect persons and abstain from all using and violence towards them, are simply participating in that vision of them and love for them which God has[18]. But what above all concerns us at the present moment is not so much the personalist norm, and its validity even for God, but the underlying truth about the selfhood of the person which is reflected in it, the truth that the person is *sui iuris* and *alteri incommunicabilis,* that is, in an incomparable sense he is himself and he is not any other.

This is what John Paul says about the *being* of the person. He also has something to say about the *acting* of the person. He makes his well-known distinction between "what happens in man" and what man "does himself", calling the former an "activation" and reserving the term, "acting", for the latter[19]. "What happens in man" would comprise instincts, drives, and whatever else springs up in us outside of our selfhood and with a spontaneity of its own. One sees how acting expresses the being of one who belongs to himself as person; it is just because the human person belongs to himself, that he does not just endure what happens in him, but can act through himself. If the human person were not gathered into himself in the sense of being *sui iuris et alteri incommunicabili* he would entirely lack the inner ontological resources, so to speak, for acting through himself.

We cannot fully understand the thought of John Paul on the acting of the person without considering the person *in his relation to truth*. He often explains himself on this point in exactly that subjective way discussed above. Thus in one place he explains it by reflecting on the experience of solitude. Placing himself into the account of Adam naming the animals, he interprets this act of naming as the act of understanding the truth about the non-personal beings around him[20]. And in understanding this truth Adam acted through himself and so came to himself, began to experience himself; in going out to the truth of things around him he returned to himself, and began to experience his personal selfhood and to develop an interiority. But in this self-experience he realized how different he was from all the beings around him, and in this realization he experienced a deep solitude. This is a solitude which we too experience in our relation to non-persons, and experience in proportion as we understand the truth about them. It is clear that this solitude is not *a merely psychological* experience, detached from the being of the person; it is nothing but an experience of this being, it is an experience of that ontological structure of belonging to oneself of which John Paul speaks. Perhaps we could even say that it is an experience of what Boethius had called, using the language of Aristotelian metaphysics, the proper substantiality of the person. The main point for us is that we act through ourselves and experience our selfhood through our relation to the truth of beings, and that we cannot act through ourselves and experience our selfhood if we lose our orientation towards truth.

He also discusses the more properly moral acting of the person, and explains why it is possible only in relation to the "truth about good". When we feel the appeal of good things, even

objectively good things, we are at first in danger of being dominated by them, of being subject to a "moral determinism" which
tends to prevent us from acting through ourselves. Only in breaking through to the "truth about good" do we gain that spiritual
distance to goods which lets us act through ourselves towards
them[21]. Through that spiritual distance we experience something
like the solitude of Adam naming the animals; we grow in that
interiority and subjectivity in which the ontological structure of
the human person is lived through and experienced.

Thanks to his subjective approach to the human person John
Paul is able to bring to light a very significant though easily over-
looked feature of our acting in relation to the truth about good.
He says that this acting should not be exclusively understood in
terms of the good to which it is directed; there is also a reflexive
element in all acting, that is, the agent also has to do with himself. This is perhaps nowhere so clear as in conscience; when we
feel some moral imperative in conscience, however strongly we
are drawn outside of ourselves by the good which imposes the
obligation, we are at the same time drawn within ourselves, and
are aware of disposing over our very selves in the performing of
the action, in other words we are aware that our acting involves
self-determination. Just as in all cognition we are not only aware
of some object, but also present to ourselves as cognizing, so in
all acting in relation to good we not only affirm some object outside
of ourselves but also determine ourselves; self-determination
is to moral acting what self-presence is to cognition.

In this probing the subjectivity of acting we can develop further our understanding of the selfhood of the person. For John
Paul often says[22] that self-presence and self-determination express
the fact that the person is an end in himself and even in a sense
exists for his own sake; if the *whole* meaning of his acting were
the cognizing of some object outside of himself or the promoting
of some good outside of himself, then he would be drawn out of
himself towards that object or that good in a manner inconsistent
with his belonging to himself.

Let us now see what follows (from John Paul's account of
selfhood and self-determination) for the understanding of the
teachings of *Humanae vitae*.

1. The personalist principle, as we saw, says that the person, being *sui iuris et alteri incommunicabilis,* must never be merely used but always also affirmed for his own sake[23]. This implies for John Paul the wrongness of one way of trying to explain the condemnation of contraception, and thus at least points indirectly in the direction of the right way of defending it. He means the "rigorism" according to which the whole meaning of the sexual union of spouses is to be an instrumental means for raising up offspring[24]. If that were so, it would of course follow that contraceptive intercourse is inherently disordered and irrational. But the premise contradicts the personalist principle; spouses would violate each other as persons if in their intimate relations they merely used each other for the sake of procreation, and God would violate them as persons if He gave them the sexual drive merely to use them for this purpose. Notice that the nobility of the purpose does not help at all in removing the moral disorder which comes from using persons.

2. But from this it does not follow for John Paul that one can give a personalist defense of contraception, *for contraception also violates the personalist principle,* and this violation goes far towards explaining the wrongness of contraception. In other words, it is not only non-contraceptive marital relations performed according the spirit of this "rigorism", but also contraceptive marital relations, which violate the truth about the person. While it is obvious that the former violate the personalist principle, it is not equally obvious that the latter violate it, and so we shall have to examine more closely the depersonalizing character of contraception. But we have made an important start by identifying the personalist principle as the principle which according to John Paul controls the ethical analysis of contraception.

3. This personalist principle helps us understand why John Paul teaches, as the Church has always taught, that the act of contraception is intrinsically wrong and can never be made right by any amount of good results which it might lead to. It is not so difficult to see that the violation of a person, as when one makes a slave of him, is intrinsically wrong, and that the good consequences of enslaving him are irrelevant to the rightness or wrongness of enslaving him. If then John Paul can show that

contraception does indeed violate the personalist principle, it will hardly be surprising if he teaches that the wrongness of contraception is an intrinsic wrongness. I touch here of course on a vast subject, which I cannot do justice to in this paper; but the subject should not pass unmentioned.

4. John Paul's understanding of selfhood and self-determination underlies his teaching on the possibility of abstinence. If abstinence were easy, the teaching of *Humane vitae* would have caused no controversy; everyone would then agree that the only medically sensible way of spacing out births would be abstinence, which would be much preferable to powerful new drugs or to unreliable devices. But very many people think that the abstinence which is typically required of a couple which refuses contraception is not only difficult but is in fact more than human nature can bear. John Paul responds that such people often fail to understand the personhood of man and woman; they think that human beings have to live at the beck and call of their drives and wants; they overlook their power of acting through themselves and of determining themselves. He often calls attention to the paradox that the same people who exalt man into a promethean position when it comes to the technological manipulation and domination of the world and of themselves, fail to treat him even as a person when it comes to the task of him mastering and forming his drives and urges: they make him first a god and then a beast, without ever getting closer to the truth that he is in fact an incarnate person[25].

b) But the human person, for all his selfhood, does not exist through himself, and does not suffice for his own happiness. "He can find himself only by making a sincere gift of himself ", as that Council text says. If the human person through his selfhood reflects God, then through his being made for communion with other persons he reflects the inner-trinitarian life of God. In his commentary on Genesis John Paul ventures the opinion, cautiously, that this being made for communion with others is perhaps an even more significant fact about man than his selfhood[26]. As we would expect, John Paul often explains interpersonal communion in a subjective way, as when, in the same commentary, resuming his discussion of solitude, he says, "Man's solitude . . .

is presented to us not only as the first discovery of the character-istic transcendence peculiar to the person, but also as the discov-ery of an adequate relationship 'to' the person, and therefore as an opening and expectation of a communion of persons'"[27].

It is important to add that John Paul not only stresses the necessity of each person living by self-donation, *but also of be-ing received by the one to whom he gives himself;* this too be-longs to the full finding of oneself in communion with other persons[28].

Now what is the most perfect form in which one human person makes a sincere gift of himself to another human person? In a marvellous passage in his early work, *Love and Responsibil-ity,* Karol Wojtyla explains the answer which he has always given to this question: the most radical self-giving of one human person to another human person occurs between man and woman in spousal love[29]. Here we have a love which is more than just benev-olence towards the other, and even more than the readiness to make sacrifices, even very great sacrifices, for the other; here we have a giving of oneself, and not only that, but a *surrender* of oneself to the other, and the will of each to come to belong to the other. Indeed, the abandonment of each spouse to the other goes so far, he observes, that one might well wonder how this aban-donment is compatible with the selfhood of each spouse. How can a person, who as person belongs to himself, ever make him-self belong to another, how can he even want to belong to an-other? "The very nature of the person is incompatible with such a surrender"[30]. Karol Wojtyla answers that in fact spousal self-surrender is *rendered possible* by the belonging of the person to himself. *Precisely because* the person belongs to himself, and is handed over to himself, he can dispose over himself by giving himself away spousally[31]. And he gives a further answer. One can see that a further answer is necessary as soon as one notices that the belonging of the person to himself also renders possible the act for example of selling himself as a slave or of throwing him-self away in some other manner; if he did not belong to himself as person he could not dispose over himself like this. The further answer is that in giving oneself away spousally one precisely does not throw oneself away but rather gives oneself in such a way as to gain oneself and to live and thrive as a personal self who is *sui*

52

iuris and *alteri incommunicabilis.* He says that spousal love bears witness in a particular manner the words of Our Lord: "He who would save his soul shall lose it, and he who would lose his soul for my sake shall find it again" (Matt. 10:39).

Notice that many modern thinkers who start from the selfhood and self-determination of the person go on to develop some notion of autonomy, or of man as a subject of rights, which excludes the possibility of self-donation. But John Paul knows how to find a new personalist approach to self-donation *precisely on the basis of selfhood and self-determination.*

But we have not yet given a complete account of John Paul's personalist analysis of self-donation; we have to consider not only the person who gives himself spousally but also his partner, the one to whom he gives himself. If I experience my partner as merely sexually attractive I will not be able to perform any act of spousal self-donation. I have first of all to apprehend my partner as person and to experience his or her sexual attractiveness only in relation to his or her personhood. And why? Why does my self-donation to the other require this cognition of the other as person? Because I can act through myself and determine myself in a properly personal way only by acting in relation to the "truth about good"; as we saw, only this truth lets me gain a spiritual distance to good and lovable beings and thus gain that spiritual space which I need in order to determine myself with respect to them. But it is almost the most important part of the truth about the goodness and lovableness of the other that he or she is a person. The fact, then, that I am a person and thus belong to myself is only a necessary but not a sufficient condition for me performing the act of spousal self-donation. I have also to apprehend the *other* as person and thus stand in the truth about the goodness of the other.

So much, then, on the paradoxical structure of the person according to John Paul. To summarize: on the one hand, the person exists in selfhood, with a being of his own, as a world for himself, but on the other hand, he is made for self-donation, and can live as personal self only by basing his existence on self-donation.

We indicated above some of the consequences which follow from the selfhood of the person for the ethical question of contraception; let us now indicate one of the main consequences which follow from the self-donation which, according to John Paul, the human person is made for.

All of his thought on spousal self-donation stands in the closest relation to his thought on marriage. In marriage a man and a woman achieve that complete belonging of each to the other for which they long as a result of their spousal love. A man and a woman with no interest in marriage could not possibly, John Paul would say, love each other with a spousal love. But more to the point of the present study is the fact that self-donation is not only the soul of marriage but is also the soul of the marital act; the whole *raison d'être* of the sexual union of the spouses, according to John Paul, is to express and to enact their spousal surrender to each other and their spousal belonging to each other. He loses no opportunity to protest against a purely biological consideration of sexual intercourse; the only way to understand it for what it really is, is to consider it from the point of view of the person, that is, from the point of view of spousal self-donation[32].

Let us suppose that the marital act had nothing to do with self-donation, and in fact that it had no deep personalist significance, and were not distorted by being considered in a purely biological way; let us suppose that it were nothing more than the gratification of sexual concupiscence. Then it would be very hard to make an ethical case against contraception; it would be impossible to make any argument based on the inseparability of the unitive and procreative meanings of sexual relations, for one would have abolished the unitive meaning, which of course does not consist in physical union but in the union of persons. Most people can readily see that there is something morally relevant about the bond between the bodily expression of spousal self-donation, and the coming into being of a new human being, even if they are often unclear as to exactly which ethical consequence they should draw; they see that such a bond is deeply meaningful, and that there is hardly any other human act or experience which would be more appropriately endowed with procreative power. But nobody could possibly find any moral relevance in the bond between the selfish gratification of sexual concupiscence and the coming into being of a new human person. On the contrary, one would have to judge this bond to be an unfortunate fact of nature, one would even have to say that such a way of coming into existence is unworthy of a new human person. When then contemporary men and women, strongly influenced by consumerist materialism, can see nothing more in sexual relations than entertainment, devoid of any deeper personalist content, then it is only natural that they will find the Church's teaching on contraception unintelligible; indeed, it would be strange and unnatural if, having driven self-donation out of human sexuality, they had any more objections to the use of contraception. But if they can learn from John Paul how spousal self-donation is the soul and the form of sexual intimacy, and why sexual intimacy becomes untruthful and depersonalized in the absence of any spousal self-donation, then they might recover some sense of the deep human meaning and mystery which lies in the procreative power of sexual union, and then the idea of sterilizing the sexual union would become for them, at the very least, ethically quite problematical.

Here we see the makings of a powerful personalist argument for the teaching of *Humanae vitae.* It is certainly not the only argument which can be made; I stress it because of the way it grows out of John Paul's analysis of self-donation. But the argument cannot be developed further without first enlarging the underlying personalism. The reader should bear in mind that the task we have set ourselves in this study is not the completion of any of the arguments for the teaching of the encyclical, but an exposition of the personalism of John Paul which makes certain of the arguments possible.

3. The Nuptial Meaning of the Human Body

There is an all-important category in the personalism of John Paul of which we have as yet said very little: the human body. If one takes a certain view of the body, if one separates it from the person, maintaining a kind of dualism of the person and his body, then one gets a personalism which really is subversive of many Catholic moral teachings. Though the term, dualism, is not regularly used by John Paul, it lends itself naturally to expressing the position opposed to his own. Since this term can express very various meanings and confusions of meanings, it is important that the reader take in exactly that meaning of dualism which emerges from the following, and that he take John Paul's critique of this dualism as a critique precisely of it and not of other dualisms[33].

An American feminist calling herself a Catholic recently defended any and all kinds of sexual relations between man and woman (and between man and man, and woman and woman), saying that *God does not care what we do with our bodies, but only how we treat each other as persons.* She apparently did not consider the possibility that a person's body forms such a unity with the person himself that the way men and women treat each other's bodies determines whether they respect each other as persons. One would misunderstand the dualism which this feminist expressed if one thought that she, or rather the mentality which she represents, rejected entirely the possibility of self-donation, or that it regarded all sexual activity as inherently selfish. No, the representatives of this mentality might speak in praise of self-donation; what characterizes their mentality is a certain "spiritualism", that is, *the idea that self-donation is not tied to this bodily expression rather than that one, and is not necessarily incompatible with any particular bodily expression. This means that self-donation springs out of the interiority of the person and has complete freedom in seeking its bodily expression, which can in principle be any exercise of sexuality*[34]. If persons get estranged from their bodies like this, then it becomes very hard indeed for them to make any sense at all of *Humanae vitae* and of other Catholic teachings on sexuality and procreation.

In the writings and addresses of John Paul we can find at least two causes of this dualism, or two reasons why it is so difficult for modern men to understand the real unity of the person with his body.

1. In his allocution of April 8, 1981, which belongs to the catechesis on human love, he said:

> The whole development of modern science, regarding the body as an organism, has rather the character of biological knowledge, because it is based on the separation, in man, of that which is corporeal in him from that

which is spiritual. Using such a one-sided knowledge of the functions of the body as an organism, it is not difficult to arrive at a way of treating the body . . . as an object of manipulations. In this case *man ceases, so to speak, to identify himself subjectively with his own body, because it is deprived of the meaning and the dignity* deriving from the fact that this body is proper to the person [my italics][35].

2. The other factor tending to estrange the person from this body is not a specifically modern factor, nor does it have any special connection with modern technology; it is the sexual concupiscence which has taken over in human nature since the fall. John Paul discusses sexual concupiscence far more extensively than the first factor, and in fact what he has to say about it forms a particularly rich part of his catechesis on human love[36]. He says that as a result of the fall there occurred

a certain constitutive break within the human person, almost a rupture of man's original spiritual and somatic unity. He realizes for the first time that his body has ceased drawing upon the power of the spirit . . . The body, which is not subordinated to the spirit as in the state of original innocence, bears within it a constant center of resistance to the spirit, and threatens, in a way, the unity of the man-person . . . The structure of self-mastery, essential for the person, is, in a way, shaken to the very foundations in him . . .[37].

As a result, the masculinity and the femininity of the human body is no longer transparent to the personhood of men and women, but begins to exercise an attractive power which is detached from the preciousness and lovableness which they have as persons. Man and woman then desire each other for sexual gratification, and not to perfect their belonging to each other. This disappearance of the person from sexuality leads to, or rather is, that dualism which John Paul deprecates.

But one might at first wonder whether, for all his deprecation of dualism, there are not elements of it in his own thought.

As we saw, John Paul's reflection on the self-determination of the person leads him to an important distinction between what happens in man and what man does through himself. This means that there are two poles in the makeup of human nature: there is the more passive pole which is the principle of undergoing, enduring, and there is the pole of selfhood and self-activity. In *The Acting Person* Karol Wojtyla is in fact willing to adopt a widely-used terminology, and to distinguish between "person" and "nature" in man, and in one place in this work he even goes so far as to say that person and nature "divide the human being, as it were, into two worlds"[38].

The problem is that the person-nature distinction is very commonly understood in a dualistic sense, and that it is very commonly used by those who argue for the liceity of contraception; they say that the biological processes which are manipulated by contraception belong to what is merely "nature" in man, and that human beings are simply exercising the self-possession which belongs to them as "persons" when they practice this manipulation.

And yet John Paul does not hold the dualism. For he maintains in this same work, and in fact argues here at length, that person and nature in man, distinct as they are in idea, are nevertheless not distinct beings, they rather belong to one and the same being[39]. The same human being who is characterized by personal selfhood, is characterized by nature; the very one who acts through himself in freedom also undergoes and endures. I cannot discuss now all of his arguments for the unity of man, I will limit myself to just one of them, a typically subjective one. "When man acts, the ego has the experience of its own agency in action. When, on the other hand, there is something happening in man, then the ego does not experience its own agency and is not the agent, *but it does have the experience of the inner identity of itself with what is happening* [my emphasis] . . ."[40]. In other words, when I act through myself in freedom, and then undergo that which happens in me, I experience not two different experiencing subjects, but one; I experience that it is the same subject who now acts and now undergoes. Person and nature, then, though sharply distinct in idea, belong to the same human being.

But if we want to find John Paul's deepest insights into the error of the dualism, we should look not just at what he says about *the ontological unity of person and nature in man,* but also and above all at what he says about *the task of integrating nature into the life of the person.* I would try to render his train of thought in the following way.

Self-donation belongs to man as person, as we saw; it belongs to him no less than selfhood and self-possession. The supreme self-donation between human persons is spousal self-donation. We explained these things above without any reference to the body. But now John Paul adds: this spousal self-donation can be fully expressed and enacted only when a man and a woman in marriage become one flesh (Genesis 2, 24). Though sexual attraction, in its origin, is a matter of nature, springing up in us on its own, and existing at first outside of our interiority, it is destined to be drawn into our interiority. Then it can lend an entire dimension to the self-donation of persons which would otherwise be missing. This means that the sexual drive is not merely related to the person as something to be dominated by the person, it is related much more intimately to the person than that, *it is related as something to be incorporated into the life of the person,* for in marriage it provides the person with a medium for a deeper and more perfect performance of an act which springs from the depths of his selfhood and interiority. This potential of the masculinity and the femininity of the human body to serve the supreme self-donation of persons is[41] what the Holy Father calls the "nuptial meaning of the human body". This aptitude of the body to serve the communion of persons, and to make possible a plenitude of communion which would otherwise be missing, gives us a profound disclosure of the dignity, the nobility of the human body, and shows forcefully the error of a Manichean hatred of the body. But more to our present point: this aptitude to be incorporated into the deepest life of the person shows that the body belongs to the being of the person and is not an object for the person, and that the person is not entirely free in seeking the bodily expression of his inner acts.

One might ask whether this entirely refutes the dualism. What if someone were to interpret the thought of John Paul as follows: the spouses can confer the meaning of self-donation on their bodily union, and then their bodily union comes to express self-donation, but only as a result of this conferral; if they do not confer this meaning then their bodily union is merely bodily union and has nothing to do with self-donation. Is this not still the dualism? This question forces us to bring out into the open the aspect of John Paul's teaching which decisively refutes the dualism. It is this: their bodies have nuptial meaning, and their bodily union has the meaning of self-donation, *independently of any subjective act of conferring which they might perform*. This is why the bodily union of man and woman in the absence of spousal self-donation and of spousal belonging to one another (that is, the bodily union of fornication or adultery) has something untruthful, it "says" as it were too much, more than is really meant. This means that a certain self-surrender of man and woman to each other is objectively effected by their sexual union, whether they want this or not; they do not have the power to render their sexual union harmless, to keep their personhood out of it, and to deprive it of its meaning of self-donation. The untruthfulness comes from the discrepancy between this objective self-surrender and the subjective absence of spousal love[42]. We spoke above of the person disappearing from sexuality; now we have to qualify this and say that there is a certain sense in which the person cannot disappear from sexuality. John Paul expresses all this, if I read him correctly, when he says that spouses, in truthful sexual relations, employ a "language" which is not of their own making[43]. We find, then, that the nuptial meaning of the body does not exist merely as conferred by the spouses, it is rather pre-formed in the nature of man and woman, and is so strong a reality that it constitutes a norm for their subjective intentions; and it cannot be ignored without persons misusing each other.

Let us now recall the ethical issue which serves to focus the personalist analysis of this study, that is, the issue of contraception. It is true that the reflection of the last paragraph only referred to the wrongness of fornication and adultery. But we do not have far to look in order to find some bearing on contraception[44].

We just saw that the subjective intentions of men and women do not suffice to render their sexual relations worthy of themselves as persons; these subjective intentions can remain good only by conforming to the objective laws governing the bodily expression of them. But then the question arises: are there perhaps other such objective laws governing the intimate bodily union of man and woman? Could it be that the nuptial meaning of the body requires other elements besides self-donation if sexual union is to be worthy of the person united? Does it also require an openness to the procreative power of sexual union? Could it be that spouses inevitably fall out of the attitude of respect for truth and respect for each other as persons when they sterilize their sexual union? *In any case, the whole discussion is put on a new level as soon as one abandons the spiritualistic attempt to explain the ethics of contraception in terms of internal intentions and begins looking for the objective laws, grounded in the nuptial meaning of the body, which govern truthful sexual intimacy.*

It would, by the way, be a mistake to think that John Paul gives up his preferred subjective approach when he comes to the task of establishing these objective laws. He thinks that these laws make themselves felt in the deeper subjective experience of men and women, and can be experienced from within precisely as objective laws. He himself often explores the nuptial meaning of the body through the subjectivity of spouses.

NOTES

1. This article is a somewhat expanded version of the paper which the author presented at the conference on *Humanae vitae* at Princeton University, August, 1988. The conference, which stood under the motto, "Trust the truth", was organized by the Roman Atheneum Foundation and the Aquinas Institute of Princeton University.

2. Cfr *Familiaris consortio*, para. 31.

3. I refer of course in the first place to the series of 133 addresses at the Wednesday audiences which began in 1979 and extended to 1984 and which was devoted to developing a "theology of the body". The definitive Italian text is GIOVANNI PAOLO II, *Uomo e donna lo creò*, Roma 1987. I will in the following quote from the English translations which appeared in *L'Osservatore Romano* and which have been published in four paperback volumes by the Daughters of St. Paul, Boston, under the following titles: I: *Original Unity of Man and Woman* (1981); II: *Blessed are the Pure of Heart* (1983); III: *The Theology of Marriage and Celibacy* (1986); IV: *Reflections on Humanae vitae* (1984). My references will be to these volumes.

4. Here we have to do primarily with *The Acting Person*, Dordrecht 1979 and *Love and Responsibility*, New York 1981. Karol Wojtyla also wrote certain papers which are important for the subject of this study: these will be introduced below.

5. *Die anthropologische Vision der Enzyklika Humanae vitae,* in *Von der Koenigswuerde des Menschen,* Stuttgart 1980, 182. This paper first appeared in "Lateranum", XLIV (1978), no. 1, with the title *La visione antropologica dell' "Humanae vitae".*

6. Cfr *Familiaris consortio,* n. 34. As will often be the case throughout this study, our reference here is not to the most important passage in John Paul's writings which illustrates what we are ascribing to him in the text, even less is it to the only such passage; it is simply to one exemplary passage.

7. KAROL WOJTYLA, *The Acting Person,* 166.

8. KAROL WOJTYLA, *Love and Responsibility,* ch. 3, section 2, "The Metaphysics of Shame". And in his commentary on Genesis he gives a *theological* reading of the experience of sexual shame.

9. On this whole subject see above *The Acting Person,* chs. 1 and 2.

10. In *Analecta Husserliana,* VII, Dordrecht 1978, 107–114. This article was just recently published in Polish in "Ethos" 2/3 (1988), 21–28.

11. If one considers, as JOSEF SEIFERT has tried to show in his metaphysical treatise, *Essere e persone,* Milano 1989, that being in the most proper sense is personal being, then it follows that the "subjectivity" through which Karol Wojtyla proposes to study man as person is a subjectivity through which the most properly objective reality is revealed.

12. Allocution of September 17, 1983; cfr *Familiaris consortio,* para. 32.

13. I refer here to the German translation, *Die anthropologische Vision der Enzyklika "Humanae vitae",* especially the section entitled "Subjektivitaet", 186–192. See my note # 5 above.

14. We will understand better the objectivity of this refusal after we have gotten acquainted with the place of the body in the makeup of human nature according to John Paul.

15. *Ibid.,* 192 (my translation from the German).

16. See above all *The Acting Person,* ch. 3. But for a briefer statement of his thought on the selfhood of the person see *Love and Responsibility,* 21–24, or his lectures *Die personalistische Konzeption des Menschen,* in *Elternschaft und Meschenwuerde* Vallender-Schoenstatt 1984, Wenisch (ed.), 27–43, especially 30–36.

17. KAROL WOJTYLA, *Love and Responsibility,* 27.

18. See for example JOHN PAUL II, *The Original Unity of Man and Woman,* Boston 1981, 116, 132. (This is the first of the four volumes which contain all the allocutions of the Holy Father's five-year catechesis on human love; see my note # 3 above).

19. *The Acting Person,* ch. 2.

20. *The Original Unity of Man and Woman,* 43–49, cfr also John Paul's address at the Catholic University of Lublin, June 9, 1987. See my commentary on this address, *Dialektyka podmiotowosci i transcendencii w osobie ludzkiej (The Dialectic of Subjectivity and Transcendence in the Human Person),* in "Ethos" 2/3 (1988), 57–65.

21. *Love and Responsibility,* 115; cfr also *The Acting Person,* ch. 3, sections 7 and 9, and ch. 4, section 3.

22. For instance in *Die personalistische Konzeption des Menschen,* 34.

23. Cfr *Love and Responsibility,* 40–44.

24. *Ibid.,* 57–61.

25. Cfr his allocution at the Catholic University of Lublin, June 8, 1987.

26. *The Original Unity of Man and Woman,* 72.

27. *Ibid.*

28. See for instance *Ibid.,* 128–134.

29. *Love and Responsibility*, 95–100.

30. *Ibid.*, 96.

31. Cfr also *Die personalistische Konzeption des Menschen*, 34–36.

32. Cfr for instance *Love and Responsibility*, ch. 5.

33. One often calls by the name of dualism the position that there is a substantial distinction between body and soul in man, that is, a distinction such as is presupposed for the continued existence of the separated soul after death and before the resurrection of the body. Obviously John Paul and any other Christian thinker as well maintains this dualism. This is dualism in a sense very different from the dualism of which we speak in the text; it is a dualism which is in no way antagonistic to the nuptial meaning of the body, and in fact further reflection would show that it is even presupposed by the nuptial meaning of the body.

34. When I speak here of "spiritualism" I do not mean a Platonic metaphysics of the soul and a failure to do justice to the unity of soul and body. I speak of spiritualism and of dualism, not in a Platonic or in a Cartesian sense, but in the sense in which FABRO in effect ascribes them to Kierkegaard when he says that Kierkegaard's thought is characterized by "a diffida contro ogni prevalere dell' esteriorita" (*Introduzione al Diaro*, I, Brescia 1980, 68). Perhaps one could say, in deliberate over-simplification, that we speak in the text of a spiritualism and dualism which in the modern world derives more from Luther than from Descartes. It is the spiritualism/dualism which underlies much Protestant situation-ethics. The Cartesian spiritualism/dualism is in any case anti-materialistic, whereas we refer in the text to a dualism/spiritualism which is commonly found among largely materialistic thinkers who want to have nothing to do with the metaphysics of a spiritual soul. This whole subject needs further investigation, which would stand very much in the service of the development of John Paul's personalism.

35. JOHN PAUL II. *Blessed are the Pure of Heart*, 263.

36. See above all *ibid.*, 19–152.

37. *Ibid.*, 50–51.

38. *The Acting Person*, 79.

39. *Ibid.*, 71–90.

40. *Ibid.*, 80.

41. Subject to the qualification introduced in the next paragraph.

42. DIETRICH VON HILDEBRAND expresses a related thought in his great work, *In Defense of Purity* (the original German title is *Reinheit und Jungfraeulichkeit*), 21–26. He says that in all sexual intimacy there is enacted an incomparable self-disclosure of each partner to the other, a unique revelation of the most intimate secret of each partner, and he says that this self-revelation is enacted whether the man and woman want it or not. This is why sexual union, as soon as it is isolated from marriage and from any spousal self-donation, effects a terrible *desecration* of each, a terrible *self-squandering* of each. This idea of self-surrender through self-revelation, and of self-squandering as the result of irresponsible sex, adds something to the analyses of Karol Wojtyla/John Paul. There is an important study waiting to be written on the understanding of man and woman, of sexuality, chastity, purity in the writing of von Hildebrand and of John Paul.

43. Cfr JOHN PAUL II, *The Theology of Marriage and Celibacy*, 313.

44. Of course the nuptial meaning of the body has a bearing on all kinds of other issues of sexual and marital morality. To give just one example: John Paul rethinks the idea that one of the purposes of marriage is the *remedium concupiscentiae*, and says that this does not mean that marriage legalizes the unbridled exercise of concupiscence, but rather that it relieves concupiscence in the sense of making sexual desire serve the union of persons and making it more dependent on the nuptial meaning of the body.

Chapter 4

THE REJECTION AND REDISCOVERY BY CHRISTIANS OF THE TRUTHS OF *HUMANAE VITAE*

The Most Reverend John J. Myers

I was honored when Fr. Stetson wrote and asked me to participate in the Symposium celebrating the twentieth anniversary of the issuance of *Humanae vitae*. I thank him for including me in this symposium.

My remarks, for the most part, will be from a personal as well as pastoral perspective. While preparing these thoughts, it occurred to me that Church teaching on conjugal morality and the reaction to that teaching has been a significant feature of my life as a priest. During my years of theological studies for the priesthood in Rome, the various Pontifical Commissions were often featured in the news as well as in the famous Roman gossip circuit. I was completing my first year as an assistant pastor in July, 1968 when, via the radio, I heard the news that the Holy Father had issued *Humanae vitae.* I remember thinking to myself, "Oh Oh. Here we go!", and an explosion did, indeed, follow.

In these remarks we will explore some reasons for the rejection of the encyclical, and consider some signs which I consider hopeful, indicating a rediscovery by both clergy and laity of the truths contained in this historic document.

I. REJECTION OF THE ENCYCLICAL

To begin with, we must frankly admit that the encyclical *Humanae vitae* was rejected by a large number of both Catholic clergy and laity when it was issued in 1968. Though we say they rejected the encyclical, what we really mean is that they rejected the received teaching against contraceptive intercourse and the supporting argumentation of Pope Paul VI. Few clergy or laity bothered to actually read the encyclical after they found out from the media what was contained in it.

To enable them to rediscover the truths of *Humanae vitae,* we must understand and address the reasons for the rejection of the encyclical in the first place. I shall address four primary causes:

1) The Historical Context

Many forces in both the Church and the world contributed to a climate in which rejection of the teaching on conjugal morality was rendered subjectively possible and even likely for many Catholics. The Second Vatican Council confronted people with ecclesial changes which, for many, were profound and often confusing. A change in the teaching against artificial contraception was just another change, according to some influential people.

Catholics, no less than others in society, were increasingly secularized and influenced by a hedonistic and materialistic culture.

66

Catholic theologians began to adopt a "university" model of theology which minimized the role of authoritative teaching. This opened the way to "privatized conscience." The media, and media personalities in the wake of the Council, became major actors in the theological process. Catholic thought and many issues in the Church captured public attention. The resultant process did then, and continues to this day to introduce ideas and forces into Church life which contain many elements contrary to the Gospel of Christ.[1]

Moreover, media hype produced a neurotic fear of "over population"—in my opinion, rooted in the fear that contemporary Western lifestyles might suffer. Coupled with this, the sexual revolution was in full swing and the "pill" was just coming into its own, offering another easy and effective solution to an age old dilemma.

As a result, the Holy Father and the bishops found themselves without the appropriate traditional support and assistance for their teaching. The faithful could pursue the easier path, claiming to hide behind high-sounding motives and the theories of well-known theologians, not rooted in rigorous ethical thought, as they pursued their search for happiness through sensuality and materialism.

2) The Inadequate Formulation of Magisterial Teaching

If one studies the history of the Church's teaching on contraceptive intercourse, it becomes clear that until very recently the magisterium *proclaimed* the teaching abstractly rather than *explaining* it effectively to the average Catholic. An explanation gradually developed under the Scholastics, but it was convincing primarily to Scholastic philosophers and those trained by them. At best it was *intellectually convincing* and, in the area of sexual morality, that type of conviction is more often than not inadequate to repel temptation. The Church required a more coherent sexual ethic which would convince the *average untrained Christian* of the *truth* of her teaching.

Until this century, the Church had depended heavily upon the connatural knowledge of the faithful and the respect for her teaching authority to convince the faithful that "each and every act of intercourse must remain open to the possibility of new life." Now, in the mid-twentieth century when the argument from authority no longer convincing (especially in matters sexual), and when Scholastic philosophy and theology were understood by only a few, even among the clergy, the lack of a fuller presentation became very costly.

As noted above, the context in which *Humanae vitae* was issued involved all manner of contrary historical forces. Obviously, a teaching which was perceived by people to be based primarily on authority, and which seemed to many to restrict freedom, was not going to fare well—and it didn't!

A final aspect which must be understood is that for almost five years, both the faithful and the clergy had been led to believe by the media (both Catholic and secular) that the teaching would change.[2] In 1968, when the long awaited papal answer was given and there was no change, they reacted with dissent and disbelief. Worse yet, the *mode* of presentation had not changed in any appreciable way. Frankly, theology and theologians had not prepared Church teachers well for the immense challenge before them.[3]

Certainly *Humanae vitae* began to use the terminology and framework of *Gaudium et spes*. These developments, however, were neither obvious enough nor dramatic enough to be noticed by many students of theology, and surely not by the average Catholic.

Please do not misunderstand me. The Holy Father was correct, his reasoning was correct, the Holy Spirit had guided his courageous teaching. But Christ's promise to guide his Church did not include a promise to present each teaching in the fullest and most persuasive manner each time.[4] In *Humanae vitae* we see an example of this. If one already accepted the Church's teaching on contraceptive intercourse, then *Humanae vitae* made eminent sense. If one did not accept it, then, for many, the encyclical lacked sufficiently convincing arguments. The conclusions of *Humanae vitae* were prophetic, the reasoning involved was true, but it did not convince the general populace. Many of the reasons for this failure could be found in the world and in the faithful whose lives and thought were too permeated with the world. One would have hoped in retrospect, that because of the intense media attention, the encyclical had been a better teaching document.

3) The Reaction of the Faithful

Having argued that the magisterium's mode of presentation in regard to her teaching on contraceptive intercourse, while certainly true, could have been pedagogically more effective, it would be well for us to look briefly at the response of the faithful to this teaching over the years to see if we can glean some insights for the future.

It is interesting to note that nowhere in theological literature or in cultural records, until our present century, do we find any widespread movement among the faithful to defend the practice of contraceptive intercourse as a "good thing," or even a "lesser evil."[5]

Indeed, one can characterize the public response of the faithful to this teaching of the Church as quite docile until the late 1950's. People sinned, but they had little problem admitting it *was* a sin and confessing it as such. The faithful, for the most part, acted on the moral instinct that sex had to do with procreation. Contraceptive intercourse rendered this unlikely, and so it was wrong. People did not possess an extremely detailed knowledge of *why* it was wrong, only *that* it was wrong. It was seen as more of a sin of weakness than of malice, but sinful it was. This "moral instinct" was reinforced by the Church in her ordinary and universal magisterium.

In the 1940's, 1950's and 1960's, people actually confessed sins of contraception. Why? Because they knew they were "supposed to." Once again, it was a time when the argument from authority was honored. People were actually convinced that the Pope and Bishops spoke in the name of Christ! Given hindsight, I think the argument from authority was at its apogee. It simply worked well enough that we did not notice it was loosing its force for many.

Coupled with this was the cultural development of the "pill generation." Pills were being developed for all manner of maladies. There was a pill for almost any medical problem. So it was only natural that when science developed a "pill" which would eliminate the worry of pregnancy, people would think it quite normal and moral. They began to ask their confessors about using this new "pill" to plan their families. This brings us to our fourth consideration:

4) The Inadequate Mediating Role of the Clergy

One of the primary roles of the parish priest has always been to take the teaching of the Church and to explain it to his parishioners in such a way that it would make sense.

One often hears the question: Priests supported the teaching on contraception in the 30's and 40's, why not now? What changed? The answer is quite simple. The faithful changed. I really wonder what would have happened if the laity of the 30's and 40's had asked the same questions the faithful raise today. In the early part of this century, the clergy stood firm on this matter because it was fairly easy to do so. Remember, at that time the primary argument *given* and *accepted* was both abstract and heavily reliant on authority. In most small towns, the parish priest was the most educated person around. If a sincere couple wanted to use contraception, they went to the parish priest to seek his advice. In moral matters, he gave "advice" in much the same manner as a doctor or judge. It was more in the realm of a decision handed down than a detailed and convincing explanation. If the inquisitive couple pressed the point as to *why* contraception was against God's Law, the average parish priest knew a few Scholastic maxims on the natural end of intercourse and the primary and secondary ends of marriage. He knew enough to *appear* knowledgeable. He was like the proverbial perfume bottle—it smelled full, though nothing was within.

My point is this: The Catholic clergy, as a group have *never* known how to defend this doctrine. They did not know in the 30's and they do not know now. The only difference is that *everyone*

70

now knows they don't know! The questions of the laity demand more convincing answers.

Among the truths about parish priests pertinent to our topic are these: they like to be liked and they do not like controversy. They have a tremendous capacity to empathize with people who are hurting. They do not like to dash peoples' hopes, especially if they have been part of the process of raising their hopes. They do not like to tell people bad news, especially if they do not know *why* they have to tell them the bad news . Unfortunately, the average parish priest of the late 60's and 70's considered the Church's teaching on contraception to be "bad news" and began, in the confessional, to waffle on the issue. This waffling continues on a broad scale to the present day. Teaching on sexual morality is practically never heard in regular preaching.

II. Rediscovering the Truths of Humanae Vitae

Up to this point in our presentation, we have concentrated on what we consider four primary reasons for the rejection of *Humanae vitae* by a large portion of the clergy and laity:

1) The impact on the faithful of historical and cultural forces over which the Church had little if any control.
2) The need for a better presentation by the magisterium in the teaching on contraception, and the need for a coherent and complete sexual ethic which would be convincing to the average Catholic in the pew.
3) The realization of the above by a large number of the clergy and faithful as well as the media.
4) The inability of the average parish priest to convincingly present and defend the Church's vision of marital morality in regards to family planning, and his consequent waffling from the pulpit and in the confessional.

While the above could give one cause for despair, these reasons are related to the hope I will explore. In each of these areas one can see the Spirit marvelously at work remedying the situation. Mind you, the situation is *not* remedied, but it is *beginning to be remedied,* and it is this which gives me hope. I should like to address three reasons for this hope.

1) The Reformulation of the Received Teaching by John Paul II

As we stated earlier, one of the primary reasons for the rejection of the received teaching on contraception was that it was largely formulated in a language which was no longer used or understood by modern man. Pope John Paul II has done the Church a tremendous service by taking the perennial truth of the Church's teaching on contraceptive intercourse and reformulating it into a teaching which appeals deeply to contemporary couples.[6]

Not only this, but he is the first Pontiff to enunciate a total theology of human sexuality within which contraception can be seen as morally wrong. I cannot emphasize too much the importance of such a development. The rejection of the Church's teaching on contraception and other sexual questions is due in large part to the lack of an integrated and appealing theology of human sexuality which could be readily explained to the faithful.

John Paul II roots the entire Christian sexual ethic not only in the *structure of the act* (though he acknowledges its importance), but rather in the meaning of the love reflected in sexual intercourse. Couples readily assent to the teaching that the *normal* meaning of intercourse is mutual love. They can also readily assent to the teaching that the *ultimate* meaning of sexual intercourse is when their love for each other can produce new life, if it be God's Will.

What they are *gradually* beginning to see is that within this context, it is morally dishonest to withhold part of that love through contraceptive intercourse.

Long before he became Pope, John Paul taught at length on sexual morality. He maintained that the only proper response to a person is *love.* For him, a person could never be reduced to the level of an *object,* a means to an end. Contraceptive intercourse, he posited, is one way in which married couples sin against one another, their own love, and the Creator, by reducing the other to a means of pleasure.[7]

Moreover, as Pope, John Paul has explored the marriage relationship more deeply. He has repeatedly explored the "language of the body." The human body, with its sexual dimension seen in the very mystery of creation, is not only a source of fruitfulness and procreation, as in the whole natural order, but includes right from the beginning the "nuptial" attribute, that is, *the capacity for expressing love—that love precisely in which the man-person becomes a gift, and by means of that gift, fulfills the very meaning of his being and existence.*[8]

The conjugal act is "true" only when the conjugal love which it expresses is true. As the Holy Father states:

> In the act which expresses their conjugal love, the spouses are called to make *of themselves* a gift, one to the other: nothing of what constitutes their *being* a person may be excluded from this self-donation.[9]

Contraception introduces a limitation on the self-giving of the other, and therefore a falsification which contradicts true married love.

Married couples are *gradually* beginning to see the core *practical* teaching of the Holy Father: That married couples may engage in conjugal relations whenever they wish, but they must *mean what they are saying with their bodies.* The theological appreciation of the language of sexual relations makes the difference between contraceptive intercourse and the abstention from intercourse of those practicing natural family planning painfully apparent.

In contraceptive intercourse the married couple is saying "We know that our love for each other can create a new life. We do not want this new life at this time. Therefore we will, by a directly willed positive act, destroy that creative part of our love. Though our bodies are saying we love each other completely, we do not love our fertility at this time. Thus we will sterilize our love."

A couple using natural family planning is saying "We know that our love for each other can produce a new life. We cannot responsibly *mean* what we would be saying if we had intercourse at this time, thus we choose to abstain from intercourse *out of respect for the meaning of intercourse.*"

The Holy Father expands on the constant teaching of the Church on the ends of marriage. He teaches that conjugal relations may never be entered into outside that context of committed marital love. Neither can conjugal acts be reflective of committed marital love (which is total love expressed through bodily union) when they deliberately destroy the procreative dimension of that love when it is present. Neither the love dimension nor the procreative dimension of intercourse can ever be destroyed by the couple and still have their conjugal union mirror the divine love. It is precisely in this destruction of one of the two essential meanings of their sexual love that sin enters into intercourse. In contraceptive intercourse we have an attitude of defiant destruction of the procreative dimension of sexual love. In natural family planning, the couple abstains from intercourse during the fertile period precisely out of a profound *respect* for the meaning of their relations at this time. They will not say with their love what they cannot responsibly mean.

It is this vision of marital sexuality which we can present to the faithful today. It is a vision which can transform their marriage and be the basis of a profound marital spirituality. It is this vision, given by Pope John Paul under the inspiration of the Holy Spirit, which gives me hope.

2) The Changing Response of the Faithful

The second reason for hope is the renewed consciousness of the faithful in regards to their sexuality. For centuries married couples viewed the sexual dimension of their marriage as isolated from their spiritual life. They could not understand how God might have a real share in their sexual love. They were not given, nor could they likely have appreciated, a vision of human sexuality which would have enabled them to appreciate this fact.

This is changing. More and more couples are beginning to appreciate the vision of sexuality offered by the Church. They are beginning to appreciate that human sexuality goes to the core of a person's being. They are beginning to understand that genital activity is not something which is casual and recreational. Rather, it is the ultimate means of communicating committed love at the physical level.

Having accepted this insight, they are gradually coming to appreciate the real *dishonesty* which is present in any type of sexual activity which violates this norm. What gives me hope is that this basic insight inexorably leads to the rejection of false theologies of sexuality which accept contraception, masturbation, homosexual acts and premarital sex as legitimate expressions of committed love. Having accepted the context of the Church's teaching, people instinctively realize these actions are dishonest.

In this regard, I have been much encouraged by the research which has made Natural Family Planning a significant option for responsible couples. Two weeks ago we were privileged to have the national convention of the Couple to Couple League in our diocese. Hundreds of couples and families attended. The presentations were both hard-hitting and helpful. Enthusiasm was high. Surely such movements give us great cause for hope.

3) The Renewed Support of the Clergy

The third reason which gives me hope is the renewed support of the clergy. Sadly, I am not speaking of all the clergy. We must frankly admit that a large number of clergy and women religious have simply closed their minds to any reconsideration of the issues involved.

I do, however, see significant reason to hope when looking at the younger clergy. They have grown up in a different age. They do not carry the emotional baggage of the middle age clergy on these issues. They have a *predisposition for assent* to the teaching of the Church.

I worry, though, that this predisposition could be squandered if we bishops do not guarantee that it is built upon in the seminary. We must face the fact that not a few moralists in our seminaries do not enthusiastically support the received teaching.

The *way* in which the teaching is presented to our seminarians is all important. There is a real difference between a teacher who *presents* a position and one who *advocates* a position.

This distinction reveals a major dilemma facing Catholic theological training at the university and seminary levels today. One can *present* a position quite adequately but not believe it at all. It is quite another thing to *advocate* a position. All kinds of things go into advocacy; the tone of voice, the enthusiasm, the body language. A student knows when a professor is an advocate or a presenter.

All too often a moral professor will adequately present the Church's teaching, and then spend the next several days presenting the dissenting views of various contemporary theologians. This in itself would not be improper methodology, since a priest ought to be familiar with the opposing views. The problem is that the unit on contraception often ends here. There is often little, if any, effort made to refute the objections to the teachings. The seminarian is left with the impression (usually unstated) that the position of the dissenting theologians is *on par* with that of the magisterium.

This is simply foreign to true Catholic theological methodology. The magisterium has a *privileged vision* of doctrinal and moral truth, since it is guided by Christ's promise to be with His Church "all days." The magisterium's teaching on moral matters, even when not infallibly defined by Pope or Council, must be the practical norm of conscience. The Church is usually *certain* that a doctrine is true long before she commits herself to the precise terminology of a *definition*.

Not a few moralists who teach in our Catholic colleges and seminaries quite simply do not believe the magisterium has such a "privileged vision of truth." One need only recall the innumerable theologians who came to the defense of Fr. Curran before his *missio canonica* was revoked by Cardinal Hickey.

As bishops we must guarantee that the theologians teaching in our institutions and seminaries are faithful *advocates* of Church teaching. This does not mean that the theologians teaching in our seminaries are mindless parrots with no creativity of

76

their own. It does mean that we choose only those who can and will *enthusiastically* support the magisterium to be the teachers of the next generation of priests. If we cannot guarantee *advocacy* of the Church's teaching on contraception in the seminary, then we can guarantee it nowhere.

We surely have the right to expect that our future priests are faithful to the magisterium's teaching within the sacramental context of the confessional. After all, it is not the priest's private forum where he can dispense "grace and favor" dispensations like the nobles of old. He is *in persona Christi,* and must realize that neither infallibility nor even "religious submission of mind and heart" are to be accorded his personal theological opinions, even if well intentioned.

III. A QUESTION?

I would like to share with you a question which has been in my thought in recent weeks. We believe that contraceptive intercourse violates the natural law. It frustrates that sexual act and sets sinful limits on the mutual self-giving of married couples.

If these things are true, as we believe they are, then it seems to me there should be discernable consequences. I believe that research which could demonstrate these consequences, though difficult, would be extremely helpful in improving the effectiveness of our pastoral teaching.

Could research establish useful information about the *quality* of the marriage relationship among couples who follow Church teaching as opposed to those who have adopted a contraceptive lifestyle? Surely, the beautiful experiences shared by many couples is a fine beginning, but could we not find a way to establish these facts more clearly? I hope so. I think it is worth pursuing.

CONCLUSION

As we come to the end of these reflections, I cannot but recall that, in the aftermath of *Humanae vitae,* I felt almost overcome. I could not see how the Church could turn it around. I

77

thought we were in for a very long period of dissent, the end of which I might not live to see. I am happy to report I was wrong. I had not counted on the prompting of the Spirit, the brilliance of Pope John Paul II, the realization by many faithful that their vision of human sexuality was flawed, and the courageous willingness of today's seminarians to meet this challenge if given the opportunity. Today, I am full of hope. However, lingering anxiety still cautions me that unless we build on these beginnings, and build quickly, we shall waste this precious second chance God has given us to teach and *convince* the faithful of the "Truth that will set them free."

NOTES

1. For an excellent analysis of the media's role in the rejection of *Humanae vitae* see James Hitchcock, "The American Press and Birth Control: Preparing the Ground for Dissent," *Homiletic and Pastoral Review,* 80 (July 1980), pp. 10–26.

2. *Ibid.* pp. 12–13.

3. Cardinal Ratzinger has pointed out "that at the beginning of the great debate following the appearance of the encyclical *Humanae vitae* in 1968, the demonstrative basis of the theology faithful to the magisterium was still relatively slim." (*The Ratzinger Report,* Ignatius Press: San Francisco, 1986, p. 87).

4. This is frankly admitted by the Congregation for the Doctrine of the Faith. See *Mysterium Ecclesiae, AAS* 65 (1973), pp. 396–408.

5. See the definitive work on the history of this teaching by John T. Noonan, Jr., *Contraception: A History of its Treatment by Catholic Theologians and Canonists* (Cambridge, Mass.: Belknap Press of Harvard University Press, 1965).

6. For an excellent summary and analysis of the Holy Father's teaching in this area see Richard M. Hogan and John M. LeVoir, *Covenant of Love* (New York: Doubleday, 1985).

7. For a more complete presentation of this line of thought see the Pope's work *Love and Responsibility,* (Farrar, Straus, Giroux: New York, 1981). The Pontiff states: "The personalistic norm says: A person is an entity of a sort to which the only proper and adequate way to relate is love. . . . This norm, in its negative aspect, states that the person is the kind of good which does not admit of use and cannot be treated as an object of use and as such the means to an end." (p. 41).

8. John Paul II, General Audience, 16 January, 1980.

9. John Paul II, "Discourse on Responsible Personhood," 17 September, 1983.

Chapter 5

THE IMPORTANCE OF THE CONCEPT OF *MUNUS* TO UNDERSTANDING *HUMANAE VITAE*

Janet E. Smith

For all the debate surrounding *Humanae vitae* it still remains to a large extent an unappreciated document. And here I am not referring to the fact that *Humanae vitae* is largely a neglected and rejected document. Rather, I am claiming that the scholarship on *Humanae vitae* has not yet probed the full dimensions of the encyclical. This is not surprising since church documents are typically succinct and in need of much elaboration and in the grand scheme of life, the twenty years we have had the encyclical in our hands is not a long time. Certainly, the articles already written on *Humanae vitae* would fill volumes and many of these articles contribute substantially to our understanding of its teaching. Yet much of the debate has been peripheral to the argument of the encyclical itself and what debate there has been has concentrated largely on only a few lines of the encyclical.

The basic teaching of *Humanae vitae*—that contraception is an intrinsic moral evil—is a point that has caused and continues to cause tremendous resistance to the document. And thus it is certainly a point most worthy of scholarly attention. Yet sometimes I think that so much energy is expended arguing over the reasons why each and every marital act must remain ordained to procreation that other truths of the document have been somewhat neglected. The truth of this observation is borne out by a reading of Pope John Paul II's lectures about the theology of the body, about marriage and about *Humanae vitae*. Most who have read and studied *Humanae vitae* are struck by the freshness of his approach, for his interpretation illuminates human sexuality and marriage to such an extent that one wonders if one understood the encyclical at all in earlier readings. Pope John Paul II would, of course, deny that he is promoting novel or original truths and insights. Indeed, he regularly uses the word "reread" and by this word "reread" he means we must think through again what truths we can find in basic texts of scripture and in Church documents. These truths are the fundamental truths of Christianity and thus nothing new. But it is also true that these truths have the depth of mystery and thus are inexhaustible. The depth of the Pope's understanding of these truths about the human person, of sexuality, and of the Christian calling that informs his reading of *Humanae vitae* is rather astonishing—one gets the sense that it would take a lifetime of study and reflection to begin to grasp the wealth of his "rereading", of his insight.

Some time ago I began to try to reread *Humanae vitae* carefully; this included reading it in Latin and consulting each of the footnote references. This method of reading *Humanae vitae* led me to realize how much the document relies upon an understanding of marriage as a Christian vocation and to see how important the concept of vocation, here, of course, the vocation of marriage, is to understanding *Humanae vitae*. It may seem obvious to many that it would not be possible to understand the Church's teaching on contraception without understanding its teaching on marriage and the family, but our age has to a large extent lost the sense of the importance of vocation, of finding one's vocation and living in accord with it. Marriage is rather routinely seen as an arrangement largely designed to provide companionship—children are often considered a mere option in marriage. In my teaching of *Humanae vitae,* I have found that providing instruction on marriage as a vocation has enabled me to teach *Humanae vitae* more effectively for I discovered that students had little understanding of Christian marriage and of the place of children within marriage. (Nor, of course, do I think this lack of understanding is limited to students only.) Much of their resistance to *Humanae vitae* dissolved as they came to realize what marriage is and why children are so important to marriage. This is not to say that I have found a surefire way of convincing the sceptical of the truth of *Humanae vitae* but I have learned that there is a better chance of success when I do not begin with HV 11—the section asserting that each and every marital act must remain ordained to procreation—but when I begin by sketching the Christian understanding of marriage.

This approach escapes the temptation of treating *Humanae vitae* as a negative document—as one which has as its sole intent the prohibition of contraception. For truly the document is much more positive than negative when understood in light of the Christian understanding of marriage since it explains to spouses how properly to live out their elevated calling to the vocation of marriage. It relies upon an understanding of the centrality of children to marriage and the centrality of the virtue of "self-giving" to marriage. It promotes the view that parents are primarily responsible for fostering the virtue of self-giving in their children and conversely that children play a key role in fostering virtues in their parents.

The first line of *Humanae vitae* invokes a concept of marriage and the Christian life that is quite foreign to our current ways of thinking. The fourth word of the encyclical, the word *"munus",* is one of particular interest to us here. It carries with it a number of ideas that provide a context to the whole of *Humanae vitae.* The first part of this paper will provide an abbreviated philological account of the meaning of the word *"munus"* to suggest how important it is for spouses to live up to the challenges of their *munus*. The second portion will develop some analogies based on the concept of *munus* that I hope will ease resistance to *Humanae vitae*'s condemnation of contraception. Finally, the third portion of the paper will explore what may be called the "interiority" of *munus*. There the argument will be made that fulfilling the *munus* of transmitting human life, or of having children, is essential to the ultimate purpose of marriage, to the sanctification of the spouses and their children into the loving, generous, and self-sacrificing individuals all Christians are called to be.

Meaning of *"Munus"*

So what does this word *"munus"* mean and why is it important to *Humanae vitae?* The very first line of *Humanae vitae* in Latin reads *Humanae vitae tradendae munus gravissimum.* This line is usually rendered "The most serious duty of transmitting human life. . . ." The translation "duty", however, does not fully convey the richness of the term *"munus".* The chief problem with the translation "duty" for *"munus"* is that for many modern English-speaking people the word "duty" has a negative sense. A duty is often thought of as something that one ought to do and something that one is frequently reluctant to do. The word *"munus,"* though, truly seems to be without negative connotations; in fact, a *munus* is something that one is honored and, in a sense, privileged to have.

"Munus" means much more than duty. One who knows classical Latin would as readily translate *"munus"* as "gift," "wealth and riches," "honor," or "responsibility" as "duty." One common classical Latin use of the word would be in reference to the bestowal of a public office or responsibility on a citizen. Being selected for such an office or responsibility would be considered an honor; the selection would entail certain duties, but ones that the recipient willingly embraces. The word is also often used synonymously for "gift" or "reward:" it is something freely given by the giver and often, but not always, with the connotation that the recipient has merited the gift in some sense; it is given as a means of honoring the recipient. In scripture and in the

writings of St. Thomas Aquinas the word *"munus"* is used to refer both to gifts that men consecrate to God and to gifts and graces that men receive from God. I would recommend that the first line of *Humanae vitae* be translated to read not "the most serious duty of transmitting human life" but "the extremely important mission of transmitting human life." Rather than being a burdensome duty, a *munus* is much closer to being an assignment or mission that is conferred as an honor on one who can be trusted and who is chosen to share the responsibility of performing good and important work. The next lines of *Humanae vitae* reinforce this reading for they speak of the "spouses fulfilling this mission freely and deliberately and thereby offering a service to God the Creator," and later in section 8 of *Humanae vitae* we read:

> It is false, then, that marriage results from chance or from the blind course of natural forces; God the Creator wisely and providently established marriage with the intent that He might achieve His own designs of love through men. Therefore, through the mutual gift of self, which is proper and exclusive to them, the spouses seek a communion of persons, by which, in turn, they perfect themselves so that in the procreation and education of new lives, they might share a service with God.

A chief meaning of *"munus"*, then, is that it is a work that one does at the behest of God and as a service to God. This word has great currency in Church documents, especially the documents of Vatican II and commonly refers to the designated tasks which different individuals have in building up the kingdom of God. Translations of Vatican II commonly render *"munus"* as "role," "task," "mission," "office" and "function." In these documents, *"munus"* is also closely linked with "vocation", "mission", "ministry", and "apostolate" and at times seems interchangeable with them. The general meaning of *"munus,"* like these words, carries the meaning of something that the Christian is called to do. While occasionally *"munus"* is translated simply as "task," it routinely refers to tasks that have the nature of a solemn "assignment." *"Munus"* quite regularly refers to a special assignment that is entrusted to one, the completion of which is vital for the successful institution of the kingdom of God. Again, it is conferred as an honor, often empowers one, and entails serious responsibilities and obligations.

The documents of Vatican II regularly identify the *"munus"* of different individuals in the Church. One primary reference of the word is to the triple *munera* of Christ of being Priest, Prophet, and King (*Lumen gentium* 31). Christians, in their various callings, participate in these *munera;* they do so by fulfilling other *munera,* specifically entrusted to them. For instance, Mary's *munus* (role) is being the Mother of God (LG 53 and 56) which also confers on her a maternal *munus* (duty) towards all men (LG 60). Christ gave Peter several *munera:* for instance Peter was given the *munus* (power) of binding and loosening and the *grande munus* (special duty) of spreading the Christian name— which was also granted to the apostles. The apostles were assigned the *munera* (great duties) of "giving witness to the gospel, to the ministration of the Holy Spirit and of justice for God's glory" (LG 21). To help them fulfill these *munera* they were granted a special outpouring of the Holy Spirit (LG 21). By virtue of his *munus* (office), the Roman Pontiff has "full, supreme, and universal power" in the Church (LG 22) and also by virtue of his *munus* (office) he is endowed with infallibility (LG 43). Bishops, by virtue of their episcopal consecration, have the *munus* (office) of preaching and teaching (LG 21). The laity, too, sharing in the priestly, prophetic, and kingly *munus* of Christ, have their own mission [*missio*]; they are particularly called [*vocantur*] to the *munus* (proper function) of "working, like leaven, for the sanctification of the world from within, and especially so by the witness of their lives. By shining forth with faith, hope, and charity, they are to manifest Christ to others" (LG 31). *Munera* are conferred by one superior in power upon another; it is important to note that Christ is routinely acknowledged as the source of the *munera* for each of the above-mentioned groups. *Munera* are not man-made but God-given.

Many Church documents use the word *"munus"* in their titles or subtitles. *Familiaris consortio,* for instance, is about the *"munus"* or role of the family in the modern world and the title of the document is routinely translated as such. The use of *munus* in the title of *Familiaris consortio* and in the first line of *Humanae vitae,* then, follow typical practice in ecclesial documents. And I think their appearance serves the purpose of linking these documents to each other and to the Vatican II document *Gaudium et spes.*

The section of *Gaudium et spes* that treats of marriage repeatedly makes reference to the *munus* of spouses, which is the *munus* of parenthood. One paragraph provides a summary statement: "In the duty [*officium*] of transmitting and educating human life, which is the special mission [*missio*] of spouses, they understand themselves to be in cooperation with the love of God the Creator and, as it were, interpreters of this love. Therefore, with human and Christian responsibility, they will fulfill their *munus* (task). . . ." (GS 22).[1] Later in the same section, there is mention of "the *munus* (duty) of procreating" and it is stated that "those who fulfill this God-given *munus* (task, *commissio a Deo*) by generously having a large family are particularly to be admired" (GS 50).

So what does *Humanae vitae* mean when it speaks of the *munus* of transmitting human life? This *"munus"* is clearly a special task chosen by God for spouses. It is a responsibility that they have but a responsibility given to one as a kind of honor. To reject this *munus* is to reject what God has ordained for spouses. We hear modern couples speaking of "choosing" to have a family, but it would be very odd for Christian spouses to speak in this way, for Christian marriage has as one of its purposes the bringing forth of children into the world and the raising them up to be worthy to be citizens of the kingdom of God. *Casti connubii* states this principle well:

> . . . Christian parents should understand that they are destined not only to propagate and conserve the human race, nor even to educate just any worshippers of the true God, but to bring forth offspring for the Church of Christ, to procreate fellow citizens for the Saints and servants of God, so that the worshippers devoted to our God and Savior might daily increase. (AAS 454)[2]

The closing of the section of *Gaudium et spes* on marriage reads

Everyone should be persuaded that human life and the task of transmitting it are not realities bound up with this world alone. Hence they cannot be measured or perceived only in terms of it, but always have bearing on the eternal destiny. (GS 51)

Spouses should not underestimate the enormity of the responsibility bestowed upon them through the *munus* of transmitting life; nor should they underestimate the importance of the task entrusted to them. God is the creator of each and every human life. Indeed, it is through a special act of creation that each and every human soul comes into existence. And all souls are destined for eternal union with God, a union that God might be described as desperately desiring. Again, spouses do not create this life, God does. He *transmits* this life through the act of sexual intercourse. It is appropriate that this act be performed by spouses only for only spouses are able to imitate God's creative act properly. That is, God's act of creation is an act that is free, responsible, and loving; a spousal relationship is the only one that has the features of being free, responsible, and loving in a way appropriate to the bringing forth of new life. Indeed, couples—particularly those hoping to conceive a child—not infrequently feel that God is present in a special way during their love-making, and this feeling has a sound foundation in reality. The emotions that flow and the bonding that takes place during love-making are of a grand and mysterious—not to say sacred—nature. Again, this is understandable considering that God is the source of love and life and that He has privileged spouses with being the transmittors of life through an act of love. Those who do nothing to contravene the baby-making possibilities of sexual intercourse have, in a sense, left God space to perform His act of the creation of a new soul, if He so chooses.

Humanae vitae, then, relies upon an understanding of the nature of the *munus* of transmitting human life that acknowledges how elevated is the task of bringing forth new life. *Humanae vitae* has as its purpose clarifying certain facets of the *munus* of spouses, the *munus* of bringing forth children and of being responsible parents to them, with a view to guiding them to be worthy of eternal union with God.

Use of *munus* to ease resistance to *Humanae vitae's* condemnation of contraception

Now at the outset of this paper, I indicated that I thought the study of *Humanae vitae* focused too exclusively on the passages that assert a prohibition against the use of contraception. But here I would like to suggest that the above understanding of *munus* may offer some assistance in explaining how contraception violates God's intent for spousal intercourse. Here I will employ a few rather imaginative analogies to show how the use of contraception would be a reneging on one's *munus* of transmitting human life, to help explain why "each and every act of marital intercourse must remain ordered to procreation" and why the procreative and unitive meanings of marital intercourse are inseparable.

The first analogy requires that we imagine a good and generous king of a country who asked one of his worthy subjects to help him build his kingdom. The king needs a responsible individual to perform this *munus* since it is important, indeed essential, to the kingdom to keep contact with a distant borough. He chooses to honor his subject George with this *munus* of keeping contact with one of the outlying boroughs. In order for George to perform this service, he gives George the use of a fine horse and buggy that will enable him to travel to the distant borough. The king has business that he wants conducted in this borough whenever George visits it and makes it clear that George should never go to this borough unless he attends to the king's business while he is there. He has another motive in providing George with the horse and buggy for he also wishes George to prosper. The horse and buggy will enable George to attend to his own business when he travels to the distant borough. The king makes it clear to George that those who live in the borough and George himself will fare better if George uses the horse and buggy as designated, for the king desires both that the kingdom prosper and that George prosper—indeed, it is quite impossible for either to prosper without the other. So George achieves two ends by the use of the horse and buggy; he advances his own prosperity and that of the kingdom. The king also tells George that business is closed in the outlying borough one week of every month and during that week George may freely use the horse and buggy for his own purposes. Moreover, since the horse and buggy are handsome and efficient it is pleasurable for George to employ them, but pleasure is an added benefit to the use of the horse and buggy, not the purpose of the horse and buggy. The king more or less leaves it up to George how often and when he visits the borough when business is in session. He simply asks George to be generous and to use his own good judgment. Now, if George were to accept this *munus* and the horse and buggy that go with it but refused to drive to the outlying borough, then he would be reneging on the *munus* that he accepted. And if he were to go to the borough but refuse to attend to the king's business while there, he would again be failing to live up to the demands of his *munus*.

There are parallels here with the *munus* of transmitting human life. God has given this *munus* to spouses because He wishes to share the goods of His kingdom with more souls and He has chosen to call upon spouses to share with Him the work of bringing new life into the world. This work is an honor and entrusted only to those willing to embrace the responsibilities of marriage. Those who perform the responsibilities of marriage in accord with God's will benefit both themselves and the rest of society. The spouses achieve the good of strengthening their relationship through sexual intercourse, i.e. the good of union, and they achieve the good of having children, i.e., the good of procreation. Both goods are goods that also benefit God's kingdom for He wishes love between spouses to flourish and He desires more souls with whom to share the goods of His kingdom. Thus, sexual intercourse is a part of the *munus* of transmitting human life, a *munus* that is intimately bound with other goods. Those who accept this *munus* need to respect the other goods that accompany it. Still, in the same way that the good king allowed George to use the horse and buggy even when business was not in session in the outlying borough, God has so designed human fertility and human sexuality, that humans are sometimes fertile and sometimes not. It is permissible for spouses to enjoy marital intercourse at any time, whether they are infertile or fertile. God seems to have designed the human system this way to foster greater union and happiness between spouses. But He has asked them to be receptive to new life, generously, and in accord with their best judgment, and not to misuse the *munus* that He has given them. To choose never to have children is like refusing to go to the outlying district ever. It is to renege on the *munus* that comes with marriage. To have contraceptive sex is like driving to the outlying borough and ignoring the king's business. The contracepting couple is repudiating the *munera* of their own fertility and altering the functioning of the body. They are pursuing pleasure while emphatically rejecting the good of procreation. They may not feel that they are engaging in an act of emphatic rejection of the good of procreation but in terms of their *munus,* that is exactly what they are doing. (It is also true that the good that they achieve, pleasure, is not the good of union, which can be achieved only if the procreative good is also respected. More will be said about this below). But the good king allowed George to use the horse and buggy when business was not in session and that is exactly what the couple is doing who are having sexual intercourse during the infertile period. They are pursuing one good, the good of union *when another is not available.* Again, the contracepting couple is repudiating a *munus* that they have accepted; the noncontracepting couple is cooperating with the complexity of the *munus* that God has entrusted to them.

Let us now use another analogy to attempt to further clarify why *Humanae vitae* makes the claim that it is impossible to separate the procreative meaning of spousal intercourse from the unitive meaning. Here we shall be daring and use the responsibilities entailed in presiding over the sacrament of the Eucharist. This analogy may seem far-fetched but we must remember that in being a sacrament marriage is more like the priesthood than it is like an appointment by a king.

What we need to focus on here is that vocations have a certain reality and make certain demands upon those embracing their vocation. *Humanae vitae* 10 speaks to this point:

> The responsible parenthood of which we speak here
> has another dimension of utmost importance: it is

rooted in the objective moral order established by God—and only an upright conscience can be a true interpreter of this order. For which reason, the mission [*munus*] of responsible parenthood depends upon the spouses recognizing their duties towards God, towards themselves, towards the family, and towards human society, as they maintain the right hierarchy of goods.

For this reason, in regard to the mission [*munus*] of transmitting human life, it is not right for spouses to act in accord with a private judgment, as if it were permissible for them to define subjectively and willfully what is right for them to do. On the contrary, they must accommodate their behavior to the plan of God the Creator, a plan made manifest both by the very nature of marriage and its acts and also by the constant teaching of the Church.[3]

By freely and deliberately accepting the calling of marriage, spouses also freely and deliberately accept the *munera* that go along with that calling in the same way that a priest in responding to the calling of the priesthood also accepts the *munera* of that "assignment." To be married but not to accept the *munus* of transmitting life, is like taking on an assignment but not taking on the full responsibilities of that assignment—and not realizing the full goods of that assignment both for one's self and for others. For instance, a man may wish to be a priest, but not wish to perform some of the sacraments; that would be a repudiation of his calling and the *munera* of his calling. The following elaboration of this parallel with the priesthood cannot be made exactly coordinate at all points, but if it is a correct parallel at some key points it should illuminate why it is wrong to attempt to separate the goods integrally united within a given act.

Participation in the Eucharist is parallel to the marital act in so far as it too conveys several goods, the good of sacramental grace, for instance, and the good of united community activity. It is possible that a priest may wish to pursue the good of united community activity without pursuing the good of sacramental grace. He may be facing a community that includes both Catholics and non-Catholics and not wish to exclude any from receiving the Eucharist. Knowing that he should not distribute the Eucharist to non-Catholics, he may do something to invalidate the consecration—he may not say the proper formula or may use invalid matter for the eucharistic bread and may then distribute it to all present. (Admittedly it makes the example somewhat preposterous to speculate that a priest who would have qualms about serving the Eucharist to non-Catholics would choose to invalidate the sacrament, but let us suspend our disbelief for the sake of the analogy!) Thus he would gather the community together but not violate the norms for distribution of the Eucharist. But it should be clear that it amounts to a sort of deception or indeed a sacrilege to pretend that one is distributing the Eucharist, while having deliberately deprived the act of one of its essential—and sacred—dimensions. The intention of the priest may be good, but he could achieve the end of unifying the community by some other ceremony; he need not violate the meaning of the Eucharist to do so. Or, he could distribute the Eucharist only to the Catholics present and tolerate the "imperfection" of a not fully united community. But he ought not to seek the good of a united community at the expense of the good of the sacrament. The ultimate irony, of course, is that he is not truly achieving the good of union if he excludes the good of sacramental grace, for it is precisely the sharing in sacramental grace that effects the truly meaningful union of the assembly. Any other sort of union is superficial in comparison.

Spouses, too, may be tempted to pursue one good achievable through sexual intercourse and not another. Yet they are faced with the same reality as the priest; to pursue one good without the other is to fail to achieve either. As noted, the priest who distributes a non-consecrated "eucharist" achieves at best only a superficial uniting of the community for he fails to effect the sacramental grace that is the source of true unity achieved through reception of the Eucharist. Similarly, couples achieve only a superficial union through contracepted sexual intercourse; they do not achieve the union appropriate to spouses. As *Humanae vitae* states, the goods of union and procreation are inseparable; spouses cannot achieve one good without due ordination to the other. Certainly couples may believe that they are achieving the good of union through contracepted sexual intercourse, but their actions do not correspond to their intentions. The fact is that contracepted sexual intercourse yields neither the good of procreation nor the good of spousal union. To be sure, some sort of union takes place, for shared activity nearly always produces some sense of union among the participants. For instance, strangers viewing a sporting event together experience a sense of union with each other, but such is a fleeting and insubstantial union. Sexual intercourse, being by its nature a very intimate activity, undoubtedly creates bonds even when engaged in with strangers but these are not the bonds appropriate to spousal intercourse. (Indeed, sexual intercourse engaged in with strangers or with non-spouses is not only a source of union [albeit superficial] but it is also a source of alienation; for the sexual partners know that they do not intend the depth of union inherently promised by the act of sexual intercourse. Therefore, although they have achieved some kind of bond it is not an authentic, trustworthy or spousal bond.)

Nor does sexual intercourse robbed of its procreative meaning create the bond that is proper to spousal intercourse, for spousal union requires that the spouses give fully of themselves to one another. Theirs is to be a total self-giving. But by using contraception they are withholding their fertility and all that being open to child-bearing entails. Being open to child-bearing is an essential feature to spousal sexual intercourse. And "being open to child-bearing" does not mean that the couple must intend to have a child with every act of sexual intercourse. Rather, it means that the couple has done nothing to deprive an act of sexual intercourse of its baby-making possibilities. Thus, those who are infertile whether through age or physical abnormality, or through the periodic infertility all women experience by nature, have not negated the procreative meaning of sexual intercourse. If engaging in sexual intercourse in a spousal way, they are still expressing the desire for a union appropriate for spouses—one that would accommodate children if children were a possibility. The meaning may be present in sexual intercourse only symbolically but it is there nonetheless.

Let us consider somewhat further the claim that being open to baby-making, at least symbolically, is essential to spousal intercourse. Consider the common description of contracepted sexual intercourse as "recreational" sex. It is sex that is engaged in for play. Now such sex obviously could be engaged in with a large number of individuals. That is, most individuals could easily find others with whom they would enjoy a romp in the hay. But when we start thinking of the baby-making possibilities of sex and start thinking of those with whom we are willing to share the responsibilities of child-rearing, the list of potential partners for such sexual activity becomes quite short. And this is because we know what kind of bond is appropriate for being parents—it is, in fact, the bond characteristic of spouses—i.e., one that is faithful and exclusive and committed to a lifetime union with another. Thus those responsibly engaging in non-contracepted sexual intercourse with another are engaging in an activity which expresses the kind of commitment or love that spouses should have for one another. Indeed, a sign that one loves another as a spouse is one's willingness to have and raise children with this individual, the willingness to interlock one's life together with another in the way that is appropriate for raising faithful Christians. Therefore, written into the desire for union characteristic of the spousal love of Christians is an ordination to having children. On the other hand, those who rob their sexual intercourse of its procreative meaning are also severely diminishing its unitive meaning; indeed it no longer expresses the kind of union that spouses are meant to desire with one another. Truly, spouses using contraception are desiring pleasure more than union for they have deliberately diminished the unitive meaning of their act.

And finally, let it be noted that just as a priest can pursue community union through other means as effectively as doing so with an invalid Eucharist (and truly more effectively when sacrilege is not present), so, too, there are many ways that spouses may express their love and foster union apart from intercourse. What is wrong is deliberately depriving a sexual act of the essential good of fertility all in the name of union—or again, more properly, all in the pursuit of pleasure. To do so is to use one's *munus* improperly; to be selective about the way that one will serve God through the gifts and responsibilities that He has entrusted to one.

The above analysis of *munus* has, I hope, shown that contraception is so very popular because spouses have such an imperfect understanding of the meaning of sexual intercourse. Were they to understand that the act of spousal intercourse is united with the *munus* of transmitting human life and that the ability to achieve meaningful spousal union is integrally united with the procreative meaning of sexual intercourse, they may not so easily tamper with the integrity of the sexual act. The fairly common view that sex is a superior form of recreation would permit few objections to contraception. But the view that sexual intercourse is part of the *munus* of transmitting human life, of performing a service for God, and of facilitating a unique human relationship and human union that is unachievable without a procreative meaning, suggests all sorts of reasons why contraception might be morally objectionable.

The Interiority of "Munus"

To this point the discussion of *munus* has focused largely upon the external dimensions of *munus,* upon its status as a task bestowed as an honor on man by God. What is needed now is a consideration of the kind of internal benefits gained by one who eagerly embraces and seeks to fulfill his or her vocation, mission, or *munus.* What we need to do is focus on the interior changes in the individual who lives his or her married commitment faithfully. And we wish to place particular emphasis on the role of children in fostering these interior changes. When *Humanae vitae* asserts that one of the defining characteristics of marriage is its fruitfulness, it states:

> [Conjugal] love is fruitful since the whole of the love is not contained in the communion of the spouses, but it also looks beyond itself and seeks to raise up new lives.

Humanae vitae cites further from *Gaudium et spes:*

> Marriage and conjugal love are ordained by their very nature to the procreating and educating of children. Off-spring are clearly the supreme gift of marriage, a gift

which contributes immensely to the good of the parents themselves.

This final portion of the paper will, very briefly, elaborate on this claim of *Gaudium et spes* and *Humanae vitae* that children contribute immensely to the good of the parents. The fundamental point is that having children and raising children is a source of great good for the parents, that having to meet the responsibilities entailed in the *munus* of transmitting human life works to transform individuals into more virtuous individuals—it works an attitudinal change that enables them to be better Christians.

Here we will be drawing upon the work of Pope John Paul II—in particular from passages in his book *Sources of Renewal*, which he wrote (as Karol Woytyla) as a commentary on Vatican II, and from *Familiaris consortio*, in itself a marvelous commentary on *Humanae vitae*. In these works, the Pope puts a great deal of emphasis on man's internal life, on his need for transformation in Christ. The focus on interiority is characteristic of Pope John Paul II; it flows from his interest in personalist values, in his interest in the kind of self-transformation one works upon one's self through one's moral choices. Pope John Paul II has labored hard to draw the attention of moralists to the personalist values, the values of self-mastery and generosity, for instance, that are fostered by moral choices. He repeatedly depicts life as a continuous process of transformation. For instance, in *Familiaris consortio* he states, "What is needed is a continuous, permanent conversion which, while requiring an interior detachment from every evil and an adherence to good in its fullness, is brought about concretely in steps which lead us ever forward. Thus a dynamic process develops, one which advances gradually with the progressive integration of the gifts of God and the demands of His definitive and absolute love in the entire personal and social life of man" (FC 9).[4] The task of life, then, is to become ever more like Christ through fidelity to the demands of one's calling in life.

In his book *Sources of Renewal* Karol Woytyla placed great emphasis on the "attitude of participation" required from Christians in Christ's mission, which he calls the "central theme of the Conciliar doctrine concerning the People of God."[5] There he makes reference to Christ's threefold power or *munus* as priest, prophet, and king in which Christians must participate. He maintains that sharing in this power or *munus* is not simply a matter of sharing in certain tasks; rather it is more fundamentally a participation in certain attitudes. He tells us that man has the power or " 'task' or 'office' (cf. Latin *munus in tria munera Christi*) together with the ability to perform it." He goes on to observe,

> In speaking of participation in the threefold power of Christ, the Council teaches that the whole People of God and its individual members share in the priestly, prophetic and kingly offices that Christ took upon himself and fulfilled and in the power which enabled him to do so. . . . The Conciliar teaching allows us to think of participation in Christ's threefold office not only in the ontological sense but also in that of specific attitudes. These express themselves in the attitude of testimony and give it a dimension of its own, as it were an interior form derived from Christ himself—the form of his mission and of his power.[6]

The claim that participating in a *munus* involves not just the power to act, nor simply the responsibility to complete an external act, but also requires an internal attitudinal change on the part of Christians adds another dimension to the complexity of this word. In *Sources of Renewal,* Karol Woytyla outlines the different attitudinal changes required to be faithful participants in Christ's threefold *munus.* He identifies a certain attitude associated with each of the three *munera* of priesthood, prophet, or king.

It is possible to crystalize these attitudes in the following way. In conjunction with the *munus* of *priesthood* shared by the laity, the attitude needed is a sacrificial one, whereby "man commits himself and the world to God."[7] To explain this attitude, he cites from a key passage in *Gaudium et spes:*

> It follows, then, that if man is the only creature on earth that God has wanted for its own sake, man can fully discover his true self only in a sincere giving of himself. (GS 24)

Sharing in the *prophetic munus* of Christ requires that spouses work to bring the truth of Christ to the world, through evangelization. And the *kingly munus* is best exercised by man not in rule over the world, but in rule over himself. Thus, to be a priest, one must be self-sacrificing, to be a prophet, one must evangelize, and to be a king, one must govern—and govern one's self above all.

It is in *Familiaris consortio* that we find more detailed instruction on how spouses are to participate in the threefold *munus* of Christ, how they are to be priests, prophets, and kings, or how they are to be self-sacrificing, evangelical, and self-mastering. *Familiaris consortio* speaks specifically about the family's part in the threefold *munus* of Christ; it states:

> The Christian family also builds up the Kingdom of God in history through the everyday realities that concern and distinguish its *state of life*. It is thus in *the love between husband and wife and between the members of the family*—a love lived out in all its extraordinary richness of values and demands: totality, oneness, fidelity, and fruitfulness—that the Christian family's participation in the prophetic, priestly, and kingly mission of Jesus Christ and of his Church finds expression and realization. Therefore love and life constitute the nucleus of the saving mission of the Christian family in the Church and for the Church. (FC 50)

In the remainder of *Familiaris consortio,* he explains how the family fulfill their participation in Christ's threefold *munus.* He identifies the *prophetic* office with the obligation of the family to evangelize, especially to its own members. The Pope rehearses the obligation of parents to be educators of their children, especially in matters of the faith. *Familiaris consortio* refers to the evangelization of children as an original and irreplaceable ministry (FC 53). It states:

> The family must educate the children for life in such a way that each one may fully perform his or her role [*munus*] according to the vocation received from God.

For the family, the *priestly* office is fulfilled by engaging "in a dialogue with God through the sacraments, through the offering of one's life, and through prayer" (FC 55). And the *kingly* office is fulfilled when the family offers service to the large community, especially to the needy. Note this powerful passage:

> While building up the Church in love, the Christian family places itself at the service of the human person and the world, really bringing about the "human advancement" whose substance was given in summary form in the Synod's Message to families: "Another task for the family is to form persons in love and also to practice love in all its relationships, so that it does not live closed in on itself, but remains open to the community, moved by a sense of justice and concern for others, as well as by a consciousness of its responsibility towards the whole of society." (FC 64)

The family participates in the threefold *munus* of Christ by being true to its own *munus*. In the previous sections of *Familiaris consortio* which laid the foundation for the discussion of the family's participation in the threefold *munus* of Christ, the Pope sketched out the interior changes to be gained when the family is true to its *munus*. What Pope John II hopes for from marriage is that it will result in the formation of a new heart within the spouses, the children and ultimately within all of society. This heart will be one that is loving, generous, and self-giving (FC 25). The family serves to build up the kingdom of God insofar as it is a school of love; as the Pope puts it, "the essence and role of the *munus* of the family are in the final analysis specified by love (FC 17). He goes on: "Hence the family has the mission to guard, reveal and communicate love." *Familiaris consortio* states that:

> The relationships between the members of the family community are inspired and guided by the law of "free-giving". By respecting and fostering personal dignity in each and every one as the only basis for value, this true

giving takes the form of heartfelt acceptance, encounter, dialogue, disinterested availability, generous service and deep solidarity. (FC 43)

The text also states:

All members of the family, each according to his or her own gift or *munus,* have the grace and responsibility of building, day by day, the communion of persons, making the family "a school of deeper humanity": this happens where there is care and love for the little ones, the sick, the aged; where there is mutual service every day; when there is a sharing of goods, of joys and of sorrows. (FC 21)

A key phrase for our purposes is the next line: "A fundamental opportunity for building such a communion is constituted by the education exchanged between parents and children, in which each gives and receives . . . and "Family communion can only be preserved and perfected through a great spirit of sacrifice. It requires, in fact, a ready and generous openness of each and all to understanding, to forbearance, to pardon, to reconciliation." These passages suggest the kinds of virtues needed for and cultivated by good family life. Successfully adapting to family life fosters love and generosity, the ability to forgive, and a whole host of related virtues. Both the parents and the children and ultimately the whole of society stand to grow in these virtues as the family attempts to be true to its nature.

Familiaris consortio confirms what a consideration of family life will reveal to the attentive observer. If we reflect upon what happens to ourselves when we marry or what happens to our friends when they marry, especially among those who work hard to have good marriages and to be good parents, we may well observe that the experience of parenting, like the experience of marriage, both requires and fosters many virtues. Having children generally does adults a lot of good. Most find that having children effects profound changes in their whole response to life. Becoming quite directly responsible for the future of others tends to be a pivotal point in most people's existence. My more reflective and articulate friends upon becoming parents have been known to exclaim "Everything has changed." They tend, for instance, rather of a sudden, to take more of an interest in community life; the quality of the schools and the neighborhood, the immorality in the media, all acquire a new importance. Many find themselves rethinking their religious views when they have children for they become concerned to hand on something substantial to their children; they find themselves striving to learn more about their faith when they realize that they are responsible for nourishing the faith of their children. Most individuals also find themselves more concerned about their moral lives when they have children—they realize the importance of example for raising kids. Some find themselves trying harder than ever to master a bad temper or to become neater in their habits. Most find themselves becoming more selfless, more patient, kind, loving, and tender when they have children. This occurs largely after they have learned how selfish, impatient, and harsh they can be, for children help one learn of one's vices before one acquires the virtues. Learning to live with children has many of the same advantages of living with a spouse; it forces one to accommodate one's self to others; it forces one to acknowledge that one has constant tendencies to be selfish. Staying awake at night with children, dealing with their daily joys and sorrows, learning to be a good example for them, contributes greatly to the maturity of adults.

If this portrait of family life is correct then it corresponds with Pope John Paul II's claim that the *munus* of the family assists individuals in becoming more self-sacrificing (as they strive to fulfill their priestly *munus*), more self-controlled (as they strive to fulfill their kingly *munus*) and more concerned to provide service to the larger community (as they strive to fulfill their prophetic *munus*).

The *munus* of transmitting life, of educating children, of being parents, then, yields multiple goods. Creating a family where self-giving and all the virtues might begin to flourish is an activity that has multiple purposes. Certainly, it works towards achieving God's end of producing more souls to share with Him eternal bliss. Having children also helps parents mature and acquire many of the virtues they need to be fully human and fully Christian. Furthermore, building families is to the good of the whole of society for generosity and love should flow from the family to the larger community, especially to the poor and needy.

Familiaris consortio, a document that is wonderfully rich in itself, should also serve to provoke more extended considerations of the goods produced by the family. Our current lamentable experiences of all the social evils attendant upon the breakdown of the family should provide us with an unparallelled appreciation for the importance of good family life.

What is key here for our understanding of *Humanae vitae* is to recognize that to reject the procreative power of sexual intercourse, is not a simply rejection of some biological power. The resistance to the procreative power of sexual intercourse that accompanies the desire to use contraception predictably involves an underestimation of the value of the family—to God, to the spouses, and to the larger society. As Pope John Paul II knew, in order to promote the teachings of *Humanae vitae,* we must promote the family. Thus, mine is not a new approach to HV; as usual the Pope is far out in front of the rest of us. He draws upon and develops the understanding of marriage worked out in earlier Church documents. But since this understanding is a patrimony that modern times have wasted, we desperately need to recover an understanding of marriage fully consonant with Christianity. If we do so, we will find that creating good and healthy families is not some avocation spouses have, but is their central vocation. Nourishing the family is primary over all other considerations—career, recreation, public works, whatever. If this is so, or rather since this is so, there needs to be a shift in the thinking of most of us. We need to take seriously the teaching of *Humanae vitae* that spouses may limit their family size only for grave reasons. Children should not be measured over against a European vacation, a second car, or a second family income. True Christian spouses are eager to have many children—for God—and deeply regret financial restraints or whatever obstacle stands in the way of their having more children. For they know that to reject the *munus* of transmitting life, to limit the number of children they have, is to limit the number of gifts and blessings that God gives to them, it is to limit the gifts that they return to God, and it is to limit their opportunities and ability to grow as Christians.

NOTES

1. Translations for the documents of Vatican II are taken from *The Documents of Vatican II,* ed. by Walter M. Abbott, S. J. (Chicago: Follett Publishing Company, 1966).

2. The translation for *Casti connubii* is mine.

3. The translations of passages from *Humanae vitae* are mine.

4. Translations for *Familiaris consortio* are from *The Role of the Christian Family in the Modern World* (St. Paul Editions; Boston, MA., no date given).

5. Karol Woytyla, *Sources of Renewal,* translated by P. S. Falla (Harper and Row: San Francisco, 1980) 219.

6. Ibid, 220.

7. Ibid, 223.

Chapter 6

INDIVIDUAL AUTONOMY AND PRIVACY: ARE THERE LIMITS?

Bruce C. Hafen

I am grateful for the underlying attitudes I have sensed about this conference. For example, I liked the statement in the Symposium Proposal about the need to appeal to people who appreciate the wisdom of religious teachings "independently of theological reasoning." The idea that religious truth can be rationally persuasive even to those who reject religion reminds me of the cartoon showing a bearded professor who has a horseshoe nailed over the door to his university office. A friend visiting him in the office notices the horseshoe and asks the professor, "you don't believe in those superstitions about horseshoes bringing good luck, do you?" The professor replies in a confidential whisper, "Oh, they say it works whether you believe it or not!"

I also liked the suggestion of James Kearns that he sees this conference not so much as a source of ready answers but as a seedbed for future interdisciplinary thought and research. Thus, open-ended reflections in the conference papers have been actively encouraged. It is in that spirit that I will think out loud with you about constitutional and related considerations concerning individual autonomy and privacy.

I would have you know at the outset that I have strongly held convictions about the transcendant significance of personal freedom. I believe deeply in the enduring, even everlasting, uniqueness of the individual personality. For me, law and religion contain rich wellsprings of nurturing support for personal development and the preservation of meaningful individual liberty. We sometimes think of laws and rules as limiting us rather than freeing us. But it is only because of the law of gravity that we can walk. Rules of grammar make communication possible. Only by adhering to the laws of physics can we send people to the moon and compose beautiful music. Obedience to law is ultimately liberating, even if that same obedience appears at first blush to be confining.

Consider an example from the application of free speech concepts to children in public schools. The term "freedom of expression" has two different meanings. It usually means freedom *from* restraints upon expression. But "freedom of expression" can also mean having the *capacity* for understanding and self-expression. If free speech is to be meaningful, a citizen must have something worth saying, together with the maturity, insight, and skill needed to say it. Thus, in order to help our children develop real autonomy, we must help them temporarily submit their immediate autonomy to the schoolmaster of discipline in ways that may appear to limit their freedom temporarily but which ultimately enhance their capacity for the exercise of freedom.

But in this modern era, we have never had so much freedom of speech with apparently so little worth saying to one another. As Neil Postman put it in his provocative book, *Amusing Ourselves to Death,* George Orwell feared those who would ban books; but Aldous Huxley feared there would be no reason to ban a book for there would be no one who wanted to read one. Postman's worry, and mine, is that Huxley's fear might be a more serious threat to our long range liberty than Orwell's.

Our view of personal freedom may be either short range or long range. In the short run, we must frequently endure limitations on our autonomy so that, in the long run, we might enjoy more meaningful personal freedom and sustain in perpetuity the social conditions that will allow our descendants to enjoy a life of freedom as well. Modern society has come to prefer a short range view of personal autonomy that will undermine the development of actual long range autonomy, both for individuals and the society. Ironically, this development has proceeded in the name of expanding personal autonomy, when in fact I believe it will contract it.

To develop this theme, I wish to discuss the 1986 Supreme Court case of *Bowers v. Hardwick,* which illustrates the place of privacy and autonomy in recent constitutional analysis. I would then like to review the history of how we have come to our present dilemma over this issue, followed by some observations on the effect of the new autonomy on some illustrative topics related to the theme of our conference.

The *Bowers* case arose from the following circumstances. A policeman in Georgia entered a dwelling looking for Michael Hardwick, who was wanted for questioning regarding some minor offense. Someone in the dwelling pointed toward a bedroom door. The policeman entered the bedroom, where he found Mr. Hardwick engaged in homosexual relations with another man. The state conducted a preliminary hearing against Mr. Hardwick on the charge of violating Georgia's sodomy law, but decided to drop the charge rather than taking it to a grand jury. Mr. Hardwick then himself brought suit in federal court to challenge the constitutionality of the law. The court of appeals for the Eleventh Circuit eventually held that the state statute was unconstitutional on the ground that it violated Mr. Hardwick's fundamental right of privacy and intimate association.

In a much publicized and highly controversial opinion, the Supreme Court two years ago reversed the Eleventh Circuit by a vote of 5 to 4, holding that the constitutional right of privacy does not guarantee the right to engage in homosexual sodomy.[1]

Justice White's majority opinion acknowledged that the Court's prior decisions, including the famous abortion case of *Roe v. Wade,* did establish a privacy right, but stated that these precedents were limited to cases involving the family, marriage, and procreation and do not extend to all forms of "private sexual conduct between consenting adults." The majority expressed its concern about the risks of subjective judicial lawmaking whenever a new substantive right is identified outside the express limits of the constitutional text, noting that the "Court comes nearest to illegitimacy when it deals with *judge-made* constitutional law having little or no cognizable roots in the language or design of the constitution."

In stating the appropriate constitutional test for determining when courts should recognize a right that is not enumerated in the text of the constitution, such as privacy, Justice White quoted earlier cases establishing such extraordinary protections *only* for personal liberties that are "implicit in the concept of ordered liberty" or "deeply rooted in this Nation's history and tradition." He found that homosexual conduct, long rejected by Western culture as deviant behavior, did not fall within these categories. The court did not directly address the question of whether the *recognized* area of constitutional protection would protect the sexual privacy of heterosexual, as distinguished from homosexual, unmarried adults. That issue could well become a major point of focus before some future Supreme Court. The question would then be whether the court's treatment of *Hardwick* was based primarily on his sexual orientation or his status as a single person.

A vigorous dissent for four justices authored by Justice Blackmun, who had written the majority opinion in the abortion cases 13 years earlier, stated that Michael Hardwick's right to express his own sexual orientation and to choose his own form of intimate association is protected by "the most comprehensive of rights and the right most valued by civilized men," namely "the right to be let alone." The dissent argued forcefully that the right of privacy protects one's intimate personal decisions, especially if those decisions involve conduct in one's own home. The rationale for this conclusion was based squarely on the assumption that individual *autonomy* is a core constitutional right: "We protect those rights *not* because they contribute . . . to the general public welfare, but because they form so central a part of an individual's life." Thus, the right to marry and have children is protected not because of some social interest in childbearing or "a preference for stereotypical households," but because "individuals define themselves in a significant way through their intimate sexual relationships with others."

The dissenting opinion expressly rejected the view that the moral values of society may be determined by a long established cultural consensus: "The fact that [homosexual acts] 'for hundreds of years, if not thousands, have been uniformly condemned as immoral' " is not "a sufficient reason to permit a State to ban them today." Indeed, the dissent continued, the ultimate test of a constitutional freedom is whether it protects the personal "right to differ as to things that touch the heart of the existing order." Having thus given personal autonomy a pre-eminent analytical position, the dissent then shifted the burden to the state to show a truly compelling interest that would justify intrusions on so fundamental a freedom. None of the state's arguments about public morality and the interests of society rose to the demanding level of the dissent's test, essentially because the dissenters found that the case involved "no real interference with the rights of others."

I have taken the time to review the dissent's autonomy theory, because *that theory* clearly represents the dominant view reflected in current literature in the scholarly legal journals. Indeed, one of today's best known constitutional scholars, Laurence Tribe of Harvard Law School, wrote the brief and argued the case for Michael Hardwick. In addition, the dissenting opinion is significant because it evidently came within a whisker of becoming the majority opinion. The *Washington Post* reported shortly after this case was handed down that Justice Lewis Powell had originally voted to overturn the sodomy statute because it permitted what he thought was a cruel and unusual punishment; however, Justice Powell changed his mind for undisclosed reasons and eventually voted to uphold the statute.[2]

In addition, the dissent's broad approach to protecting sexual privacy has been widely encouraged by the popular media and has already been adopted by some prominent state supreme courts. For example, *Time* magazine published an essay shortly after the opinion was announced entitled "The Individual is Sovereign."[3] This essay summarized the history of morals legislation, particularly as applied to homosexuality, and noted that "customs do change." Citing John Stuart Mill's famous libertarian principle that the only justification for limiting individual liberty is to prevent harm to others, the essay concluded that there had been no "harm" shown in the *Hardwick* case that would justify an intrusion on a homosexual person's autonomous choice. Moreover, it said, "most sexual activity has very little to do with procreation" and state interference with sexual choices violates the fundamental principle of free thought.

At the level of *lower* courts, most states have not reached definitive decisions on these issues, but the highest courts of New York and Pennsylvania had, not long before *Hardwick,* upheld rights of sexual privacy among all consenting adults. The New York case granted unmarried adults the right to seek "sexual gratification" in a case where the "private settings" involved included vehicles parked on city streets in the early morning hours.[4] The Pennsylvania case gave constitutional protection to sex acts performed in a public lounge between dancing performers and lounge patrons, holding that a law prohibiting deviate sex acts between unmarried persons discriminated against them on the basis of their marital status.[5]

Court decisions of this kind have a very different effect from legislative decisions that remove statutory penalties or otherwise "de-criminalize" sexual conduct. If a *legislature* removes criminal penalties against, say, fornication, this action will protect unmarried cohabitants from *criminal* prosecution. But it will not give their relationship the same constitutional status as marriage. Thus, unmarried couples would not have the same rights to tax preference, inheritance rights, or marital property interests. In addition, the state would have an easier time imposing regulations that regard unmarried cohabitation as potentially *harmful,* even if it is not criminal. For example, even if a legislature repealed its criminal laws against fornication, that state could still, upon a reasonable showing of likely harm, prevent a child custody placement with a cohabiting parent, or it could decide that a pregnant but unmarried elementary school teacher is setting a bad example for impressionable students.

However, if a *court* finds that a state's fornication or sodomy laws violate a *constitutional* right of privacy and autonomy, sexual conduct between unmarried people would be not just legally *permitted,* but would be constitutionally *protected.* As a result, the state's interest in protecting traditional sexual morality in a variety of non-criminal ways would then be far more difficult, because its regulation in *custody* placements or its standards affecting the personal lives of school teachers would invade constitutional rights.

For instance, after the New York Court of Appeals struck down that state's anti-sodomy law on constitutional privacy grounds, a lower New York court permitted one adult homosexual to *adopt* another adult homosexual, thereby creating a "family" relationship even though homosexual marriage is not permitted in the state of New York (or elsewhere). The lower court noted that prior New York case law would have barred such adoptions as violating public policy, but the adoption court found that the Court of Appeals' sexual freedom opinion disposed of the public policy issue, having conveyed "eloquent pronouncements that have considerable import for the wider public policy considerations of public morality."[6]

In other words, the adoption of a personal autonomy theory by the U.S. Supreme Court would have far more profound social effects than legislative action to decriminalize sexual conduct. If the Supreme Court should overrule *Hardwick* or if it should uphold a right of sexual privacy between unmarried heterosexual adults, we would probably see a ripple effect in the public consciousness very similar to the effects of the abortion cases since 1973, which have clearly made public opinion more tolerant of abortion. Those who favored Michael Hardwick's position before the Supreme Court were not concerned *primarily* with protecting Mr. Hardwick against *criminal* prosecution, since no prosecution was actually pending at the time they filed suit. Rather, they saw the judicial process as the ideal forum in which to urge the courts to assume bold leadership in altering the public consciousness, and they believe that the Court is and should be at the cutting edge in giving leadership to the formation of a new cultural consensus.

Incidentally, that very issue—whether society's moral values should originate within the majoritarian electoral and legislative process or whether the moral values of the culture should be shaped by judges who respond to the value claims of minorities—was at the heart of the controversy a few months ago involving Judge Robert Bork. One of Bork's primary arguments against judicial positions of the kind taken by the dissenting opinion in the *Hardwick* case was *that,* in the absence of clear-cut directions in the text of the Constitution, our constitutional system allocates the inherently subjective process of shaping the community sense of moral values to democratically elected representatives.

By contrast, those scholars who favored the *Hardwick* dissent argue that deference to the traditional moral values of the majority inherently violates the civil liberties of minorities. In their view, the core constitutional value of personal autonomy should make it impossible for *any* majoritarian policy or process to limit the individual choices of individuals, in the absence of serious and demonstrable harm. In other words, society itself should carry the burden of proof, being required to justify legal restrictions that grow out of traditional values. According to this view, the right of individuals outside the social mainstream to choose "deviant" behavior is at the heart of what the Constitution is all about. It is for such reasons that today's interest in personal autonomy as a source of constitutional protection has such significant potential implications for our social and political system.

Let us consider briefly how we have arrived at the point where the issue of autonomy has become so pivotal. One part of this perspective arises from the long range development of our intellectual history and the other from a more immediate summary of the Supreme Court's developing position.

Since ancient times, people have sought for a frame of reference that gives order and meaning to "life"—not only a meaning for life in general but a meaning for one's own individual life as well. One of the major contributions of classical Greek thought was the idea that there is a natural order to the universe and that mankind should live in meaningful harmony with that natural order. In other words, the meaning of "my life" was to be found with reference to a surrounding natural framework for "life" in a larger and more objective sense.

In the development of Western civilization prior to 1500 A.D., the dominant frame of reference for several centuries was a religious world view. Within that framework, the meaning of *"life"* in a universal sense was defined by religious teachings and the meaning of *"my life"* was defined as living in harmony with those teachings.

The revolutionary age that began with the Renaissance did not alter Western culture's underlying assumption that the universe was based on ordering principles of natural law; rather, those revolutions—particularly influenced by the scientific revolution—shifted the prevailing assumptions from a *religious* explanation of the cosmos to a *scientific* explanation. Even with so profound a shift, Western man *continued* to take for granted that there is a large, natural, and objective order within which each person can find a sense of harmony and purpose. The natural law inheritance of our constitutional theory reasons directly from this set of premises: "We hold these truths to be *self-evident*," wrote Jefferson in the Declaration of Independence, "that all men are created equal, that they are *endowed by their Creator* with certain unalienable rights, that among these are life, liberty, and the pursuit of happiness."

The history of our civilization over the last hundred years, however, has been the story of a gradual erosion of confidence in the idea of an external framework for our thinking about life— not just skepticism about the particular ordering principles furnished thus far by religion or science, but skepticism concerning whether there is *any such thing* as a set of natural, pre-existing principles at all. This is a very different development from the shift in emphasis from religious to scientific explanations, because the modern era doubts the very *idea* of a comprehensive order of meaning.

This is, of course, a major theme of 20th century life. As Tevya sang in the famous musical, without our traditions our lives would be as shaky as a fiddler on the roof. And as Viktor Frankl wrote in *Man's Search for Meaning,* "The traditions that had buttressed man's behavior are now rapidly diminishing. No instinct tells him what he *has* to do, and no tradition tells him what he *ought* to do; soon he will not know what he *wants* to do. More and more he will be governed by what *others* want him to do."[7] Or as Edna St. Vincent Millay wrote about "this furtive age" that "never speaks its mind," there "rains from the sky a meteoric shower/ of facts . . . they lie unquestioned, uncombined./ Wisdom enough to leech us of our ell/ Is daily spun; but there exists no loom/ To weave it into fabric . . ."[8] With the rejection of traditional forms of all kinds, twentieth century art, music, and literature have accurately mirrored this intellectual turmoil. As summarized by Western historian Thomas Greer, when Nietzsche said in the late 19th century that "God is dead," he "meant not only the God of the Judeo-Christian faith but the whole realm of philosophic absolutes, from Plato down to his own day."[9] And thus have we been living through a century of existential anxiety, its unsettling effects aggravated by the near universality of education and communication, which cause the philosophical problems that once bothered only the elite few, now to bother almost everybody. And in the middle of all this has raged a central fear; if there is no objective order, no natural framework for "life" in general, then all values are relative and "my life" is without foundation and without meaning.

Western *legal* theory and jurisprudence have developed in ways that parallel these sweeping movements in our thought. The influence of natural law, which had dominated legal thinking from Aristotle to Aquinas to John Locke, has been in a state of obvious decline for many years now, having been strongly challenged by legal positivism, legal realism, and most recently by the critical legal studies movement. I won't take time to address the way these schools of legal thought have corresponded to the decline of other traditional worldviews, but there is a clear similarity between jurisprudential developments and developments in other fields, as one would naturally expect with intellectual movements of such broad scope. However, I do wish to note one telling and significant recent development in legal theory, and that is what some writers call neo-natural law.

Neo-natural law is a development of the last quarter century. Its central figures include Ronald Dworkin and John Rawls. I am consciously glossing over all kinds of important distinctions and qualifications that could be observed regarding the work of these and other contemporary writers in order to make one observation that is relevant to our discussion about privacy and autonomy. This group of thinkers argues that there are indeed some moral absolutes, which distinguishes their thought from the pure relativists of recent times. For many of them, the beginning premise for any reasoning about the new moral absolutes is the *primacy* of individual autonomy. They also frequently emphasize the autonomy of the least advantaged—those whose personal rights have been most abused by traditional assumptions of law and social power during the recent past.

Under this analytical model, especially given the fragmented twentieth century context, we need pick up only one piece from our shattered cultural consensus, and that is the piece we have called "my life." Now we can *reconstruct* a framework for meaning that begins not from a larger set of surrounding principles in reference to which one finds purpose for his or her life—perhaps because we assume there *are* no fixed, surrounding principles. Rather, society and the universe must find their meaning by reference to *my life.* This is a complete reversal of the presuppositions of both the religious and scientific eras, in which individual meaning was determined with reference to larger spheres of meaning. It is also more than the cold acceptance of meaninglessness and absurdity that we associate with the existentialism of the 1960s. Now there is new respect for the notion of moral absolutes, but the absolutes begin with the individual, whose endowment of natural right comes not from God but from within himself. Thus does Dworkin assume that individual *rights* rather than legal "rules" should dictate judicial decisions in close cases. And thus does Rawls argue that individual dignity should be assigned an independent status that does *not* derive from maximizing the social good. Moreover, inequalities should be arranged not according to the greatest good for the greatest number, but according to the greatest benefit of the least advantaged.[10]

This new assignment of absolute priority to personal autonomy is consistent with the dissent in *Bowers v. Hardwick,* with its stress on the right of autonomous self-definition and its insistence that "the length of time a [political and social] majority has held its convictions or the *passions* with which it defends them" is insufficient to ensure judicial deference to a society's expression of its collective best good.

To provide some sense of the significance of this view, I note that these ideas arise from the incoherent ashes of existential alienation. They represent individual man not in a state of nature with others who rationally form a social contract, but individual man standing atop the rubble of a disintegrated urban civilization proclaiming not that God is dead but that each man or woman is her own God. This assertion of personal value is in many ways *understandable* and even *appealing* to me. The most stirring response to existential absurdity has always been the assertion by the lonely individual of his own responsibility for his life.

I also sense the anxiety we all feel today, living through an explosion of electronic-age technology and a massive growth of governmental power that create the capability of overwhelming physical and psychological intrusion and surveillance, by government, by other institutions, or simply by our neighbors. These developments have poured down on the heads of a mega-society already quaking from an underlying fear of imminent nuclear destruction. Thus I can understand why Justice Douglas, who first wrote of a constitutional right of privacy in 1965, would have believed that the right of privacy (or, as Justice Douglas and the dissenters in *Hardwick* liked to call it, the right to be let alone) addressed "the most critical constitutional battleground for human dignity in the modern age."[11]

But clothed in the robes of a preferred constitutional right, this extreme version of autonomous privacy not only *reverses* the relationship between the individual and her traditional sources of meaning, it reverses our way of thinking about constitutional relationships in ways that put at risk both our long term social stability and our capacity to develop meaningful personal autonomy as individuals.

As a way of illustrating what I mean by this concern, I will summarize briefly the development of constitutional theory that led to the view of the *Hardwick* dissent. The Supreme Court first mentioned a constitutional right of privacy in 1965 in the case of *Griswold v. Connecticut,* which held unconstitutional a state law that prohibited the use of contraceptives by married couples. The best known opinion from that case, although it did not speak for

114

a majority of the justices, was the plurality opinion of Justice Douglas. Douglas expressly acknowledged that the Court should not recognize constitutional rights that are not part of the constitutional text. He recalled the heavy criticism that was directed at the court in the 1930s when it had wandered from a base fixed in the founders' language. He then proceeded to locate the constitutional right of privacy within the emanations and shadows of several express provisions of the Bill of Rights.

Other justices who agreed that the state could not constitutionally regulate contraceptive use by married couples feared that the Douglas theory was too much of an invitation for judges to roam freely, breaking new constitutional ground wherever their fancy took them. They preferred to ground the concept of marital liberty in what they saw as a kind of natural law approach, recognizing that a few obviously cherished personal rights were so well established and so universally accepted in our traditions and our social consciousness that our collective sense of justice *required* their recognition. Such cases included the right of persons accused of crimes to be protected by the rudimentary safeguards of a fair hearing, or the right of parents to direct the upbringing of their children, or parents right to resist any attempt by the state to limit the size of their family. The strength of this test as a justification for recognizing interests not explicitly protected by the constitutional text was its reliance on the *universality* of the protected interest as evidenced by long tradition and widespread acceptance. Evidence of such universal recognition gave external validation to the fundamental character of the right in question, thus ensuring that a constitutional right would never represent only the subjective bias of a few judges.

The Court began running into difficulty within a half dozen years after *Griswold,* when it extended the right to obtain contraceptives to unmarried persons on an equal protection theory. Then in 1973 came *Roe v. Wade,* which relied expressly on the right of privacy to protect a woman's right to obtain an abortion. Our ongoing and passionate national debate about the merits of abortion ranks *Roe* among the most controversial cases ever decided by the Court. But quite apart from the rightness or wrongness of abortion itself, Justice Blackmun's *analysis* in *Roe* created hopeless confusion by indiscriminately mixing the concept of tradition with the contradicting concept of personal autonomy as its justification for recognizing a right not enumerated in the Constitution.

As I have analyzed the Supreme Court's cases that deal with the privacy theory, the personal liberty theory, or variations on those themes, I reach the conclusion that all of those cases *can* be understood as flowing from the preferred position of kinship and family life in our constitutional heritage.[12] Under *that* view, these cases don't create a right of personal autonomy; rather, they seek to protect the traditional institutions of kinship and formal marriage, in significant part because of the importance of family life for the continuity of democratic society. The majority opinion in the *Hardwick* case confirms my interpretation of these cases. However, the broad personal autonomy view came very close to prevailing in *Hardwick* and I sense that it has already gained widespread acceptance among the legal scholars and lower court judges from whose ranks our future Supreme Court justices are likely to come.

Perhaps I can illustrate more specifically why I regard the autonomy theory as having so much potential significance. As suggested earlier, this theory begins with the *assumption* that individual preference should prevail over social traditions unless the defenders of those traditions can mount a compelling case to prove that tangible harm would result from upholding the individual preference. This approach is fundamentally different from the tradition-oriented justification for the majority opinions in both the *Griswold* case and the *Hardwick* case. It also reflects the new view of neo-natural law, that we should allocate legal rights according to the greatest benefit of the least advantaged member of society, regardless of the social consequences.

In a more practical sense, the autonomy approach is also the exact *opposite* of the longstanding assumption that those challenging the status quo have the burden of proof. And that is my point: autonomy as a core constitutional value alters our analytical assumptions by 180 degrees. I acknowledge the argument that sometimes it is precisely our traditional social values that must be changed, as potently illustrated by the case of racial discrimination. But in the area of personal and social moral norms—those "habits of the heart," as Tocqueville called them—a special set of problems still obtains from the way a core constitutional preference for autonomy can alter our entire attitude on so fundamental a question as whether there are *any* normative values at *all* in our society, especially in cases where it is impossible to prove in the short run whether a particular practice is in fact harmful.

John Stuart Mill argued a century ago that society has the right to regulate personal conduct only to prevent harm to others. The Supreme Court has not yet accepted this basic postulate as a general proposition, although it has flirted with doing so. But what do we do when we simply cannot tell whether given behavior harms others in the society? Who should bear the *risk* of harm?

Consider an example. A crucial issue in *Roe v. Wade* was when does life begin. If fetal life were thought to begin in the early stages of pregnancy, the obvious interests of an unborn child would have prevented the legalizing of nontherapeutic abortions. On the other hand, if life were thought *not* to begin prior to viability, a pregnant woman's choice about abortion could be constitutionally protected. Unfortunately, as the Court said, the medical, religious, and other relevant communities were not in agreement about when life begins. In the absence of empirical proof on the question, the Court had to make an *assumption* about the nature of life and when it begins. Under traditional constitutional tests, the Court would have deferred to the assumptions of the legislature on such an important but subjective matter. But in the abortion cases, the Court *began* its analysis with the unexplained assumption that a pregnant woman has a right of privacy. This assumption shifted to the state the burden of proving that a fetus is a living being. This the state could not prove, just as the opposing side could not prove that a fetus is *not* a living being. The Court modestly stated that it was not determining when life begins, but then allowed its *a priori* assumption about privacy and autonomy to shift the burden of proof and thereby decide the outcome.

It is similarly impossible to *prove* or *disprove* conclusively the individual and social risks at stake in following or abandoning many of the normative values that underlie our culture. Just to take one obvious example, the available social science research is simply inconclusive on the question of whether non-violent pornography is personally or socially harmful. It may be harmful, but we can't yet *prove* that—perhaps because we lack adequate empirical testing methods. Just as we may not be certain whether we have irreparably harmed the ozone layer of the atmosphere until it is too late to turn back, we may not be able to prove that sexual permissiveness can destroy a society until it is too late. Because of the sheer gravity of the risks at stake in such questions, we have previously assumed that we should make cautious choices and resolve our empirical doubts in ways that protect the overriding interest of society in its own continuity. But the new moralistic passion for personal autonomy as a first principle could change all that.

If I were to illustrate my point by drawing a cartoon, I would show a bloody and tattered lawyer standing in rags before a judge whose desk and chambers were a pile of rubble. Holding up a few shreds of paper, the lawyer would say, "*Now* I think I can show, your Honor, that those practices were harmful to society."

The effects of the new commitment to autonomy can be illustrated in a wide variety of ways, which can be divided into at least two general categories: effects on our view of one's obligations to the larger social interest and effects on our view of one's obligations to other persons within one's intimate circle of contacts.

Just to illustrate briefly the relationship between individual autonomy and *social* interests, the importance of marriage once turned primarily on the significance of marriage as a social institution, but its importance is now widely thought to turn primarily on its significance to *individuals*. Changes in general attitudes toward *divorce,* for instance, have clearly been influenced by a declining belief that marital partners should feel any obligation for social stability.

A commitment to individual autonomy also affects one's view of obligations within personal relationships. Consider, for instance, the evident reluctance in popular discussions about AIDS to require marital partners (or unmarried partners, for that matter) to disclose a contagious condition to one another. Note also the unwillingness of the courts to let a husband interfere with his wife's decision about an abortion, despite the husband's obviously equal interest in the future of the unborn child.

In the interest of time, I will choose only one example for more extended final illustration—the area of adolescent pregnancy, which provides a particularly unsettling demonstration of what can happen to our common *sense* when the emotional power of an implicit belief in personal autonomy resolves any doubt or uncertainty in favor of leaving people alone. The prospect of unmarried adolescents having children has enormous implications both for society and for the more immediate circle of influence, which particularly includes the impact of a teenage pregnancy on an adolescent's parents and on the future life of the new baby.

My reading on this topic has failed to identify *any* serious scholar or policymaker who honestly believes it is a good thing for America's adolescent population to be sexually active. There is widespread agreement, even among people of very different persuasions, that teenage pregnancy is a huge national problem and must be addressed. But our mechanisms that influence both policymaking and the social consciousness are often immobilized because of the reticence some feel to interfere with society's new sense of respect for privacy and autonomy, which manifests itself in a variety of areas that affect young people.

For example, we are increasingly reluctant to talk with our children or others in ways that suggest there are right and wrong attitudes or right and wrong ways to do things, especially when matters of intimate choice are concerned. When the public is sufficiently outraged, we *may* become willing to label certain conduct as wrong, as reflected in the recent momentum of campaigns against drunk driving, smoking, and drug abuse. But those are the exceptional categories. The Surgeon General's recently distributed brochure on AIDS, for example, states, "No one should shoot drugs. It can result in addiction, poor health, family disruption, emotional disturbances, and death." The same brochure is much softer in its treatment of sexual choices: "You are going to have to be careful about the person you become sexually involved with, making your own decision based on your own best judgment. That can be difficult." The distinction between these approaches is subtle, but it is not trivial.

The medical counseling model also inhibits our willingness to sound directive with young people. Because of the need to encourage patients to share confidential information with medical personnel, because of the legal importance of informed consent and the recognition for other reasons that patients should consciously choose their own medical care, physicians tend to sound non-judgmental when giving advice, even when it is perfectly obvious to them that the patient would be a fool to choose one alternative rather than another. Despite their appearance as authority figures to young people, we assume it is not the place of medical personnel to sit in judgment on the behavior of their patients. As this medical model is reflected in the general public posture toward teenage sex, adolescents receive a message that assures them of their confidential right freely to choose their own conduct.

Another source of reticence in advising the young is our growing awareness about the constitutional prohibitions against the establishment of religion. Just weeks ago, the Supreme Court upheld by a 5–4 vote the federal Adolescent Family Life Act against a vigorous and almost successful challenge by the ACLU. From the time it was first enacted, the media had perjoratively dubbed it "the chastity law," thereby creating the impression that any governmental attempt to discourage adolescent sexual activity makes a good target for belittling, quite apart from the involvement of religious organizations. A similar example was the media's treatment a few years ago of a federal law requiring parental consent prior to dispensing contraceptives to minors, which it playfully called the "squeal law."

Even though the Court upheld the Adolescent Family Life Act, I believe the net effect of the media's *amusement* with such litigation is to cast a chilling effect on the teaching of behavioral standards that might seem to reflect *religious* teachings—despite the fact that those same standards are not only defensible but necessary from a purely secular point of view. This phenomenon is similar to the way the treatment of religious subject matter disappeared from public school textbooks and discussions after the Supreme Court struck down classroom prayer and ritualized bible reading in the schools. As some groups now recognize, the Court never intended to create a sense of *embarrassment* about the place of religion in our history and our literature, but that is nonetheless what happened.

The visual media of movies and videotapes seem particularly out of control, relying passionately on intellectual autonomy and free speech arguments while legitimizing premarital and extramarital sex with an irresistible appeal. Our fear of the perjorative label of censorship successfully creates a hands-off attitude about this subject, as we implicitly acknowledge the privacy and autonomy of both filmmakers and viewers, adult and adolescent. Yet—ironically—at the same time as current films graphically and routinely portray adolescents making love with an explicitness that would have been unthinkable a generation ago, the Supreme Court has unanimously held that the first amendment does not protect child pornography. The Court stated in 1982 that "the prevention of sexual exploitation and abuse of children constitutes a government objective of surpassing importance," noting the serious harms inflicted on youngsters through the exploitation of "crass commercial interests."[13] Precisely that same exploitation of young people by commercial interests fills our theatres and stocks our video shelves, but even to say as much as I have would suggest to some a lack of commitment to the core principle of privacy and autonomous expression.

We could look in similar ways at other manifestations of the adolescent sexuality problem, but I will only touch a headline or two. In our *welfare* laws, the concept of providing aid to families with dependent children was originally established to protect the innocent victims of divorce or the death of a breadwinner, but that concept has now become—almost unintentionally—a powerful financial incentive to single mothers that clearly encourages illegitimacy. In constitutional law, the Supreme Court has sought to protect adolescents against the risk of pregnancy and venereal disease by assuring their right to obtain contraceptives, but did so in an opinion that unnecessarily and erroneously creates the impression that young single people also have a constitutional interest in making private sexual choices, including the choice to have a child out of wedlock.[14] And in order not to yield on their basic premise that most of society's ills are caused by sex discrimination, some voices in the extreme corner of the feminist movement urge that attempts to limit the sexual freedom of teenagers is but one more form of female repression.[15]

121

Each discrete context I have mentioned, from medicine and church/state issues to the media, welfare, and feminism understandably seeks to guard against intrusions on its core concerns. Often, there are understandable reasons for this reticence, but its aggregate effect is to render all but impossible the creation of ongoing social, political, and legal policy tools to rescue our youth and the society from what nearly everyone agrees is a growing disaster area. I find it especially disheartening to sense that much of this policy paralysis arises from the fear of some adults that making adjustments in the social climate in order to protect children will dampen an atmosphere of privacy and autonomy that these adults have come to enjoy. For example, a team of distinguished researchers concluded a large study of increasing rates of pregnancy with the observation that, "for ourselves, we prefer to cope with the consequences of early sex as an aspect of an emancipated society, rather than pay the social costs its elimination would exact."[16]

This candid admission is but an echo in the adolescent pregnancy context of what is emerging as a major theme in contemporary writing about children: the abandonment of children by an adult society preoccupied with a concern for its own autonomy. As stated by *Time* magazine's Lance Morrow in a recent major story about the current status of American children, today's children "struggle to understand right and wrong in a society that has lost its bearings . . . The problem is not so much that *children* have changed. The *world* has changed . . . The messages [of the media] . . . suggest orgiastic sex. Public health officials counsel 'safe sex.' Prudence—and morality—would recommend no sex to children, who have no clear idea of what sex is anyway. . . . But TV has a certain authority in loco parentis. It is there when the kids come home. . . . A motif of *absence*—moral, emotional and physical—plays through the lives of many children now. It may be an absence of authority and limits, or of emotional commitment. . . ." Whatever it is, "there appears to be a new form of [adult] neglect: absence."[17]

It seems to me that today's emerging commitment to short-range personal autonomy will impair our ability to maintain a society of meaningful personal liberty in the long run. We must *prepare* our children for the *responsibility* that goes with adult

122

autonomy, rather than abandoning them to a malnourished concept of autonomy that leaves them and our future society without the capacity to sustain themselves. We must balance our commitment to individual interests with a commitment to social interests. Otherwise, the search for autonomy, divorced as it now is in the public mind from a search for commitment and duty, is a search that will compound our sense of alienation, not eliminate it.

NOTES

1. Bowers v. Hardwick, 106 S. Ct. 2841 (1986).
2. Washington Post, July 13, 1986, p. A1.
3. Time, July 21, 1986, p. 80.
4. People v. Onofre, 415 N.E.2d 936 (1980).
5. Commonwealth v. Bonadio, 415 A.2d 47 (1980).
6. In re Adoption of Adult Anonymous, 435 N.Y.S.2d 527 (1981).
7. (1959), p. 168.
8. Collected Sonnets (1941), p. 140.
9. T. Greer, A Brief History of the Western World (4th ed. 1982) 535.
10. See Bodenheimer, Jurisprudence 157 (2nd ed. 198–).
11. J. Simon, Independent Journey 348–49 (1980).
12. See Hafen, "The Constitutional Status of Marriage, Kinship, and Sexual Privacy: Balancing the Individual and Social Interests," 81 Michigan Law Review 463 (1983).
13. New York v. Ferber, 458 U.S. 747 (1982).
14. See Carey v. Population Services Int'l, 431 U.S. 678 (1977).
15. See Willis, "Teen Lust," *Ms.,* July/August 1987.
16. M. Zelnik, J. Kantner & K. Ford, Sex and Pregnancy in Adolescence 182 (1979).
17. Time, August 8, 1988, p. 32.

Chapter 7

HUMANAE VITAE AND THE *INSTRUCTION* ON HUMAN LIFE AND REPRODUCTION: A COMMENT BY AN ECONOMIST

Jacqueline R. Kasun

1. Does the Church's teaching on human life and reproduction appear anachronistic to an economist? Does this teaching shock or violate a modern economist's understanding of what is true about human nature and human behavior?

Not at all. Economics posits rational human beings who make choices freely, who attempt to make the *best* choices for themselves and their families and others for whom they are responsible, who make those choices in the light of their beliefs regarding what is good and just, and who willingly endure costs—sacrifices, if you will—in order to achieve what they regard as worthy ends. I am happy, in fact, to have this opportunity to tell you what economics really teaches about human beings, as opposed to the caricature of what we teach that is rather frequently reported by other persons. One of my friends, a historian, was fond of calling economists "the Neanderthal men," because of what he believed to be our understanding, or misunderstanding, of human nature. He had in mind the utility-maximizing robot far too frequently presented as the model "economic man" by persons who do not understand our use of mathematics and special language and concepts, such as "marginal utility", in our efforts to be logical.

I am happy to be able to assure you that the parents who scrimp and save in order to send their children to church schools where they will receive a Christian education fit perfectly our models of utility maximization. As do the families who fast periodically in order to improve their spiritual lives or to share with the poor. Every year the incoming president of the American Economic Association makes an address to the members on a topic of special interest. The most recent address, by Professor Gary Becker, was on family economics. A major focus of Professor Becker's thought is the topic of altruism.

One of the fundamentals of economic understanding that dovetails neatly with Church teaching is, to put it in economese, that "it is impossible to make interpersonal utility comparisons." That is to say, no human being can know the true personal cost or benefit of anything to another human being. And it is these inviolably personal judgments regarding costs and benefits that constitute what economists humanly-determined ends. Human beings do not exist for the good of business or the Party or the State and no one can assign a value to another human being. What we are saying above all is that each person is uniquely precious. It is perfectly compatible with our professional assumptions and methods to believe that human beings exist and have their freedom because that is the will of our Father in Heaven, but we do not believe it is our mission as economists to give religious instruction.

Indeed, clear and forthright teaching by the Church can only be helpful to economic analysis. We economists often call our field the science of choice. However, choice theory obviously cannot do its work if we don't know what our choices are or what they imply. One of the most baffling features of our present social malaise is that distinctions have become blurred, slogans have obscured facts, and perspectives are distorted. The Church can perform a valuable service by bringing some of these confused perceptions into clear focus, with whatever plain speech that may require. To be specific, spokesmen for the Church can and should state that the Christian teaching from the earliest times has always been that the only licit way to conceive a child is by natural sexual intercourse between husband and wife; sexual intercourse is licit only within lawful marriage; and the only licit way to prevent births is by abstinence, either totally or periodically. It is not even necessary that the teaching be defended every time it is stated. The important thing is that modern people have a right to know this. I know Catholics who do not know this. Spokesmen for the worldly views are not reluctant to make their views known; they are incessantly talking. The Church has the best of reasons to speak up; the Truth with which the Church has been entrusted is to be carried to "all nations."

2. Do I have some suggestions as to ideas in this connection that may reward further exploration? Yes, I do. But first let me offer, as a worker in the field of economics, some suggestions about specific things the Church can do, or avoid doing, that would, I believe, encourage this fruitful exploration. I offer these suggestions in the spirit of the cat looking at the queen. The Church's mission is holy and eternal. I am a mere economist.

First, I would hope that the Church would speak primarily from its authentic position as the Catholic authority on the timeless tenets and requirements of the faith. The world teems with so-called "experts" in every modern field of knowledge. The Church cannot outdo, or even in most cases catch up with, these persons in their own fields of expertise. Thus if it makes statements on the economy, for example, it is likely not to contribute much of significance either to economic or Christian understanding, unless—and I stress the "unless"—it speaks mainly of the timeless requirements of the faith. And here I would like to stress that governments are not individuals. Governments cannot be compassionate or caring or cruel or insensitive. Governments cannot love, but people can. Governments will not come into the

Judgment but people will. And when people vote for social programs such as child care to be provided through government with the costs imposed on other people, they are not performing acts of Christian charity, and I can also tell you as an economist that they are not seeing to it that child care is made available in the most efficient or fair way.

Second, I would hope that spokesmen for the Church would be extremely wary of accepting or appearing to accept any contemporary perspective on the human situation. For example, modern psychology has led many churchmen far astray. The myths regarding the alleged evils of "overpopulation" have seduced a number of the Protestant denominations. The so-called "teenage pregnancy crisis" has led still others into the quagmire.

The latter provides some handy examples of the kinds of dangers that await those who are too quick to adopt the thought forms of the Zeitgeist. A sincere priest of my acquaintance, apparently alarmed by the threat of teenage pregnancy, endorsed, probably without reading it, one of the most explicit and morally relativistic sex education programs currently available. Do we have a teenage pregnancy problem? The *rate* of births among women of age 15–19 in this country has fallen by almost half since 1957. The *number* of births to mothers in this age group has fallen by almost 180,000 since 1970. The rate of pregnancy in this group declined between 1957 and 1971 but has risen by about half since then, with the explosive increase in abortions preventing almost half (more than half in my state) of those pregnancies from ending in births.

Certainly there has been an increase in the number and proportion of births out of wedlock—the majority of births to mothers under 20 now occur out of wedlock—but is this a pregnancy problem or a marriage problem? The great majority of births to this group of women still occur, as they always have, to mothers over 17 years of age—that is, it is not primarily a problem of schoolgirls, although this is what the media would have us believe. But what is different now is that they do not marry before having children. I found that in California if the same proportion of women under age 20 were married as in 1970 and if the marital fertility rate were the same as it is now, our proportion of

128

births out of wedlock would be only 9 percent—less than one-fifth what it is now. Why don't they get married?

And why do we continue to do the things that don't work in the prevention of premature sex experimentation among the young, while failing to do the things that work? Years of research have shown that youngsters who receive sex education in school have a higher probability of engaging in sex at an early age. Girls who have to obtain their parents' permission to obtain contraceptives or abortions have lower rates of pregnancy, abortion and births. Young women who have to pay for their own abortions rather than receiving them at the expense of the state have fewer abortions, pregnancies, and births. School clinics which provide easy access to contraceptives and abortions do not reduce pregnancy or births. There are intriguing suggestions here regarding the power of families to influence the behavior of their offspring. There are also intriguing suggestions as to the power of economic incentives to influence personal behavior. Both of these lines of thought deserve more study. And we should give additional thought to the policies that will implement our best knowledge. We will not embark on these studies, however, as long as we allow ourselves to be held captive by the popular, secular definitions of our problems.

The reductions that occur in pregnancy, abortion, and births among minor girls when they are required to get their parents' permission for birth control or abortions are remarkably large— in Minnesota, within two years after the passage of the law requiring parental consent for minors' abortions the teenage abortion rate had fallen by 20 percent, the pregnancy rate by 16 percent, and the fertility rate by 13 percent. This suggests not only the remarkably strong and good influence that ordinary parents have on their children but also the very large damage which we must be doing with social programs which diminish parental responsibility and control. In his presidential address Gary Becker said, "Throughout history the risks faced by the elderly, young, sick, and unemployed have been met primarily by the family, not by state transfers, private charity, or private insurance. Children usually cared for elderly or infirm parents, the unemployed looked to their families for temporary support, and parents have spent much time, money, and energy to rear and train

129

their children. . . . Parents in richer countries have more re- sources to spend on children and to protect against the hazards of old age. Why then have public expenditures on both the young and old grown rapidly during the [last] 100 years [in] western countries as they have become richer?" He suggests some rea- sons, including the "weakening" of "social norms."

His question, however, led me to think about the numerous ways in which we now tax parents in order to provide govern- ment benefits for their children and also tax children in order to provide government benefits for their parents. Economists have long realized that social security payroll taxes reduce family after- tax income and reduce the ability of families to produce and sup- port and educate children. The promise of social security benefits also reduces parents' need for children as a means of support in old age. These combined disincentives can result in fewer chil- dren being born than are necessary to support the social security system. This appears to be happening now in western industrial- ized countries.

But beyond this, I notice another effect in the growth of the so-called government "safety net," and this is the one suggested in the data on parental consent laws. It is that when government provides goods, services, and incomes, it does so on the govern- ment's terms. For example, a family providing support for a college student will usually attach some family-determined conditions— make your grades, stay out of trouble (my husband and I required our students to study the history and literature of Western civili- zation). And the family will monitor the fulfillment of those con- ditions fairly closely. Not many families will continue to support a student who is involved with drugs or sex or is devoting his time to free speech agitation. But the government student aid program will. The incentives for providing the aid are, in fact, entirely different. The parents are trying to make sure that their individual student acquires the best possible preparation for the rest of his life. They are likely to believe that discipline, especially self-discipline, is an important part of this process. On the other hand, the administrators of student aid are trying to maximize enrollment, and the competition with other colleges in order to get students gives them the incentive to minimize any unpleasant- ness. Thus they will want to offer fun rather than discipline. And

130

so we now have mixed-sex dormitories, "peer counselors" rather than chaperones, a "relaxed" attitude toward drugs, and programs that tend to be rather heavy on recreation. One element of stringency remains: students know that unless they complete a program that leads to a job, the good times will not last forever for most of them.

I suspect the same thing is occurring in many other parts of our government-operated social programs, and I hope that research and thought will go into these areas. I wonder how much of the same thing explains our national drug problems. How many people are receiving income support from government without the supervision and discipline that their families would provide if they were giving the money and not just paying the taxes so that bureaucrats can give the money? If my line of thought stands up to testing, it suggests that we need to move in exactly the opposite directions from the way that we have been going for most of this century. And perhaps what we need to think of first is an expanded requirement for parental consent for minors to obtain services from the state as well as tax credits for families who provide the kinds of benefits and services for their members that would otherwise create expenses for the state. Coming readily to mind, of course, are tax credits for child care provided by the child's own mother in his own home, for home care of the elderly and the disabled, and for private education, including home schooling, as well as Social Security tax credits for dependent children. Given the scope of our present government social programs, however, absorbing the bulk of public revenues, the possibilities are far greater than this short list would suggest. The object, of course, must be to restore to the family some measure of the responsibility which it bore toward its members throughout the ages before we invented governmental "social programs." We must try to reverse our generation's headlong unmooring of individuals from the ties which make them responsible and therefore truly human. The government "safety net" should be primarily for those cases in which the family fails, surely a far smaller number than those now receiving government aid.

* * *

The Church can best help in dealing with our problems not by trying to be up-to-date on the current "crises" as defined by special interest groups but by keeping ever before us the central truths of the Faith. I do not suggest that Church spokesmen should remain oblivious to all contemporary concerns but that they should respond to those concerns with the perspective gained from the ages of historical experience enlightened by the Holy Spirit that leads us into all Truth. Nor do I mean to ask the impossible of spokesmen for the Church. By and large it is my humble opinion that they have done their difficult tasks rather well. The essence of my request is that spokesmen for the Church should speak up clearly and forthrightly now. There was never a better time or a greater need for the message they bear.

Chapter 8

MARITAL CHASTITY: A BLESSING FOR MARRIAGE, FAMILY AND SPIRITUAL LIFE

R. Patrick Homan

I want to start by defining my terms. "Natural family planning," or "NFP," is the first term. That is simply the observation of easily observed physical changes that occur in a woman's cycle to determine when she is in a fertile or nonfertile time, so that a couple can decide whether to achieve or postpone a pregnancy by engaging in, or abstaining from, intercourse during that period. This is quite a bit different from the Planned Parenthood version of NFP which counsels that if a couple does not want to achieve a pregnancy during a fertile time, then they simply should use barrier methods. I must make that distinction because

133

there is a growing group in Planned Parenthood that talks about NFP. We call their method "fertility awareness."

Within the NFP field there are two methodologies, both of which are good. I want to state that in the very beginning. There is the ovulation method which is basically best known by the work of John Billings and Mercedes Wilson, and the sympto-thermal method, which we use. Both methods use the external observation of cervical mucus, which the Lord in his wisdom lets appear as the woman is starting her fertile cycle. It starts as a thick, tacky substance and usually changes rapidly to a very thin, stretchy, slippery, clear substance and finally dries up and goes away, indicating the fertility is over.

We both teach that symptom, and to that cervical mucus symptom sympto-thermal adds the observation of the post-ovulatory rise in the basal body temperature. We use the two symptoms then as a cross-check which some couples need. We also add other symptoms, such as the internal observation of mucus and the condition of the cervix itself. Those symptoms were largely based on the work of Dr. Ed Keith in New York, who is probably one of the unrecognized pioneers in the modern NFP field.

At the Couple to Couple League ("CCL") we do not just teach the biological functions of CCL natural family planning. We do not teach just the mechanics, nor do we just teach against contraception. We add morality, religion, and values, because we are not just trying to teach Catholic birth control. What we are offering is the thought that, while practicing marital chastity, each and every act of marital union is a renewal of the marriage covenant, so that living marital chastity then becomes a constant source of grace. That also helps to keep in mind that we need this grace because the ultimate goal of spouses is the mutual attainment of eternal salvation.

Therefore, marital chastity is the use of natural family planning in a setting that is a living example of *Humanae vitae,* rejecting all unchaste activities and being both generous and open to life, exercising responsible parenthood as outlined in Paragraph 10 of *Humanae vitae.*

One of the unfortunate but very real current realities is that young couples, often Catholic, come to marriage with erroneous

134

ideas of what is or is not chaste behavior. We are often told by young couples that our classes are the first place that they have ever heard that the Church has a teaching on birth control. We are also getting an increasing number of requests for information from couples after they are married on just what is and is not permitted during this period of abstinence. Some are really shocked to find out that what they thought, or were taught, or were led to believe, is permissible, is in fact not permissible.

When one thinks of hotbeds of erotic activity, one usually does not think of North Dakota, but last year we received a very specific letter from a gentleman in North Dakota telling us, in a helpful tone, that we had a serious marketing problem with natural family planning. He said that we were on to a very good thing because the pill and IUD's had many problems, condoms were not that effective, and so on, so that NFP was a great help, but he felt that we were missing the boat because we were preaching abstinence, total abstinence, during the fertile time. What we should do instead, according to this gentleman, is to teach alternate methods for relief of sexual tension during this period of abstinence. To make sure that we did not misunderstand him, he proceeded to tell us specifically what he meant: mutual masturbation, oral sex, sodomy, an entire catalogue of perverse activities. To him, and as we found out, to many other ignorant but well-intentioned people, abstinence refers only to the specific act of intercourse; everything else is fine.

The number of requests that we have received for this kind of guidance has grown to the point that John Kippley, with valuable help from Father John Harvey, has produced a paper on what is marital sexuality. This is such a serious matter that we have decided to seek an *imprimatur* on it, because of the critical importance of the questions.

For this and similar reasons, we have always included this information on moral values and theology in our classes. Just last year, Pope John Paul in an address to NFP providers specifically begged them to include the teachings of morality and not to teach NFP as a biological function. Yet, I regret that, of the international providers, it appears that we alone do include moral values in our teachings. In fact, I know of only two diocesan programs that insist that all classes on NFP include moral values.

The reality is that we are often criticized by dioceses and others in the NFP field for including these values and not just sticking to biological certainties.

I do not want to dwell on that, but on some of the positive aspects. But morality and values are so integrally connected with natural family planning that to properly get into the next section, I had to mention it. What I want to share is the blessings of participating in true NFP, or marital chastity as we call it, concentrating on three areas: first, that it leads couples to a better marriage; second, that children are seen as a blessing; and third, that the couple attains a deeper, stronger spiritual life.

To illustrate this, I must share some of my own journey, actually that of my wife, Ellen, and myself, and some comments from letters that we have received at CCL. To the secular world, the marital chastity that we promote is a contradiction. The very thought that abstaining in marriage for any reason is beneficial, instead of being harmful, that children are not to be avoided but to be sought, and that a strong spiritual life is necessary, are all contradictory to our secular humanist world.

Marriage is a journey, and there are many stations along the way. Often we arrive at these points without realizing that we have arrived at them. Some couples never seem able to board the train of marital happiness, and some are derailed or sidetracked early and end up in divorce. Others are on board but are seemingly unaware of the journey; I am referring to those couples who are practicing Catholic birth control, using NFP for almost contraceptive reasons. They are not without hope because they are open to God's grace and, to be quite honest, most of us started using NFP for much less than pure reasons; we started because it was the next thing on the list, because the pill had failed, for this reason, for that reason. Rarely did we come to NFP for some perfect rationale.

I think that Ellen and I are typical of couples who were married in the early 1960's. We did not use anything at first. In fact, at the end of four months of marriage, I thought that we had a fertility problem because Ellen was not pregnant. The following month, that was resolved; the Lord is generous. Four years later, in March, 1967, while I was an Army officer on active duty, I was blessed with the arrival of our third child, my first son, and also

136

orders to Vietnam. At that point, I did not want to leave a pregnant wife; I was very concerned about that. So we went to our Catholic chaplain, a good priest, and explained the dilemma to him. The priest said, "Well, use the pill. It is a wonderful thing that is going to come out. The Church is going to approve it; it has already been approved by a papal commission. All it does is to suppress ovulation; it is a very natural fact. You have nothing to worry about."

So we started on the pill. In fact, I was in Vietnam when *Humanae vitae* came out. I remember exactly where I was because it was such a surprise. I came home, and Ellen told me that she had already seen our parish priest, again a good priest, who, following his conscience and trying to do the right thing for his parishioners, had told Ellen that she could use the pill. He said that she could use it because she had highly irregular cycles and we were using the pill not to prevent birth but to train her body to be regular, which was one of the myths that was going around in 1968.

So we did that. I continued on in what was quite frankly induced bliss, ignoring the occasional pangs of my conscience, that little voice that hit me at two in the morning when I could not sleep anyway. I was able to ignore that, but Ellen was not. This bothered her very much, much more than I realized at the time. Finally one night she came to me and said, "This is wrong; it is not right. I am sorry, but I can no longer do this. I will do anything you want, but I will not use the pill. If we have 50 children, we have 50 children."

I was stunned; I was shocked; but way deep down, I knew she was right, and I was relieved. Years later, I finally got around to reading *Humanae vitae;* like many good Catholics who spoke eloquently on the subject in the late sixties and early seventies, I had never read the encyclical. When I finally got around to reading it, Paragraph 17 was a real shock, because that is where the Pope gave the prophetic message that a husband who relies on contraceptive devices can lose respect for his wife, treating her not as a God-given gift but simply as a sexual toy. I am paraphrasing, of course. This is precisely what I had done, and that hurt. It was a bitter pill for me to swallow, because I knew that I had done that.

Let me back up in time a bit. I have had many blessings over the years. In my senior year of high school I was blessed in having Father Leo McKenna of the Society of Jesus as my religion instructor. Father Leo gave us wondrous insights on marriage that we eighteen-year old know-it-alls needed. He told us, for example, that spouses rarely lose or attain heaven separately; they either gain it or lose it together. He also told us that marriage is a constant compromise: each person has to give in 95 percent of the time. We did not believe that then, but those who have been married a few years know that it is 100 percent of the time.

The one thing that he said that really hit home was that if a young man wanted a good wife, and understood that the purpose of a wife was to lead him to heaven, then he had to pray for that. He also very bluntly told us that, left to our own devices, we would inevitably choose some young lady for the wrong reason and could easily end up going the other way. That made a great deal of sense to me, so I prayed for that.

My Irish grandmother used to tell me that we should never pray for something unless we really want it, because the Lord will give it to us. She was right, and the Lord was generous: he sent me Ellen. He sent me this remarkably beautiful girl; not only remarkably beautiful physically, but a very beautiful woman spiritually. When I realized years later that, during this time when we had used the pill, I had unjustly treated his gift, that I had rejected the gift he sent me, it was a shock. It still is a shock. All I can do now is to look back and admit how foolish I was, and again thank the Lord for sending me a courageous wife who put me back on the right path.

What Ellen and I did after that point was to develop our own method of rhythm, because Ellen was very irregular. We knew that she would never conceive before day 10 or after day 30, so we abstained from day 8 to day 35, and eventually cut it down after a couple of months to about 20 days, maybe a little more. The first thing I learned was that nobody dies from abstinence. The clergy know that already, but it was a bit of a shock to me then. We were even able to plan the next children to some degree, and we were very careful. We tried to cut down from each end of the abstinence phase very carefully to figure out when we would conceive another baby. We did this twice. Actually we planned

138

three times, but each time we never made it through the first month. The Lord blessed us with Matthew and Sarah, and then just about the time we really learned NFP we were able to achieve Joe. I am not sure whether to credit that to NFP or to our own crude method, but in any event Joe was our sixth.

It was in late 1977 we first began hearing about something called natural family planning, with some written explanation of what it was about. In early 1978 the Diocese of Oklahoma City had some classes going; they sent an instructor team down to Lawton, where we were living, and we attended our first class. It was some time after that that the first big blessing of NFP really came home to me. I think it was after we had moved back to Cincinnati. I had changed jobs and Ellen had lost her father to a very tough malignancy. In other words, it was not a good time in our lives at all. It dawned on me that we had gone through these compounded crises and had come through quite well, that in fact we had something special. It took me a while to figure out why. This was about the same time that many of my classmates and her classmates were divorcing. This was quite a shock to us, and led us to ask ourselves why they were divorcing and we were not.

I began to realize that the Lord was being generous to us, because we were doing something for him. When we had been practicing our crude method of rhythm, we really did not handle the abstinence well. But one of the things we had learned in natural family planning, besides how to replace our own guess-work with solid facts, was how to handle this period of absti-nence, or "Phase II" as we call it in CCL. What was happening was that the Lord was blessing us with an abundance of graces, and while we were not necessarily aware of the graces, we were definitely aware of the benefits. This abstinence period was not easy, and it was definitely a contradiction to the secular world, but it was this voluntary denial of our sexual love at a time when it was most desired that made our marriage better.

Let me now present a part of the first letter that I wanted to share with you. It says, "I believe that NFP is a gift from God. It contains at least three of his spiritual fruits: patience, faithfulness, and self-control, with emphasis on the latter. It is unfortunate that the world views NFP as the least desired form of contraception when in truth it is the best, and more than just a contraception, it is a healthy beginning for a new or revived marriage. Does NFP work? No, it does not work, but our Lord Jesus, from which all things come, does work and he honors NFP especially for the earnest believer."

The woman who wrote these words has touched on many of the key factors. The first is that NFP gives us a courtship phase in which we abstain, in which we have to go back to courting. I have to court Ellen once a cycle, and that is a good thing for our marriage. I have to talk to her. We have to be physically close but not maritally intimate. It is good to talk to her and with her, not just at her. This has drawn us, and draws all couples, closer together. We learn self-control, and self-control is essential to be successful in any form of life, but especially in marriage.

In reality, as always, it is a cross. Christ told us that we daily have to pick up our cross and carry it. Maybe this is just one of those little crosses we have to pick up. To be honest, it is not easy. The Lord did give me a beautiful wife and it is difficult to turn away from her at these fertile times of the month, but that is the path we have chosen at this time. So I pick up my little cross. It is very difficult to sit in front of a crucifix and complain. If I start feeling sorry for myself, I go and look at Christ on the cross and realize that my problems are so minimal. If we pick it up the Lord will never let it get too heavy. Every time it starts to get too heavy and we say, "Enough!" he lifts the load; but usually we do not even have to tell him that. He knows it and lifts the load. Because he is always more generous than we are, he bestows on us abundant blessings. It is a courtship phase, and we know that the courtship phase will always end and is always followed by a honeymoon phase. It is no surprise to me, therefore, that NFP couples have about a one percent divorce rate.

The next two blessings seem to be noticed about the same time. It is difficult to decide which comes first, so I will arbitrarily select the blessing of children. This happens for a couple of reasons. First, the couple has now studied and rejected the secular view of sex and marriage. Sex is not only for me and my pleasure and right now; it is a matter of "us" and it is a mutual sharing of love, not just of physical pleasure. When we reject the selfish view of sex the Lord showers his grace on us. Then we begin to see through the other views of the secular world and especially the secular view of children. They are not a disease; pregnancy is not a disease. Children are not a burden, but a wondrous blessing. We learn to accept children as a blessing and therefore, as a gift. They are not something that we can demand; they are a gift, and a gift given by a loving God.

Again, from a couple of the letters that we have received: "In a few months we will be celebrating our eighteenth wedding anniversary with the birth of our seventh child. He was very much planned and very much wanted." "Praise God for people like you who stand up for what is good and right. I am blessed and encouraged every time I read the CCL News. My husband and I have six children. We will be married ten years this August. My, how time flies when we are having children. We wanted a large family and the Lord blessed us with one."

Mark Hayden, our national field representative, gave me a beautiful thought about a year ago: when a married couple kneel down in front of a cross and ask God to bless them with a child, and then share the marital embrace, they know that if God does answer their request, they have participated in the creation of something that will endure forever, an eternal soul. I find that a marvelously beautiful thought.

Because God knows better, we have to accept that sometimes he will not bless us as we want, so that some couples are not blessed with children despite their prayers and earnest pleas. Therefore, it is wrong for us to judge the generosity of a family by merely looking at the number of children that they have, because we never know how much they wanted more, if they did or did not, or what their circumstances are and why they decided at what point to limit the size of their family. As the Pope points out in *Humanae vitae,* this is a decision that each couple has to come to on their own in a prayerful and generous spirit.

The final blessing is a richer spiritual life. We often get letters that refer to a conversion experience. Somewhere in the practice of NFP, and it seems to come between the second and third year, couples often begin to realize how much the Lord is touching them in their lives. They pray more; they are more aware of God's presence. I understand this; my wife and I went through it.

Another letter: "I wanted to share with you the joy and peace that CCL has brought us. As a matter of fact, my wife and I credit CCL with turning us back to the Catholic faith." We get letters like this all the time, totally unsolicited. It is, I think, God's way of keeping us inspired to press on.

It is a wonder to me how God is constantly flooding us with grace, when we do his will, for whatever reason. I do firmly believe, as my sainted Irish grandmother said, that if we open the door or the window just a little bit for God, he will blow it open with his grace and love. We cannot stand up to that. We have learned to surrender to him and to his will. We have learned to be more open to God. He is constantly then reciprocating, outdoing us at every step of the way. When I look back at my own life, I have to stop and reflect on how marvelously good God is; on how foolish I was for so many years, to have turned my back on him; and on how good it is now to be where I am, to know that each day it gets better and better.

I have to be honest. Ellen and I do not have a perfect marriage. Ellen and I still have arguments, our spats, our disagreements. The children are not angels. Problems still abound: the car broke down last week; the roof needs repair; the tuition went up. We are just like every other couple, but we do have a peace, a love, a tranquility, that gets us over the hurdles. When it is finished and all the dust is gone, and we are memories, there is this wonderful thought that, with the help of the Lord, Ellen and I will share an eternal life together in the fullness of God's love in heaven.

Let me briefly sum up by sharing with you a letter that is a sad letter. It came on a very bad day, when things were not going well. Yet it is an inspired letter. It reads as follows:

Dear CCL,

I want to thank you for helping us to strive for the best marriage we could possibly have. Though my husband and I had only four short years together before leukemia claimed his earthly life, I thank God we took NFP classes during our engagement, and instilled the CCL values of loving, selflessness, respect and communication in our married life. Because of this, and with the help of Marriage Encounter, I believe we had a great four years together and very few regrets. We made the best of the time we had. I am also very thankful for my beautiful blue-eyed daughter. She looks just like her dad. She is a wonderful reminder of the life we shared and the principles we held dear.

That sums up better than anything that I can say as to why we do what we do. Basically we welcome that marriage is good and life is good. And God is great.

Chapter 9

THE FERTILITY GAP: THE NEED FOR A PRO-FAMILY AGENDA

Allan C. Carlson

"So God created man in His own image, in the image of God created He him; male and female created He them. And God blessed them, and God said unto them, Be fruitful and multiply, and replenish the earth." God's first command to humankind was the charge to be fertile. Humankind's first act of rebellion against God was the quest by Eve and Adam to "be as gods," equal to the Creator, presumably immortal, and so free of the need and obligation to procreate. In this sense, the fertility question has been with us from the beginning.

Published in *This World,* Summer, 1989, No. 26, pp. 34–45. Reprinted here with permission of the Rockford Institute, Rockford, Illinois.

145

The affirmation of human fertility as pleasing in the sight of God lies at the heart of *Humanae vitae.* This courageous document, so at odds with its time, affirms "the very serious duty of transmitting life" and the status of married persons as "free and responsible collaborators with God the Creator." *Humanae vitae* describes openness to fertility as part of "the natural moral law." It labels the generation of new life a "mission," and endorses "the thoughtfully made and generous decision to raise a large family" as in consonance with the world's natural order.[1]

But in general, the population of the Western world has chosen not to hear. Since the appearance of *Humanae vitae,* human fertility has been in a downward spiral among the once-civilized, once-Christian nations. Families have shrunk dramatically; in consequence of the rising rejection of marriage, they have begun to disappear altogether. In some locales, such as West Germany, Denmark, and even Italy, average fertility is moving toward only one child per couple, a crude formula for extinction. God's gift of fertility, it appears, has been rejected by many of His children.

There are signs that this rejection is not solely the result of human pride, human selfishness, and human sin, pervasive though they are. Some evidence suggests that the decay in fertility must also be understood as a consequence of a new dissonance in the world, where our culture, our economy, and our mode of government have become—in an altogether new way—hostile to family and fertility. Calls to faithfulness such as *Humanae vitae* do not occur in a vacuum. Our understanding of Western man's failure to respond must take into account, I believe, this new dissonance in our lives. I will suggest that where once the "normal" man and woman could, with relative ease, abide by the will of God in matters of fertility, only the "heroic," and hence the unusual, man and woman can do so today.

My approach is to answer three questions: Is actual fertility below desired fertility? If so, why? And what are the implications for future action? My answers to these questions will be constructed largely on the findings of social science, in the belief that honest investigations of human activity ought to reveal insights that are in consonance with the truths of human nature.

Looking at the Western world, then, can we say that actual fertility is below desired fertility? Is there a "fertility gap"? While the problems of accurately measuring "desired fertility" are considerable,[2] the answer appears to be "yes." One recent assessment of American data showed that never-married women tended to expect more births, once married, than they subsequently had.[3] Looking specifically at Catholic Americans, demographer William Mosher found that while Catholic women, prior to marriage, tended to expect significantly more children than non-Catholics, the difference disappeared as expected births were compared after marriage.[4] For some ethnic populations, the fertility gap is considerable. Among Mexican-American women, for example, 44 percent wanted more children in 1973, but only 29 percent actually had them five years later.[5]

In Europe, the fertility gap may be larger. A study of 4,000 Norwegian women found that of those saying, in 1977, that they wanted another child within five years, only 55 percent actually had one by 1982. Among women ages 30–34, a mere 43 percent of those planning a child actually fulfilled their plan.[6] Another research team, assessing the desire for children among West German couples, found that while newlyweds desired an average of two children, they subsequently shifted the desired number to only one child.[7]

Why does this fertility gap exist? The answers may lie in a better understanding of the overall causes of the fertility decline.

From the 1930s until recently, analysts understood the decline in fertility as one component of what they called the demographic transition. Seen as the population component of modernization, the demographic transition accompanied the rise of industry and great cities and other social changes that marked the end of the old world and the emergence of the new. The process—it was said—took tradition-bound, agricultural societies marked by a balance between high death rates and high fertility and transformed them into urban, industrial societies now balancing low mortality and low fertility. The seemingly natural balance at either end of the change contrasted with the imbalance of the transition period, where mortality reduction preceded fertility reduction and produced, for a time, rapid population growth.

This mechanistic, neo-Malthusian interpretation accorded fairly well with population developments in Europe and America between 1800 and 1940. While at one level merely descriptive, the concept of the demographic transition did carry with it a sense of inevitability or determinism that implied historical causation.

Yet experiences after 1940 began to suggest the need for a more complex theory of fertility decline. In the West, the "baby boom" of the 1950s mystified demographers, particularly the real increase in completed family size seen in the United States, Canada, and Australia.[8] Similarly inexplicable was the turn by the same Western societies to sub-replacement fertility after 1970, and the growing instability of demographic projections of any sort.[9] Religious and ethnic groups in the United States also exhibited odd departures from expected behavior in this period. Moreover, developments in the non-Western world began to cast doubt on the universal value of the existing model.

A vast quantity of new research on the causes of fertility decline has appeared in recent years, work that has both illuminated and obscured the subject through its sheer mass. Analyses of gender roles have shown, perhaps unsurprisingly, that a traditional gender role orientation among women results in higher fertility, while egalitarian attitudes among women are associated with fewer births.[10] Numerous studies also reveal a strong, regular relationship between the employment of married women and reduced fertility.[11] The evidence is strong, too, that an increase in the real wages of men will raise fertility, while an increase in the real wages of women will delay child bearing and reduce the number of children.[12]

Studies of intentional childlessness, a growing factor in declining fertility, show that its practitioners view parenthood as daunting, expensive, and involving loss of control in their lives, while they see the absence of children as preserving marital harmony and a comfortable routine. However, independent studies also suggest that childlessness actually derives from psychological roots: the childless tend to be distanced emotionally from their own parents, while intentionally childless men tend to grow up without fathers, and are left with a deep fear of entering into permanent commitments.[13]

Some forms of government intervention are also indicted by the research. Detailed studies of the impact of Social Security on fertility "consistently support the conclusion that increases in current Social Security benefits decrease fertility in the United

States," since social insurance undercuts the economic value of children. Looking at an international sample, Charles Hohm of San Diego State University found that the reverse relationship also proved true: a lower fertility rate is causally related to higher Social Security benefits. So from Austria to Zambia, it appears that higher old age benefits cause fewer babies, and fewer babies cause higher benefits, with no apparent stopping point.[14]

Ann Marie Sorensen of the University of Arizona, had documented how pronatalist values wither under the impact of assimilation into a new culture. Among Mexican-Americans, she shows that high fertility is a function of continued identification with Mexico: with other factors (including income and fathers' occupations) held constant, Mexican-American homes in which English is spoken average 2.3 children; but in those where Spanish is dominant, 2.9 children.[15]

While direct studies are curiously non-existent, indirect evidence also suggests that fertility reduction came in part through the direct actions of the political opponents of fertility, specifically their efforts to increase the number of sterile adults in America. In an influential 1958 article, Richard Meier urged the movement of women into jobs that would make a stable home and community life impossible: tasks such as engineering, sales, fire fighting, and management. Such a movement began, of course, in the 1960s, stimulated by many arguments, including the Malthusian complaint. Eight years later, Edward Pohlman argued that "the population avalanche may be used to justify . . . large-scale attempts to manipulate family size desire, even rather stealthily." A cultural redefinition of a family with three or more children as "selfish" and "immoral" would be particularly useful, he said: a goal largely achieved by the early 1970s and reflected in the 1972 Report of the President's Commission on Population Growth and the American Future. More recently, David Yaukey of the University of Massachusetts explained that policy makers must seek to alter marital patterns in order to reduce the motivation for having children. Along with welfare measures that would encourage divorce and discourage remarriage, he called for strategies to increase the death rate of husbands. He acknowledged that the tactic of directly raising the male death rate "would seldom be a permissible policy." However, Yaukey did conclude that "greater emphasis could be placed on reducing female mortality than male mortality," and so "maximize the proportion of women who were widowed." We have yet to see how well this new strategy works among us fellows.[16]

The most surprising evidence has come from research into the effects of education on fertility. U.S. data from the mid-1970s World Fertility survey showed that the number of children expected by married women was a nearly perfect negative function of their level of education: the more years of schooling they had, the fewer desired children.[17] Demographers David Bloom and James Trussell found the level of education to be an important determinant of both delayed child bearing and permanent childlessness, a linkage "reaching strikingly high levels" in recent years among women continuing their education beyond high school.[18]

Among Catholics, too, education is significantly related to fertility decline. Canadian demographers report that the sharp decline in the fertility of Quebec Catholics during the 1960s was linked to a prior shift in style of education, from a traditionally classical approach to one oriented to modern professions.[19]

This vast catalogue of possible causes of fertility decline—ranging from gender roles and the employment of mothers to social security and education—has generally affirmed what common sense tells us. Yet here, as elsewhere, the specialized nature of research and the array of explanation seem to leave us with no simple answers or real policy alternatives. In this decade, though, several social scientists have sought to build a new, integrated theory of fertility decline, drawing together the many answers toward one. The studies of John C. Caldwell and Norman Ryder provide, in particular, illuminating new angles to our question. Significantly, they both emphasize the dominant role of mass or state education, and the ideology driving it, as the cause of fertility decline.

I should note at the outset that both Caldwell and Ryder operate within a neo-Malthusian perspective. They see excessive fertility as the primary human population problem, and generally seek to understand fertility change in order to reduce the growth in human numbers. In short, they would not consider themselves friends of *Humanae vitae*. My contention, though, is that their work does cast light on the meaning of this document for the modern world. Their work also reflects the best thinking from a serious discipline, and it deserves our attention.

John Caldwell's *Theory of Fertility Decline* appeared in 1982, and represents and attempt to apply the result of anthropological research, primarily in Africa and Australia, across the board. Caldwell asserts that fertility declines only when there is a change in economic relations within the family. In traditional societies with a "familial mode of production," the flow of wealth is from children to parents. Children are thus perceived as economic assets, and fertility is high. However, as the modern "labor market mode of production" breaks through in a society, the flow of wealth reverses, now going from parents to children. Educated children, Caldwell explains, expect to be given more and to be demanded of less by their parents, and their economic importance for parents evaporates.

In an important turn of his argument, Caldwell emphasized that it is not urbanization or the rise of industry, per se, that causes this change in family relations. Rather, it is the prior development, importation, or promulgation of new, individualist ideas through mass education that causes the critical shift in the parent-child relationship. Mass schooling, particularly the modernist phenomenon of state mandated education, served as the driving force behind the shift in preference from a large to a small family and the construction of the modern family as limited and egalitarian, with its members participating in economic activity only outside the family.[20]

Evidence from the United States gives strong support to Caldwell's emphasis on the changing roles of children as the primary explanation of fertility decline. The fall in American fertility between 1850 and 1900 has long puzzled demographers, for throughout that period the U.S. remained predominantly rural and absorbed masses of young immigrants, situations normally associated with high fertility. Caldwell's interpreters speculated, though, that the leadership role of the United States in introducing a mass state education system might explain the change. And indeed, U.S. data from 1871 to 1900 show a remarkably strong negative relationship between the estimated fertility of white women and an index of public school growth developed by L. P.

Ayres in 1920. Fertility decline was particularly related to the average number of days that children attended school in a year, the percentage of children who attended school during the year, and the percentage of enrolled students in public high schools. Even among rural farming families, the negative influence of public schooling on fertility was strong. in the late 19th century, each additional month that a child spent in school decreased family size by .23 children: that is, a child with nine months in school would come from a family averaging 5.3 children, a child with no schooling at all from one averaging 7.4 children. Moreover, the early U.S. fertility decline was concentrated in the Northeast, the section of the country also sporting the earliest development of a comprehensive public education system.[21]

With his usual bluntness, Norman Ryder, Professor of Sociology at Princeton and Director of the University's famed Office of Population Research, had offered a variation of the Caldwell theory, one giving greater emphasis to "mortality decline" as a mechanism forcing change in family structure. Yet his theory also continues to reveal the role of state education and state power as a destroyer of family integrity.

Writing recently for the *Population Bulletin of the United Nations,* Ryder emphasizes that any viable social system must have regularized arrangements by which productive adults are committed to the care of young and old dependents. Family continuity over time rests on the crafting of an intergenerational contract, where productive adults share resources with their own elderly parents, in the hope of receiving similar, future support from their own children. This broad human household, rooted in nature, is authoritarian, patriarchal, and oriented to the common good of the family over time. Its success, as that of any social organism, rests on its ability to resist deviance and pass on its web of obligations to future generations. Family stability is most easily achieved, Ryder asserts, in a rural society based on subsistence agriculture.

The breakthrough of the modern world upsets this equilibrium, particularly the intergenerational contract. Simple improvements in public health that reduce the death rate, for example, may delay the time when the younger generation might succeed the older, or may increase the number of surviving sons clamoring for their father's estate. Migration and delayed marriage might restore equilibrium for a time, but at the cost of family dispersion. Meanwhile, specialized new institutions emerge that compete with the family, performing functions in a more efficient manner than kin groups are capable of doing. Industry, for example, enhances productivity by exploiting the division of labor, as employers make contracts with individuals "emphasizing initiative and self-reliance, themes contradictory to the way the family works." Mobility and individualism also undermine the unity of the family.

Mass education, Ryder continues, further threatens family life. It serves as modern society's agent in the release of the individual from obligations to kin. "Education of the junior generation is a subversive influence. Boys who go to school distinguish between what they learn there and what their father can teach them. . . . The reinforcement of the [family] control structure is undermined when the young are trained outside the family for specialized roles in which the father has no competence."

A related struggle goes on between the family and the state for the allegiance of the individual. As Ryder puts it: "[Modern] society has interest in the rational allocation of human resources to serve aggregate economic and political ends, and expresses those interests by substituting individualistic for familistic principles in role assignment. Political organizations, like economic organizations, demand loyalty and attempt to neutralize family particularism. There is a struggle between the family and the State for the minds of the young." In this struggle, he continues, the school serves as "the chief instrument for teaching citizenship, in a direct appeal to the children over the heads of their parents." The school also serves as the medium for communicating "state morality" and a state mythology designed to supplant those of families.

At the same time, Ryder goes on, the state creates a social security system that replaces the economic bonds between generations of a family with a redistribution system that leaves the state as the new locus of economic loyalty. Bans on child labor also reduce the potential economic value of children, while extended, compulsory education dramatically raises their cost. State welfare authorities assume ever more control over child rearing, be it as a service said to "help families" or in the name of preventing "neglect" and "abuse." For a time, the family may reorganize around the nuclear unit of procreation, severing most bonds with the extended family, yet maintaining a division of labor by gender and a residual patriarchal authority. Yet this structure, Ryder suggests, seems to give way, in turn to a much different, more compatible form, resting on egalitarian gender roles and a pure commitment to the individual. In either structure, though, fertility is progressively diminished, and the individual is left alone and unprotected in a dependent relationship with the state.[22]

Within their secular frame of reference, the Caldwell and Ryder explanations of fertility decline are, I believe, essentially on target, and they hold important implications for the defenders of fertility.

First, there is Caldwell's important conclusion that fertility decline is not a necessary part of the emergence of industrial society. Rather, the decline of fertility begins for independent reasons, rooted in ideas or ideology, and the method of education which a society employs to spread these ideas.

Second, spiritual exertion can defend human fertility for a time, but natural fertility cannot indefinitely be sustained in the face of a hostile culture and State.

There are several recent examples of religious communities defying the times. The 1945–67 era, for example, produced an extraordinary flowering of Catholic fertility in America. While births rose far more rapidly and continued longer among Catholics, suggesting that the celebrated "baby boom" was in truth largely a Catholic phenomenon. Indeed, the turn to larger families was found exclusively among Catholics. In the early 1950s, only 10 percent of Catholics under age 40 reported having four or more children, a figure close to the 9 percent for Protestants. By 1959, the Protestant figure was unchanged, but the proportion of Catholics with large families had more than doubled to 21 percent.

It appears that this resurgence in Catholic fertility derived, in part, from a consistent, vocal celebration of the large Catholic family throughout the Church's leadership, from Pope Pius XII to the American bishops to parish priests. Most surprisingly, this development flourished among the best-educated Catholics:

154

Catholic women who had attended college were bearing significantly more children than those Catholics without a high school degree. Through the mid-1960s, moreover, each new group of young, college-educated Catholic parents was more pro-natalist in its attitudes than the group before. And their actions had a clear religious focus: more frequent attendance at Mass was tied to more births.[23]

Yet in the 1968–1975 period, this religiously-driven affirmation of Catholic fertility collapsed. By the latter date, Protestant fertility was higher than that of Catholics. Moreover, the large family ideal vanished. One survey found that in 1967, 27 percent of "devout Catholics" wanted five or more children; by 1971—a mere four years later—only 7 percent did. The fall in expected fertility was sharpest among the better educated, while frequency of attendance at Mass also disappeared as a factor predicting fertility.[24]

This return of American Catholics to normal modern behavior has usually been attributed to the current of ideas affecting Catholicism in the mid and late 1960s, particularly the encouragement of debate on the birth control question in the mid 1960s, followed by the stunning reaffirmation of orthodoxy in *Humanae vitae*. This is no doubt true. My point, though, is that the resurgence of Catholic fertility after World War II occurred in defiance of modernity: it might be characterized as a spirit-driven protest against the emerging post-family world, and the tension with the world could be sustained only so long as doctrinal certainty was absolute. While extraordinary, the Catholic baby boom proved unable to survive the first serious internal crisis of authority: social, economic, and cultural currents swept this act of mass heroism aside.

Starting in the 1970s, American Mormons began displaying a very similar defiance of the times. While the U.S. fertility rate continued to decline sharply in this decade, Utah's fertility climbed by six percent to a level twice that of the national rate. The change appears to be related to the upsurge in temple construction and mission work that marked the denomination in this period. Indeed, as with the earlier Catholic episode, Mormon fertility is now positively related to frequency of attendance at services, and to the observance of daily worship activities within the family. Moreover, high Mormon fertility is also tied to education: college-educated Mormons have more children than those with only a high school degree.[25] Whether this surge in fertility, and group defiance of the age, can withstand a future internal crisis must, of course, remain speculation.

Yet it does seem evident that a sustained opposition to the anti-family pressures of the modern world is difficult. Scattered marginal groups, such as the Amish and the Hutterites, have managed to achieve it for a century or more, but even they now seem to be succumbing to the "trend of the times," and their average family size is shrinking. For a large human community to be in harmony with the will of God, it appears that the social and economic order must also be in harmony with the purposes and structure of the natural family.

The *third lesson drawn from recent demographic theory is that the modern state cannot be relied on to save the family.* Most family policy agendas involve new governmental "supports" for families: state-funded health care, state-sponsored child care, and so on. But, as Ryder so ably explains, the state is not a benign partner for families. Rather, in the broad sweep of history, it is the principal rival of the family in a struggle for the loyalty of individuals. A state-family partnership is the rough equivalent of a wolf-rabbit alliance. Virtually all programs of the modern liberal state, at some level, work to subvert the family. The challenge is seldom direct. Usually, it comes through the benign offering of a more efficient or less-demanding "alternative" to a product or service provided by the family.

The fourth lesson is that a proper pro-family agenda should aim at restoring, to the degree possible, the natural family economy, and the natural relationship of men to women, parents to children, and ancestors to posterity. The task may be less daunting than it sounds. Possible actions toward this goal extend from the public policy arena to activities at home, and include:

—first, targeted income and payroll tax relief, keyed to the number and age of dependent children, and designed to allow families to keep more of their earned income, and simultaneously reduce the resources available to government;—second, alternatives to state old-age pensions, particularly reforms that would gradually restore incentives to inter-generational support and care

156

within families;—third, the dismantling of those state agencies designed to police parents and families (often with pernicious results);—fourth, the encouragement of what economists call "home production," or economic functions in the home. These range from such traditional tasks as the care of our own children, meal preparation, gardening, and canning to the production of handicrafts and even Toffler's "electronic cottage";—and fifth, family-centered education, be it either through the rapidly growing home-schooling movement, or through religious schools truly committed in their curricula to a support of families and a defiance of the times.

My essential point is that actual fertility will again equal desired fertility, and fertility itself will again be natural at a society-wide level, only as the family is restored to an economic and social function that is in harmony with the world.

If I am correct here, then a dilemma of sorts faces the Church for a dominant element of its social teaching since *Rerum novarum* has been to make its peace with the modern liberal state. With the notable exception of its spirited defense of parochial education, the Catholic church, much like many Protestant counterparts, has regularly urged the expansion of state welfare and state benefits. These are justified in the name of compassion or justice; yet the unintended effects of state growth may have been to substitute state power for family power, and so weaken the material basis for conjugal life and fertility.

In its urgent warning about the extraordinary dangers of public authorities using the practice of contraception for their own ends, *Humanae vitae* leaps back in time and draws on the spirit, if not the specific protests, of the last Pontiff to stand fully athwart the engine of progressive change, shouting "halt." Pius IX, in a passage eerily resembling the descriptions of Caldwell and Ryder, explains how certain men, misguided servants of the modern state, "declare that domestic society or the family derives all its reason of existence solely from the Civil Law; and consequently all the rights of parents over their children emanate from and depend upon the Civil Law—especially the right of instruction and education." In protesting this belief, Pius stressed how the modern state undermined Christian life by corrupting the minds of youth and separating them from their families. In our era of school-based sex clinics, government-funded abortions, and welfare mothers,—without husbands—wedded to the state, this warning from 125 years ago is prophetic. And it is that same spirit of protest—lodged in the hearts of men and women and in the Church that must shelter them from the schemes of princes and bureaucrats—that our age so urgently needs.

NOTES

1. Pope Paul VI, *Humanae vitae,* trans. by M. A. Caligari (Cincinnati, OH: The Couple to Couple League, 1983).

2. See: Norman Ryder, "Fertility and Family Structure," *Population Bulletin of the United Nations* 15 (1983): 18.

3. M. O'Connell and C. Rogers, "Assessing Cohort Birth Expectations: Data from the Current Population Survey, 1971–81," *Demography* 20 (1983): 369–84.

4. William D. Mosher, David P. Johnson, Marjorie C. Horn, "Religion and Fertility in the United States: The Importance of Marriage Patterns and Hispanic Origin," *Demography* 23 (1986): 375

5. George Sabagh, "Fertility Expectations and Behavior Among Mexican Americans in Los Angeles, 1973–82," *Social Science Quarterly* 65 (1984): 606.

6. Turid Noack and Lars Ostby, "Fertility Expectations: A Short Cut or Dead-End in Predicting Fertility?" *Yearbook of Population Research in Finland* 23 (1985): 48–59.

7. Friedmann W. Nerdinger, Lutz von Rosentiel, Martin Stengel, and Erika Spiers, "Kinderwunsch und generatives Verhalten—Ausgewahlte Ergebnisse einer Langsschnittstudie an jungen Ehepaaren," *Zeitschrift für Experimentelle und Angewandte Psychologie* 31 (1984): 464–82.

8. See: Frank D. Bean, "The Baby Boom and Its Explanations," *The Sociological Quarterly* 24 (1983): 353–65.

9. See: Evelyne Lapierre-Adamcyk, "Les aspirations des Quebecois en matiere de fecondite en 1980" *Cashiers Quebecois de Demographie* 10 (1981): 171–88.

10. Patrick MacCourquodale, "Gender Roles and Premarital Conception," *Journal of Marriage and Family* 46 (1984): 57–63; Wilber J. Scott and Carolyn Stout Morgan, "An Analysis of Factors Affecting Traditional Family Expectations and Perceptions of Ideal Fertility," *Sex Roles* 9 (1983): 901–13; and Elizabeth Thomson, John L. Czalka, and Richard Williams, *Wives and Husbands' Demand for Children,* Center for Demography and Ecology Working Paper 84–6 (Madison, WI: University of Wisconsin, 1984), 14.

11. See: M. Frances Van Loo and Richard P. Bagozzi, "Labor Force Participation and Fertility; A Social Analysis of Their Antecedents and Simultaneity," *Human relations* 37 (1984): 941–67.

12. National Center for Health Statistics. U.S. Department of Health and Human Services, *Working Women and Childbearing: United States,* DHHS Publication No. (PHS) 82–1985. (Hyattsville, MD: NCHS, 1982), 4–5; and Alessandro Cigno, *The Timing of Births: A Dynamic Theory of Consumption, Employment and Fertility Decisions,* Hull Economic Research Paper, No. 126 (April 1985), University of Hull, Department of Economics and Commerce, Hull, England.

13. Elaine Campbell, "Becoming Voluntarily Childless: An Exploratory Study in a Scottish City," *Social Biology* 30 (1983): 307–17; Victor J. Callan, "The Impact of the First

Birth: Married and Single Women Preferring Childlessness, One Child, or Two Children,'' *Journal of Marriage and the Family* 48 (May 1986): 261–69; and Wilma Munkel, "Geburtenrückganges Folge veranderten generativen Hadelns des Mannes," *Zeitschrift für Bevolkerungswissenschaft* 10 (1984): 193–207.

14. Steve Swindler, "An Empirical Test of the Effects of Social Security on Fertility in the United States," *The American Economist* 27 (Fall 1983): 51–57; and Charles F. Hohm, et al., "A Reappraisal of the Social Security—Fertility Hypothesis: A Bidirectional Approach," *The Social Science Journal* 23 (Dec. 1986): 19–68.

15. Ann Marie Sorenson, "Fertility Expectations and Ethnic Identity Among Mexican-American Adolescents," *Sociological Perspectives* 28 (1985): 339–60.

16. Richard L. Meier, "Concerning Equilibrium in Human Population," *Social Problems* 1958): 163–75; Edward Pohlman, "Mobilizing Social Pressures Toward Small Families," *Eugenics Quarterly* 13 (1966): 122–126; and David Yaukey, *Marriage Reduction and Fertility* (Lexington, MA: Lexington Books, 1973), 86–87.

17. John D. Kasarda, John O. G. Billy, and Kirsten West, *Status Enhancement and Fertility: Reproductive Responses to Social Mobility and Educational Opportunity* (Orlando, FL and New York: Academic Press, 1986), 89.

18. Victor J. Callan, "Comparisons of Mothers of One Child by Choice with Mothers Wanting a Second Birth," *Journal of Marriage and Family* 47 (1985): 155–63; and David E. Bloom and James Trussell, "What Are the Determinants of Delayed Childbearing and Permanent Childlessness in the United States?" *Demography* 21 (1984): 605–07.

19. Natalie Kyriazis and J. Henripin, "Women's Employment and Fertility in Quebec," *Population Studies: A Journal of Demography* 36 (1982): 432.

20. John C. Caldwell, *Theory of Fertility Decline* (New York: Academic Press, 1982), particularly chapters 4 and 10.

21. Avery M. Guest and Stewart E. Tolnay, "Children's Roles and Fertility: Late Nineteenth Century United States," *Social Science History* 7 (1983): 355–80.

22. Ryder, "Fertility and Family Structure," 20–32.

23. See: Judith Blake, "The Americanization of Catholic Reproductive Ideals," *Population Studies* 20 (1966): 39–40; Lincoln H. Day, "Natality and Ethnocentrism: Some Relationships Suggested by an Analysis of Catholic-Protestant Differentials," *Population Studies* 22 (1986): 27–30; William D. Mosher, David P. Johnson, and Marjorie C. Horn, "Religion and Fertility in the United States: The Importance of Marriage Patterns and Hispanic Origin," *Demography* 23 (1986): 367–69; and Gerhard Lenski, *The Religious Factor: A Scoiologist's Inquiry* (Garden City, NY: Doubleday, 1961), 203, 215–218.

24. See: Charles F. Westoff and Elise T. Jones, "The End of 'Catholic' Fertility," *Demography* 16 (1979): 209–11; Leon F. Bouvier and S. L. N. Rao, *Socioreligious Factors in Fertility* Decline (Cambridge, MA: Ballinger, 1975), 1–4, 84–91, 156–58; and Charles F. Westoff and Larry Bumpass, "The Revolution in Birth Control Practices of U.S. Roman Catholics," *Science* 179 (12 Jan. 1973): 42.

25. James E. Smith, "A Familistic Religion in a Modern Society," in *Contemporary Marriage: Comparative Perspectives on a Changing Institution,* ed. Kingsley David (New York: Russell Sage, 1985), 291, 296; and Tim Heater and Sandra Calkins, "Family Size and Contraceptive Use Among Mormons, 1965–75," *Review of Religious Research* 25 (1983): 102–13.

Chapter 10

THE MEDIA AND THE TEACHINGS OF THE CHURCH

Phyllis Zagano

I. INTRODUCTION

I have prepared for you today by reading John Milton and *The New York Times.* I hope in a half hour or so you'll agree with me that they are closely related.

The substance of our conference here at Princeton is *Humanae vitae,* fact and text. Human life. What other words call forth such dignity, such respect? What other words call forth such practical questions and discussions? But at the start of every single question, at the root of every discussion, is the *fact* of human life. It *is.* We *are.* We exist as mirrors up to the nature of God (and not the other way around), and from that we claim our dignity and our respect. That is the fact.

And then there is the text. The text of *Humanae vitae* set into motion a whole industry of practical questions and discussions. It made—and broke—the reputations of a number of moral theologians. The nature of the discussion has been such that it depends on which side of the fence you sit whether you think one or another moralist is famous or infamous, whether one or another moralist has had his reputation made or broken.

But I said I was going to talk with you about John Milton and *The New York Times.* You of course will recall Milton's great epic, *Paradise Lost,* which tells:

> Of Man's first disobedience and the fruit
> Of that forbidden tree whose mortal taste
> Brought death into the World, and all our woe
> With loss of Eden, till one greater Man
> Restore us. . . . (*Paradise Lost,* I:1–5)

Its succeeding twelve books describe Satan's attempts to recruit more followers to the primary sin: that of intellectual pride. As Milton tells it, there were rumors about that a new world was to be created, and with the approval of his council, Satan goes off to have a look about. He manages to hide himself, first within the sun and then within the garden, and, well, you know what happens. Women have been getting bad press since Eve. In Milton's telling, the Archangel Michael shows the fallen couple a vision of the suffering of all humanity, but explains that the Son of God has already offered himself in ransom for mankind. Michael also promises them that mankind—in and through the son of God—will ultimately be victorious over Satan.

One tends to wonder these days whether Michael could be right. While we are thinking of the fall, if I may, let me read to you a brief article from the business pages of *The New York Times.*

A pediatric surgeon has patented a new contraceptive based on protein found in fetal tissue. The patent also covers a method for enhancing female fertility, based on antibodies to the same substance.

The protein, known a Mullerian inhibiting substance, or MIS, prevents a human egg from maturing to the point that it can be fertilized by a male sperm. The substance is normally present in a fetus just before and just after birth, when it temporarily stops the process of cellular division.

If the substance is present when a woman is ovulating, the ovum does not develop, according to Dr. Patricia K. Donohoe, chief of pediatric surgery at the Massachusetts General Hospital in Boston. Dr. Donohoe has already patented a method of producing MIS through recombinant DNA technology. So far, the contraceptive has been tested only in animals.

Dr. Donohoe received patent 4,753,794.[1]

Without belaboring the point too much, I think we genuinely must consider the kinds of experimentation quite possibly involved in research like this. About a month after this story, the *Times* wrote:

For years, scientists who wanted to do research involving human embryos and fetuses have found themselves in a Catch-22 situation. They could do their work with impunity, and receive Federal funds for it, so long as an ethics advisory board approved their proposals. The catch is that the board does not exist, and has not for nearly a decade.[2]

The defunct ethics board functioned between 1974 and 1980; it was created in response to some rather bizarre experiments, such as that of Stamford University scientists who, in the early 1960s, obtained 15 fetuses by abortion and then immersed them in saline solutions to see if they could absorb oxygen through the skin. One lived for 22 hours.

This Federal ethics board would rule on the appropriateness of Federally-supported human subjects research where the human subjects would be embryos, or fetuses. If the Federal board talks about them the way the Federal government has in the past, that is, "the bread belongs to the baker," we may not be far from all that Aldous Huxley promised us in *Brave New World*. What, after all, would be the harm of breeding flaxen-haired Deltas?

The point is, of course, that according to *The New York Times,* there may be nothing wrong with it at all. After all, the only nemesis to research is that same medieval institution that refuses "Fairness in Foster Care" (the title of a recent editorial)— the Catholic Church. The proud *Times* sonorously warned not long ago that ". . . Catholic agencies have refused to offer the birth control counseling many experts believe is an essential service for teen-age girls."[3]

Experts. This is an interesting term to use when the questions at hand refer to human life.

II. THE MESSAGE AND THE MEDIA, OLD AND NEW

While we can console ourselves all we want with the fact that the argument from authority is the weakest one possible, it is still a fact that "expert testimony" has considerable weight, whether in a courtroom or in the *Times* or on NBC Nightly News. Today's media need experts the way college freshmen need footnotes. The time—or the preparation—to explain the argument just isn't there. You may or may not be surprised to learn that the total number of words spoken on an entire network evening news broadcast is fewer than those on the average front page of *The New York Times*. If we want to accuse *The New York Times* of lack of depth, whatever can we say about TV news? A picture is worth a thousand words? Please.

Has it always been so? Well, if we put ourselves into another century, we'll find that the primary information source, particularly about Church matters, was the person in the pulpit. There was a single text to be taught (although the details of how it was arranged might still be being worked out), and it was generally agreed that if you were of the Church, you taught what it taught: Jesus Christ, true God and true man, was born, lived, died and was buried, and on the third day he arose from the dead. And we were redeemed. We too—if we cooperated with grace—could enjoy resurrection of the body and life everlasting.

There were variations on the theme, certain stories of Him and His followers to be told. Sometimes with Church sponsorship and sometimes without, brilliant artists depicted what people could only imagine. Poets told tales both out of scripture and out of school. When they spoke without need of official approbation, they risked heresy or ridicule. Their imaginations often ran afoul of authority, then as now. Our contemporary, Jean-Luc Goddard certainly caught it with his recent cinematic rendition of *Je vous salus, Marie*. Even our friend John Milton raised hackels about 25 years before *Paradise Lost* with his *Aeropagetica* and the *Doctrine and Discipline of Divorce*.

Still, my own reading of much of the art up to and including the 17th century in the west is that it is, in large measure, a form of communications and, in fact, a large part of what it communicates is religious belief. Our religious belief. Much great literature continues this tradition up to about the mid-nineteenth century, when the natural condition of man and his superior intelligence becomes that upon which the story turns. As you know, the center of the universe in art and intellectual life then shifted dramatically from God to man, and the altar of history began to replace the altar of God.

For many, in both prose and poetry the notion of God becomes outmoded and merely quaint. In fact, as we enter the twentieth century there are fewer and fewer writers for whom the dignity of human life depends on our relationship to God. My own early work on Gerard Manley Hopkins and R. S. Thomas[4] is described as work on "religious poets," that is, poets for whom God is most important—as if that is not the norm for all, poets or not. But of course we know that it is not.

III. PACKAGING THE MESSAGE

As more and more people gained literacy in the west, they sought political freedom along with what they considered to be freedom from certain Church restrictions and strictures. What some saw as freedom from the constraints of religion became as well freedom from the need to believe in God. Intellectual freedom began to be the new norm. New Gods of course replaced the God they had known or heard about, but few would or could admit that. Improved methods of moving information created information. Free discussion presented a political reality: people who wanted to say—and think—whatever they wanted without fear of any authority's hand restricting them or chastising them.

Soon enough the new thing on the block—the newspaper—exploded the old ways of thinking about methods of moving information or creating inspiration. Painting and sculpture could tell a story all right, but that was more inspirational than informational. The oral tradition—the poetry of the bard and the minstral—continued, but branched out into newer forms of written art. Novels and stories began to grow, and were printed in dailies, weeklies, or monthlies, in periodicals which had as common denominator the fact the they were relatively cheap and generally accessible to the common man. As for preaching, it did exist, but it now had more words to compete with. As we all know, it also had a great many more ideas with which it had to contend.

This brewing kettle of confusion boiled over altogether in the past 50 years. First telegraph, then telephone. Radio. Television. Satellite transmission. Computer linkage. Now FAX. Information is moving, both privately and publicly, faster than our ability to comprehend it, and even faster than our ability to comprehend the speed with which it moves. And as fast as it moves, that fast is it being created. There are over 8,000 radio stations[5] and 1241 television stations[6] in the United States today; there are over 450,000,000 radio receivers[7] and 89,130,000 television sets[8] in this country, in addition to hundreds of thousands of personal computers capable of sending and receiving information. Beyond, anyone with a few thousand dollars can set up a desk top publishing operation; for a few thousand more you can have a satellite dish in your backyard.

With this as backdrop, if you will step back a bit with me to look at it all, I think you will see that our beliefs and the teachings of the Church have been thrown into this great vortex along with everything else. I think, in fact, you'll agree that for the average person, catching sight of *Humanae vitae* is like staring at the window on a washing machine trying to see if your socks are in there.

Even if you do catch sight of it, there is a great deal of confusion as to what the message is, who delivers it, and how it is delivered. Five hundred years ago the message was, at least compared with now, fairly accepted. The fact of its existence was its authority. The reading of a Papal Bull was not dismissed as so much Papal chatter. The man in the pulpit had ample regalia to emphasize the authority of the message he read, and his authority to read it. He read it well or not so well, but it was delivered from a place of authority—the altar or the pulpit. (It might be well another time for us to think a bit about the difference between what is said and read at the altar, and what is said and read from the pulpit.) Beyond this pulpit, the message was embellished in the ways that artists will, but no one really sought to argue with the message at its root.

But this is not the time of Guttenburg. Nor is it really, except in the stratosphere of intellect and finance, a period ruled by *The New York Times*. Popular culture has created new idols to compete with Jesus Christ and Mr. Marx. Think a bit, if you will, about Superman. Or even, Mickey Mouse. Television, radio and the movies (with all their combinations and permutations) have both assumed and subsumed all the old stories—it doesn't matter now whether you're thinking of the old myths or of the realities of the scriptures—sound and pictures have replaced, have replaced what?

Sound and pictures have replaced sound and pictures. It is as if we have skipped a few hundred years and raced right into the past. Where once the painter or the bard presented life's tales, questions and answers, now it's the producer and the PR man who control most of the information you receive. Our friend John Milton has been replaced, not so much by Tom Brokaw, but by Tom Brokaw's producer.

And the focus of authority has shifted from the origin of the message to a combination of who delivers it and how it is delivered. The stole of authority is not worn by the preacher in the pulpit so much as it draped across the morning paper or the nightly news. And, following the pattern of development of American print journalism, there is an apparent egalitarianism in television journalism which would on the surface at least allow the news to seem unbiased. The result, as well we know, is that those who speak with genuine authority without having to speak from authority are sandwiched in between "the opposing viewpoint" and a Heinz ketchup commercial.

And the pulpit, which used to be conveniently located within a few steps of the altar of sacrifice, is now all over the lot. The pulpit is in the subway and on the television; it's at St. Patrick's Cathedral and over at the *National Catholic Reporter;* it is radio and it is magazines; it is the movies and it is the papers.

And who is in this new expanded pulpit? Pope John Paul II? Yes. And John Cardinal O'Connor, and Bishop Lefevre, and Mother Teresa along with Anne Landers, Charles Curran, Phil Donohue, Dr. Ruth, and you, me, the butcher, the baker, and the guy who does candles.

So, with the wisdom of Solomon, Tom Brokaw's producer needs to "balance" the story on the Catholic Church and contraception—15 seconds of Pope John Paul and 15 seconds of Catholics for a Free Choice. And that would be the best split one could hope for. More likely, it would be 15 seconds of Monsignor Authority, preferably with a Roman collar and a tight smile, and 15 seconds of good old regular Father Somebody, Professor of Moral Theology.

Over at *The New York Times,* the night city editor is searching for a balance to the teachings of the Church—(which, incidentally, are increasingly becoming viewed as the "opinions" of the Church)—that night city editor is splitting the quotes and the photos equally between the Most Reverend Francis J. Mugavero, Bishop of Brooklyn, and Marquette University theology professor Dr. Daniel C. Maguire. Do I exaggerate? Take a look at *The New York Times'* coverage of the "Instruction on Respect for Human Life in its Origin and on the Dignity of Procreation: Replies to Certain Questions of the Day" of March, 1987.[9] That is exactly what happened.

We are in a situation now where the media is overpowering the message. The media is now not only controlling who delivers the message and how it is delivered, but also what that message is. That is, the content of the message is now in large measure controlled by the medium which conveys it. Rather than function as a simple conveyer of information, the media are now shaping the content of the information which they appear to merely convey.

We are more than a step removed from the preacher in the pulpit, because even if we are inclined to agree with whatever it is he or she might have to say or convey, we are still often at the mercy of the media as to with what authority we receive the message.

IV. When Media Overpower the Message

We are at the mercy of the media insofar as we are receiving the message through it. In a 15th century world of few books and no minicams, street preachers could still complete with the people in the pulpit if they dared, but now the situation is reversed. It is the preaching and the teaching of the Church which has lost authority, and the opinions of the street preachers which has gained a following.

The new understanding of the human condition comes to us through the magic of television, and the cathode ray tube is what lends credence to the message. If you can get on television, you must have something to say. The airwaves, in fact, have become the cathedral of the twentieth century. Independent of anything else, people have become used to receiving authoritative information from public commercial broadcasting. The stole of authority they wear claims fair and unbiased presentation of the truth. Anyone else is suspect of presenting a tendentious argument, a slanted viewpoint.

And so, even though it may be Lions-3, Christians-0, we compete in the arena we are thrown into.

I don't think we are doing much better than our predecessors.

Think about television. Who are the unbiased authorities, the presenters of the truth? They are Dan Rather, John Chancellor, Tom Brokaw, Peter Jennings, Sam Donaldson and Bryant Gumble. Who are the "opinion makers" who come to us through the tube? They are Oprah Winfrey, Ronald Reagan, Johnny Carson, Pope John Paul II, and Carl Sagan. What has happened? The exigencies of the situation are such that the vast majority of people in this country, if not in this world, see a six-inch high Pope on a stage in San Antonio, and what he says and what he does is related to them by a commentator. That commentator may have nothing to base his commentary on, for it is entirely possible that the actual text of the Pope's talk, no matter where he is or what he is doing, may not be generally available to the press *in advance* of the event.

To give you a concrete example: I personally stood in the United Nations' public information office last June five minutes before Augostino Cardinal Casaroli was to deliver the message of the Holy Father to the UN's Third Special Session on Disarmament *begging* for a copy of the statement which was there, only to be told that the Holy See gave strict instructions that the text was not to be released to the press in advance. When I did get a text, only English was available, not the French of it's delivery.

But we were talking about Bryant Gumble and the six-inch high Pope. The people in front of those 89 million television sets are not all able to tell the difference between "Hill Street Blues" and Midnight Mass from the Vatican. One entertainment show is as good as another. The reality of the Christian message becomes just one more information bit competing for a spot on the dial, and the Chair of St. Peter is easily juxtaposed with reruns of "Miami Vice." What is worse, the broadcast of a religious event—say a cathedral procession or an open-air mass, looks like one more news story. So we are left with only an impression of what was said and done, and still have no real grasp of the substance of the message.

This destruction of the substance of the message is in part due to the nature of the ways in which it is delivered. The traditional distinctions have collapsed, and it is the medium which determines the message (because of the nature of media), it is the medium which delivers it (not the person of authority who is being broadcast), and it is the medium which determines how it is delivered (because commercial enterprises are just that.)

At the very best, the Pope becomes just one more TV preacher. The pity is, he is not among the more successful ones; no one appears to hear what he says.

V. PROUD FAILURE OR HUMBLE SUCCESS?

No one is hearing in part because of the cacophony of competing messages, and in part because of the apparent failure of the Church to deal with the communications techniques of the coming century. Karl Marx wrote in newspapers; Fidel Castro broadcast from Havana Square by radio; the Ayatolla Khomeni was known all over Iran through television and wall posters. They may not have totally controlled the media with which they dealt, but they adapted the method of delivering their respective messages to the media they used.

I happen to think that the Church's teachings are pretty easy to understand, and therefore pretty easy to explain via various media, but I think we have been too proud to "reduce" ourselves to dealing with the techniques of publicity and public relations when it comes to presenting these teachings. We are still depending on our own extraordinarily well-organized operation which gives near ultimate power to individual bishops and pastors, and because of that we are loathe to cross diocesan or parish lines with that new-fangled wireless invention. And when we do make use of it on our own—rather than depending on begged or borrowed or scene-stealing news time—we get so excited about controlling the information that virtually nothing is said.

It does not have to be this way. I think the possibilities are endless, but only if we loosen up a bit. We do need to counter the bad information already out there, by dint of genuine error or of malice, but we need to pay attention to every single part of the equation.

Not all preaching is done in the cathedral. Honest clerics and catechists do a wonderful job, but every diocese needs a proactive professional communications office to reach the people whose opinions of the Church are formed through Father Mulcahy on "MASH" or the editorial writers for *The New York Times*. That office might prepare an answer to this statement from a recent *Times* editorial:

Once, the United States was a leader in international efforts to help those millions of women whose early, uncontrolled child-bearing condemned them to parched lives and early death. Since 1984, however, the Reagan Administration, yielding to a small group of noisy activists, has steadily backed America away from its previous membership in worldwide, multilateral family planning efforts.[10]

Since when is the Catholic Church "a small group of noisy activists?" That professional communications office will answer it only if it is headed by an intelligent professional. Or maybe it won't answer it. Public affairs is a very delicate and very serious business. I don't think the Church takes it seriously.

Are we too proud to stoop to this arena? Well, we're in it already, whether we like it or not. And when you are in someone else's game, you have to play by their rules. The Church will always be able to control somewhat what is said and taught within its walls, but Messers. Guttenberg, Bell, Marconi, Paley and Watson have opened up whole new areas of consideration the likes of which St. Paul, or St. Augustine, or St. Dominic and his preachers, could never have imagined.

There is nothing wrong with the message we have. *Humanae vitae* is not unreasonable. But it has been badly taught, especially in this country. It has been so badly taught that most people do not distinguish between abortifacient and other methods of contraception;[11] it has been so badly taught that most women do not know they can legitimately protect themselves from the possibility of pregnancy through rape, including when the rapist is one's husband; it has been so badly taught that the blurred lines between abortion and contraception are making abortion a more ordinary "contraceptive measure."

In fact, so many of the Church's teachings have been so badly mangled (in part, I believe, because of our attitude toward the media) that the Church is once again viewed as the only bastion in the way of progress. When it says there are some ways we need not know, some ways we need not investigate, the Church is accused of raining rocks upon some strange "academic freedom" in which truth has become a subjective norm and the fall of man is non-existent.

But when it becomes too bureaucratic to overlook a few geographical boundaries in order to extend its vision to the world as it will be, it falls short of being able to deal with the electronic global village that we live in already.

We began by talking about John Milton and *The New York Times.* Each has a story to tell, each has a perspective. I am convinced that the relationship among scripture, John Milton, *Paradise Lost,* and what we know about the fallen human condition are frighteningly parallel to the relationship among Mickey Mouse, "pro-choice" Catholics, *The New York Times,* and the world's growing ignorance of the sin of pride.

Mickey Mouse, "pro-choice" Catholics, *The New York Times,* and an unbridled curiosity sometimes disguised as "academic freedom," are already well among us. I think if we ourselves are not too proud to do so, we will be able to pay a bit more attention to scripture, and thereby avoid coming to another, different, yet still very destructive kind of fall.

NOTES

1. "A Contraceptive Based on Fetal Tissue Protein," *The New York Times,* July 2, 1988, p. 32.

2. "Ethics and Fetal Research: Government Begins to Move" by Gina Kolata, *The New York Times,* July 31, 1988, p. E-7.

3. "Fairness for Foster Care," unsigned editorial, *The New York Times,* July 2, 1988, p. 22.

4. Phyllis Zagano, *R. S. Thomas and Gerard Manley Hopkins: Priest Poets,* unpublished doctoral dissertation, 1979.

5. *The Hammond Almanac, 1983,* Maplewood, NJ: 1983 lists 8,359 radio stations for 1977.

6. 941 commercial stations and 300 educational stations according to *The World Almanac, 1988,* NY: Pharoah Books/Scripps-Howard, 1988.

7. *The Hammond Almanac, 1983,* lists 450,000,000 radio receivers for 1979.

8. *The World Almanac, 1988.*

9. Phyllis Zagano, " 'Equality' Before the Press: Survey of Coverage of Vatican Birth Technology Statement," *Crisis,* May, 1987, pp. 29–34.

10. Unsigned editorial, *The New York Times,* August 4, 1988, p. A-24.

11. "One source of this confusion and ignorance, purposeful or not, is clearly the conflation in the press (and in the minds of Catholics) of the questions of birth control and abortion. In teaching *Humanae vitae,* the American bishops made the quite serious educational mistake of not separating, and separating clearly, abortifacient methods of birth control from other methods. Their philosophical laziness has now returned to haunt them, and there is still no real education as to the distinctions. Birth control and abortion *are* separate arguments, yet some methods of birth control are really early abortions. This is not taught, because it seems to give legitimacy to other, nonabortifacient methods of birth control. It could be that the trainers are not trained." Phyllis Zagano, "The Church and Abortion: Perception and Reality," *Commonweal,* March 23, 1984, p. 175.

Chapter 11

LOVE AMONG THE TEST TUBES: LOUISE BROWN TURNS 10; *HUMANAE VITAE* TURNS 20

Donald E. DeMarco

July 25, 1988 commemorates the 20th anniversary of *Humanae vitae*. It also marks the tenth birthday of Louise Brown, the first baby who was conceived in a laboratory dish. The two events this date recalls represent the antipodes of the moral discussion concerning the inseparability of the unitive and procreative dimensions of human sexuality. For many people, the very existence of Louise Brown is the definitive refutation of *Humanae vitae's* essential meaning. At the same time, however, the extraordinary technical innovations that *in vitro* fertilization has demanded and

Published in *Fidelity,* November 1988, pp. 28–32. Reprinted here with permission. (*Fidelity* Magazine's address is: *Fidelity,* 206 Marquette Ave., South Bend, IN, 46617.)

ushered in over the past decade have convinced many that initiating new life apart from the conjugal union embrace is not only wrong in itself but sets into motion attitudes concerning marriage and the family that are even more pernicious.

Doctors Steptoe and Edwards, the gynecologist and physiologist who did the pioneering work that made the birth of Louise Brown possible, displayed an unusual amount of persistence before they finally achieved their desired result. It is estimated that over a period of twelve years they discarded 99.5 per cent of the ova fertilized in their laboratory.[1] These embryos had been judged unfit for reasons as various as obvious abnormality, and development beyond the optimum stage for implantation in the uterus. In a report to the Royal College of Obstetrics and Gynecologists, the doctors detailed the final countdown to their success: 68 women who underwent laparoscopy (a method of egg retrieval), 44 yielded appropriately mature eggs, of which 32 were fertilized, and four were successfully implanted, resulting in two live births. Louise Brown was born in July 1978. Steptoe and Edwards' second success Alastair Montgomery, arrived the subsequent January.[2]

The media, which more often prefer bad news to good, hailed the arrival of Louise Brown, and paid scant attention to the failures that preceded her. The public embraced the idea that *in vitro* fertilization could bless infertile couples with children of their own. In August 1978, *Parents Magazine* published a Harris poll in which 85 per cent of the women who responded found *in vitro* fertilization an acceptable procedure for couples otherwise unable to have children. A Gallup poll showed 60 per cent of men and women "in favor." *McCall's* captured the spirit of the time with a heart-warming article on "Our Miracle Named Louise." *In vitro* fertilization clinics sprang up around the world. Within a few years, the United States had 200 of them, and entrepreneurs were calculating that by 1989, every city would have one.

One Problem

There was a problem, however; the same problem Steptoe and Edwards had encountered; an extremely high failure rate between egg retrieval and child delivery.

The biological root of this problem is the fact that, during her reproductive career, a woman produces, on average, only one fertilizable egg per month. The high cost of *in vitro* attempts (financial, physiological, psychological) demands a faster pace of natural egg production. Thus women are superovulated to produce as many eggs as possible for each *in vitro* fertilization trial.

Howard Jones, the director of what has become the most successful IVF clinic in the western hemisphere, in Norfolk, Virginia, failed to achieve a single success in his first 10 months of operation. During this period he had allowed his patients to ovulate naturally. His first success occurred when, on the advice of Australian fertility experts, he decided to "control ovulation" by using hormones. Dangers are associated with ovulation-inducing drugs, but they may spare the woman further exposure to the trauma of anesthesia and laparoscopic surgery.

Ovulation-inducing drugs have stimulated the production of as many as 20 eggs in one cycle, more commonly, from four to seven. The additional eggs offset failures during fertilization, implantation, and gestation, and thus help to insure that at least one egg makes it through fertilization to birth.

Surplus Eggs

Surplus eggs may be donated to infertile couples of whom the wife is unable to provide her own eggs or her eggs may have a genetic defect. Concerns are expressed, however, about the possibility of immunological rejection of donor eggs as well as the risks assumed by a woman in her 40s (or even older) whose pregnancy was initiated by a donor egg. Further, donor eggs create the possibility of bifurcating maternity since the genetic mother who provides the egg is not the same woman as the gestational mother who carries the pregnancy to term. There are legal problems here. When inefficiency is expected, and even planned for, efficiency then becomes undesirable. Doctors at the IVF unit of Toronto East General hospital were somewhat unpleasantly surprised when all five fertilized eggs they implanted in one of their patients survived. In this case, Mrs. Collier, of Holland Landing, Ontario, gave birth to quintuplets. Thanks to ovulation induction, multiple births are a common feature of *in vitro* fertilization. It is currently estimated that as many as 15 to 20 percent of pregnancies were multiple IVF embryos are involved may result in multiple gestation.[3]

The Collier babies were the world's third "test-tube quints." Toronto East General has had 21 sets of twins, and six triplets, among the 120 babies born since the unit opened in 1983. The Collier babies were delivered by Caesarian section, 11 weeks prematurely. The lightest was one pound 12 ounces, the heaviest two pounds 10 ounces. All five were put on the respirator.

A technology that remedies one problem creates another. Ovulation induction remedies nature's low rate of egg production at the risk of multiple pregnancies. The superovulating drugs, like anesthesia and laparoscopic surgery, are traumatic to the reproductive system and can permanently reduce its capacity to achieve pregnancy.

Embryo Freezing

Embryo freezing was developed to offset the problems of multiple pregnancies and post-operative trauma. It provides a temporary storage for surplus embryos, and allows the woman to recover her strength so that in a subsequent cycle successful implantation is a greater likelihood.

The world's first frozen embryo was born in Melbourne, Australia in March 1984. Her mother, when superovulated, had produced 11 eggs. Ten of these were fertilized. Three were lost in unsuccessful implantations; seven were frozen. Of these, one was rejected as unsuitable, and four did not survive the freezing. The remaining two were implanted, and one survived, was delivered by Caesarian section, and named Zoe Leyland.[4]

Embryo freezing has been criticized on the ground that a doctor should not create a situation in which he has more patients that he can possibly keep alive. Some have expressed outrage that human embryos are treated as "industrial waste." But the aim of freezing embryos is neither reckless nor malicious. It is a logical extension, and an inevitable refinement, of *in vitro* fertilization.

178

The success rate in freezing, thawing, and implanting embryos is low, as might be expected with a new technology that involves a delicate subject. Dr. William Karow, director of the Southern California Fertility Institute, where embryos are routinely frozen, estimates the chances of producing a "freeze-thaw" baby at 2 to 3 per cent. He is nonetheless optimistic: "My philosophy," he says, "has always been to try everything that's humanly possible."[5]

Twins Born 18 Months Apart

Embryo freezing allows a woman to avoid the hardship of carrying many children at one time. In 1987, a British woman delivered a baby 18 months after the birth of its twin sister. One embryo was implanted and the resulting pregnancy was carried to term. The twin was frozen, then thawed and implanted 18 months later. The frozen embryo remained on hold, as it were, until its mother gestated its sister and then recovered from the experience. It was born 27 months after conception.

Because the frozen embryo is kept in a metal cylinder, its welfare is not directly linked with the welfare of its mother. It would not be affected if its mother were to die. One might even construe this independence as a possible advantage for the frozen embryo.

An extraordinary case occurred in Australia that illustrates what can happen when a frozen embryo is orphaned. In 1981, Elsa Rios of Los Angeles had several of her eggs fertilized *in vitro* with sperm from an anonymous donor. The IVF team at Australia's Queen Victoria Medical Centre tried to implant some of them in Mrs. Rios, and froze two others. The implants failed. Shortly thereafter, Mrs. Rios and her husband were killed in an plane crash in Chile.

Frozen Embryo, Dead Parents

Mario Rios, a 57-year old Californian, was a millionaire property developer. The Rios couple had no other heirs. Australian law had no provision for dealing with frozen embryos whose parents were dead. There was public speculation that a surrogate mother could rescue the embryos and claim a share in the millionaire's estate.

The legal uncertainties of the situation provide excellent grist for a fiction writer's imagination. Could a woman become an heir by serving as the gestational mother of the two children? Once having secured this title, could she then exercise her perogative and abort the children without forfeiting her claim on the estate? Or could she hold the children hostage in the womb, to assure getting what she wanted? Would a woman be entitled to a sizable share of the fortune if complications during pregnancy left her infertile? Should there be two gestational mothers; and on what grounds should they be selected?

The Australian Parliament, after much debate, ordered the embryos to be destroyed. The Medical Centre refused the directive, however, and mounted a national publicity campaign to gain sympathy for the embryos, inviting volunteers to serve as surrogate mothers. The campaign was successful, but alas, the attempts to rescue the frozen embryos were not.

Despite various snags, there is progress at the frontier of embryo freezing. Recently Toronto East General Hospital established embryo freezing as an extension of its *in vitro* fertilization service, as part of its LIFE program.

The modern world moves at dizzying speed; it is not easy to keep up, and efforts are made to make many things easier and faster to assimilate. For motorists, "through" becomes "Thru" and "crosswalks" become "X-walks." Newspapers replace sentences with truncated expressions called "headlines." Commercial advertizing employs slogans and jingles to bypass reason and go straight to the emotions. There is simply not enough time to analyze and reflect upon the passing scene.

The most radical form of linguistic contraction is found in the acronym, where complex identities that take so long to articulate they would be taxing to the memory are neatly compressed into a single word. A well-chosen acronym not only saves time, but carries a built-in moral endorsement. Perhaps nowhere is this more evident than in the field of bioethics, where VIP stands for Voluntary Interruption of Pregnancy, and its equivalent, MR, is

Menstrual Regulation. In hospital slang, GORK abbreviates God Only Really Knows, and describes a patient who (the doctors suspect) has not hope of recovery. In the world of reproductive technology, GIFT is a gift of life through Gamete IntraFallopian Transfer, and TOT through Tubal Ovum Transfer.

The Inaccuronym

C. S. Lewis, in his science fiction novel *That Hideous Strength*, created the acronym NICE to represent the National Institute for Coordinated Experimentation, a malefic bureaucracy possessing the power to destroy society, showing the moral distance that may exist between an acronym and the reality it camouflages—acronym as inaccuronym.

The LIFE acronym stands for Laboratory Initiated Fetal Emplacement. "Laboratory Initiated" conjures the distracting and infelicitous spectacle of promiscuity among the test tubes; unless the laboratories themselves are understood to be amorous. The word "fetal" is wrong, since it is an "embryo" that is transferred to the uterus. "Emplacement" is misleading: the desired end is "implantation."

A booklet for the LIFE Program calls the freezing of embryos "cryo-preservation." It presents this procedure as a "therapy." The terms suggest optimism rather than realism, since the technique is more likely to kill the embryo than preserve it.

To freeze an embryo, the temperature is slowly reduced below freezing. But when the temperature reaches minus-eight degrees centigrade, ice crystals begin to form which damage the embryo's cellular structure. In order to prevent this, chemicals are introduced to diminish the size of the crystals, or dehydrate the embryo so that ice will not form in and around it. These chemicals are called "cryoprotectants." Their effect on the human embryo is not yet established. About half of the thawed embryos will not survive in culture. One-tenth of these, or one in 20 of the embryos originally frozen, are expected to be born.

While the proportion of embryos that survive freezing, thawing, and implantation is small, the results are cumulative. The more embryos frozen, the better the chances. By September last year, 150 babies had been born from thawed frozen embryos; innumerable others are on the way.

The Life Program

A couple who has a child through the LIFE Program may not want another. Husband and wife may have frozen embryos they do not want kept. In this case, LIFE offers several options. The couple may donate these embryos to another patient, donate them to research, or have them destroyed. A woman can give surplus eggs to the clinic's ovum donation program for the use of a patient who has produced an inadequate number of eggs, or does not wish to use her own eggs because she carries some genetic disorder.

On the other hand, new circumstances may arise after freezing. If the couple changes its mind about having a child, if there is disagreement between husband and wife, a divorce, or if either dies, the LIFE Program is empowered to dispose of the embryos. The embryos may be destroyed if the parents fail to communicate their intentions for six months, or if they fall six months behind on the storage payments, or if the mother turns 40, or if the program itself goes out of business and cannot transfer the frozen embryos to another IVF center.

Here is an unintended paradoxical effect. Techniques designed to help a woman have her own child, and thus give her more control over her reproductive system, end up giving her less authority over her progeny. Under the present laws of most western countries, a pregnant woman can abort or carry a child to term without the approval of the child's father: her will is sovereign. But when her embryo is frozen in liquid nitrogen, joint consent is needed if she hopes to give birth to the child, for the father has a veto power he would lack were the child in the womb. Further, the clinic may override the couple's decision, though both husband and wife wish to keep their embryos alive. With embryo freezing, disposal rights shift from the woman to the father and to the clinic, giving them "prochoice" options previously reserved to the pregnant woman and limiting the authority she has over her own pregnancy to the kind of power a minority stockholder has in determining company policy. The more the woman is enmeshed in reproductive technology, the more rights she must surrender to external agencies.

Embryo freezing is a logical response to particular problems created by *in vitro* fertilization: surplus embryos, multiple pregnancies, and the repeated, traumatic effects of ovulation-inducing drugs, anesthesia, and laparoscopic surgery. It improves the chances for infertile couples to have their own child, but without guaranteeing the elimination of these problems. For example, a woman who has six fertilized eggs may choose to freeze three and have three implanted. She need not worry about giving birth to sextuplets, but, whether she wants them or not, she might still have triplets.

The Final Solution

The final solution for the redundant embryo has been designed by a four-man team of doctors at the University Hospital in Leiden, the Netherlands. It is a technique called "pregnancy reduction." A needle is inserted through the woman's abdominal wall, and under ultrasonic guidance is directed to the embryos in the uterus. A solution of potassium chloride is injected into the hearts of those judged to be supernumerary. In due course, these embryos dissolve and are absorbed into the mother's body.

While pregnancy reduction is going on in the uterus, attempts at inducing twinning is being conducted in the Petri dish. Carl Wood of Australia's University of Monash has been trying to stimulate embryo division at the zygote stage, in the hope another viable embryo may be produced who is the identical twin of its parent zygote. One-celled protozoans reproduce in a similar fashion. The intention is to improve a woman's chance to have a child *in vitro* when she begins with only one fertilized ovum.

Each of the many technologies that IVF has spawned is consistent with its original purpose of serving the needs of the infertile couple. Despite this apparent tidal wave of progress, the overall "take-home-baby-rate" is, according to the international weekly *Medical Tribune,* a disappointing 5.6 per cent.[6] And there is reason to worry for the babies themselves. A survey conducted by the Australian government in 1985, of 900 pregnancies, found *in vitro* babies four times more likely to be stillborn, and twice as likely to have congenital abnormalities than babies conceived in the traditional way. One *in vitro* pregnancy in 20 was ectopic (the child developing outside the uterus), and one in four ended in miscarriage. Premature delivery was common, and 43 per cent of deliveries were by Caesarian section.[7]

A Grave Danger to Humanity

For reasons such as these, some IVF specialists have abandoned their work. Dr. Jacques Testart, who facilitated the first French test tube pregnancy and was involved with freezing human embryos, made the following statement in an interview with the Paris newspaper *Le Monde:* "I will not go on in this. One cannot apply the logic of progress to something which will become a grave danger to humanity."[8]

Patrick Steptoe once remarked that in pioneering IVF, all he wanted to do was "help women whose child-producing mechanism is slightly faulty." His mistake was to view the woman's procreative power as consisting of an assemblage of mechanisms in the first place.

Several years ago Edward Grossman wrote in *Atlantic* that a day would come when a woman's two laparoscopy scars will be as commonplace as our smallpox vaccination mark. At age 20, every female will be superovulated, and her eggs will be collected and frozen, since babies conceived by women of that age are less likely to suffer from Down's Syndrome and other congenital defect. Thereafter, whenever a woman wants to become a mother, she will simply have one of her eggs thawed, fertilized in a dish, and gestated in an artificial incubator. The uterus will become vestigal, though the ovaries will remain important. No woman will lose her figure in childbearing.[9]

According to such a scenario, the only part the woman plays in the development of her motherhood is in furnishing the egg (which she accomplishes with a complete absence of conscious effort). Everything else transpires independently of her. Thus, she does not grow into motherhood, motherhood is prepared for her, apart from her. When she becomes a mother, she does so instantly. But the nagging question remains. Will women be ready for instant motherhood when it is ready for them? Will they be able to cultivate maternal feelings and responsibilities while their children are developing away from them? IVF inaugurates a pattern that progressively externalizes procreation. As this process develops, incarnate motherhood progressively diminishes.

Multi-Man

The scenario Grossman depicts appears relatively tame when compared with what other prognosticators envision. Following the first stage of human life, the zygote is *cleavage* during which the single initial cell undergoes successive equal divisions with little or no intervening growth. The resulting cells—or blastomeres— become progressively smaller, while the size of the total aggregate remains approximately the same. After three such divisions, the aggregate contains eight cells.[10] In experiments with mice, it has been shown that if two such eight-cell aggregates, each of different parentage, are fused into a sixteen-cell unit, the resulting single organism can develop to adulthood. In this instance, the adult has four genetic parents. One social commentator has remarked: "If multi-mouse is here, can 'multi-man' be far behind?"[11] If such a technique could be developed, it would offer hope for a lesbian couple to have a child of its own, though two other male parents would also be involved in contributing to the genetic makeup of the child. Two zygotes would be formed *in vitro* in separate dishes by four different progenitors. At the eight-cell stage, the two embryos would be fused into a single entity thereby establishing a 16-cell embryo who would develop to adulthood, bearing the traits of each of his four genetic parents.

All women ask of *in vitro* fertilization is to make them a mother: not to create surplus embryos to be frozen or disposed of or donated for one purpose or another; not to create multiple pregnancies to be reduced or carried to term at much risk; not to induce the maturation of a prodigality of eggs which are frozen or donated.

A bare desire cannot be directed into the organic network that commands the initiation of life without disturbing at that moment a myriad of ancillary operations. The body does not restrict its responses to our desires. It has a mind of its own, so to speak; it is not wholly submissive to our will. And so, reproductive technology is an excursion into unpredictability. The myth of progress creates the illusion that technology can grant our desires without burdening us with unrequested tribulations. Reality remains stubbornly organic; touch a nerve and the whole system trembles. We choose what is convenient and what is inconvenient chooses us. It is the central irony of our modern technocracy.

Unexpected Wisdom

Conquering nature and yoking human generation to our desires will continue to elude us. And well it should since within the body is ingrained a balance and a wisdom we disregard at our peril. The ten years that have elapsed since Louise Brown should have re-educated us to the fact that motherhood and fatherhood are uncompromisingly personal. But it has tempted us to believe that they are replaceable. The new world of technologized parenthood must indeed be brave, for it ventures into *terra incognita* with more faith in reason than reason would find reasonable. By contrast, *Humanae vitae* contains a message of perhaps unexpected wisdom, namely that preserving the integrity of the unitive and procreative ends of intercourse also preserves the integrity of parenthood and personhood.

NOTES

1. Eugene Diamond, "A Call for a Moratorium on *In Vitro* Fertilization," *Linacre*, Nov. 1979.

2. Gena Corea, *The Mother Machine* (New York: Harper & Row, 1985).

3. The Ethics Committee for the American Fertility Society, *Ethical Considerations of the New Reproductive Technologies*, Sept. 1986, p. 588.

4. Jo Wiles, "The Gift of Life," *Star World*, April 24, 1984, pp. 24-6.

5. "Baby Craving: Science and Surrogacy," *LIFE*, June 1987, p. 41.

6. Rick McGuire, "Charge Baby Biz Programs Still 'Oversold and Overrated,' " *Medical Tribune: International Medical News Weekly*, June 21, 1988, p. 17. See also *"Procréatique et désinformation,"* Le Monde (Paris), 17 décembre 1987 which puts the average birth rate per total IVF attempts at very much below 7 per cent *("trés inférieur á 7*

per cent"). It should be remembered that a small percentage of couples would have conceived naturally had they not employed IVF. Such a figure, obviously, is undeterminable.

7. Ann Pappert, "Critics worry women not told of fertilization program risks," *Toronto Globe & Mail*, Feb. 6, 1988.

8. *Lifelines*, Vol. 14, no. 2, April 1988, pp. 18–19.

9. Edward Grossman, "The Obsolescent Mother: A Scenario," *Atlantic*, May 1971, p. 49.

10. N. Le Douarin and A. McLaren (eds). *Chimaras in Developmental Biology* (New York: Academic Press, 1984).

11. Alvin Toffler, *Future Shock* (New York: Random House, 1970), p. 205.

Chapter 12

CATHOLIC TEACHING ON THE LABORATORY GENERATION OF HUMAN LIFE

William E. May

July 25, 1978 is a memorable date in history. It is, first of all, the birthday of Louise Brown, the "test tube" baby, the miracle child of modern technology. Although she was not the first baby to be conceived *in vitro,* she was the first child conceived in this way to be born. What is most significant about her birth is that it marks the first time in human history when new human life was born after having been conceived outside the body of a human person, that is, the mother. New human life can now come to be in the laboratory and not in the body of a woman.

Artificial insemination, whether by husband or vendor[1], had already severed the generation of human life from the act of sexual union, and *in vitro* fertilization necessarily requires this separation, the significance of which will occupy us later. Artificial insemination, insofar as it requires biological technology and expertise and entails the severing of the bond between sexual intercourse and the generation of new human life, was the beginning of the shift from generating human life bodily through sexual union of man and woman to producing it in the laboratory. Accordingly, artificial insemination will be included as a mode of laboratory generation of human life. Nonetheless, with artificial insemination the life generated still comes to be in the body of a woman, and some mystery still shrouds its origin and early development. With the advent of *in vitro* fertilization, or the laboratory generation of human life in a more complete way, however, there has been, as it were, a "demystification" of the inception of human life. The contingencies beyond human control affecting its origin have been significantly reduced, and the origin and early development of new human life have now been brought, to considerable degree, under the control of human will and planning. We can now literally "make" babies, and our capacity to do so has become, within the decade since the birth of Louise Brown, much more sophisticated and "successful" than it was when Dr. Steptoe and Edwards managed the conception, gestation, and birth of Louise[2]. July 25, 1978 is memorable, secondly, because it is the tenth anniversary of Pope Paul VI's encyclical on marriage and the generation of human life, *Humanae vitae*. In his encyclical Pope Paul affirmed that there is "an inseparable connection, willed by God and unable to be broken by man on his own initiative, between the two meanings of the conjugal act: the unitive meaning and the procreative meaning"[3]. The Pope appealed to this "inseparable connection" as the fundamental truth undergirding the Church's teaching on the intrinsic immorality of contraception, insofar as the choice to contracept severs the bond between these two meanings of the conjugal act. He had, it should be noted, given other reasons to show that contraception is intrinsically disordered; for example, he explicitly noted that contraception is immoral because it is directly opposed to the divine gift of fertility, something good in itself[4]. But

190

his principal claim was this: the Church's teaching that "each and every marriage act must remain open to the transmission of human life" is "founded upon" the "inseparable connection" between the unitive and procreative meanings of the conjugal act[5]. In addition, Pope Paul emphasized that the conjugal act, by reason of its intimate structure as an act most closely uniting husband and wife, "capacitates them for the generation of new lives *(eos idoneos etiam facit ad novam vitam gignendam),* according to laws inscribed in the very beginning of man and of woman"[6].

Pope Paul's concern in *Humanae vitae* was with contraception and not with the laboratory generation of human life. Nonetheless, his teaching on the "inseparable connection" between the two meanings of the conjugal act plays a central role in the March 1987 *Instruction on Respect for Human Life in Its Origin and on the Dignity of Procreation,* in which the Congregation for the Doctrine of the Faith formally addressed the moral issues raised by various reproductive technologies. This document, drawing on the teaching about marriage and human procreation developed in the light of the Catholic tradition by Popes Pius XII, Paul VI, and John Paul II, insists that the generation of human life, if it is to respect the dignity of both parents and children "must be the fruit and sign of the mutual self-giving to the spouses, of their love and fidelity'"[7]. In its treatment of heterologous fertilization, in which gametes, whether ova or sperm, from parties other than the spouses are used to generate new human life, the *Instruction,* not surprisingly, concludes that this way of generating human life is gravely immoral. It is so because heterologous fertilization is "contrary to the unity of marriage, to the dignity of the spouses, to the vocation proper to parents, and to the child's right to be conceived and brought into the world in marriage and from marriage'"[8].

Although some individuals find this judgment of the *Instruction* too limiting and restrictive of human freedom[9], most people, whether Catholic or non-Catholic, can see its wisdom. In getting married a man and a woman "give" themselves exclusively to each other, and the "selves" they give are sexual and procreative in nature. Just as they violate their marital covenant by attempting, after marriage, to "give" themselves sexually, in coition, to another, so too they violate that covenant by choosing freely to exercise their sexual power of generating life with someone other than their spouses, the person to whom they have irrevocably given themselves, including their power to generate life. Moreover, a sperm or ovum "vendor," by freely choosing to bring new life into being by selling his sperm or her ovum for the purpose of generating human life, becomes a parent, a father or mother. Yet such a person refuses to accept the responsibilities of parenthood; and the child who comes to be as a result of their choice and who is, in truth, their own flesh or blood, will not even know them and will be deprived of their care, something to which it has a right. For all these reasons—briefly yet accurately set forth in the *Instruction*—most people can see why it is morally bad to generate human life by laboratory methods that are heterologous in nature. For those who for some factor or another cannot grasp these reasons the tragic story of "Baby M" should be instructive[10].

The "hard" case taken up by the *Instruction,* and the one in which Pope Paul's teaching on the "inseparable connection" plays such a key role, is that of homologous fertilization, when the gametes used to generate new human life are provided by the husband and wife. At times this entails artificial insemination to the wife by the husband; at other times it entails *in vitro* fertilization of the wife's ovum by sperm provided by her husband, with subsequent embryo transfer into her own womb. In this "hard" or, viewed somewhat differently, "simple" case there is no use of gametic materials from third parties; the child conceived is genetically the child of husband and wife, who are and will remain its parents. In this case there need be no deliberate creation of "excess" human lives that will be discarded (perhaps through a procedure that some term, euphemistically, "pregnancy reduction"[11]), frozen, or made the objects of medical experimentations of no value to them. In this case there need be no intention of intrauterine monitoring with a view to abortion should the unborn child be found "defective." Nor need there be, in this case, the use of immoral means (masturbation) to obtain the father's sperm. In this case, apparently, there need be only the intent to help fulfill the legitimate desire of a couple, unable either by reason of the wife's blocked fallopian tubes or the husband's low sperm production or other causes, to have a child of their own and give it a home. Many people, both Catholic and non-Catholic, think that resort to the laboratory generation of human life is morally legitimate in this "simple case" of *in vitro* fertilization. They ask, quite reasonably, what could be morally offensive here? What wrong is being done? What evil is being willed?

Yet the *Instruction,* in company with Pope Pius XII and his successors, claims that even this type of homologous fertilization is morally wrong because it involves the deliberate willing of an evil. And to support this claim the *Instruction* appeals, first and foremost, to the teaching of Pope Paul VI on the "inseparable connection, willed by God and unable to be broken by man on his own initiative, between the two meanings of the conjugal act: the unitive meaning and the procreative meaning"[12]. The evil willed in homologous fertilization is the "separation" of these meanings that, in God's plan, are inseparably connected. Applying this teaching to homologous fertilization, the *Instruction* appeals to the authority of Pope Pius XII, who had said that "it is never permitted to separate these different aspects to such a degree as positively to exclude either the procreative intention [as is done in contraceptive intercourse] or the conjugal relation"[13]. The *Instruction* then concludes that

> fertilization is licitly sought when it is the result of a "conjugal act which is *per se* suitable for the generation of children to which marriage is ordered by its nature and by which the spouses become one flesh." But from the moral point of view procreation is deprived of its proper perfection when it is not desired as the fruit of the conjugal act, that is to say, of the specific act of the spouses' union[14].

In summary, a principal argument given in the Vatican *Instruction* to show that homologous fertilization, even in the "simple case" described previously, is morally bad employs as its major premise the teaching on the "inseparable connection" between the unitive and procreative meanings of the conjugal act. This document also uses two other lines of argument to support its conclusion, and these will be considered below, namely, the argument that generating human life in the laboratory is a form of "production" and hence an act that violates the dignity of the child produced; and the argument that generating human life in this way falsifies the "language of the body." But here our interest centers on the argument based on the "inseparable connection" of the two meanings of the conjugal act; a teaching central, as we have seen, to Pope Paul VI's encyclical, *Humanae vitae*. The argument's conclusion, namely, that homologous fertilization is in itself immoral, follows *if* the premise on which it depends, namely, the inseparable connection between the unitive and procreative meanings of the conjugal act, is true. I hold that this premise is true. Yet it is not self-evidently so. People can reasonably question whether it is. The premise was used in *Humanae vitae* to show that marital contraceptive intercourse is morally bad, and it was used in the *Instruction* to show that homologous fertilization is morally bad. But it is possible that the premise about the inseparability of the two meanings of the conjugal act is itself a conclusion, derived from the premises (1) that it is always wrong to contracept and (2) that it is always wrong to "make" or "produce" children. I shall consider this possibility below. But first I wish to offer some considerations, drawn from Catholic understanding of marriage, that provides support for the truth of the proposition affirming the inseparable connection between the two meanings of the marital act, even if these considerations, derived in part from divine revelation, do not constitute, in themselves, demonstrative proof of the truth of this proposition.

Marital Rights and Capabilities, the Marital Act, and the Generation of Human Life

When the teaching of Paul VI in *Humanae vitae* and of the Congregation for the Doctrine of the Faith in its *Instruction* is examined from within the Catholic tradition, one can see, I believe, that these documents look upon the question of human procreation within the framework provided by the constant teaching of the Church on marriage and its relationship to the generation of human life, and that they regard this teaching as supporting the proposition about the inseparable connection

194

between the unitive and procreative meanings of the conjugal act. An important point of departure is provided by what Pope Pius XII had to say in 1949, when he took up the question of homologous artificial insemination. In rejecting this way of generating human life, Pius XII spoke as follows:

> We must never forget this: It is only the procreation of a new life *according to the will and plan of the Creator* which brings with it—to an astonishing degree of perfection—the realization of the desired ends. This is, at the same time, in harmony with the dignity of the marriage partners, with their bodily and spiritual natures, and with the normal and happy development of the child[15].

Pius XII was evidently of the mind that God wills the generation of human life only in the marital act. Thus the choice to generate it outside the marital act is a choice that goes against the will of God. In 1951 he returned to this matter, saying,

> To reduce cohabitation of married persons and the conjugal act to a mere organic function for the transmission of the germs of life would be to convert the domestic hearth, sanctuary of the family, into nothing more than a biological laboratory. . . . The conjugal act in its natural structure is a personal action, a simultaneous natural self-giving which, in the words of Holy Scripture, effects the union "in one flesh." This is more than the mere union of two germs, which can be brought about artificially—i.e., without the natural action of the spouses. The conjugal act as it is planned and willed by nature implies a personal cooperation, the right to which parties have mutually conferred on each other in contracting marriage[16].

The thought of Pius XII here is rooted in the Catholic understanding of marriage as a specific sort of human reality whose author is God Himself[17]. According to this understanding, married persons have capabilities, rights, and duties that nonmarried persons do not have. What are these?

By giving themselves to one another in marriage, husbands and wives not only acquire rights that nonmarried men and women do not have but they also give to themselves capabilities that nonmarried men and women do not have. Nonmarried men and women have the natural capacity, by virtue of their sexuality and their endowment with sexual organs, to engage in genital sex and to generate human life through such sexual activity. Yet they do not have the *right* either to engage in intimate genital acts or to generate human life. Although I cannot here show fully why they do not have the right to engage in genital sex[18], I can briefly say why this is so. The reason is simply that they have not, by their own free choice, capacitated themselves to respect each other as irreplaceable and nonsubstitutable persons in their freely chosen genital acts. Such acts between nonmarried men and women do not *unite two irreplaceable and nonsubstitutable persons;* rather, they *join two individuals who are in principle replaceable and substitutable, disposable.* But human persons ought not to be treated as replaceable, substitutable, disposable things. Similarly, nonmarried men and women do not have the right to generate human life precisely because they have not, through their own free choice, capacitated themselves to receive such life lovingly, nourish it humanely, and educate it in the love and service of God[19]. Practically all civilized societies, it should be noted, rightly regard as irresponsible the generation of human life through the random copulation of unattached men and women. [It is a sign of a new barbarism that many in our society now assert the "right" of single men and women to have children, whether generated by heterosexual intercourse or by making use of the new "reproductive" technologies.]

Husbands and wives, on the contrary, have the right to the marital act, whose nature will be more fully investigated below. They have this right precisely because they have given themselves the capacity, through their irrevocable gift of themselves to one another in marriage[20], to respect one another as irreplaceable and nonsubstitutable spouses. Likewise they have given to themselves the capacity to receive human life lovingly, nourish it humanely, and educate it in the love and service of God, for by marrying

196

they have made themselves capable of receiving any new human life that should be given to them and of giving to it the home where it can take root and grow under the living tutelage of its own father and mother, persons who are not strangers to one another but who are rather made one by *being* married.

An analogy may be helpful. I do not have the right to diagnose sick people and prescribe medicines for them. I do not have this right because I have not freely chosen to study medicine and to discipline myself so that I can equip myself with the knowledge and skills needed to do these tasks. But doctors, who have freely chosen to submit themselves to the discipline of studying medicine and acquiring medical skills, do have this right. They have this right because they have freely chosen to give themselves the capacity to do what doctors are supposed to do. Similarly, nonmarried men and women do not have the right to engage in intimate genital relations or to generate human life because they have not, through their free choice, given themselves the capacity needed to do these things. But husbands and wives have made the free choice to capacitate themselves to do these things because they have freely chosen to give themselves to each other in marriage and to do what married persons do, namely, give themselves to one another in the marital act and receive, through that act, the gift of new human life. The act proper to them is the "marital" act. Thus some comments on its nature are pertinent.

The marital act is not simply a genital act between a man and a woman who "happen" to be married. Husbands and wives have the capacity to engage in *genital* acts, as do nonmarried men and women, because of their sexuality and endowment with genitals. But they have the capacity (and the right) to engage in the *marital* act because they married, i.e., because they are husbands and wives. The marital act, therefore, is more than a simple genital act between a man and a woman who happen to be married. It is an act that inwardly participates in their marital union, and it is one, furthermore, that respects the "goods" of marriage, i.e., the good of steadfast fidelity and of exclusive marital love and the good of children[21]. The *marital* act, therefore, as distinct from a *genital* act between a man and a woman who happen to be married, is one that is (1) open to the communication of spousal love and (2) open to the reception of new human life. A

197

genital act forced upon a wife by a drunken husband seeking only to gratify his sexual urges and unconcerned with her legitimate desires is a genital act, but it can not be regarded as a true marital act[22]. Similarly, a genital act between husbands and wives that is deliberately made hostile to the reception of human life, i.e., an act of *contra*-ceptive intercourse, is also one that violates the marital act and is hence nonmarital precisely because it is an act deliberately made inimical to one of the goods of marriage[23].

Thus the marital act is itself inwardly an act that is unitive or love-giving and procreative or receptive of the gift of life. It is so because it is *marital,* i.e., an act participating in marriage and its goods. The bond, therefore, that joins its two meanings, unitive and procreative, is the bond of marriage itself. "What God has joined together, let no man put asunder." There is an "inseparable connection, willed by God and unable to be broken by man on his own initiative, between the unitive and the procreative meanings of the marital act" because this act is the expression and sign of the marriage itself, a human reality inwardly open to the communication of conjugal love and to the reception of human life as a gift from God.

While husbands and wives have the right and capacity to engage in the marital act and, through it, receive from God the gift of life, they do not have a right to a child. They do not have this sort of right because a child is, like them, a person, not a thing that others can possess, nor is it an act to which others can have rights.

I believe that these considerations, drawn from the Catholic understanding of marriage—an understanding that in part derives from divine revelation—provide the context for the teaching on the "inseparable connection" of the unitive and procreative meanings of the conjugal act and help provide support for this teaching. Still, they do not demonstrate the truth of that proposition independently of Catholic faith, although they certainly make this proposition reasonable. A more demonstrative argument to establish the truth of the proposition about the "inseparable connection" will be advanced below. But before advancing it I want to examine a second line of reasoning advanced in the *Instruction* to show that all ways of generating human life other than by the marital act are morally wrong. This is the argument that the laboratory generation of human life regards the child as a "product" and is therefore a violation of the child's dignity.

"Procreating" Human Life vs. "Reproducing" Human Life

According to the *Instruction* of the Congregation for the Doctrine of the Faith, the child "cannot be desired or conceived as the product of an intervention of medical or biological techniques." Why? Because, it teaches, "that would be equivalent to reducing him to an object of scientific technology. No one may subject the coming of a child into the world to conditions of technical efficacy which are to be evaluated according to standards of control and dominion"[24]. The *Instruction* then concludes:

> Conception *in vitro* is the result of the technical action which presides over fertilization. Such fertilization is neither in fact achieved nor positively willed as the expression and fruit of a specific act of the conjugal union. In homologous IVF and ET, therefore, even if it is considered in the context of *de facto* existing sexual relations, the generation of the human person is objectively deprived of its proper perfection, namely, that of being the result and fruit of a conjugal act in which the spouses can become "cooperators with God for giving life to a new person"[25].

The *Instruction* is surely correct in judging that the generation of a child through artificial homologous fertilization (including artificial insemination of an ovum within the body of the wife) is a technological procedure, an instance of "making," and hence quite different in kind, as a human act, from the generation of life in and through the marital act. When human life is given through the marital act it comes, even when ardently desired, as a "gift" crowning the act itself. The marital act is not an act of "making," either babies or love. The marital act is something that husbands and wives "do"; it is not something that they "make."

But what is the difference between "making" and "doing," and what is the human significance of this difference?

In "making" the action proceeds from an agent or agents to something produced in the external world. Autoworkers, for instance, produce cars; cooks produce meals; bakers produce cakes; etc. Such action is transitive in nature because it passes from the acting subject(s) to an object fashioned by him or her (them). In this kind of activity, which is governed by the rules of art, interest centers on the object made (and ordinarily those that do not measure up to standards are discarded—at any rate, they are little appreciated, and for this reason are frequently called "defective"). Those who produce the products made may be morally good autoworkers or cooks or bakers or they may be morally bad, but interest in "making" is in the product made, not the producers, and we would prefer to eat good cakes made by morally bad bakers than indigestible ones baked by saints who are incompetent bakers.

In "doing" the action abides in the acting subject(s). The action is immanent and is governed by the requirements of prudence, not of art. If the action is good, it perfects the agent(s); if bad, it degrades and dehumanizes them[26]. I should note here that every act of making is also a doing insofar as it is freely chosen, for the choice to make something is something that we "do," and this choice, as self-determining, abides in us. But the important point here is the difference between "making" and "doing."

As we have seen, the marital act is not an act of making. Rather, it is an act freely chosen by the spouses to express their marital union, one open to the reception of life and the communication of marital love. As such, the marital act is an act inwardly perfective of them and of their life as spouses, the life of which they are co-subjects, just as they are co-subjects of the marital act itself. Even when they choose this act with the ardent hope that, through it, new human life will be given to them, the life begotten is not the product of their act but is "a gift supervening on and giving permanent embodiment to" the marital act itself[27]. When human life comes to be through the marital act, we say quite properly that the spouses are "begetting" or "procreating." They are not "making" anything. The life they receive is "begotten, not made."

200

But when human life comes to be as a result of various types of homologous fertilization, it is the end product of a series of actions, transitive in nature, undertaken by different persons. The spouses "produce" the gametic cells that others use in order to make the end product, the child. In such a procedure the child "comes into existence, not as a gift supervening on an act expressive of the marital union . . . but rather in the manner of a product of a making (and, typically, as the end product of a process managed and carried out by persons other than his parents)"[28]. The life generated is "made," not "begotten."

A human child, however, is not a product inferior to its producers. Rather, it is a person equal in dignity to its parents. A child, therefore ought not to be treated as if it were a product.

To this the proponents of producing babies might argue: desire for the good, the coming to be of a new human person, leads to the choice, not wrong in itself, to bring the possible person into being. Granted, it would be preferable, if possible, to procreate the baby through the marital act. However, any disadvantages inherent in the generation of babies apart from the marital act are clearly outweighed by the great good of new human lives and the fulfillment of the desire for children of couples who otherwise cannot have them. They still wonder, what could be wrong with this?

This objection deserves an answer. The project of producing a baby precisely is to bring a possible baby into being to satisfy the desire to have a baby, and the choice precisely is *to produce a baby*. So, a choice to bring about conception in this fashion inevitably means willing the baby's initial status as a product. But this status is subpersonal, and so the choice to produce a baby is inevitably the choice to enter into a relationship with the baby, not as an equal, but as a product inferior to its producers. But this initial relationship of those who choose to produce babies with the babies they produce is inconsistent with and so impedes the communion of persons endowed with equal dignity which is appropriate to any interpersonal relationship.

Naturally, those who choose to produce a baby make that choice only as a means to an ulterior end. They may well intend that the baby be received into an authentic child-parent relationship, in which he or she will live in the communion which befits those who share personal dignity. If realized, this intended end for the sake of which the choice is made to produce the baby will be good for the baby as well as for the parents, But, even so, the baby's initial status as a product is subpersonal, and as a result the choice to produce the baby is a choice of a bad means to a good end. Moreover, in producing babies if the product is defective, a new person comes to be *as unwanted*. Thus, those who produce babies not only choose life for some, but—can anyone doubt it?—quietly dispose at least some of those who are not developing normally[29].

I believe that the foregoing argument shows that it is wrong to "make" babies, and that homologous fertilization is a mode of making babies. I also believe, although I am not going to show why here, that contraception is immoral because it is a contra-life choice[30]. Since producing babies is always wrong and since contraception is always wrong, the only morally acceptable way to engage either in love-giving or life-giving actions is by engaging in the kind of sexual act that is open to new life and to the communication of love. But this, as we have seen, is the marital act. It is for this reason that there is the inseparable connection between the unitive and procreative meanings of the conjugal act.

The "Language of the Body" and Laboratory Generation of Human Life

There is a third line of reasoning found in the *Instruction* to show that it is morally wrong to generate human life outside the marital act. This line of reasoning is based on the "language of the body." The *Instruction* observes that

> spouses mutually express their personal love in the "language of the body," which clearly involves both "spousal meanings" and parental ones. The conjugal act by which the couple mutually express their self-gift at the same time expresses openness to the gift of life. It is an act that is inseparably corporal and spiritual. It is in their bodies and through their bodies that the spouses

consummate their marriage and are able to become father and mother[30].

The *Instruction* then continues,

> In order to respect the language of their bodies and of their natural generosity, the conjugal union must take place with respect for its openness to procreation, *and the procreation of a person must be the fruit and result of married love.* The origin of the human being thus follows from a procreation that is "linked to the union, not only biological but also spiritual, of the parents, made one by the bond of marriage." Fertilization achieved outside the bodies of the couple remains by this very fact deprived of the meanings and values which are expressed in the language of the body and in the union of human persons"[31].

According to this argument, *in vitro* fertilization, which occurs outside of the bodies of a husband and wife and outside of the bodily act by which their marital union is uniquely and properly expressed, is a way of generating human life that fails completely to respect the "language of the body." It is a way of generating human life that simply refuses to acknowledge the deep human significance of the personal gift, bodily and spiritual in nature, of husband and wife to one another that is aptly expressed in the marital act, a personal gift that is itself fittingly crowned by the gift of human life.

This argument, derived from the beautiful "theology of the body" developed extensively by Pope John Paul II[32], is basically, so it seems to me, a variant of the argument based on the inseparable connection between the unitive and procreative meanings of the conjugal act. The truth central to it is that the marital act is a *bodily-spiritual* act wherein husband and wife "give themselves" to each other and truly become "one flesh." It is an act that "consummates," i.e., perfects and fulfills, their marriage by expressing in a bodily way their "gift" of themselves to one another as bodily, sexual, procreative persons who differ complementarily in their sexuality. In this act the husband gives himself to his wife in a receiving sort of way, and she in turn receives him in a giving sort of way. In this act the "nuptial significance" of the body, as a sign of the gift of the male-person to the female-person and vice versa, is revealed and displayed, and upon it the blessing of fertility can descend.

How different is this act, one immanent in nature and participating in the marriage of husband and wife and open to the gift of life, from the series of transitive actions involved in the laboratory generation of human life. The latter is in no way a bodily act of which the spouses are co-subjects, nor is it one in which they speak the language of marital love. Through the "language of the body" husband and wife open themselves to the gift of life and cooperate with God in its procreation. Through the laboratory generation of human life they merely provide materials, through distinct individual acts of their own and not through the act proper to them as spouses, that others will use to "make" life, to bring into being a "product" subject to technical control.

LTOT, GIFT and TOT

Before bringing this paper to conclusion, I want to discuss briefly the compatibility of some new reproductive technologies other than *in vitro* fertilization and embryo transfer with the teaching of the Church. My concern here is with the procedures known as LTOT (Low Tubal Ovum Transfer), GIFT (Gamete Intra-fallopian Transfer), and TOT (Tubal Ovum Transfer)[33]. Although the *Instruction* did not specifically address these procedures, it did, following the lead of Pope Pius XII[34], articulate the basic principle to be used in determining whether or not these procedures are morally right and compatible with Catholic teaching. According to the *Instruction* a technical procedure "can be morally acceptable" "if [it] facilitates the conjugal act or helps it reach its natural objectives." But "if . . . the procedure were to replace the conjugal act, it is morally illicit"[35]. Thus in what follows my purpose will be to determine whether LTOT, GIFT, and TOT serve as substitutes for the marital act or serve to *facilitate* it and *help it reach its natural objectives.*

204

In LTOT an oocyte is removed from the wife's ovaries by laparoscopy and then, unfertilized, is then reinserted in the mid or lower portion of the fallopian tube or in the uterus itself. Husband and wife then engage in the marital act and fertilization, should it occur, takes place as the natural result of this marital act[36]. In my judgment LTOT meets the criterion of a technical procedure that facilitates the conjugal act and helps it to achieve its natural objectives. As such, LTOT assists and does not replace the marital act. It is, therefore, in my judgment morally permissible and compatible with Church teaching.

GIFT is quite a different procedure. Developed originally by Ricardo Asch and his associates at the University of Texas in San Antonio, when first used it obtained the husband's semen by masturbation. Ova were removed from the wife's ovaries by laparoscopy. The semen and oocytes were then placed in a catheter separated by an air bubble to prevent fertilization outside the wife's body. The catheter tip was then inserted into the fimbriated end of the fallopian tube and the contents gently injected. Fertilization of the oocytes then took place within the wife's body[37].

Since GIFT, as originally practiced, obtained sperm from the husband by masturbation, it was not in accord with Catholic teaching. The procedure was then modified to obtain the sperm in a morally acceptable way. In its modified form husband and wife engage in the marital act, using a perforated condom. Sperm collected in the condom are then placed into the catheter along with an ovum (or ova) removed from the wife's ovaries and separated by an air bubble to prevent fertilization from occurring outside the wife's body. The catheter is then introduced into the end of the wife's fallopian tube and its contents injected, with subsequent fertilization taking place within the wife's body.

Although some Catholic moralists have given their approval to the GIFT procedure[38], claiming that it assists the marital act and does not substitute for it, I believe that it is not compatible with Catholic teaching. With Donald DeMarco and others[39], I think it must be said that in the GIFT procedure the conjugal act is in truth incidental and not essential to the achievement of pregnancy. The bond between the marital act and the GIFT procedure is not essential. This is quite obvious from the fact that this procedure as such does not require the marital act. There is a complete dissociation between the marital act and the technical method which leads to conception. The *only* reason to engage in the marital act is to obtain the husband's sperm in a nonmasturbatory way. But this is only incidental to the GIFT procedure as such. Conception does not take place as a result of the conjugal act, the personal, one flesh union of husband and wife. Rather, it takes place as a result of a technological procedure which, of itself, is not essentially related to the marital act. GIFT, therefore, *substitutes* for the marital act so far as the conception of the child is concerned and does not facilitate it or help it to achieve its natural objectives.

Although the acronym "TOT" would make it seem that this procedure is similar to "LTOT," a close examination of this procedure shows that this is not the case. Developed by David S. McLaughlin, it differs from LTOT first in that the environment in which prospective fertilization is to take place is as high in the fallopian tube as possible (hence the elimination of the "L" in the acronym LTOT). But, secondly, it differs from LTOT in that fertilization does not take place as the result of a subsequent marital act. Rather, fertilization takes place after sperm (obtained from the husband either by masturbation or by the use of a perforated condom during a marital act) are introduced into the fallopian tube along with the wife's ovum after having been placed in a catheter, using air bubbles between sperm and ovum to prevent fertilization outside the body. In other words, TOT is more similar to GIFT than it is to LTOT. Its relationship to the conjugal act is, like that of GIFT, accidental and not essential insofar as the marital act is resorted to only in order to obtain the sperm used in a nonmasturbatory way. Conception does not follow from the one flesh unity of husband and wife in the marital act, rather it follows from the technological introduction of sperm and ovum via a catheter into the distal region of the fallopian tube, and this technological intervention is *not* essentially related to the marital act. Thus in my judgment TOT, like GIFT, is in essence a way of generating human life that substitutes for the marital act and does not in truth facilitate that act's achieving its natural objectives. It is thus a procedure that is not compatible with Catholic teaching.

Conclusion

In this paper I have tried to show the reasons why it is morally wrong to choose to generate human life outside the marital act and to support the truth of Catholic teaching on this subject. I am convinced that, at the very deepest levels, a profound theological truth is at the heart of this teaching. According to Catholic faith, the Eternal Word of the Father was "begotten, not made." Catholic faith holds that human beings are the living images of God Himself, the "created words" that His Uncreated Word became precisely to show us how deeply God loves us and wills to give us His very own life. It follows therefore, that His created words ought, like His Uncreated and Eternal Word, be "begotten, not made."

NOTES

1. I use the term "vendor" advisedly. On this see George Annas, "Artificial Insemination: Beyond the Best Interests of the Donor," *Hastings Center Report* 9.4 (August, 1979) 14–15, 43. Annas, a lawyer, noted that those "providing" sperm do so on the basis of a contract according to which they are paid. "The continued use of the term 'donor,' " he wrote, "gives the impression that the 'vendor' is doing some service for the good of humanity," which is not in fact true.

2. The revealing, if inadvertent, remark of Dr. Robert Edwards after the birth of Louise Brown is worth noting. Edwards said: "The last time I saw *her, she* was just eight cells in a test tube. *She* was beautiful *then,* and she's still beautiful *now*" (*Science Digest,* October 1978, 9; emphasis added). Surely Edwards' statement is an eloquent testimony that human life begins at fertilization.

3. Pope Paul VI, *Humanae vitae,* n. 12: "Huiusmodi doctrina, quae ab Ecclesiae Magisterio saepe exposita est, in nexu indissolubili nititur, a Deo statuto, quam homini sua sponte infringere non licet, inter significationem unitatis et significationem procreationis, quae ambae in actu coniugali insunt."

4. IBID., n. 13: "Pariter, si rem considerent, fateantur oportet, actum amoris mutui, qui facultati vitam propagandi detrimento sit, quam Deus omnium Creator secundum peculiares leges in ea insculpsit, refragari tum divino consilio, ad cuius normam coniugium constitutum est, tum voluntati primi vitae humanae Auctoris. Quapropter cum quis dono Dei utitur, tollens, licet solum ex parte, significationem et finem doni ipsius, sive viri sive mulieris naturae repugnat eorumque intimae necessitudini, ac propterae etiam Dei consilio sanctaeque eius voluntati obnititur."

5. Ibid., n. 12, text cited in note 3.

6. Ibid., n. 12: "Etenim propter intimam suam rationem, coniugii actus dum maritum et uxorem artissimo sociat vinculo, eos idoneos etiam facit ad novam vitam gignendam, secundum leges in ipsa viri et mulieris natura inscriptas."

7. Congregation for the Doctrine of the Faith, *Instruction on Respect for Human Life in Its Origin and the Dignity of Procreation,* Part II, A, 11, with a reference to Vatican Council II, *Gaudium et spes,* n. 50.

8. Ibid., II, A, 2, with a reference to Pope Pius XII, Discourse to Those Taking Part in the Fourth International Congress of Catholic Doctors, 29 September 1949, *AAS* 41 (1949) 559.

9. Many people, particularly in the affluent Western democracies, are quite favorably disposed to all the new reproductive technologies, even those involving use of gametic cells from third parties, the use of surrogate mothers, etc. One of the most extreme views, unfortunately not uncommon, is set forth in great detail by Joseph Fletcher, *The Ethics of Genetic Control: Ending Reproductive Roulette* (Garden City, N.Y.: Doubleday Anchor Books, 1972).

10. The "Baby M" case refers to the tragic story of a little girl, referred to as "Baby M," conceived by the artificial insemination of Mrs. Mary Beth Whitehead with sperm "provided" by Dr. Stern, whose wife did not wish to become pregnant because of a mild case of multiple sclerosis. Mrs. Whitehead, who had grown attached to the child, did not wish to give her over to the Sterns after her birth, and a lengthy, well-publicized trial took place, eventually giving custody of the child to the Sterns.

11. "Pregnancy reduction" is the expression used by some doctors who deliberately kill within the womb "excess" children who have been conceived *in vitro* and implanted in their mother's womb to enhance the possibility of at least one child surviving pregnancy. In this type of case several babies are deliberately conceived *in vitro* and subsequently implanted in the mother's womb. But, since multiple pregnancies raise problems about the survival of all the unborn and since the parents are interested in having only one or possibly two children of their own, the "excess" number of unborn children is "reduced" by killing several.

12. *Instruction. . . ,* Part II, B, 4, a, citing Pope Paul VI, *Humanae vitae,* n. 12 (text cited in note 3).

13. Ibid., II, B, 4, a, citing Pope Pius XII, Discourse to Those Taking Part in the Second Naples World Congress on Fertility and Human Sterility, 19 May 1956, *AAS* 49 (1956) 470.

14. Ibid., II, B, 4, a; emphasis omitted.

15. Pope Pius XII, Discourse to Those Taking Part in the Fourth World Congress of Catholic Doctors, 29 September, 1949, *AAS* 41 (1949) 561.

16. Pope Pius XII, Apostolate of the Midwives: An Address to the Italian Catholic Union of Midwives, 29 October 1951, text in *The Catholic Mind,* 50 (1952) 61.

17. On the constant Catholic teaching that God is the author of marriage see the following: The Council of Trent, Session 24, 1563, in *Enchiridion Symbolorum* ed. Henricus Denzinger and Adolphus Schoenmetzer (ed. 33, Romae: Herder, 1984), nn. 1797–1812; Pope Leo XIII, Encyclical *Arcanum Divinae Sapientiae,* in *Official Catholic Teachings: Love and Sexuality,* ed. Odile M. Liebard (Wilmington, N.C.: McGrath, 1978), nn. 3, 5, 6; Pope Pius XI, Encyclical *Casti connubii,* in Liebard, nn. 31, 64, 66; Vatican Council II, *Gaudium et spes,* n. 48; Pope Paul VI, *Humanae vitae,* nn. 8–9; Pope John Paul II, *Familiaris consortio,* n. 11.

18. For a fuller discussion of this point, see my *Sex, Marriage, and Chastity: Reflections of a Catholic Layman, Spouse and Parent* (Chicago: Franciscan Herald Press,1981), chapter 5. Also see my "Sexual Ethics and Human Dignity," in *Persona, Verità e Morale: Atti del Congresso Internazionale di Teologia Morale (Roma, 7–12 aprile 1986)* (Roma: Città Nuova Editrice, 1988), pp. 477–495, especially pp. 488–489.

19. Centuries ago St. Augustine rightly noted that one of the chief goods of marriage is children, who are to be received lovingly, nourished humanely, and educated religiously. See his *De genesi ad literam,* 9.7 (PL 34.397).

20. On this see Vatican Council II, *Gaudium et spes,* n. 48.

21. The Augustinian teaching on the threefold good of marriage (progeny, steadfast fidelity, and the "sacrament") was set forth by him in several places (see, for example, *De bono conjugali, De nuptiis et concupiscentia,* passim). This teaching was accepted by later theologians and by the magisterium of the Church. The doctrine of the threefold good of marriage is central to Pope Pius XI's Encyclical, *Casti connubii,* and the Fathers of Vatican II made it clear, in *Gaudium et spes,* n. 48, with corresponding footnotes to sources in Augustine, St. Thomas, the Council of Trent, and Pius XI, that they made Augustine's teaching their own.

22. Here the teaching set forth by Pope Paul VI in *Humanae vitae,* n. 13, is pertinent. There he noted that a "conjugal act" (using this term in a purely descriptive sense) imposed by one of the spouses upon the other against the reasonable wishes of the other violates the requirements of the moral law.

23. On the issue of contraception, which cannot be taken up here, see the essay by Germain Grisez, John Finnis, Joseph M. Boyle, Jr., and William E. May, " 'Every Marital Act Ought to Be Open to New Life': A Clarification," *The Thomist* (July, 1988); also printed in the book by the same authors, *The Teaching of "Humanae Vitae": A Defense* (San Francisco: Ignatius Press, 1988).

24. *Instruction. . . ,* II, B, 4, c.

25. Ibid., II, B, 5, with an internal citation from Pope John Paul II, *Familiaris consortio,* n. 14.

26. Classic sources for the difference between transitive and immanent activity and the significant of this difference are : Aristotle, *Metaphysics,* Bk. 9, c. 8, 1050a23–1050b1; St. Thomas Aquinas, *In IX Metaphysicorum,* Lect. 8, n. 1865; *Summa theologiae,* 1, 4, 2, as 2; 1, 14, 5, ad 1; 1, 18, 1.

27. Catholic Bishops Committee on Bioethical Issues, *In Vitro Fertilization: Morality and Public Policy* (London: Catholic Information Services, 1983), n. 23.

28. Ibid., n. 24.

29. The previous three paragraphs paraphrase material developed by Grisez, Finnis, Boyle and May in the essay referred to in note 23.

30. *Instruction. . . ,* Part II, B, 4, b, with a reference to Pope John Paul II, General Audience on 16 Jan. 1980; *Insegnamenti di Giovani Paolo II* III, 1 (1980) 148–152.

31. Ibid., with a reference to Pope John Paul II, Discourse to Those Taking Part in the 35th General Assembly of World Medical Association, 29 October 1983; *AAS* 76 (1984) 393.

32. On this see Pope John Paul II, *Original Unity of Man and Woman: Catechesis on Genesis* (Boston: St. Paul Editions, 1981).

33. The best treatment in English that I know of dealing with those procedures is Donald DeMarco, "Catholic Church Teaching and TOT/LTOT/GIFT," a paper given in February, 1987 at the meeting of the Bishops of the United States and Canada in Dallas, TX, on reproductive technologies, sponsored by the Pope John XXIII Medical Moral Center.

34. Pope Pius XII, Discourse to Those Taking Part in the Fourth International Congress of Catholic Doctors, 29 September 1949, *AAS* 41 (1949) 560.

35. *Instruction. . . ,* Part II, B, 6.

36. On this see Pope John XIII Medical Moral Center, "Should Catholic Hospitals Encourage Low Tubal Ovum Transfer?" *Hospital Progress,* March 1984, 55–56.

37. Ricardo Asch, et al., "Pregnancy after Translaparoscopic Intrafallopian Transfer," *Lancet,* Nov. 3, 1984, 1034–1035.

38. E.g., Lloyd W. Hess, "Assisting the Infertile Couple," *Ethics & Medics* 11.2 (1986).

39. See note 33.

Chapter 13

ARTIFICIAL PROCREATION AND CATHOLIC TEACHING

Richard H. Berquist

Donum vitae, the Vatican's *Instruction on Respect for Human Life in Its Origin and on the Dignity of Procreation,* is concerned with many issues. Among them are respect for embryonic life, the sanctity of marriage, the use of donor gametes, and surrogate motherhood. The central issue, however, is artificial procreation; other issues appear in the document primarily because of their relevance to this one.

Artificial procreation is a particularly difficult moral question. Many people can understand why the Church is opposed to abortion and even to contraception. There is a negative, unnatural aspect to these practices that even those who would permit them can recognize. They can also understand why the Church considers the use of donor gametes a violation of the sanctity of marriage. What they can't understand is why a wife may not be artificially inseminated with her husband's sperm or why her ovum may not be fertilized in vitro with her husband's sperm if the resulting embryos are to be transferred to her womb. These practices seem positive, life affirming, and consistent with sanctity of marriage. They do not seem essentially different from other medical procedures intended to help nature achieve its ends.

My purpose in this brief paper is to sketch an approach to explaining the Church's teaching on artificial procreation. It is based on a presentation made at a conference on infertility in February of 1988. The conference took place at the College of St. Thomas in St. Paul, Minnesota and was jointly sponsored by the College and the Twin City Couple to Couple League.

The Church teaches that artificial procreation is intrinsically wrong. This means that artificial procreation as such is opposed to human dignity. Obviously, it is not opposed to human dignity insofar as it is procreation. It is opposed, therefore, insofar as it is a sub-human **mode** of procreation, a mode of procreation that is beneath the dignity of the man and woman who procreate and unworthy to be the starting point of a new human life. It differs essentially from the natural act of love which is precisely suited to the dignity of human nature.

This, in outline, is the heart of the argument, as it appears to me. To clarify it, I would like to consider (a) human dignity (intrinsic value) as distinguished from utility value, (b) artificial procreation in relation to medicine, and (c) artificial procreation in relation to human dignity. I will conclude with a couple of brief reflections about the possible social consequences of the practice of artificial procreation.

Intrinsic Value and Utility Value

Imagine using an exquisite Ming vase as a refuse container. Our immediate reaction is that such a use of so lovely a work of art would be inconsistent with its "dignity." A Ming vase has a higher, more "noble" purpose. It has a value beyond utility—or rather, a value beyond the low level utility of a refuse container. To the extent that it transcends utility, it appears as intrinsically valuable, as possessing a kind of dignity.

In the final analysis, of course, the Ming vase is no more than an object of utility. It possesses intrinsic value or dignity only in a relative sense, as compared to a refuse container. Dignity in the strict sense is possessed only by beings whose essential value is altogether beyond utility, beings which exist for their own sake. Dignity may be defined as the value of a being which exists for its own good as its ultimate purpose. (The expression "own good" can refer to a common good, a good shared with others, as well as to a merely individual good.)

Human beings possess dignity in this strict sense of the term by their very nature. An easy way to see this is to compare human beings to animals. What is unique to us is the power of reason. We are capable of understanding our own good and of distinguishing it from the good of others. Hence we naturally seek it as our ultimate end and refuse to accept the status of an object of utility, i.e., the status of a being which exists for the good of others. Note that infants, the unborn and severely retarded adults also possess this dignity. Although they lack the use of reason, in whole or in part, they are human beings, oriented by nature to their own good as an ultimate end. Our dignity arises from the life we are naturally **meant** to achieve, not from the actual achievement of it.

Animals, on the other hand, lack reason. They instinctively seek their good as a **proximate** end but are unconcerned with their **ultimate** purpose. If my dog is well fed and kindly treated, he is content; the fact that I think of him as existing ultimately for my benefit and not for his own is irrelevant. But for a human being this is even more important than being well treated. In fact, it is precisely because we exist for our own good and **know** that we exist for our own good that we insist on our right to be treated with respect.

Artificial Procreation and Medicine

Most couples who seek artificial procreation believe that it is an extension of the ordinary medical therapies for curing infertility. But this is not true. To understand why artificial procreation is **not,** properly speaking, a medical procedure, it is helpful to consider the original purpose of technology. For medicine is a kind of technology applied to the human body.

Technology, defined in terms of its purpose, is the intervention of the human hand or human instruments in order to perfect what is imperfect or to remedy what is defective in the material world. To grasp the meaning of this definition, let us reflect briefly on the creation of the world as related in the Book of Genesis.

At the time of Creation God gave man and woman dominion over the earth so that it might be perfected by being ordered to their service. This is why He commanded Adam and Eve to cultivate the Garden of Eden. For although God's creatures were perfect in their own natures from the very beginning, they were not yet perfected for human use. The environment needed to be domesticated and "humanized" to become a suitable habitat for human persons.

Technology, therefore, was present from the beginning of human history. It was necessary so that the earth might be raised from its natural state and recreated, so to speak, in the image of man and woman, who alone, of all material creatures, were made in the image of God. Just as the image of God in man and woman reveals His Lordship over them, so the image of man and woman in transformed nature reveals their lordship over the earth.

In the beginning, technology did not touch the human body, at least not in any significant way. (An exception might have to be made, I suppose, for personal grooming—cutting hair, for example.) For there was nothing imperfect to be perfected or defective to be remedied. Only after the fall, when we began to suffer from diseases and other physical evils, did it become necessary to intervene technologically upon the human body so that it might be restored as much as possible to its natural state and functioning. Hence the origin of medicine, the most noble of all the uses of technology. For medicine touches the human body itself, the only part of material creation which shares essentially in the dignity of the human person.

Let us now consider artificial human procreation. It does not fall under the original purpose of technology—to perfect inferior creation for human use—since it is concerned with something essentially human. Nor does it fall under the purpose of medicine, since it does nothing to restore the human body to its natural state and functioning. For this reason, it cannot be a medical therapy in the proper sense of the term. It should be classified rather as a form of bioengineering.

There is an essential difference between artificial procreation and medical therapies intended to remedy infertility. Some of these attempt to restore lost function to reproductive organs—for example, opening a blocked fallopian tube. Others—for example, LTOT—are meant to assist the natural act of love in achieving conception.[1] These interventions are essentially medical; the procreation which results is **human procreation** technologically assisted. Artificial procreation, however, is not human procreation in the proper sense of the term; it is **technological procreation** applied to human beings.

The fact that artificial procreation requires medical expertise does not prove that it is a genuine medical procedure. Any form of technology can be misused. Nor is this proved by the fact that it serves a human desire. A quick way to see this is recall a well known incident in the life of Van Gogh. He cut off one of his ears to send to a girl friend. Suppose he had asked a physician to do this for him. What physician would have complied with such a request? Medicine is not a technology which serves human desires per se; it is technology which recognizes the dignity of the human body and which serves the human person precisely by restoring the body to its natural condition—that is, to health.

The Van Gogh example relates more closely to abortion (and also to contraception and contraceptive sterilization) than it does to artificial procreation. Abortion, like cutting off a healthy ear, is anti-medical; both procedures are opposed to the natural state or functioning of the human body. (To get around this, some people have tried to define an unwanted pregnancy as a disease. By the same logic, we could define an unwanted ear as a disease and cutting it off as therapeutic.) Artificial procreation, on the other hand, is not so much anti-medical as it is a-medical, outside the sphere of medicine altogether. It neither promotes nor hinders the natural functioning of the body. This is why it is bioengineering rather than medicine.

215

The Vatican *Instruction* refers to artificial procreation as a form of technological domination over the human person. The preceding reflections make clear why this is so. In artificial procreation, technology asserts the same kind of authority over human procreation that is has traditionally and rightly asserted over inferior nature. We **dominate** inferior nature, that is, we treat sub-human beings as objects of utility, which exist not for their sake but for ours. Consequently, we do not respect their natural manner of procreation as a matter of principle any more than we respect their lives. Artificial procreation, by reducing human procreation to technological procreation, asserts this same kind of domination over human persons.

How is it that we do not recognize artificial procreation as a form of technological domination? One reason is that couples desperate to have a child willingly submit themselves to this procedure and hence do not feel dominated by it. However, the element of domination is intrinsic to artificial procreation and is therefore present even when the procedure is willingly undergone. In the same way, the murderer, by the act of murder, asserts domination over the life even of a willing victim and the sadist, by his sadistic acts, asserts domination over the willing masochist.

Another reason is simply lack of reflection. We are in the habit of looking at technological procedures primarily in terms of their utility—i.e., the desirable and undesirable consequences which follow from them. Artificial procreation does produce a desirable result; it enables infertile couples to have children. Undesirable consequences, if any, are not obvious. Therefore, we feel justified in making use of it.

But there is another question which, too often, we do not ask. Is artificial procreation suited to the dignity of the human person? By not asking this question, we fail to recognize the moral distinction between applying techniques of artificial procreation to animals and applying them to human beings. We treat human beings, by default, as though they were on the same plane as animals, equally subject to technological manipulation. We fail to consider that what is appropriate for beings whose value lies ultimately in their utility may not be appropriate for beings who exist for their own sake.

Artificial Procreation and Human Dignity

In order to see clearly why artificial procreation is inconsistent with human dignity, it is helpful to examine the natural manner of human procreation more closely. This can best be done by contrasting it with reproduction in animals and plants.

The first step is to distinguish between the **fact** of reproduction, which is common to all living things, and the **mode** of reproduction, which varies from one species to another. Every kind of living being naturally reproduces in a way that is suited to the kind of life it possesses. Life is self-motion, self-direction, autonomy. Because some kinds of living things are more perfectly self-moving than others, their natural modes of reproduction are more excellent.

At the lowest level are plants. They have very little control over the processes by which their germ cells are brought together. They depend on wind, insects and other external agents for this purpose. Their reproduction, as a consequence, expresses self-motion only to a very limited degree.

The higher animals, on the other hand, unite their germ cells by their own act, the sexual act of male and female. This is a more excellent mode of reproduction corresponding to the more perfect kind of self-motion found in animals based on sense awareness and instinct. If animals had dignity, i.e., if they existed for the sake of their own natural fulfillment, we would have to respect their natural mode of procreation. It is because they are ultimately objects of utility that we are morally free to reproduce them technologically.

Human beings are even more perfectly self-moving than animals since they act not from instinct but from understanding. The human procreative act recapitulates the kind of self-motion found in the sexual act of animals, but in a higher, more perfect way, as one dimension of a personal act of love. It is therefore a mode of procreation precisely suited to human nature, a mode of procreation **at the human level of existence.** Because human beings are not objects of utility but creatures whose ultimate purpose is the achievement of a way of life which expresses and perfects their nature, the human mode of procreation must be respected. Artificial procreation strips the procreative act of precisely those aspects which make it appropriately human and is therefore inconsistent with human dignity.

In summary, the procreation of human beings, like all forms of sexual reproduction, requires the bringing together of germ cells. From the point of view of utility, it matters little **how** the germ cells are brought together. From the point of view of human dignity, however, it matters a lot. Human procreation must be an expression of human nature itself, of the natures of man and woman, and not an expression of the technology by which we dominate plants and animals which exist for our use.

Some Consequences of Artificial Procreation

Thus far we have been considering artificial procreation in relation to the dignity of the human person. Let us now briefly reflect on some of its possible consequences.

I believe that the practice of artificial procreation will contribute to the loss of respect for embryonic life and will lead to an increased tolerance of procreation outside of marriage. Both of these problems are discussed in the *Instruction.* The sub-human quality of artificial procreation leads us to think of embryos as sub-human "things" and their availability (in in vitro fertilization) opens the door to many possible abuses. Artificial procreation within marriage leads naturally to artificial procreation outside of marriage since it removes the personal intimacy normally associated with procreating children.

Because it debases the mode of procreation, the practice of artificial procreation also debases the human relationships involved in procreation. Human embryos, for example, come to be valued not in themselves but as a means for satisfying the desire to have a child. If embryos are objects produced to satisfy desires, the husband and wife need not themselves supply the raw materials. Procreation ceases to be a natural expression of the love between husband and wife and becomes similar to the breeding of animals.

As I stated at the outset, artificial procreation is a difficult moral problem. I am convinced that the key to its solution lies in a more developed understanding of human dignity and its implications than we have thus far achieved. I hope that the preceding reflections will contribute in some small way to this understanding.

NOTES

1. LTOT stands for low tubal ovum transplant. This procedure bypasses a blocked fallopian tube by surgically removing an ovum from the ovary and transplanting it in the lower part of the tube where it may be fertilized through sexual intercourse. See the discussion in *Ethics and Medics,* 8(10), October, 1983.

Chapter 14

THE PERMANENCE OF MARRIAGE AND THE MENTALITY OF DIVORCE

The Most Reverend Edward M. Egan

On September 6, 1986, the *New York Times* ran an article entitled, "Britannica Computer Foils Tampering with the Facts." The story was this. Toward the end of the previous July, one of the 130 editors of the *Encyclopaedia Britannica* was served notice that his employment was terminated. Hurt and angered, he came to his former office by night and fed into the computer that contained the almost completed 1987 edition of the encyclopaedia, several pieces of misinformation which, because of the nature of the computer process, soon made their way here and there into all thirty-two volumes.

When the situation was discovered early in August, it was feared that it might not be possible to issue the 1987 edition. Indeed, the misinformation seemed to have so thoroughly "infected" the entire publication that in a rather unusual memorandum to all employees, the Senior Editor, Mr. Norman Braun, is reported by the *Times* to have lamented, "Our hard work has been turned into garbage."

Happily, Mr. Braun proved to have been overly pessimistic. For having guessed who was responsible for the misdeed and knowing his so-called "computer password," in something less than six hours a master technician managed to extract all of the misinformation from "the world's oldest reference work still in publication," restoring it to its usual and much-vaunted level of accuracy. The "sabotage" had failed, Mr. Braun announced at a press conference. The 150,000 sets of the 1987 edition of the *Encyclopaedia Britannica,* each containing 44,000,000 wondrously truthful words, would appear as per schedule.

* * *

It is the thesis of this paper that something similar appears to have happened over the past twenty-five years to the Catholic understanding of marriage, particularly in the English-speaking world. Not out of hurt or anger, to be sure, but regrettably, nonetheless, a good deal of misinformation seems to have made its way into the computer. And if it has, I would suggest, it needs to be gotten out as soon as possible, lest Catholic belief about the fundamentals of marriage be seriously prejudiced.

To identify the alleged misinformation, it will be necessary to start with what I would presume to term the facts, the reality, the simple, even if prosaic, truth about marriage. However, in order to do this effectively, it might be well to make two preliminary observations. First, marriage is a phenomenon which can be analyzed from many points of view. Thus, it can be both fairly and sensibly discussed in terms of philosophy, theology, psychology, spirituality, even economics and poetry. It should not therefore come as a surprise to anyone that, inasmuch as marriage is commonly thought to entail rights and obligations, it can also be discussed juridically, that is to say, in terms of law.

Second, some things in life are by their nature complicated and elusive. Computers are perhaps an example. Others are more simple and accordingly understood, at least in their essentials, by the vast majority of adults of ordinary intelligence. Marriage clearly belongs in this second category. True, over the past quarter of a century and more, religious, and especially Catholic, authors from various disciplines have claimed to have discovered all manner of intricacies and nuances concerning it. Still, in its basics, virtually everyone knows what marriage is and knows, moreover, that he or she knows it. "Teflon-like," marriage has allowed even the most recondite of ambiguities to slide off rather easily, leaving little trace behind, at least in the estimate of the average citizen, the proverbial man or woman on the street.

* * *

This said, we move on to what I at least would term juridical misinformation regarding marriage.

The word, "marriage," has in most languages, if not all, at least two meanings. The first is the manifestation of the will to be married on the part of a male and a female. (This is often described as the exchange of marriage consent.) The second is the state of being married which results from the aforementioned manifestation of will. (This is often described as the marriage relationship, the condition of being married, or—if I might be permitted a bit of rather well-known Latin—the marital "society" [*societas*], "union" [*unio*], "communion" [*communio*], "partnership" [*consortium*], and even "bond" [*vinculum* or *ligamen*].)

Now I ask: How is marriage in its first meaning achieved? Please note every word. John and Mary consent to marriage by giving to and receiving from each other a commitment to do and not to do certain things. They enter a contract, form an agreement, constitute a covenant (all of these expressions are and always have been quite acceptable) in which they exchange rights and obligations or, to be perhaps more precise, in which they exchange a very specific right and obligation.

And what is that right and obligation? In classic Catholic teaching it is the exclusive and permanent right (from the standpoint of the receiver) and obligation (from the standpoint of the giver) to perform together that act which has not surprisingly come to be called the "marriage act," that act, namely, to which a male and female are drawn under a physical impulse from their Creator and whereby they make of themselves candidates to become co-creators.

Later on we will treat in some detail whether this is indeed the only right the couple exchanges when by "doing" marriage in its first meaning, they consent to and constitute marriage in its second meaning. At this point, however, I would simply invite you to attend to exactly what has been said. John and Mary consent to be married by mutually giving and receiving a right which at least in traditional Catholic teaching is claimed to be the exclusive and permanent right to the marriage act.

* * *

Who in the world, you are perhaps asking yourself, would disagree with any of this? Many, I would reply. And their disagreements are intimately bound up with the misinformation of which I spoke above, the misinformation which I believe has somehow been fed into the computer of Catholic teaching about marriage and which in my judgement urgently needs to be gotten out.

I have never been altogether sure why the first piece of what I style misinformation has been so widely and enthusiastically proclaimed. Whatever of this, about the breadth and warmth of its proclamation there can hardly be any doubt. For example, in a book published in 1982 by an American theologian on the nature of marriage according to Catholic thought, it is repeated over twenty times in a variety of formulations.[1] Similarly, in an article published in 1987 by an Italian canonist, it appears, again in variety of formulations, over a half dozen times.[2] In simplest terms it is this: According to perennial Catholic doctrine, the object of marriage consent is the procreation and education of offspring.

Certainly, one can understand an occasional "lapsus calami" about a matter such as this. However, grammar, if nothing else, should forestall relentless repetition. The object of marriage consent (marriage in its first meaning) is manifestly the state of being married (marriage in its second meaning). Standing before the altar on his wedding day, John does not consent to procreation

224

and education of offspring; he consents to marriage. And incidentally, John knows this, Mary knows it, and even the local registrar of marriages knows it.

Why, then, the confusion? Frankly, as admitted above, I am not sure. Still, I would note that mistaking the classic, Catholic object of marriage consent does lend itself to a kind of "straw man" argument which may be thought by some to be an efficient means of casually dismissing the wisdom of centuries. The rhetoric might flow something like this: "Traditional Catholic teaching has championed so narrow and inappropriate a view of marriage as to suggest that when a man and woman marry, they consent to something extrinsic to themselves, something which does not even yet exist, something which may never exist, something solely on the physical or, worse yet, animal level, something to which they may have given little thought, something for which they may have little enthusiasm."

Confronted by such reasoning, the ancient philosophers used to warn: "Ex falso sequitur quodlibet." ("From a false premise anything follows.") For our purposes here it will be enough to observe, first, that the premise of the argument, if an argument be intended, is patently wrong, inasmuch as the object of marriage consent is not the procreation and education of offspring but rather the marital state, and second, that we will have occasion to address some of the conclusions later on at length.

* * *

The second piece of what I am defining as misinformation is no less widespread. It is this: Marriage consent may be fairly described in juridical terms as the giving of self to one's partner and the receiving of self from one's partner. Indeed, almost all who speak in this vein regularly claim that the giving and receiving of the selves in marriage consent, if it is to be effective juridically, must somehow be "total."[3]

Here I must ask you to allow me a disclaimer. As mentioned above, marriage can be rightly and properly examined under many aspects, among them the poetic. In fact, we might add now, the poetic frequently expresses about marriage, as it does about many things, truths which other endeavors, including law, are

225

hard-pressed to articulate. Joyce Kilmer allows that trees have "hungry mouths" which are "prest against the earth's sweet flowing breast." And he is, of course, correct, no matter what horticulturists and geologists may think about the matter. Still, we would have little good to say of the horticulturist who, having read Kilmer's "Trees," dug into the roots of elms and oaks expecting to find there oral cavities, any more than we would feel much confidence in a geologist who, having contemplated the same poem, came to hold that the earth is a mammal.

I have no problem whatever about someone's speaking or writing in a theological, spiritual, or poetic context of a person consenting to marriage by giving his or her self to another and receiving that self of that other, totally or otherwise. I fully expect to find such statements in books of theology, spirituality, and poetry. Indeed, I am not even upset to discover them in books of a legal sort, as long as I can be assured that no one is drawing legal conclusions from them.

Gaudium et spes speaks of marriage in this way.[4] So does *Humanae vitae*.[5] And so too does the new Code of Canon Law.[6] You may on first hearing find this last statement a bit unsettling. Yet, if you reflect upon the history of legal codes, you will soon be calmed. The opening pages of the first book of the Code of Justinian, you will recall, is a theological, moral, and spiritual disquisition on the meaning and implications of the Mystery of the Trinity.[7] Even codes are at times permitted to take flight.

No, there is no problem in stating in any context that marriage consent is wrought by a couple's giving and receiving themselves and, if you like, giving and receiving themselves totally. A problem is, however, created if what is thus stated is somehow transformed into a premise in a juridical analysis and juridical conclusions are drawn from it. Juridically, no one has himself or herself to give another; much less can the self of one person be received, juridically speaking, by another. All of which is true whether the expression, "totally," be added or not. For philosophically and juridically, self is an indivisible totality. If it could be given and received (and it cannot), the only way in which this could be done would be totally, as long as we are thinking and reasoning about marriage in the altogether legitimate sphere of law and things juridical.

I have personally seen any number of sentences, that is, judicial decisions, in which Church tribunals have declared marriages invalid because the man in question was found to be selfish or the woman in question was found to be grasping, and it was concluded that such persons had to be at the time of their marriage unable to give themselves to another, and especially to do this totally. If you wish just one example, I might refer you to a decision given at the Roman Rota "coram Egan," as they say, on March 29, 1984, which reversed the judgement of a diocesan tribunal that had pursued this manner of argument.[8] I speak here of a piece of misinformation, as I view misinformation, which has made its way far deeper into the computer than many might imagine.

* * *

The third and last piece of misinformation to which I would respectfully draw your attention is the most common and easily the most damaging. It can be articulated in many ways. All, however, come down more or less to something such as this: When a couple consents to marriage, they do it perhaps by exchanging an exclusive and permanent right to the marriage act, but also and particularly by exchanging the right to some additional thing or things without which the marriage would be invalid. These further objects of the exchanged right are one or more of the following: an interpersonal relationship, a community of life and love, self-completion, self-development, self-fulfillment.

What are we to say of this? I will endeavor to be as brief and clear as possible.

First, the expression, "interpersonal relationship," in this context can have only two possible meanings. They are either the marital state pure and simple or the marital state with the proviso that it is to achieve at least a modicum of human, personal gratification for the parties, or to put it all quite badly, that it is to be at least reasonably successful, basically happy.

If one has in mind the first meaning, the marital state pure and simple, obviously no right to it can be exchanged, first, because consenting to marriage by giving and receiving a right to marriage is a meaningless redundancy, and second, because even if it were other than a meaningless redundancy, John cannot be given a right to marry Mary, any more than he can give Mary a right to marry him. (The same, of course, holds true for Mary vis-à-vis John.) The generic right to marry is a reality derived from the natural law. The specific right to marry this person or that does not, and cannot, exist.

If one has in mind the second meaning of a marital interpersonal relationship, that is, the state of being in a marriage which is at least in some fundamental sense happy, again no right to it can be exchanged, first and foremost because there exists no such thing as a right to a happy marriage. Moreover, even if there did exist such a thing, it is unlikely that any juridical conclusions about the validity of a particular marriage could be derived from it. For happiness is a most personal, individual, and fluid reality. Accordingly, one can hardly imagine a criterion whereby to measure how much of it a particular person or couple must be able to provide in order for their marriage to be counted as valid. Nor, we might add, has anyone ever been able to identify a criterion whereby to measure how much this particular person or couple were actually able to agree to provide on their wedding day, except, of course, in the case of someone who was so manifestly incapable of marriage on other grounds that there would be no reason to bring up such plainly unreal considerations as the exchanging of a right to a happy marriage.

This last remark brings us to what I at least would consider the heart of the matter. As everyone knows full well, long before discussions began in the Church about giving self in marriage, marital interpersonal relationships, and the like, canonical doctrine and jurisprudence had spelled out with remarkable logic, clarity, and thoroughness, what precisely is required by the natural and positive law for the validity of a marriage. When treating the capacities of the partners to the marriage, the requirements were quite impressive. In order to marry validly, it was determined,

1. One had to be of a certain age and free of such impediments as consanguinity, a previous marriage bond, or religious vows;

2. One had to know that marriage is a society of a man and a woman which is ordered to the begetting of offspring through corporal contact;
3. One had to enjoy the use of reason;
4. One had to be able to consider the wisdom of marrying with the kind of mature deliberation that a matter of such import requires;
5. One had to be endowed with both external and particularly internal freedom to marry;
6. One had to be both physically and psychologically capable of the marriage act;
7. One had to be able to commit oneself to an exclusive marital union;
8. One had to be able to commit oneself to a permanent marital union.

Now let us suppose for a moment that, in order to marry validly, it were necessary to give and receive a right to some basic, minimum measure of marital happiness. Is it even thinkable that a person could meet all the classic requirements for being able to marry validly as outlined above but could not do whatever is the minimum that could be reasonably demanded as regards marital happiness? The individual person is, as everyone knows, a substantial unity, operating with one mind, one will, one body, and one set of emotions. If he or she is of legal age to marry and without invalidating impediments, clear about the meaning of marriage, endowed with the use of reason, able to deliberate about a serious matter in a mature manner, externally and internally free, physically and psychologically capable of the marriage act, and capable as well of both an exclusive and a permanent union with another, he or she will certainly not find the reasonable and legitimate demands of the interpersonal relationship approach beyond his or her capacities. Without doubt it is possible to conjure up in one's imagination a person who is able to do all that canon law has traditionally required of those who would marry but who is at the same time unable to do what is alleged to be demanded by the need to give and receive the right to a marital interpersonal relationship in its second meaning, that is to say, the right to a marriage with a basic minimum of happiness. The imagining, however, would, at least in my estimate, stand apart from the real, everyday world in which marriages are made and lived.

Regarding the right to a community of life and love and the right to self-completion, self-development, and self-fulfillment, I would repeat much of what has already been observed about the right to a marital interpersonal relationship. If by the right to a community of life and love you mean nothing more than the right to the marital state, pure and simple, with your chosen spouse, I would again assert that there exists no such right. If you mean something more, namely, the right to a basically agreeable, successful, or—in plainest language—happy marriage with your chosen spouse, I would again contend there exists no right to that either. Moreover, I would add, as was done above when discussing the right to a marital interpersonal relationship, that even if you insist that the last-named right does exist, you can rest assured that any problem which might arise because of its not having been exchanged in a particular marriage will be susceptible of adequate handling according to the principles of traditional canon law. For no one could measure up to all that the law demands in a person for a valid marriage without being able to provide, from the standpoint of his or her personal capacities, whatever are the behaviors or attitudes thought to be necessary by exponents of the community of life and love analysis for the validity of marriage. And precisely the same is to be said, *congruo congruis referendo,* as regards the alleged right to self-completion, self-development, and self-fulfillment.

Nor am I ignorant of the fact that among the defenders of the community of life and love approach, not a few place special emphasis upon the love dimension of the formula, maintaining that it cannot be subsumed under the general heading of basic, legitimately required marital happiness. To these, however, I would dare to repeat yet again what I proposed to the theorists of the interpersonal relationship, the fundamental community of life and love, self-completion, self-development, and self-fulfillment. And it is this: If a person be capable of doing all that canon law has been regularly requiring of those who would marry validly, he or she will be capable of giving and receiving the supposed right to that essential modicum of loving without which one might seriously and fairly determine that a marriage would be invalid. Recall once more, I dare to invite you, that canonical doctrine and jurisprudence warmly recognize the invalidity of the marriage of anyone who is under legal age and beset by invalidating impediments, unclear about the meaning of marriage, without the use of reason, unable to deliberate about a matter as serious as marriage in a mature manner, lacking external or internal freedom, physically or psychologically incapable of the marriage act, or incapable of either an exclusive or a permanent union with another.

* * *

Very well, then, let us assume for a moment—

1. that when marriage consent is given, the parties consent to marriage and nothing else,
2. that when marriage consent is given, the parties may be conceived of as exchanging themselves in whole or in part, but that no juridical conclusions can be legitimately derived from such a conception;
3. that when marriage consent is given, the right of one party to marry the other is not exchanged, inasmuch as no such right exists,
4. that when marriage consent is given, the right of one party to marry the other happily is not exchanged, inasmuch as there exists no right to this either, even if it be shrouded in such attractive language as the right to an interpersonal relationship, the right to a community of life and love, or the right to self-completion, self-development, and self-fulfillment,
5. that when marriage consent is given, parties who are capable of all that canon law has over the centuries postulated for a valid marriage will be capable of engaging in as much relating, living, loving, completing, developing, and fulfilling as might be fairly required by a judge who has somehow divined how much relating, living, loving, completing, developing,

and fulfilling is needed for a valid marriage and how much a person at the time of his or her wedding would have been able to provide during the course of married life.

* * *

And having assumed all of this, allow me now to inquire aloud how we might be able to remove the contrary information from the computer of Catholic thinking about marriage. Or to press the analogy even further: What is the "computer password" which we master technicians will have to use in order to extract what needs to be extracted?

At the risk of sounding simplistic, I would submit that the password is in briefest terms "the mentality of divorce." This is what has somehow taken hold even among a goodly number of good Catholics, not in the sense that they openly and avowedly deny the permanence of the marriage bond, but in the sense that they have allowed themselves to make their peace with the "reasonableness," the "logic," above all, the "value" of putting an end in an orderly and civilized fashion to marriages which have not proved to be sufficiently "relational," lively, loving, completing, developing, and/or fulfilling.

Once that mentality takes hold, all else follows with relative ease. The necessary formulae come to mind. Philosophers and theologians, psychologists and poets, join the parade. And of a sudden everything appears to make such good, modern, progressive sense. The notion of marriage consent is dismissed on grounds that are groundless. The male-female element of marriage cedes to preoccupation with the self. Exclusivity bows to relationship. Permanence is overwhelmed by completion, development, and fulfillment. In a relatively short span of time, nineteen hundred years of disciplined thought are upturned. We come to forget that marriage is not something about which all manner of ambiguities can be solemnly affirmed without, in due course, losing in the minds of many its identity, its reality, its God-given truth.

In 1983 and 1984 I published two long articles in English on the subject of capacity for marriage in a well-known European canon law journal.[9] Each was accompanied by judicial decisions in Latin which I had written during my years as a judge of the Roman Rota and which were intended to illustrate what I had set forth in English. To my knowledge, what I had to say in these articles, all very much in criticism of current canonical positions regarding the nullity of marriage, was totally ignored, at least in print, until a few months ago. Last May, to be exact, there appeared an article in a Canadian canon law journal in which my objections were to be answered.[10] And the answer? Ecclesiastical authorities must know what is being done in Church tribunals. If they are silent, we may fairly presume their acquiescence.

Such thinking is in my estimate altogether unsatisfactory. For, again in my estimate, it bespeaks an attitude which can take hold only when the mentality of divorce has found its way deep into the computer, only when we are looking for an escape from thought about or responsibility for what we are doing. Who weds the spirit of one age may be a widow—or a widower—in the next. Certainly, we have lived through an era in which marriage has been challenged on all sides, an era in which the permanence of the marriage bond has been thought, even assumed, in many quarters to be quite indefensible. Whatever of this, marriage in all of its authentic, God-determined reality may be reappearing on the horizon. Indeed, I am persuaded that there are signs of this all about us; and I wonder if we may not one day find ourselves "hustling," as they say, to catch up with something that should never have escaped our grasp.

* * *

In a report issued last May by the City of New York concerning what we in Gotham should expect in the year 2000, page after page provides statistical proof that our children are being destroyed physically and psychologically, for lack, above all else, of stable family life, with father and mother in the home and the children being reared there by them.[11] Two years ago Senator Moynihan in a widely-acclaimed treatise on the family and the nation[12] and last year M. A. Glendon in a masterful work on divorce and abortion in America made the same point.[13] Both, moreover, added that, while all of society is being damaged by the breaking-up of families, those who are suffering the most are the most vulnerable, the children and the women. I am reminded of Chesterton's remark of seventy years ago: "The triangle of the father, the mother and the child . . . can destroy civilizations which disregard it."[14]

And of late the same theme has been played as well in other contexts in a more cheery, upbeat key. This past June, for example, scholars from the University of Illinois informed us through the major newspapers of the nation that an American child can be expected to be academically successful in direct proportion with the number of years he or she has lived in a stable, complete family.[15] Similarly, the current number of the review, *Public Interest*, reports on studies by a number of universities which are said to demonstrate that the adults in this country who are likely to be the most healthy are those who are married and staying married.[16] Small wonder that on my desk as I type this paper there lies a popular tabloid in which virtually an entire page is dedicated to reporting that a candidate for the presidency, who has never evidenced much concern for things familial, made a brief appearance yesterday in Erie, Pennsylvania, where he addressed himself to the family no less than nine times.[17]

In the light of all this, perhaps we Catholics would do well to consider our current direction as regards marriage and the family. The world may be preparing to move again down a different road, and we may be left behind. It may be time to take a careful look at our computer to be sure that everything in it bespeaks solid, Catholic truth.

In Tom Wolfe's *The Bonfire of the Vanities,* a novel which has been on the best-sellers list for almost forty weeks,[18] the hero is often tempted to break his marriage vows. On each occasion we hear him arguing with himself; and the argument regularly turns on the assumption that he, as a successful Wall Street bond trader, one of the "masters of the universe," as he puts it, should not be held to the pedestrian rules which have traditionally governed marriage. His musings are clearly intended to bring a smile to the reader's lips. Still, behind them lurks a truth which upon reflection may be rather disturbing. The laws of marriage and the family are not the business of the "masters of the universe." They belong exclusively and permanently to the one *Master* of the universe. We are not in a position to change them or even adjust them, no matter how important or self-important we may be. And if such a position sounds a bit radical in these days of freedom and change, so be it. Nineteen hundred years ago it sounded radical, indeed, shocking, to the Apostles too.[19] All the same, at the Master's insistence, His will regarding marriage and the family was fed into the computer; and there it is to remain until—how shall I put it?—until the last edition comes off the press.

NOTES

1. T. Mackin, *Marriage in the Catholic Church: What is Marriage?* (New York: Paulist Press, 1982).

2. M. F. Pompedda, "Incapacity to Assume the Essential Obligations of Marriage," in *Incapacity for Marriage, Jurisprudence and Interpretation* (Romae: P.U.G., 1987).

3. The origin of the word, "total," in this connection seems to have been the word, "omnis," in the definition of marriage commonly attributed to the Roman jurisconsult, Modestinus. (Cf. "consortium omnis vitae" in *Iustiniani Digesta*, 23, 2, 1: Mommsen-Krueger, p. 330.) For the Romans its meaning was probably something akin to our "in good times and in bad" ("in prosperis et adversis").

4. Cf. # 48.

5. Cf. # 8.

6. Cf. Canon 1057,# 2.

7. *Codex Iustinianus*, 1, 1, 1–27. Krueger; pp. 5–12.

8. *Chicagien.*, coram Egan, March 29, 1984, n. 3.

9. "The Nullity of Marriage for Reason of Insanity or Lack of Due Discretion," in *Ephemerides iuris canonici*, XXXXIX (1983), pp. 13–54; and "The Nullity of Marriage for Reason of Incapacity to Fulfill the Essential Obligations of Marriage," in *Ephemerides iruis canonici*, XL (1984), pp. 9–34.

10. W. H. Woestmann, "Judges and the Incapacity to Assume the Essential Obligations of Marriage," in *Studia canonica*, 21/2 (1987), pp. 315–323. (This volume appeared in the Spring of 1988.)

11. R. J. Wagner, ed., *New York Ascendant: The Report of the Commission on the Year 2000* (New York: Harper and Row, 1987).

12. D. P. Moynihan, *Family and Nation* (San Diego: Harcourt-Brace, 1986).

13. M. A. Glendon, *Abortion and Divorce in Western Law: American Failures, European Challenges* (Cambridge, Mass.: Harvard University Press, 1987).

14. Cf. G. K. Chesterton, *The Superstition of Divorce* (New York: John Lane, 1920), p. 66.

15. *New York Times*, June 29, 1988, "Single Parent Homes: The Effect on Schooling."

16. Cf. B. J. Christensen, "The Costly Retreat from Marriage," in *Public Interest*, 91 (Spring, 1988), pp. 59–66.

17. *New York Daily News*, July 25, 1988, " 'Family,' Sez Duke, Again and Again."

18. T. Wolfe, *The Bonfire of the Vanities* (New York: Farrar-Straus, 1987).

19. Cf. Matthew 19: 3–12; and Luke 10: 2–12.

Chapter 15

THE MULTI-GENERATIONAL EFFECTS OF DIVORCE

Francis D. Andres

The consequences of divorce have been dealt with quite extensively lately in the literature, but the tendency these days is to focus on the effects of divorce on children. Also there has been a fair amount of research done on the mortality, if you will, and morbidity factors after a divorce, particularly as it relates to the husbands: there seems to be an increase of morbidity and mortality, especially with husbands, after a divorce.

The children go through the whole range of psychological difficulties. In general, it can be said that the earlier the divorce occurs in the person's life, the more permanent are the effects of the divorce psychologically. Young children regress and then spend the rest of their lives trying to find the parent with whom they do not live. Older children go through all kinds of symptoms, particularly in school, where typically their grades suffer. Teenagers these days are the ones that on the surface appear most vulnerable because they act out problems, especially with drugs, alcohol, sex, and suicide. In my practice, that is also the kind of effect that I am now seeing, with parents bringing in a child having one of these difficulties. We could spend a lot of time on the consequences of divorce. Rather than do that, however, I thought that I would go through some of the ideas that have to do with family systems theory, as developed by Dr. Murray Bowen at Georgetown University. Some of the terms are used in a way that is different from the meaning that they have in common usage, and I will try to explain them as I go along. The theory's connection with the effects of divorce will become obvious as we progress.

The multi-generational effects of divorce have yet to be fully defined. But considering the current situation in the world from a theoretical frame of reference, we can probably form a reasonable hypothesis about some of the things that can happen as a result of divorce. To start off, I would say that the study of family structure, size and function, particularly from a multi-generational perspective, can be used to discover certain aspects of family vulnerability that lead to divorce. In addition, the current trend towards keeping family size far below the natural level at which a family functions at its full capacity, feeds the process of future family dysfunction. Simply reducing the size of the family can create quite difficult problems.

Likewise, the attempt to produce a perfect family size with optimal environmental conditions actually inhibits reproduction and creativity. The current trend to have two children in a family with the husband and the wife both working outside the home is going to produce problems down the road that we have not yet imagined. This occurs by making the family emotionally compressed and thus exaggerating or bringing into play pathologic mechanisms that are designed to handle anxiety in an emotional fusion.

Let us try to define those mechanisms. Before two people marry, each has a certain amount of emotional autonomy. But after the marriage gets going, they emotionally connect, so that by applying an emotional stimulus to one spouse, a physiologic reaction can be produced in the other. Once the family relationship begins, the onset of anxiety in one spouse leads the other to react in kind. And then the reaction of the second spouse becomes itself a stimulus to the first. As a result, there is a buildup of tension in the relationship. This is something that can be measured. It does not happen in the relationship before the marriage. Within a year after the marriage, however, the spouses develop a relationship that is much closer, as measured just from the standpoint of how much one spouse is affected by an emotional stimulus applied to the other. When this happens, there are certain mechanisms by which the system automatically tries to adapt to the anxiety of the spouses.

There are four mechanisms by which this happens. One is *distancing:* the spouses pull away from each other. The second one is *conflict.* Conflict consists of one spouse blaming the other, and when they both do it they end up in a battle. The third mechanism is *dysfunction,* in which one spouse over-functions and the other under-functions. For example, one spouse stops thinking, and the other spouse ends up essentially carrying the relationship. The under-functioning spouse eventually becomes physically ill. The under-functioning will get physiologically depressed, or will develop an ulcer, for example, or act it out in some way, such as by drinking in excess.

But the principal mechanism that has to do with the multi-generational process is *triangling,* or the projection of the problem onto the child. It is particularly important because once children enter the scene, there are mechanisms for moving the immaturity of the parents down to the next generation. This is where the multi-generational projection process comes into play. It consists primarily of a situation in which the father distances from the relationship with the child. The mother-child relationship becomes overly intense. The father remains involved with both the mother and the child, but in not nearly so intense a way as they are related to each other. The mother becomes anxious, and the child then reacts to the anxiety in the mother. The more the child reacts, the more the mother focuses on the child as the problem. The father remains outside the process and permits this overinvolvement, while at the same time holding the relationship together. The anxiety of the mother sets up an anxiety pattern in the child, and the child ends up with certain immaturities that he carries with him for the rest of his life.

This has led some people in this field to set up what they call the "differentiation of self" scale. I myself do not like the term "differentiation," which is borrowed from a biological concept. It represents an attempt to translate emotional processes in the family into predictable emotional, physiologic events, so as to make them scientific. In order to be scientific, an approach must be predictable. So the term "differentiation" is used and what it amounts to is a scale for measuring maturity and immaturity. It is a theoretical scale but it is useful in defining the multi-generational phenomenon that I will describe later. In other words, if one were to try to define a maturity scale from the least mature to the most mature, one could take 100 as the theoretical maximum of maturity, and zero as the theoretical minimum, with the average being 50. On such a scale, a level of around 20, more or less, would define what is known as schizophrenia.

The elements that define the scale are worth noting because the scale can sometimes be used for evaluating situations in a family. People at the lower end of the scale are quite different than those at the upper end, and they are different in certain identifiable ways. People at the higher end of the maturity scale are principle-oriented as opposed to feeling-oriented or emotion-oriented. Principle-oriented means that more mature people tend to think through problems ahead of time. They have a concept of the future. They are able to work through a problem logically, come to a conclusion and then act on the conclusion. People on the other end of the scale, however, do not do that; they are best described as reactive. Their decisions are based more on what feels good and what is comfortable.

Most people in the schizophrenia range of the scale are interested in the day-to-day comfort that they can achieve, and in this situation comfort is determined by the nature of the environment. In other words, they will look for the situation that is most anxiety-free. For example, when one member of a family is psychotic, one approach is to try to reduce the amount of emotion in that family so that the member who is psychotic will be more comfortable. When the anxiety level goes down, the psychotic symptoms go away. The environmental influence on somebody who is this immature is of major importance: you can change that person's world by changing the level of anxiety around him.

Another way to describe the feeling-oriented, non-thinking, reactive end of the scale is in terms of being "other-oriented". The way in which an immature person is "other-oriented" is different from the way in which a mature person is "other-oriented", which we could instead call being "perceptive." The person who is other-oriented in the immature sense deals with other people mainly by trying to figure out what will please the other person, and puts a lot of energy into that effort. Paranoia is a form of being "other-oriented" in this sense. A person who is paranoid sees hostility outside of himself when it is not there. He is intensely tuned in to what is going on around him. A person in the upper range of maturity will be perceptive of the feelings of those around him, but can still make decisions on independent grounds. In other words, his orientation toward reality puts him in a position where he does not rely on how others feel. He can see what is going on but can evaluate it for what it is. Somebody in the lower range of the maturity scale is less inclined to do that.

Theoretically, it is possible to place any given person at an appropriate place on the scale. Using this approach, it is possible to describe schizophrenia as the product of what takes place over many generations, taking into account that people tend to marry others of the same level of maturity and that the maturity level of the parents often gets reduced in one or more of their children. If we start off, for example, with two people who are, say, at a level of 50 on the scale, and they have three children, then one of the children may end up at a level of 52, another at a level of 50, and the third, let us say for the purposes of exaggeration, at a level of 40. Now the child at a maturity level of 40 is likely to marry a person who is also at a level of 40 and let us suppose that they in turn also have three children. One of these children may end up a level of 50, the same as the grandparents, another may be at a level of 40, the same as the parents, and the third at a level of 35. The child at a maturity level of 35 then marries another at the same level, that is, 35, and eventually the process lead to descendants having a maturity level of 20, which is schizophrenia. This kind of thing actually happens, although the process tends to take place over a longer period of time, from 10 to 20 generations, and it is actually closer to 20 than to 10.

The level of maturity in this hypothetical family has gone from fairly mature down to fairly immature, although, as I say, it takes quite a while to do that. If this is accurate, and there is evidence that it is, then we should think about other things that accompany that process. For example, there are references in the literature to what is described as the "extincting family." These are difficult cases to research because of the need to go back so many generations and reliable data is difficult to obtain. An extincting family is one in which the number of people in the family keeps decreasing over successive generations. Let us say that we start off with 50 people in a particular family, including grandparents, aunts, uncles, cousins, and so on, and after 10 generations there are only five. Interestingly enough, the data that is available shows that the number of physical and emotional problems increase as the family size decreases. With each succeeding generation there are more and more physical problems and more and more emotional problems. Not only does the number of problems increase, but the intensity of the problems increases as well. If one looks hard enough one can find families like that.

Now let us see what happens if we factor in the mechanisms for dealing with tension and anxiety in a marriage: distancing, conflict, physical and emotional dysfunction, and most importantly, triangling. The operation of these mechanisms in the nuclear family, and especially in the relationship between the mother and the child, will have an influence on what is going to happen in the next generation. When the relationship between the mother and child is highly influenced by anxiety and when the mother projects the problem on the child, that is, sees the problem as being in the child and is constantly trying to fix it, what results is a child who is less mature or less emotionally differentiated than the parents.

Let me illustrate the point in the following manner. If we define maturity as a kind of emotional "differentiation," we end up with at least one individual in each generation who is less mature than the others. If there is already a certain amount of immaturity in the family, then the other children are also recipients of the family immaturity in the form of "undifferentiation" which has more or less spread out and been diluted among the various children. In other words, a measurable degree of immaturity will be passed down to the next generation. Easily, one of the children will be the most triangled and end up more immature than the others. The others are apparently more mature than this one, but they, too, have picked up a certain amount of this process.

If the number of children in the family is not five but two, then the two children end up carrying the load that would have been carried by five. If there is only one child, then the impact of the whole process lands on that one child, who is profoundly affected. Although this one would have been affected in any event by the immaturity within the family, the impact is increased by the fact that there are no other children.

If this process continues for several generations, the problems can become enormous. In a family with, say, 50 members in various relationships, the immaturity within the family might be hidden because it is diluted among the many members. Some of the members might be reasonably mature, which means that they can adapt to stress; they may develop some problems under stress, but the problems will go away fast. For the less mature members of the family, stress will only bring on more problems, which will then persist. Thus, a seemingly normal family can still be vulnerable, although this would probably not be recognized until a lot stress was put on the family, in which event the family might well find itself unable to adapt.

If the number of descendants is suddenly reduced from 50 to, say, five, and this is not inconceivable, the projection process is forced into a cylinder, as it were, so that the problems are going to increase both in number and in intensity for that reason alone. As a result, even in one generation the process that normally takes 10 to 20 generations can collapse, so that the problems come on a lot faster. And they include not only more divorce, but also other physical and emotional problems, including schizophrenia.

When this process is then brought into play over several generations, there results a multi-generational projection process with decreasing numbers of people and increasing numbers of physical and emotional problems. At some point, the participants are either so impaired that they cannot marry or they are so dysfunctional they are actually infertile. At this point, the family extincts.

Some families can be recognized as being in the middle of this process long before they actually extinct. With some of the families that I see, a family history almost always shows that on both the husband's side and the wife's side the size of the family has been decreasing and the number of problems has been increasing, although the family has not extincted yet. It happens so often as to be uncanny. It will even repeat itself in terms of the kinds of the problems that are being encountered.

In terms of dysfunction, these families often have members who are overtly psychotic or schizophrenic; sometimes they have multiple physical defects, deformities, and an abundance of illnesses. The family extincting process, however, occurs over many generations and is biologically subtle. If doctors would take a multi-generational history, they could see this process going on, but most of them do not take a family history over a long enough period of time, so they do not recognize the implications of what is happening. Alarmingly, this mechanism may be accelerated by conscious reduction in family size, so that if a family is already in this situation, it is accelerated by deliberately keeping the size of the family small.

China, for example, will be in deep trouble, if it succeeds in its campaign to restrict every family to having only one child. If suddenly across an entire generation there is only one descendant from each couple, this multi-generational projection process may well be greatly exaggerated. They may reduce their population to one half, but half of them will be knocking on the door of bedlam.

Let me mention at this point that there is, in fact, a "normal" number of children for a family to have. In order to have a wide-ranging sibling constellation, it is necessary to have about six or seven children. If a family has six or seven children, that little society in itself has a large influence on how those children develop. It is an important factor from several points of view. There is some evidence, for example, that as much as a third of one's personality is formed by sibling influence. And when parents divorce, the older siblings play an important role in whether or not the younger children develop problems later on. In addition, the older children of divorced parents have their own problems since they are given a level of premature responsibility that can incapacitate them in later years—a kind of premature emotional burnout. So the sibling constellation is important from a number of different angles, and the number of children participating makes a big difference.

In addition, divorce itself accelerates the process of family extinction. Divorced people tend to have unresolved emotional issues and attachments in their relationships with their own parents. They have tried sometimes to handle these problems by excessively distancing from their parents into spousal relationships in which they have become emotionally fused. The spousal relationship then becomes so intense and uncomfortable that the couple in turn distances from each other into other relationships of equal intensity, rather than face up to and resolve the problems of the fusion in their own relationship. The result is that any children they may have become overly attached to the custodial parent, which is usually the mother. This attachment then, lacking the balance of the other parental tie, intensifies the fusion with the children and makes them more vulnerable to the multigenerational projection process.

There is a strong tendency in our society to pull away from the parental family and operate on one's own. It has the tone of "I can do it myself," but it is even more intense than that. There are many things in our society that are anti-family and contribute to perpetuating this phenomenon. Most people have a certain degree of unresolved difficulty with their parents, an unresolved kind of dependency they never quite deal with. Many people, however, will cut themselves off from their parents rather than grapple with unpleasantness.

Then they take all that intensity and channel it into the spousal relationship, making it so intensely exclusive that they may even drop their social systems. Everybody probably needs about seven relationships with other mature adults in order to have a balanced life, but these people do not do that. They isolate themselves and then they have children. That happens first. Then because they have cut themselves off from parents, other relatives, and friends, they get overly involved with each other. This becomes so difficult and uncomfortable that they end up going to the other extreme and begin to distance from each other. Usually one spouse will begin to distance first, often these days into a relationship with another person. The grass looks greener and the distancing spouse gets into the second relationship in order to get out of the first. This second relationship feels good so the errant spouse abandons the first relationship and plunges headlong into the second, only to do the whole thing over again.

When that leads to divorce, it is usually the father who is removed from the scene and the mother who functions as the responsible parent and takes care of the children. Then the mother takes the intense exclusivity that she used to share with the father and shifts it into the relationship with the children. If the father had stayed around, the relationship between the mother and the children would not have become so intense. But with him gone, the inter-generational relationship between mother and children becomes exaggerated and brings on an abnormal situation. The children become subject to the anxiety of the mother. If the mother becomes anxious for one reason or another—usually over the hard reality of trying to support the family—the children are so closely tied to her emotionally that they pick it up. As a result, there are young people who are immature but who are being asked to handle anxiety in themselves that is more appropriate for adults. Thus, they end up with an even bigger problem than they would have had.

Children who could have otherwise ended up more or less normal then go on to the next generation and carry that artificial abnormality with them. Even if the maturity level is such that symptoms do not occur, the process is so exaggerated in the one generation that the next generation is adversely affected. *By divorcing, the parents affect the maturity level not only of their children, but also of their yet unborn grandchildren.*

This process, additionally, can be so intense that there may not be any grandchildren. Fertility and infertility do seem to be related to the intensity of the fusion process, not only in the relationship between the parents themselves, but in the relationship between the parents and the children, so that the children may be unable to reproduce because of this dysfunction. Children of divorced parents not only have more divorce but they have fewer children and these children have even more problems than they would have had normally.

246

Most couples who are divorcing fail to see the implications of their behavior, not only on their children and their grandchildren but also on their own life course. They fail to see that staying with the relationship not only gives them the opportunity to discover the nature of their own problems, but also makes it possible for them to find answers that were otherwise inaccessible. By walking away they lose the once in a lifetime chance that they have to learn the value of perseverance. Many of the couples who come in to see me are at the end of the line, ready to divorce, and ask, "Will this affect our children?" I usually tell them that if they do not have any children under the age of 16, it probably will not be too bad, but if there is a child under the age of 16, that child will be permanently affected, and their grandchildren even more so. Parents do not like to hear that. I also tell them that the grass is not greener; that if they get out of their present relationship only to get into different ones, they are going to repeat the whole thing and will be back in to see me in about five years. Five years later they are back.

Chapter 16

RESPONSIBLE PARENTHOOD IN THE WRITINGS OF POPE PAUL VI AND POPE JOHN PAUL II

The Most Reverend Adam J. Maida

When the Second Vatican Council directed that the liturgy of the Church be renewed, it observed that, with the passage of time, certain features crept into the rites of the sacraments and sacramentals which tended to obscure their nature and purpose (*Sacrosanctum Concilium* #62). Hence, it was necessary to take a close look at the rituals and purify them of the accretions of time which tended to diminish the impact of the spiritual realities

Reprinted with permission from *Linacre Quarterly,* Vol. 55, No. 4. November, 1988. pp. 25–31. 850 Elm Grove Road, Suite 11, Elm Grove, WI, 53122. Subscription rate: $24 per year; $6 per single issue.

which the sacraments both symbolized and effected. A study of the history of the liturgy would reveal that certain elements were consistently present in the practice of the sacraments, and certain elements were peripheral and transitory. In every age, culture and current philosophies have their impact upon human life and practice, even in the religious sphere.

One could observe that the culture and current philosophies have a similar impact upon human behavior. It is not a futile exercise then, to step back from a historical event and examine it from the more distant perspective of time, and to discover its essential message and its enduring value, to uncover what is permanent and to assert it in a more persuasive way.

Our reflection on the Encyclical Letter of Pope Paul VI, *Humanae vitae,* 20 years after its publication, pursues that objective. I do not presume to improve on the message of the encyclical. Its language is classic and precise. On the other hand, Pope John Paul II, in his 1981 statement on the Christian family (*Familiaris consortio* #31), urges theologians and bishops to explain ever more clearly the teaching expressed in *Humanae vitae.* This precisely is our present and common endeavor.

My focus in this brief presentation will be on the concept of responsibility. What is encompassed in the expression "responsible parenthood" as it is used by Pope Paul VI in his encyclical?

Let me begin with a *contrasting* view.

The late Dr. Alan F. Guttmacher, a well-known leader of the Planned Parenthood Federation of America, at the 1970 commencement at Smith College, gave his definition of responsible parenthood. I quote:

> What does one mean by responsible sexual behavior? It does not preclude premarital sexual activity, for premarital sex is not inherently evil. It may be eminently right and proper when practiced by the right couple under the right circumstances. Such a judgment no one can make except the two persons involved.

In Guttmacher's view, there is, however, a moral and immoral arena. He continues:

Whenever sex relations take place in or out of marriage, they are patently immoral if the most effective birth control technique is not used, unless the child is mutually desired. The first line of defense against undesired pregnancy must be *contraception*. For physical and psychic reasons, abortion must be relegated to backup status for failed, or failure to use, effective contraception.

Guttmacher's position is starkly put. Since 1970 some have learned to convey the same message, but in a less blunt way. This clearly indicates how far removed from this secular view is the Christian view of responsible parenthood.

Twofold Dimension

There is both a natural and a faith dimension to the Christian view of responsible parenthood. Basic to the Christian understanding of the universe is the acceptance of a rational and divinely-intended orientation to all of creation. That plan of creation is discernible, and deliberate human interference with that plan is viewed as a *moral deviation*. This applies to human sexuality and to parenthood as well. The essential elements of the Christian understanding include 1) the role of the natural law; 2) a concern for the *common good as well as the good* of the couple; 3) promoting the dignity of persons; 4) the primacy of donative love over romanticism in married life, and the gift of God's grace.

The most basic meaning of *Humanae Vitae*'s teaching on responsible parenthood is that a married couple must be willing to cooperate with the creative intention of God in the totality of their marriage and family life, in all their various dimensions, and in each and every act of marital intercourse. Hence, it is important to discern the creative intent of God, or what we more usually refer to as the moral law. It is inherent in nature and is discernible.

Beyond a knowledge of the natural moral law, responsible parenthood implies a knowledge of the pertinent circumstances affecting responsible parenthood. *Humanae vitae* (1–10) acknowledges that the exercise of responsible parenthood takes into account "physical, economic, psychological and social conditions." Pope John Paul II, in *Familiaris consortio* (#31), recognizing a factor which receives great emphasis in the secular view on this subject, also acknowledges:

> The Church is certainly aware of the many complex problems which couples in many countries face today in their task of transmitting life in a responsible way. She also recognizes the serious problem of population growth in the form it has taken in many parts of the world and its moral implications.

(There may indeed be serious moral reasons for limiting the size of one's family.)

But taking into account the circumstances in which responsible parenthood must be exercised does not nullify the primacy of the basic natural law governing parenthood. Pope John Paul II continues on this subject.

> However, the Church holds that the consideration of these problems offers a new and stronger confirmation of the importance of the authentic teaching on birth regulation proposed in the Second Vatican Council and in the encyclical *Humanae vitae:* the use of natural means rather than mechanical or contraceptive methods.

Gaudium et spes also considers the pertinence of circumstances in the exercise of responsible parenthood. It states that married couples, in exercising their proper mission of transmitting human life and educating their children, should do this with a sense of human and Christian responsibility.

> (This) involves a consideration of their own good and the good of their children already born or yet to come, an ability to read the signs of the times and of their own

situation on the material and spiritual level, and finally, an estimation of the good of the family, of society, and of the Church. It is the married couple themselves who must in the last analysis arrive at these judgments before God. (#50)

Pope John Paul II, aware of the confusion and the rejection of sound moral thinking in the modern world about marriage, the family and sexuality, has devoted a considerable amount of attention to these subjects. He reminds us that love between husband and wife will be damaged if the moral law is not respected. As he says, "A true contradiction cannot exist between the divine laws pertaining to the transmission of life and those pertaining to the fostering of authentic conjugal love." The connection between these two elements is seen clearly in the inseparable connection between the unitive and procreative dimensions of the conjugal act (Address at general audience, July 25, 1984).

Conjugal Act Unitive, Procreative

When we talk about the conjugal act being unitive and procreative, we are talking about its very nature and structure. This is why Pope John Paul II and Pope Paul VI before him, following consistent moral teaching, state that the intention of those using contraceptive practices "does not change the moral character which is based on the very structure of the conjugal act" (Address at general audience, Aug. 8, 1984). This is why there is an essential difference between acts using natural means to regulate births and those using contraceptive means. When using natural means, a couple is acting in accord with nature; when using contraceptive means, they are obstructing nature.

The significance of this for responsible parenthood is that it demands a submission to the natural moral law. The Holy Father makes clear that this is not easy. Quoting *Humanae vitae,* he says:

. . . there is no doubt that to many it may appear not merely difficult but even impossible to observe. . . .

Hence, this law demands . . . a resolute purpose and great endurance. Indeed, it cannot be observed unless God helps with His grace. (July 25, 1984 address)

In the Christian perspective, responsible parenthood includes the expectation that the couple turn to God in prayer for the help necessary to carry out their moral obligations.

Responsible parenthood, in the Christian view, similarly expects the couple to be informed. The Vatican II document, *Gaudium et spes,* stresses that, to follow the moral law, married people must realize that they may not simply follow their own fancy but must be ruled by a conscience formed in the light of the teaching authority of the Church (#50).

Another dimension of responsible parenthood, which if not ignored is belittled, dismissed as impossible, or ridiculed in the secular perspective, is stated by *Humanae vitae* and stressed by Pope John Paul II, namely, working to insure that *reason* and *will* dominate the innate drives and emotions of man (Aug. 1, 1984 address). Discipline and self-control have never been popular counsel in a secular culture (to a generation raised in an age that expects instant gratification, easy answers, and quick fixes, the concepts of sacrifice and self-denial seem foreign,) but they are integral to Christian morality. Pope John Paul II has given particular attention to this matter in his talks on *Humanae vitae*. It is this discipline, this virtue of marital chastity, which dignifies Christian marriage and the people themselves.

It seems obvious that the source of the problem about human sexuality today is a flawed metaphysics and philosophy of man. The Holy Father tells us, in effect, that our starting point must be a correct concept of man. He says that man is precisely a person because he is master of himself and has self-control (Address, Aug. 22,1984). He is not a helpless victim of his passions nor of society's manipulation.

Man must maintain the proper relationship between what *Humanae vitae* calls "domination . . . of the forces of nature" and "the mastery of self." Modern man's problem, Pope John Paul II tells us, is that he shows a tendency to transfer the methods proper to the control of the forces of nature to those proper to the mastery of self (Address, Aug. 22, 1984). Quoting *Humanae vitae* on this, he says that man has tried to extend this domination, wrought by modern scientific and technological advances, over every aspect of his own life—even over the laws that regulate the transmission of life (Address, Aug. 22, 1984). Man seeks to use new technologies in order to gain a greater control over his life, thus reducing the need for self-discipline. The result of this confusion is ultimately a loss of man's dignity because self-mastery, which gives man his uniqueness, is surrendered, and this leaves him open to manipulation.

In many of his addresses on marital love, Pope John Paul II has spoken of the "language of the body." A person uses the medium of his/her body to express personhood. The body is especially a means of expressing the maleness or femaleness of a person in the reciprocal relationships between man and woman (ibid). Pope John Paul II says that this body language has a sacramental dimension. It expresses and fosters the marital relationship. He puts it this way:

> By means of gestures and reactions, by means of the whole dynamisms, reciprocally conditioned, of tensions and enjoyment . . . the body in its action and interaction, by means of all this, the person, speaks (ibid).

This language of the body, however, is subject to the demands of truth, the whole truth. The whole truth is that the conjugal act, as a major source of the expression of this language, signifies not only love, but also potential fecundity, and therefore it cannot be deprived of its full and adequate significance by artificial means. In the more traditional language of moral theology, the unitive and procreative acts may not be separated (ibid). When there is an artificial separation of the unitive and procreative dimensions of the conjugal act, there is, of course, still a bodily union, but it does not correspond to the interior truth and to the dignity of personal communion. When this occurs, not only is there no true self-mastery, but there is also neither any true reciprocal gift or reciprocal acceptance of self between husband and wife. This violates the interior order of conjugal union and, as such, constitutes the essential evil of the contraceptive act. The contraceptive mentality makes it easier for each party to use the other for selfish purpose of sexual satisfaction alone. This is what Pope John Paul means by manipulation.

Derivation of Responsible Parenthood

Even though the full notion of responsible parenthood derives from the natural law and is necessary to insure true human dignity, one has to reckon with human weakness, human sinfulness. Adherence to the natural law is achieved only through self-denial. What is demanded, therefore, is the development with God's help, of the virtue of marital chastity or continence.

Continence, the Holy Father explains, "has the essential task of maintaining the balance between the communion in which the couple wish to mutually express only their intimate union and that in which they accept responsible parenthood" (Address, Oct. 31, 1984). Continence enables one to submit his or her emotions and passions to reason, instead of being controlled and subjected to them. The primacy of reason makes it possible to give oneself to another in marriage in the fullest sense because one has gained the kind of right ordering of one's passions and emotions. It is continence which enables a person to give oneself fully to the other in accordance with the design of God. Continence also expresses the truth that love and affection have varied expressions.

Just as sexuality cannot be abstracted from the rest of the human personality, so continence cannot exist in isolation from the other virtues. It is linked, as Pope John Paul states, "with prudence, justice, fortitude and, especially, charity" (Address, Oct. 24, 1984). This parallels the notion that in the Christian life, one is called to develop all the virtues as much as one possibly can, with Christ as model.

There is a social as well as a personal consequence to the substitution of technological control for self-control. C. S. Lewis, in his book, *The Abolition of Man,* explains the process. By using technological techniques to control his own actions, man risks losing his freedom. Technology in the hands of the strong, without moral imperatives guiding them, can subjugate everyone else. Thus, with his new technological magic, man displaces self-mastery built on the natural law with technological subjugation. Recall the once visionary scenario of George Orwell's *1984*.

Finally, responsible parenthood implies more than the generation of life. It extends to nurturing life. Pope John Paul, in *Familiaris consortio,* develops with great insight and beauty the remaining dimension of responsible parenthood: rearing and educating the child. The obligations of responsible parenthood do not end with the birth of a child, but with his/her maturation. For this reason, Pope John Paul explains, conjugal and family morality find their proper place and appropriate perspective in the family. *Familiaris consortio* specifies the elements of the nurturing process: educating in the essential values of human life, educating in love as self-giving, educating in a concern for and a willingness to undertake service to others, especially the poor.

When we attend to the various elements of responsible parenthood, we can better understand the teaching put forth in *Humanae vitae.* The emphasis on self-giving, the development of virtue, and the commitment to regulate one's life by the moral law all affect the parents' ability to educate their children. As Pope Paul VI wrote in *Humanae vitae:*

> This self-discipline brings to family life abundant fruits of tranquility and peace. . . . It fosters in husband and wife thoughtfulness and loving consideration for each other. It helps them to repel the excessive self-love which is the opposite of charity. It arouses in them a consciousness of their responsibilities. And finally, it confers upon parents a deeper and more effective influence in the education of their children.(#21)

The encyclical *Humanae vitae* speaks as eloquently and as clearly to the needs of family life today as it did when it was issued 20 years ago.

Today's society has received the legacy of disintegrating family life, eroding social and symbol systems, a loss of identity experienced by numerous members, and a future generation threatened by chemical dependency and the fallacy of absolute self-sufficiency.

This is not the legacy of Christian parenthood, nor is it the result of technology alone. It is, instead, the result of a people preoccupied with self-fulfillment, subjective moral standards, a search for power and money and easy solutions to complex questions.

In contrast, the encyclical and the concept of responsible christian parenthood challenge us to a love that is self-giving, thoughtful, personal, and human—a striving for the redemptive and faithful love of God Himself.

Chapter 17

THE PASTORAL CARE OF THE HOMOSEXUAL PERSON

The Reverend John F. Harvey, O.S.F.S.

I. DOGMATIC AND MORAL PRESUPPOSITIONS FOR A PASTORAL PROGRAM

A. The Teaching of the Church

The Letter to the Bishops of the Catholic Church on the Pastoral Care of Homosexual Persons sums up the teaching of the Magisterium. One must distinguish between homosexual orientation and activity. Even the orientation is an objective disorder, because, if acted upon, it leads to sin. But the disorder itself is not a sin. Only homosexual acts are sinful, and grievously so, if one

259

does them deliberately and freely. Often the person involved in homosexual activity is compulsive, and this means that his culpability is significantly diminished. Nonetheless, he/she does have responsibility to learn how to control compulsive drives through spiritual support systems modeled on Alcoholics Anonymous (A.A.).

In the Letter to the Bishops the teaching of the Magisterium throughout the centuries is shown to be the living tradition within the Church which alone has the right to give the faithful a correct interpretation of Holy Scripture on the subject of the morality of homosexual acts. It is to be noted that in this document the argument from Holy Scripture goes beyond references to specific texts to the general thrust of biblical teaching concerning the nature of human sexual acts and their meaning in marriage. The first two chapters of Genesis, and Jesus' interpretation of them in Matthew, Ch. 19, are important parts of the scriptural argument against homosexual activity. This is a much better approach than references to the classical specific texts on homosexual activity which may be used as additional arguments against homosexual activity.[1]

While the Church condemns homosexual activity as always immoral, she shows respect for the individual homosexual person, recognizing his or her dignity, and seeking to provide him/her with adequate spiritual guidance. The Church is aware of the controversies concerning the origins and treatment of the homosexual person, but she takes no stand for or against a variety of theories. She is concerned with the moral and spiritual dimensions of the homosexual condition as it reveals itself in the individual person. To the extent that empirical findings seem to impinge upon the moral dimensions of the person she is interested. If empirical studies reveal, for example, that the relationship between young men and their fathers was very poor, possibly contributing to homosexual orientation, then the Church will encourage better communications between fathers and sons as part of family education. And so forth. She makes no judgments about empirical studies as long as they remain within the scientific method, and are not used to prove that certain kinds of homosexual activity are morally acceptable.

Finally, the Church calls upon the living Tradition of the Church to interpret the Scriptures in their clear approval of heterosexual marriage and their clear condemnation of homosexual activity.

B. The Ability of the Person to Fulfill the Commandments of God

One conclusion flowing from Catholic teaching is that the homosexual person must abstain from homosexual activity. This is a difficult obligation to fulfill, and indeed is possible only by the grace of God. Everyone is bound to chastity according to his/her state in life. The homosexual person is no exception to this truth that God always gives us the grace to fulfill His commands.

Any theory of morality, therefore, which teaches that the homosexual person, possessed of free will and divine grace, is not capable of chastity is contrary to the teaching of Scripture and the Fathers. St. Augustine states that God does not ask of us the impossible. He will give us the power to do whatever He commands us to do.[2] Frequently in the *The Confessions* he says: "Da quod jubes, and jube quod vis. Lord, give me the grace to do what you command, and command whatever you please"[3] The Council of Trent, moreover, teaches that if anyone holds that it is impossible to fulfill the commandments of God, he is heretical.[4]

The culture, however, assumes that everyone must have genital sex if one wishes to be fully human, and therefore it is unreasonable for the Church to demand that homosexual persons practice sexual abstinence. Such an assumption is at the root of rationalizations justifying steady-lover homosexual relationships. Unfortunately, the culture fails to distinguish between the basic human need for intimacy and friendship, and the desire for physical genital activity. Everyone needs intimate human friendships, but many persons, both lay and religious, have learned with God's grace to lead a completely human life without genital activity. Since it has been proven time and again that men and women can live a celibate life out of love for God, our focus in this paper is to propose spiritual programs that help the homosexual person to live such a life.

As I have done in previous writings, I distinguish between the classical one-on-one approach and group spiritual direction. As the result of A.A., many of us have learned that individual spiritual direction in certain areas is inadequate, and that in many instances it needs to be supplemented by group spiritual direction. However, just as the use of group therapy methods does not eliminate the need for individual therapy, so also group spiritual direction does not do away with the need for individual spiritual guidance; indeed it presupposes that the individual who comes to the group will also seek out a personal spiritual director. One form of direction complements the other. To be sure, there are excessively dependent individuals who do not function well in a group, and they ought to remain with an individual spiritual director who can work along with a professional therapist. With this exception, group spiritual support systems can help a person to lead a celibate life.[5]

A. The Program of Courage

First I shall outline the Courage program, and then comment on other spiritual support systems, as I have done in my book.[6] The purposes of Courage, written by the members themselves, reveal its nature. Purpose Three speaks of the need to share with one another the difficulties of a homosexual orientation so that no one will have to carry the burden of homosexuality alone. Many homosexual persons keep their orientation a secret, discussing it with no one, living in isolation, afraid to tell even the closest of friends. In this way they make the practice of celibacy so much more difficult, because it prevents them from finding the right kind of support for a virtuous life, namely, the companionship of others in the same boat. Such group support is not friendship, but it leads members of the group to form chaste friendships with one or another in the group.

These friendships are very necessary to sustain the person in a chaste way of life. They do not happen overnight. It takes time and experience to learn how to trust another human person. Purpose Four states that chaste friendships are not only permissible, but necessary for a chaste life. At Courage meetings different aspects of friendship are a recurrent topic. I have seen good friendships develop over the past eight years. To be sure, there are difficulties, and I shall touch upon some of these later.

The Importance of the Twelve Steps

It took me a few years to realize that weekly meetings needed a focus other than academic. Gradually I began to adapt the Twelve Steps of A.A. about the same time many of my Protestant colleagues were doing so. The Twelve Steps are truly spiritual, and can help anyone who is the slave of an addiction, and they work with persons who are not addictive. They are concerned with the way a person lives. They are a form of spiritual discipline which anyone who uses them knows. I found that I could harmonize them with the spiritual plan of life I had developed for the homosexual person (or should we say "integrate"?). The late Dr. John Kinnane noted that the use of the Twelve Steps was the only effective approach to the compulsive person, whether he be alcoholic or homosexual or both.

The point is that a spiritual support system is primarily a spiritual program which demands an ascetical way of life. While one derives self-knowledge and psychological insight from participating in such a program, the first consideration is liberation from the enslaving power of lust. The program is not concerned with deep sea diving into one's past, or the exploration of the unconscious, which is the proper province of the professional therapist who is so inclined. For this reason I stress the central importance of the prayer of the heart, or meditation. Nothing is more important than prayer (Step 11 of A.A.). Just as we stress the need to break out of isolation into friendship with at least a few persons, so we recognize that in so many instances the homosexual person has ceased praying. He has deprived himself of the friendship of God, and he needs to find an intimate relationship with the Lord. As Leanne Payne tells her audience, prayer of the heart is hard work, and has to be done every day.

Another element of a group spiritual support system is the need for regular attendance at meetings. One cannot really share in the group without being a regular participant. We have people who come only occasionally, and wonder why they "get nothing out of it." Some come regularly, contribute to the discussion, and welcome new members during the social after the formal meetings; others show up only once in a while and contribute little to the dialogue, because they have lost track of the group. Some expect someone to draw them out instead of making a contribution of their thoughts to the group. All have to realize that it is a sharing situation. One must give as well as receive. This is what Step 2 of A.A. means: I turned to a power greater than myself to overcome the insanity in my life. In practice, one of the greatest obstacles to good group discussion is the passivity of many members. Some act as if they were waiting for something to happen instead of making it happen.

Another element of this spiritual program is that each individual person present must do his homework before he comes to the meeting. By this I mean that each member has a spiritual plan of life which includes prayer of the heart, spiritual reading, daily examination of conscience, regular spiritual direction, attendance at Mass as often as possible, and so forth. Since the purpose of the group is to strengthen the interior life of the person, it is necessary that at each meeting time be given to prayer.

Ordinary Format of Meetings

There are many ways of running a meeting, and I propose the one which I have found most satisfying. It consists of three parts: prayer, discussion period, and informal social. All told, the formal part of the meeting should last about 90 minutes, and the social for about an hour. The prayer period should begin the meeting, and should not last more then ten minutes. It can consist in reflection upon a scriptural passage which one of the members, or the spiritual director, has found to be most helpful. Recently I gave some thoughts from St. Francis de Sales in *The Introduction to the Devout Life.* It is important that the opening prayer period be brief.

The discussion period usually focuses on one of the Twelve Steps. The person presenting does well if he gives a handout to the members. They have a chance to read it before the discussion begins. By following the Twelve Steps each presenter has a program as a basis for discussion. This is not always easy. Some members do not want to reflect upon the proposed step as it relates to their personal lives. If one is discussing Step Four, the fearless moral inventory, some members may go off into abstractions about the Church, such as sex education in the seminary, instead of telling others how they practice the fearless moral inventory. The Chairman has to bring the group back to the subject proposed for the meeting. The tendency to dwell upon abstractions instead of applying the Step under discussion to oneself is a form of denial. It is really difficult to get members to talk about themselves in relation to the topic of the meeting.

The formal section of the meeting is concluded with a brief prayer, in the chapel, if possible. The members are invited to refreshments in a suitable place. This part of the evening is very important to chat informally with newcomers, or to arrange informal lunches among the members. It is a time when good relationships are born. Oftentimes the priest-director is busy seeing individuals for part of this period, because there is no other time to see them.

The above is the usual format: prayer, discussion, social; but once a month we vary the program with a First Friday Mass, and a brief discussion period. We also welcome guest speakers; Bishops, psychologists, sisters from prison chaplaincies.

DIFFICULTIES IN THE OPERATION OF THE PROGRAM

I should like to present some of the difficulties which individuals in the program experience. The first is sexual compulsion. How responsible are persons whose sexual behavior either borders on the compulsive or is compulsive? The moral aspects of compulsion need review.[7] In the person's past there is no way of assessing responsibility if the pattern of behavior were compulsive, that is to say, if it had gone beyond the person's ability to control it. But no matter what happened in the past, the homosexual person has the responsibility to take adequate measures in the present to regain control of his life. This person needs an ascetical plan of life, such as the Twelve Steps with its group support. Sometimes he also needs the help of a professional therapist, and to allow the spiritual director and the therapist to consult together on what is best for him. There are, however, other elements in compulsion, the first of which is fantasy.

Compulsion has its strongest grip in fantasy life, which, in turn, is tied to loneliness and isolation and feelings of self revulsion. Someone doing well for a period of time may suddenly find himself beset with strong erotic fantasies whenever he is alone, and he may fear that he will return to the bars, rest rooms and porno shops. The fantasies are there before the porno. This is a serious situation in which he should talk to the Lord in prayer. Sometimes it is better to look temptation in the eye than to become tense and fearful. Consider, for example, how ridiculous the temptation is. Why give up the peace of the Lord for this act? Sometimes it is best to turn abruptly from the scene. I have noted the almost causal relationship between fantasy and pornography and masturbation and acting out with another. But I think we need to look deeper into the person to find the roots of compulsion. A person who hates himself/herself will tend not to live in the real world, but to retreat into fantasy and pornography, which is a form of fantasy.

I encourage the person given to fantasy to reach out into the real world. All of us have had the experience of daydreams interrupted by the phone ringing, or someone knocking on the door. As we respond to the phone or the door, the fantasy world disappears, and gives place to the real world. The attractiveness of sin is part of the unreal world of fantasy. So I try to help persons possessed with fantasy to live in the real world. Of course, this requires the practice of mental discipline from morning until night so that one can cut short dangerous fantasies. At the same time one makes the effort to relate to others, to form at least a few solid friendships.

CELIBACY AND LONELINESS

Recently at a meeting in New York, a new member who was also a recovering alcoholic remarked that his perception of Courage, shared with others, was that the members were engaged in "white-knuckling" their sexual abstinence, that is to say, it was a burden which they carried resentfully by sheer force of will power. Unfortunately, such perceptions have kept many from joining Courage, and wherever Courage is established, care must be taken to present a positive view of sexual abstinene. Benedict Groeschel's little book, *The Courage to be Chaste,* dedicated to the men and women of Courage, has done much to dissipate this negative view of celibacy.[8] For this reason we endeavor to show that celibacy accepted out of love for Christ becomes a source of interior peace for the homosexual person. In my book I recount autobiographical experiences of members who have found interior peace in celibacy. Usually this is joined to a life of service to others. It is utterly dependent upon prayer.

This is not to deny the loneliness which many homosexual persons experience because they cannot marry and raise a family. They must find intimacy and friendship in another way, and that is the way of the practice of the Twelve Steps. On the human level the cultivation of good friendships remains crucial. A point that I make from time to time is that homosexual activity does not take away loneliness and restlessness, but only increases the power of lust within. Research on sexual addiction, as found in *Out of the Shadows,* and in the experience of spiritual support groups, Catholic, Protestant, and secular, reveals that sexual abstinence is the first step toward inner healing of the person. More about this later.

Formation of Friendships

Novices at Courage are sometimes discouraged that they have not been able to form friendships in a brief time. There are many reasons why this is so. The person may not have revealed anything about himself in discussions. He is not willing to talk about himself, and no one gets to know him. He may come with a soul full of distrust because of past experiences. Again, the person may not understand the difference between friendship and mere acquaintanceship in a way of behavior. A teen-age girl, inclined to heterosexual promiscuity, responded to my remark that she was very lonely by saying that she had many friends. I responded that none of them really knew her, and she admitted that I was on target. As Groeschel points out in his excellent little book, you must be willing to share of yourself with the person you desire as friend. It is a two-way street.

The Introduction to the Devout Life of St. Francis de Sales and *The Four Loves* of C. S. Lewis give some excellent advice on good and bad friendships, and the difference between solid friendship and excessive emotional attachments. In more recent times Fr. Henri Nouwen in his essay, "The Challenge of Love" in *Intimacy* (Notre Dame, Fides, 1969) shows some of the difficulties which must be faced in forming good friendships.

What Can Be Learned form Other Spiritual Support Systems

In my book, *The Homosexual Person,* I have outlined relationships between Courage and Homosexuals Anonymous (H.A.), showing similarities and differences of approach and of philosophy.[9] Since writing the manuscript in late 1986 I have noted more the work of Sexaholics Anonymous, (S.A.), Sex and Love Addicts Anonymous (S.L.A.A.), Regeneration, Desert Streams, Love in Action, Metanoia, Harvest, Outpost, and Sexual Compulsives Anonymous (S.C.A.) All the others except the last I have already referenced in my chapter on programs.[10]

In relating to these other groups I point out to counselees that if possible they attend meetings of S.A., and H.A., to help in overcoming compulsive tendencies. While it is true that H.A. endeavors to change a person's sexual orientation, going beyond sexual abstinence, and the counselee may not feel that at his stage of life (often in the late thirties or early forties) he wants to seek a change in sexual orientation, nonetheless he can get insight from such groups which also have a step program. (S.A. has 12 steps; H.A., 14 steps) Compulsives need all the support meetings that they can attend. Witness the advice given to the alcoholic who wishes to recover: 90 meetings in 90 days. Again, H.A. presents a solid scriptural foundation for its repudiation of homosexual activity, and this corresponds to the Catholic position. I have had a good experience sending persons to these meetings, not only in New York, but in other large cities. Indeed in some cases, where there is no Courage unit, I have sent persons to these other organizations, particularly young persons desirous of changing their sexual orientation. I always add the caution not to be disappointed if a complete change of sexual orientation is not forthcoming; even if such be the case, learning to overcome the slavery of lust is a form of true healing and liberation.

I have also learned from the Protestant groups the importance of seeking forgiveness and granting forgiveness to significant persons in the past of the person. This helps to overcome sexual compulsions.[11]

The Search for a Practical Spiritual Program for Courage

Over the past eight years I have developed a program for Courage meetings which will meet the spiritual needs of the group. Adapting the Twelve Step Program to the needs of Courage members has taken time. We do not question the use of the steps inasmuch as S.A., S.L.A.A., H.A., and other groups have used them successfully. But we have run into difficulties. First, some members of Courage have resented the use of the Twelve Steps, because in their perception it implied that all members of Courage were sick; and, secondly, some members have great difficulty in talking about personal sexual difficulties, and they are perfectly willing to be passive listeners to the life situations of others, or they wander into abstract issues that have nothing to do with change of behavior and growth in the spiritual life.

To overcome these difficulties, one must stress that the Twelve Steps are used as a spiritual program by persons who are not involved in any compulsive activity. One must get beyond the particular problem to which the Twelve Steps are applied, and discern the universal spiritual principles upon which they are based.[12] The second difficulty, a reluctance to speak to the group about personal sexual problems, can be overcome as a spirit of trust grows within the group, and as persons have a deeper realization that the group supports them no matter what their sexual obsessions may be. Yet this remains a slow process. Recovering alcoholics and drug addicts will tell you that it is more difficult for them to talk about sexual matters than about other forms of compulsion. At the same time they are the best presenters and chairmen of groups, because they already have positive experience of its efficacy at A.A. or Syn-Anon meetings. They are keenly aware of the phenomena of denial at work among other Courage members, and they know how to draw a person out. It should also be recalled that it is only in the last five years that we have become acquainted in a comparatively superficial way with the dynamics of sexual compulsion. We need to explore it further, and to discern its spiritual roots in deep self-hatred, emptiness, and isolation.[13]

MORE RESEARCH ON HOMOSEXUAL COMPULSION

During the last decade many members of A.A. and Narcotics Anonymous, have come to realize that they also have had a sexual compulsion. This has led to studies concerning the interconnections among drugs, alcohol, and sexual behavior. This in turn has led many people to explore their sexual identity. From pastoral experience I have met individuals who were alcoholics, but who denied that they were homosexual until later years. In my judgment, the sexual addiction is the most difficult to overcome because individuals who have recovered from alcohol or from drugs continue to be enslaved by sexual compulsions.

PRAYER AND COMPULSION

The many different Protestant groups who work under the umbrella of Exodus International, have provided a copious literature about the healing effects of prayer in overcoming homosexual compulsions, and by homosexual compulsions I mean not only external sexual behavior, but also compulsive fantasy and masturbation. The works of Leanne Payne, *The Broken Image,* Frank Worthen, *Steps Out of Homosexuality,* Ed Hurst, *Homosexuality: Laying the Ax to the Roots,* and the tapes by Colin Cook,

"Homosexuality and the Power to Change", are examples of this movement to find healing in prayer.

There is need to explore more deeply the relationship between lack of forgiveness and the persistence of homosexual dynamics, such as anger, self-pity, resentment, and particularly early deprivations.

CONCLUSIONS

1. That a 12-step program can help homosexual persons to regain control over sexual tendencies.
2. That the individual must participate regularly in meetings and develop a solid prayer life.
3. That sexual abstinence is possible for the homosexual person, provided he/she adheres to a spiritual plan of life in the context of group support.

NOTES

1. See The Letter, paragraph 5: "The Church's doctrine concerning this issue is thus based, not on isolated phrases for facile theological argument, but on the solid foundation of a constant biblical testimony. . . . It is likewise essential to recognize that the Scriptures are not properly understood when they are interpreted in a way which contradicts the Church's Living Tradition."

2. *De natura et gratia*, ch. 43, no.53 PL 44.271. Augustine refers to 1 John 5:3 and to Matt. 11:30.

3. *Confessions*, 10,9,40; 10,31,45 and 10,37,60. E. Gilson calls this statement of Augustine the essential theme of the Confessions *(L'Introduction a l'étude de saint Augstin.)*

4. *Council of Trent*, Session VI, ch. 11 (Justification) D.S. 1536.

5. See *The Social Justice Review*, March, 1987, "Homosexuality and Hope: New Thinking in Pastoral Care," for further details on the relationship between individual and group spiritual direction. See also my book, *The Homosexual Person: New Thinking in Pastoral Care,* Ignatius Press, Harrison N.Y., 1987.

6. *Op. cit.,* ch 7, 119–174.

7. Patrick Carnes, *Out of the Shadows* 1983 Compcare Publications, 2415 Annapolis Lane, Minneapolis, Minn. ch. 6, "Twelve Steps to Recovery," pp. 141–167; John Ford and Gerald Kelly, *Contemporary Moral Theology,* Newman Press, Westminster, Md., p. 230; Rudolph Allers, "Irresistible Impulses: A Question of Moral Psychology", *American Ecclesiastical Review,* vol. 100, 1939, p. 219.

8. Paulist Press, N.Y., 1985.

9. *Op. cit.,* pp. 127–137.

10. For information on S.C.A. write to P.O. Box 1585, Old Chelsea Station, New York, NY, 10011 or call 212-340-8985. See my book, ch.7, nn. 22–25.

11. See the work of Leanne Payne, *The Broken Image,* Crossways, 1982.

12. Philip St. Romain, *Becoming A New Person: Twelve Steps to Spiritual Growth,* Liguori Publications, Liguori, Mo., 1984. The author adapts the steps to help persons overcome their "addiction" to selfishness and to grow in true self-love.

13. Patrick Carnes, *Out of the Shadows,* Compcare Publications, Minneapolis, Minn. 1982.

APPENDIX 1

A.A. and S.A. From Pat. Carnes, *The Sexual Addiction,* 144–145.*

THE TWELVE STEPS OF ALCOHOLICS ANONYMOUS

THE TWELVE STEPS OF ALCOHOLICS ANONYMOUS ADAPTED FOR SEXUAL ADDICTS

1. We admitted we were powerless over alcohol—that our lives had become unmanageable.

2. Came to believe that a Power greater than ourselves could restore us to sanity.

3. Made a decision to turn our will and our lives over to the care of God as we understood Him.

4. Made a searching and fearless moral inventory of ourselves.

5. Admitted to God, to ourselves, and to another human being the exact nature of our wrongs.

6. Were entirely ready to have God remove all these defects of character.

7. Humbly asked him to remove our shortcomings.

1. We admitted we were powerless over our sexual addiction—that our lives had become unmanageable.

2. Came to believe that a Power greater than ourselves could restore us to sanity.

3. Made a decision to turn our will and our lives to the care of God as we understood Him.

4. Made a searching and fearless moral inventory of ourselves.

5. Admitted to God, to ourselves, and to another human being the exact nature of our wrongs.

6. Were entirely ready to have God remove all these defects of character.

7. Humbly asked Him to remove our shortcomings.

8. Made a list of all persons we had harmed, and became willing to make amends to them all.

9. Made direct amends to such people wherever possible, except when to do so would injure them or others.

10. Continued to take personal inventory and when we were wrong, promptly admitted it.

11. Sought through prayer and meditation to improve our conscious contact with God, as we understood Him, praying only for knowledge of His will for us and the power to carry that out.

12. Having had a spiritual awakening as the result of these steps, we tried to carry this message to alcoholics, and to practice these principles in all our affairs.

*The Twelve Steps reprinted for adaptation by permission of AA World Services, Inc. Copyright 1939.

8. Made a list of all persons we had harmed, and became willing to make amends to them all.

9. Made direct amends to such people wherever possible, except when to do so would injure them or others.

10. Continued to take personal inventory and when we were wrong, promptly admitted it.

11. Sought through prayer and meditation to improve our conscious contact with God, as we understood Him, praying only for knowledge of His will for us and the power to carry that out.

12. Having had a spiritual awakening as the result of these steps, we tried to carry this message to sexual addicts, and to practice these principles in all our affairs.

APPENDIX 2

Note on Masturbation and Homosexual Activity.

Years ago, when I first counseled homosexual persons, including a neurologist, I was advised by the latter that masturbation was often a safety valve for the homosexual person, because it prevented him/her from acting out with another person. I was not certain that he was correct on that opinion, but I insisted that the act of masturbation was immoral. Since then I have learned in working with both heterosexual and homosexual persons that masturbation that is habitual, and in many instances compulsive, does not really keep the person from seeking sex with another person. The habit of masturbation, then, must be taken seriously, not only because it leads to acting out, but also because it creates havoc within the person. The feeling that one has no real control over his sexual impulses, the self-condemnation, and the guilt have serious effects on the internal disposition of the person. Prayer, for example, becomes a burden. Irritability with self and others and a lack of energy are also frequent phenomena. The person has the sense of being enslaved to a habit which he does not want.

This is not merely a "Catholic" sin; many non-Catholics experience the same feelings described above. At S.A. meetings (which include both heterosexual and homosexual person) individuals will tell the other members of the group of their disappointment if, perchance, between meetings they have fallen back into masturbation. Dissenting theologians and pop psychologists to the contrary notwithstanding, masturbation remains a form of enslavement to the power of lust, and steps must be taken to eliminate it from one's life. Again, I share this conviction with members of S.A., H.A., Courage, and many other groups. Be it noted that group support helps the individual to overcome what has been called in classical moral theology the "solitary sin".

The way out of compulsive masturbation, and that is what we really are concerned with, is not easy. It demands a regular attendance at spiritual support group meetings in which the individual shares with others his helplessness to overcome this imperious drive alone. To be sure, like other compulsions, such masturbation is related to an interior emptiness and loneliness, a profound isolation from fellow humans and from God. He/she needs to develop the prayer of the heart, and spend time on the effort every day. Since compulsive fantasy is at the root of the habit, he needs to cut it off as soon as he is aware of its presence. This can be very difficult in the beginning, because the individual has lived in the world of fantasy. Very often he has loads of pornography, which feeds fantasy and leads to masturbation. Older persons often are addicted to the porno TV on late at night. This must be stopped first.

There is need likewise to seek out real relationships with real people, cultivating deeper relationships with some members of the spiritual support group who are literally suffering the same condition. The more he is occupied with work or voluntary acts of charity, the better. He must stay in the real world. When he is tempted to masturbate, call a fellow member of the support group. Thus, prayer, group support, and the cultivation of real friends can help the compulsive masturbator to regain gradually freedom from this enslavement. I stress GRADUALLY, because, barring a miracle of grace, it will take time. As one sponsor put it, "it takes patience and persistence in prayer." I would add, yes, and persistence in following out all the above recommendations.

Selected Bibliography

Harvey, John F., O.S.F.S. *The Homosexual Person: New Thinking in Pastoral Care.* San Francisco, CA: Ignatius Press, 1987.

———. "Homosexuality and Hope," *Social Justice Review,* March, 1987.

Carnes, Patrick. *Out of the Shadows.* 2415 Annapolis Lane, Minneapolis., MN, Compcare Publications, 1982.

Groeschel, Benedict. *The Courage To Be Chaste.* New York: Paulist Press, 1985.

Payne, LeAnne. *The Broken Image.* Westchester, IL: Crossway, 1982.

St. Romain, Philip. *Becoming a New Person.* Ligouri, MO: Ligouri Press, 1984.

Cook, Colin. *Homosexuality: An Open Door.* Boise, Idaho: 1985.

———. *Homosexuality and the Power to Change.* 14 Tapes, American Tape Ministry, P.O. Box 992, Harrisburg, PA 17108.

Homosexuals Anonymous, P.O. Box 7881, Reading, PA 19603.

Sexaholics Anonymous, P.O. Box 300, Simi Valley, CA 93062.

Sex and Love Addicts Anonymous, Box 529, New Town Branch, Boston, MA 02258.

Sexual Compulsives Anonymous, Old Chelsea Station, P.O. Box 1585, Old Chelsea Station, New York, NY 10011.

Courage, St. Michael's Rectory, 424 W. 34th St., New York, NY 10001.

Hazelton Educational Materials, Pleasant Valley Road, Center City, MN 55012-0176.

Shaefer, Brenda. *Is It Love, Is it Addiction?* Hazelton Foundation, 1987.

Chapter 18

THE TEACHING OF THE CHURCH ON POPULATION

The Most Reverend James T. McHugh

The teaching of the Church on population has developed in a relatively short period of time. International population conferences, reaching back before 1974, have been an impetus or an encouragement to the Church to try to develop a consistent ethical or moral theory dealing with the question of population. The Church has also, by its participation in the population conferences, tried constantly to interject into international population discussions some sense of ethics and morality in the way population policies themselves are developed or worked out, either by international convocations or by individual countries.

What I would like to do is to make some introductory remarks and some pertinent distinctions; to speak for a while about the teaching of the Church, the magisterium, in regard to the question of population; to advert briefly to some ethical thinkers in this field, some who are Catholic, most who are not; and finally, to draw some conclusions from the practical experience of those of us who have been involved in the international debates about population.

I might say at the beginning that Cardinal Gagnon was the chief of the Vatican delegation in 1974 at Bucharest, of which I was a member, and in his role with the Pontifical Council for the Family, he has followed the whole question of population through all of these years. Members of his staff have been also members of the delegations to the international conferences, and so there has been a continuity within Rome, within the Roman Curia, on the question of population, and there has been a very careful team-work worked out between those in the Curia and those of us who are associated in one way or the other with the Holy See. My particular association is with the Vatican's Mission to the United Nations in New York.

Introductory Remarks

First of all, I am going to speak about population, and inevitably about population control. It is good to make the distinction at the beginning that this is different from birth control. Quite obviously, there is a point at which the two come together, but population control is what governments do; birth control is what people do, what couples do. Our primary focus today is on the role and the actions of governments in trying either to motivate and persuade on the one hand, or sometimes to coerce on the other, the behavior of couples.

The second thing to keep in mind is that we are dealing very often with the science of demography. Demography is a relatively new science; its own tools of measurement are not so sharp and precise as demographers would like them to be. While we have a tremendous amount of empirical information derived from demographic studies, the demographers themselves are constantly amazed at how they missed some of the major demographic events. It took them a long time to discover precisely why we had what seems to have been a population explosion following World War II, and to see the implications and repercussions of it in the decades that came thereafter. Obviously, it was easy to measure it, because birthrates kept going up and population rates kept going up. But it was much more difficult to assess the underlying causes; they came upon that rather late. In many other areas the demographers find themselves at a loss to explain empirical data that is all too apparent to them. So we ought not to canonize demographers; yet we ought to treat them with respect. Princeton University, of course, is the seat of one of the major centers in the country for population studies, and one of the first. The Office for Population Research here was initiated before many of the others, and has compiled a fairly good track record in terms of demography. But demographers are not all so value-free as they would like you to think; they come to their science with a little bit of bias, and they pick up a little more according to who funds their research and for what purpose; that has in a sense qualified the objectivity to which the science otherwise might lay claim.

There is an interesting new book entitled, *Population Control Politics: Women's Sterilization—A Reproductive Choice,* by Thomas Shapiro, published by the Temple University Press. He gives a short history of population affairs, and says that there are three different approaches to population questions or population control. The first is the Malthusian or neo-Malthusian approach. Malthus seemed to think that population would continue to grow in such an unlimited fashion that sooner or later there just would not be enough food left, enough wherewithal for people to survive. He saw this particularly as a problem of the poor, and he felt that in a sense poor brought it on themselves; they had such large families, so many children, that they created a situation that was simple unmanageable. He really was not a promoter of birth control, because he did not believe in birth control. The Neo-Malthusain have adopted his basic premise that population increase is such a serious problem that it threatens the planet, threatens the well-being of peoples. However, they maintain that there is a solution, namely, birth control, contraception, sterilization, and abortion. Thus, the challenge to humanity is to disseminate information about these means of birth control and make them accessible to all, so that we will solve the population problems that face us.

A second dominant element in the population field has been the eugenicists, who claim that it is usually the poor, the mentally deficient, and the inept who have children, and if we could just some way or other cut back on their capacity to procreate, then we would have smaller numbers and higher quality.

The third group of actors have been those in the women's movement at various points along the line. Contemporaneously, what are probably the more radical segments of the women's movement have been a strong voice in favor of, primarily, reproductive freedom, but in order to achieve reproductive freedom, they would have to have "ready-access" and absolute freedom in regard to abortion, sterilization and all means of contraception.

Actually, I think most people see the debates about population revolving around two camps. The first is the "developmentalist" camp, which contends that, if there is good development, especially in a developing nation, or if there is a good, stable socioeconomic situation in a developed nation, then there is sufficient productivity to meet the needs of the people and that population seems to even off by itself, so that population growth is not a serious threat. The other school of thought would say that the development process of the socioeconomic stability is endangered by population growth, especially in developing nations, which are the major concern of people dealing with population growth. In this view, unless there is a curtailment of population growth, a curtailment of birthrates, in other words, unless family planning comes first and is effective, all efforts at development will ultimately fail.

In the debates that have taken place, mostly in the United Nations, but also at the Council of Europe, which are the two main fora for discussions of population questions, the Vatican has taken a prominent role, and has always chosen to be in the developmentalist camp. That is, the Vatican's position has been that assistance by the developed nations to the developing nations of the world will enable them to cope with population growth and distribution, and will also enable them to draw from their own resources to service the need of their peoples, and that responsible parenthood, properly understood, will enable both couples and peoples to deal with population growth. I will come back to the whole question of responsible parenthood a little further on in the discussion.

The last introductory comment that I would offer is that, in its involvement in population questions, the Holy See has sought to play three roles. First of all, a prophetic role: to proclaim in these international fora the position of the Roman Catholic Church and how it bears upon population discussions. The second thing that the delegations of the Holy See have attempted to do is to be a restraining influence on the more direct and compulsive type of birth control/population control programs, that are often suggested as a means of coping with population growth. And finally, the Holy See has tried to serve as a catalyst, to develop some kind of consensus among those who come with an open mind to try to grapple with the whole question of population growth.

Summary of the Present Situation

Let me briefly summarize the world-wide population situation as it exist today. During the ten years from the 1974 World Population Conference to the 1984 World Population Conference, world population increased by about 770 million people. But over the same period, the *rate* of growth of the entire world began to decline. The actual numbers probably make very little impact in a discussion like this, so I will primarily use descriptive terms. At the beginning of the 1980's the growth rate was 1.7 percent world-wide, down from 2.1 percent. The United Nations forecasts indicate that the growth rate in the year 2000 should be about 1.5 percent. Most economists, demographers and sociologists would consider a 1 percent growth rate practically no problem at all; a 2 percent growth rate would vary according to the stability and the socioeconomic development of the of the nation itself.

Mortality trends since 1974 have also declined, though they differ from region to region throughout the world. Incidentally, as a matter of background, usually the United Nations deals with regions of the world, rather than individual countries, so essentially we are dealing with the major continents as regions of the world. Life expectancy has increased in both the developed and developing nations, though at a slower pace in developing nations. Particularly noteworthy are the declines in infant mortality, although once again, infant mortality has declined more slowly, and sometimes not at all, in the developing and least developed nations of the world.

During the 1970's fertility rates continued to decline world wide. The total fertility rate declined by 22 percent. In the developed countries of the world rates have fallen to very low levels, and it is expected that the total fertility rate for the world will decrease again from what it is now and probably come to some stability in the year 2025.

Urbanization has increased since 1974. It is likely to continue and it is creating enormous problems, especially in the developing nations. The flows of permanent migrants have generally declined over the past decade; the flows of temporary migrants have varied from region to region, usually prompted by some political or social upheaval. While not much attention is paid to migration, it still is one of the most important aspects of the population picture, and it is probably the most volatile as well. Finally, the phenomenon of aging has grown, not only in the developed countries of the world, but now also in the developing nations as well.

In very general and descriptive terms, what all this adds up to is that, first of all, we do not have, and probably have never had, a population explosion. In fact, what we have is a variety of population problems in the world today. In Western Europe, in the English-speaking nations, and in the most developed nations of the world, we have what Wattenberg describes as the "birth dearth"—declining population growth because of very, very low fertility rates and birth rates, which raises the prospect not only of a decline in population, but also of real gaps in the population structure, which themselves can threaten the very future of a nation.

West Germany, of course, is the classic example: if the birth rates continue to decline, West Germany could well go out of business. The Germans themselves know this, but seem unable to bring themselves to establish or to adopt policies that will in fact be pro-natalist and will encourage an increase in births. They talk about solving their socioeconomic problems by migration, and yet they are unhappy with the migrants who come as what are hoped to be "guest" workers; that is, who would come, work their years, and then go home to wherever they came from. What happens, of course, is that more and more of the workers come, like it there, and then stay. They create colonies of their own, intermarry, and become a part of the social fabric of the nation, but even this is not going to ensure West Germany of sufficient population growth.

In any case, I take West Germany as the most graphic example because the rates of decline are perhaps most apparent there, and Germany is still a little isolated from other nations. But the same thing is happening in most of the English-speaking world, including the United States. We do not see the repercussions of it here in the United States quite so much because we have enough illegal migration coming into the country, and some migration from places like Puerto Rico, which supplies the lowest level, blue collar, unskilled working class. But sooner or later the migrants to the United States are going to be mainstreamed into the society, and we are going to feel the pinch, because there is going to be no one to do what is usually the lowest level of unskilled labor. In the United States we have also had proposals over the years to close the borders, because the migration patterns have been considered a problem in themselves, but I do not think that we could close the borders and still survive economically.

At any rate, the problem of the Western world and of the English-speaking developing countries is largely one of population decline. In some parts of the developing world, such as southern Africa, there are nations where population growth is indeed a problem, where growth rates and birth rates are high, where the social and political organization of the country is so unstable that the resources that are actually there, or that are provided by the U.N. or by bilateral agreements, just never reach the people. In such countries there is real suffering, there is real crisis. To some degree it is correlated with birth rates, but because of the political, economic and social instability of these nations, one cannot attribute all of the problems simply to birth rates or to population growth. Nonetheless, we know that in some nations of the world, population growth is indeed a problem. And that as I said before is pretty much a regional phenomenon.

Teaching of the Church

Let me move now to the Church's teaching and the Church's involvement in proposing that teaching in the international fora, dealing with the question of population.

The development of Catholic teaching in regard to population, and especially to population policy, is very much a modern phenomenon, expressed in the writings of Pope Paul VI, the Second Vatican Council, and the present Pontiff. Concern about the government's role in regard to population appeared in the encyclical of Pius XI, *Casti connubii,* in the writings of Pius XII, and in the encyclical of John XXIII, *Mater et magistra.* In these documents, however, the emphasis was more on admonishing or cautioning governments against forcing individuals to use means of birth control prohibited by the Church; in other words, the focus was very narrow: it dealt simply with protecting the freedom of couples to choose morally acceptable methods of family planning, that is, not to have the use of immoral methods imposed on them. It was probably *Populorum progressio* and *Gaudium et spes* that began to look at population more in the context of development, and more in terms of the Church's teaching on development. The encyclical *Humanae vitae* deals with the population question only very briefly, but constantly refers to *Populorum progression* and to *Gaudium et spes.* Again, *Humanae vitae* deals with the freedom of the couple and the obligation of governments to develop supportive family policies to meet the needs of couples and families. In *Gaudium et spes* the passages pertinent to population questions are not found in the sections on marriage and family life, but rather in paragraph 87, which deals with development; in *Populorum progressio,* the relevant passages are sections 36 and 37. In any case, both *Gaudium et spes* and *Populorum progressio* are almost identical in their treatment of the subject; perhaps *Populorum progressio* is a little bit more detailed in spelling out the role of government.

I will try to summarize very briefly the major points of these documents, which pervade the rest of the writings of Pope Paul VI, such as his address to the FAO in 1970, his Apostolic Exhortation *Octogesima adveniens,* the documents of the Secretary of State and the Council of the Family in preparation for the 1974 World Population Conference, and the addresses of Paul VI to the United Nations officers who were in charge of the 1974 conference, and finally, those addresses of Paul VI in June of 1978, before he died. The main points which are found in *Gaudium et spes* and *Populorum progressio* come back time and time again through all of these other addresses and documents and contain these basic points.

First of all, since rapid population growth may impede the development process, governments have rights and duties within the limits of their own competence to try to ameliorate the population problem; in other words, some role for government is recognized. But these efforts on the part of the government are always described in terms of providing information concerning the impact of population growth, and in terms of legislation and social policies that will meet the needs of families within the confines of individual nations.

The second point that is common to all of the documents is that decisions regarding the size of the family and the frequency of births should be made by the parents, without pressure from the government. Such decisions are premised on a correctly formed conscience which respects the Church's authentic interpretation of the divine law in regard to the means of birth control that are used. Couples should take into account their responsibilities to God, to themselves, to the children they already have and to the community or society to which they belong. *Populorum progressio* is the most explicit in spelling out these criteria of responsible parenthood. This is the classic statement of the principle of responsible parenthood. I will come back to it later on, because I will compare it with a statement that has also been formulated and found its way into most of the documents of the United Nations dealing with population. Obviously, absent from the United Nations documents is any reference to responsibilities to God.

Those in the population field, particularly those in the Catholic community dissatisfied with the Church's teaching on birth control, tried to assert and to maintain this principle of responsible parenthood, qualifying it in some way, usually by saying that the problem of growth created such a major threat to the common good that there was justification to set aside or give only tacit allegiance to the teaching of the church in regard to the methods of birth control.

The third point that is common to the documents is that the family is the basic social unit. It should be protected from pressures that prevent it from pursuing its legitimate goals, especially in terms of family size, and it should be provided with assistance by society in regard to health, education, stable social conditions, employment, housing, etc.—the usual socioeconomic policies that would benefit the family and enable it to fulfill its functions in society.

The fourth point is that in many countries there is a need to adopt new methods of farming and new forms of social organization. Some antiquated customs, even those related to family life, such as the inheritance of land and dowry system, should be changed or abandoned if they impede the development process and, especially in terms of the dowry system, if they are directly contrary to the dignity of the human person.

Most of these four points are expressed in all of the documents of the papal magisterium, particularly in the intervention of then Bishop Gagnon as the chief of the delegation at the 1974 Population Conference, as well as in the addresses of Paul VI to the United Nations officers in charge of the conference. Thus, with the 1974 conference, the Vatican took a more involved, one might even say aggressive, role in regard to discussions of population policy than it had prior to that time. Actually, it did not have much of a prior occasion: there was only one previous World Population Conference, and it was really more of a technical conference. The 1974 conference was more of an open conference, directed to legislators, politicians, policy makers, as well as the demographers and sociologists. So the Vatican not only attended or observed the 1974 conference, but it took a more active role and sent its delegation with a message on behalf of the Holy See that clearly proposed the teaching of the Church in regard to these issues. The Holy See then followed up by active participation in the conference to try to bring this teaching to bear on the development on the "World Plan of Action", which is the document formulated by any kind of a United Nations World Conference.

The same thing took place in 1984, but I will come back to that, because there were some further developments between 1974 and 1984.

At this point, I would like to say a few things on the question of responsible parenthood. The principle of responsible parenthood is really a technical-ethical principle. It has been honed very carefully in the Catholic tradition, and it has been adopted very easily in the international sphere.

In the preparations for the 1984 World Population Conference there was a long document, the title of which was, "Recommendations for Further Implementation of the World Population Plan of Action of 1974." There were two weeks of meetings in New York at the United Nations to develop this basic document. One of the leading voices at that meeting was that of the delegation from the United States, which was then faced with some conflicting tendencies or trends.

First of all, going into the 1974 conference, the assumption had been that the world was in the throes of a population explosion, and this would be the "do-gooder" conference that was going to show everybody how to diminish the problem. Actually, in 1974, most of the developing nations of the world did not accept the thesis that there was a population explosion, or that population was their major problem. They thought that the absence of development was their major problem, so they qualified the central thrust of the document going in to the 1974 conference. Going into the 1984 conference, demographic data had proven that this was true: in fact there was no population explosion, and development was indeed a much more serious problem than population growth. So the United States and other Western countries, still intent on bringing down population growth rates, was walking into a conference where there was no great receptivity for their particular viewpoint, and where, in fact, many of the developing nations of the world had acquired an expertise in dealing with population increases and with better articulating their own needs in terms of the development process.

Nonetheless, the United States and the other Western nations wanted to keep attention focused on the need for established and acceptable policies dealing with population growth. To do that, they interjected into the discussions a strong emphasis on freedom of the couple. I would say that, to the credit of the United States delegation, they not only interjected it, but they sustained it by argument and by coalition building, so that in the draft document going into the 1984 conference, there were strong protective paragraphs for the autonomy of the couple to determine how many children they would have, the timing of births, and the means to plan that they would use the means to plan the timing and ultimate number of births.

In the actual debate at Mexico City, a lot of those protective paragraphs were merged into a few provisions, and they found their way into some of the introductory documentation, and then were recited once again. Let me read one of the recommendations, which is very brief, so that you will be able to compare the way in which the principle of responsible parenthood is articulated in the secular world with the way it is perceived from a Roman Catholic moral perspective. Recommendation 30 says, "Governments are urged to insure that all couples and individuals have the basic right to decide freely and responsibly the number and spacing of their children, and to have the information, education and means to do so. Couples and individuals in the exercise of this right, should take into account the needs of their living and future children and their responsibilities towards the community." Recall that a Roman Catholic formulation, as found in *Populorum progressio* or *Gaudium et spes,* of the concept of responsible parenthood involves the following elements: a free, informed mutual decision by the married couple regarding the frequency of births and the size of the family, based on their conscientious assessment of their responsibilities to God, to themselves, to their children and family, and to the society of which they are a part, enlightened by the authentic teaching of the Church's magisterium regarding the objective moral order and licit methods of spacing or limiting pregnancies.

One point of comparison, of course, is that the second statement embodies a great deal more of the moral and ethical thinking within Roman Catholicism, a great deal more of the commitment, not only of *Populorum progressio* or *Gaudium et spes,* but also the document that we attend to in this symposium, that is, *Humanae vitae.*

A second point of comparison has to do with the basic thrust of the United Nations formulation: "Governments are urged to insure that all couples and individuals. . . ." The reference to "individuals" is a direct strike at the family, and the inclusion of those words, "and individuals," has been the major stumbling block for the Vatican in both the 1974 and 1984 conferences, preventing the Vatican from joining the consensus on the adoption of these plans of action that emerged from the the two international population conferences. In effect, the assertion is that the couple, but also any individual, has a right to information about birth control, and access to the means of birth control, so that he or she can engage in those acts that are supposed to be *per se aptos ad generationem.*

In any case, the inclusion of "individuals" really extends the United Nations thinking into a permissive sexual ethic, which oftentimes, then, creates a situation wherein the Vatican cannot go along. However, the Vatican is not usually alone in not being able to go along. Increasingly, many of the developing nations of the world find themselves more at home with the Vatican's thinking on these issues, than they do with the more permissive thinking of the Western world.

Let me very briefly touch upon the developments that took place from 1974, maybe 1978, that is the death of Paul VI, through the years of John Paul II. John Paul II addressed the question of population very early in his pontificate, indeed in January of 1979, in his first visit to Mexico. And then there were a series of talks, mostly on his pastoral journeys, in which time and time again, especially in the developing nations, he would make some reference to population questions.

The synod of 1980 took up the question of population, and from the bishops—not from the Roman Curia, not from the Pope— emerged one of the toughest and most direct statements on the population question, aimed at the developed nations of the world. Having been at the synod, and having read most of the English-language news reports of the synod (which never quite impressed me, since they were not, obviously, reports of the synod that I attended) I found it interesting that there was such a tremendous agreement among the writers either, on the one hand, to assert certain things that they wanted to be believed, or, on the other, to ignore other things that they did not want to be believed. One of those things was the reaction of Third World bishops against any kind of population control programs, because they were convinced that those programs were directed against the well-being of their people, and particularly against the Catholic population, especially where Catholic populations are very small proportions of the overall population.

Finally, the most direct statement by John Paul II was, again, an address just before the 1984 conference, and in that address, John Paul II once again went back to the dignity of the person as a fundamental point, a fundamental principle from which all concerns and all discussions on population ought to emerge. The importance of the family and its autonomy from governnmental control or influence was also emphasized.

A new point that was made more strongly was the value of the child. John Paul II made this point in his first visit to the United Nations in 1979 and has repeated it many times since in his addresses to specific groups, mostly United Nations groups. Again, there was emphasis on the rights of parents and how those rights should be safeguarded and not invaded by governments. There was a new emphasis on the limited role of government, that is, to assist families, rather than to coerce families. There was a new emphasis on the roles and rights of women, particularly that women, while they are assuming new roles in modern societies, should not be thereby forced to forego child bearing and child rearing, especially not to give up child rearing in those precious early years of the child's life. There was a new emphasis also on aging, because aging is a new demographic phenomenon in the 1980's and promises to be a major demographic phenomenon in the years ahead.

Finally, there was an expansion of the consideration of development in *Populorum progressio* and *Gaudium et spes.* In preparation of the 1974 document, we dealt with development as it was proposed to us by the developmentalists, that is, people in economics, development theory, population theory. But in the documents for the 1984 conference, and especially the address of John Paul II, there was also a recognition that there are different types of development theories, but that, from a Roman Catholic perspective, fundamental to them all is a concern for the dignity and the rights of the human person, and also a concern to maintain and sustain the common good at the level of principle, rather than to try to develop economic or socioeconomic theories.

Before I go to the concluding principles, one last digression. In the 1974 World Conference on Population, there was no mention of abortion. The planners of the conference did not want any mention of abortion, because they were afraid that it would disrupt the conference, and those of us who were there on behalf of the Vatican considered our own prospects for raising the issue, and were pretty well convinced that had we raised it, we would have been overwhelmed by the Western nations, and there would have been a mention, and it would have been one that sustained free access to abortion.

In 1984, there was quite a different mood. There has been a great deal of notoriety given to the position of the United States. In fact, the so-called "Reagan Doctrine" goes back to 1969, to the development of the first family planning bill in the United States. It has been the policy of both parties; it has been sustained by both the Congress and the presidency, regardless of who was President; and it has been sustained under challenge by the Supreme Court of the United States, that government need not provide money to those family planning programs that include abortion as a method of birth control. It is a very limited type of policy statement, but, very significant, because through all of the years, especially all of the years of the abortion controversy, it has prevented the flow of federal monies into abortion services, domestically, as well as world-wide.

At the 1984 conference, this was probably the central point of the statement of the United States government. But in the debate, where the policies were hammered out, the delegation of the United States took practically no role whatsoever. The delegation of the Vatican submitted the proposal that abortion should not be considered a method of birth control, and funds should not be provided for abortion, and a number of developing countries readily supported this proposal made by the Vatican. Interestingly, many of the countries of Western Europe also supported this same policy.

Yesterday, Bishop Egan made reference to a book entitled, *Abortion and Divorce in Western Countries,* by Mary Ann Glendon, recently published by Harvard University Press. Glendon's book is probably a landmark book in the abortion area, as well as in the divorce area. It summarizes and compares the laws of the United States with those of the Western Europe. The main thesis of the book is that in the United States, these laws are devoid of any kind of value orientation, whereas in Europe the laws dealing with divorce and abortion, while they might practically end up being as permissive as those of the United States, in fact, also at least pay lip service to some underlying values, that is, the dignity of the person, the importance of fetal life, and the importance of family relationships. I think that Glendon makes her case well. Certainly, that was our experience at Mexico City. The nations of Western Europe were willing to support a formulation that said that abortion is not a good thing, and should not be a central part of a population policy. There was strong opposition to that from China and from some of those nations, mostly in Africa, that had family planning programs heavily funded by the International Planned Parenthood Federation. But through the hours of debate, the proposal ultimately drew the consensus and was accepted by the International Population Conference.

I digress to make a point of this for all of us who are Americans, because repeatedly in the press today, we see reference to the so-called "Reagan policy" of no funding of abortion in family planning programs. That is part of an attempt to associate that policy simply with Ronald Reagan, so that then we can be rid of it, sometime within the next six months, regardless of who becomes President of the United States. The effort has been made, and I think successfully, to identify the prohibition of abortion funding with Ronald Reagan himself, so that when he leaves office it can then be argued that this was a very narrow-minded, personal thing, and that a more "enlightened" view will find some loopholes by which a government can meet the "legitimate" claims of some women who need abortion services. This is

292

why I emphasize that this policy is not Ronald Reagan's policy, but the policy of the United States government since its first family planning bill. It has been sustained by Congress as well as by the White House; it has been sustained by both parties; and it has been sustained by the Supreme Court of the United States. As a matter of fact, in the international forum, it was put forth, not by the United States, but by somebody else who usually does not have much power at United Nations conferences, and it was supported, not only by the Third World, but also by many of the nations of Western Europe. It is a policy well worth keeping in place because it has, at least in a minimal way, prevented the spread and the systemization or institutionalization of permissive abortion world-wide.

Conclusions

Now in light of all of this, let me draw some basic conclusions. The conclusions are my own, derived from the careful reading of the various documents.

In light of the development of the moral and ethical principles proposed by the Holy See in its involvement in population conferences, in view of the writings of population ethicists and moral theologians who have dealt with it, it seems to me that any attempts to establish a population policy based on human dignity and responsive to human needs should include the following goals:

1. A population policy should put primary emphasis on social and economic justice, international development, and increased efforts by the developed nations to assist the developing nations.
2. A population policy should sustain adequate population growth and distribution to enable any nation to pursue its development policies. In some cases, it is desirable and morally acceptable for a nation to moderate its population growth, to keep pace with its development strategies, with its food and

economic resources, and with its socioeconomic policies.

3. A population policy should be part of a larger policy of social development. It should look to the development of sufficient resources to service the existing population and its projected increase. Each step the government takes in urging people to meet demographic goals, should be paralleled by efforts to improve social conditions, and extend the full range of social opportunities, jobs, housing, health care, education, etc. to all its citizens.

4. A population policy must support the family unit, enabling the family to pursue its own goals while fulfilling responsibilities to the overall society.

5. A population policy should preserve adequate freedom for the individual couples to bear and support the number of children they desire. It is the positive duty of government to help bring about conditions that will relieve pressures on couples to limit family size.

6. When a population policy involves education and assistance in family planning, it should include only those means of family planning that are in accord with moral teaching and the dignity of the human person. Sterilization should be excluded as a means of family planning. Acceptance of family planning assistance should be voluntary, with legal prohibition of coercion, particularly of the poor, who are often considered the target of family planning programs.

7. Protection of the right to life at all stages, especially in regard to the unborn and the aging, must be included in all population policy. Euthanasia and abortion should be prohibited as a means of population control.

8. Research into all phases of the family life cycle and the effects of social trends on the family should be part of a population policy. There should also be funding for demographic research

and for the scientific work that will lead to the further development of safe and morally acceptable methods of family planning.

9. A population policy should provide a full range of prenatal, maternal health, and pediatric services, as well as nutritional care.

10. In order to benefit families, a population policy may also include ancillary services, such as education in human sexuality and in marriage and family living, and pre-marriage and marriage counselling.

I submit that the ten points are a summary of the ethical thinking and of the teaching of the Church in the area of population and population policy. I doubt that they are the final word, because we will certainly experience new challenges before the next population conference, which I think is planned for 1994, in China. But I think also that the Church's thinking and constant proposal, affirmation and assertion of its teaching in this area has, first of all, had beneficial effect, not only for Catholics, but for others as well, and has indeed motivated the international community to think in terms of ethics when dealing with something as fundamental as population.

Chapter 19

EDUCATING YOUNG ADULTS IN CHASTITY

John S. Hamlon

In this presentation I would like to describe, in a very brief and practical fashion, the course on marriage and the family that I teach for the St. Ignatius Institute at the University of San Francisco.

Whenever I have taught about family life issues, whether in natural family planning courses, in high schools, or whenever, I have always taught in the context of *Humanae vitae*. I have always spoken about the unitive and the procreative meanings of the conjugal act, despite the fact that many times my audience knew little about the Catholic Church and its teachings. Admittedly, there were times when it was difficult to do this. However, in 1981 the Holy Father issued the Apostolic Exhortation *Familiaris consortio* and, speaking for myself, this document was a source of much-needed encouragement. Soon thereafter, the Bishop of St. Cloud, Minnesota, where I was living at the time, asked me if I would write a brief commentary or study guide for *Familiaris consortio* and I agreed to do so. Many months later, after studying the document backwards and forwards, I came up with a study guide that was published by the Human Life Center at Collegeville, Minnesota. It was not written for the academic, but for the ordinary person sitting in the pew.

With the new encouragement that *Familiaris consortio* gave me, I started to educate in a new way—with adults, in marriage courses, and with any young people that came along. My approach now was to start with *Familiaris consortio* and then teach *Humanae vitae* within the context of *Familiaris consortio*. I found that, for me, this worked better than starting with Pope Paul VI's encyclical on human life. Thus, when I began to help administratively at the St. Ignatius Institute two years ago, I started thinking about a course along these same lines. I proposed it to Father Joseph Fessio, who was the director of the Institute at that time, and he agreed to have a one-unit course offered under his name, called "John Paul II's Vision of Marriage and Family". He hired me as his teaching assistant, so I was the one to teach it, but it was Father Fessio who took responsibility for the course. When last year Father Maloney succeeded Father Fessio as director of the institute, he, too, took responsibility for the course.

I would like to describe this course to you because, in my experience, the course has been successful on the undergraduate level. There are 10 sessions and the first five are devoted to *Humanae vitae* and *Familiaris consortio*. In the first session, I introduce Pope John Paul II to the students by giving them some background material on his life. Then in the second session I give a preliminary explanation of the Pope's teaching on the theology of the body. In session three, we examined the situation of the family in the modern world, for which I set the stage by reading a letter in the San Francisco *Chronicle* written by a Catholic woman. The last paragraph of the letter is enough to show where the woman stands:

Since research shows most Catholics not only don't practice the Church's "Russian roulette" forms of birth control but instead rely on better forms of birth control, one would think that the Church would come into the present century. Having given assistance to priests who had AIDS or were known homosexuals and having given assistance to elderly nuns living in poverty, and countless young pregnant Catholic girls, I ache at the Church's hypocrisy. Such "hear no evil speak no evil" thinking is not only patriarchical and sexist, but socially irresponsible.

We talk about that situation, about the dark shadows and the signs that something is going wrong in the world. It does not take very long for the students to reach many of the same conclusions that the Pope presents in part one of *Familiaris consortio* about the situation of the family in the world today. I tell them, for example, the story of the 14-year-old Catholic high school girl who went to a pregnancy center in San Francisco to get a pregnancy examination. She was given a slip of paper that indicated the results of the test, which were negative. When the nurse congratulated the girl on her supposed good fortune, the girl said that she was not surprised at the result because she was not having sex. The nurse then asked her why she had bothered to take a pregnancy test if she was not sexually active. The girl held up the slip of paper with the results on it and said, "This little piece of paper is what I need to show my friends, so that they will *think* I'm having sex."

Such is the power of peer pressure. My wife went to the same high school when she was young and can testify that in her time such a thing would have been absolutely unthinkable. There is no question, then, that we have seen some big changes over the past twenty years.

I also mention Paul Vitz's book on the cult of self-worship, since John Paul II points to it as the underlying problem here. But I also go over with my students some of the signs that Christ is amongst us, those more positive signs that Pope John Paul calls attention to in *Familiaris consortio:* greater awareness of personal freedom, greater emphasis on quality relationships, women's dignity, etc.

Then we get into Part Two of the document, particularly Article 11, which is a capsulization of his theology of the body. He says it very simply, and I offer a paraphrase of it here:

> Man is created in the image of God, who is love. Love, therefore, is the fundamental vocation of every human being. Man, an incarnate spirit, is called to love with his total being. Love, therefore, includes the human body. Sexuality reflects the human person's innermost being, and therefore total physical self-giving. Total *physical* self-giving must be the sign and fruit of total *personal* self-giving.

Then I present the Pope's emphasis on marriage as the only place where this total self-giving can happen, in the way that God intended it to happen. As John Paul II points out, marital fidelity does not interfere with personal freedom, but rather enhances it.

In the same part of that document, the Pope speaks about virginity and celibacy. I present these in juxtaposition to marriage, and point out to the students that virginity and celibacy are a higher charism in the Church. It is important for the students to know and to discuss this. From this they can see that only when marriage is highly esteemed is the value of virginity and celibacy truly protected. By the same token, virginity and celibacy protect marriage from devaluation and deterioration.

From here, we move to Part Three of the document and examine what John Paul II refers to as the four roles of the Christian family: forming a community of persons; serving life; participating in the development of society; and sharing in the life and mission of the Church. We talk quite a bit about the first of these roles, that is, forming a community of persons. The students come to understand why the Pope teaches that communion within the family begins with the communion between husband and wife. Through this document they also learn that because of Christ, because of Christ's Incarnation and Redemption, the Creator's original plan for man and woman can be realized. We cannot recover the innocence that humanity enjoyed before the Fall, but we can get back to regarding each other in the proper way.

We also stress that the educational exchange that takes place between parent and child facilitates the communion between them. We go over what the Pope says in this part of the document about the equal dignity of men and women, about women in society and women in the home, and about the husband's responsibility for the unity and development of his family, which is a big job.

Some of you may recall that back in 1983 Senator Jeremiah Denton held a series of Senate hearings on broken families. This was the occasion for several very good papers on the state of the family in the United States. Many psychiatrists and psychologists made comments that left a lasting impression. For example, one of them said that if the father is in the home and takes an active role in nurturing the children, caring for them, exercising discipline, and doing all of the other things the father is supposed to do, then those children will have a better sexual identity, and will do better in school, and so on.

We also go over what the Pope teaches about the elderly: that they are an integral part of the family and often can help to bridge the generation gap. I know this only too well from personal experience. My wife's mother has been living with us for a year. In some ways she can be a difficult woman to live with: she is 81 years old, the victim of a stroke, and needs a lot of attention. But there is one thing about her that I would never change: her devotional practices during the day. She prays and prays, and then she prays some more, and always with the complete confidence that those prayers will be heard. My young son—he was about five at that time—began visiting his grandmother in her room very early in the morning, in those predawn hours when only the very young and the very old are naturally awake. They would have long conversations, going back and forth in what often sounded like excited, and at times heated, exchanges. Then one day he brought home a drawing that he had done in his kindergarten class in public school. On the left side of the drawing was Christ on the cross, and on the right side of the drawing was a heart with little pins in it. He explained that on the left was Jesus on the cross and on the right was his pierced heart. He said that he had learned that from Grandma. His grandmother had been tutoring him in the faith. He now knows more about his religion than do my other two children, both of whom are teenagers, thanks to his early morning conversations with his elderly and infirm grandmother.

Now this is just an example of what I am talking about, but in my class I tell this kind of story, and then the students bring in their own examples.

We go on to consider the second role of the family, which the Pope calls "serving life." It is here that *Humanae vitae* comes in so strongly and so beautifully. We devote a whole session to *Humanae vitae,* with its teaching on responsible parenthood and conjugal love, on the unitive and procreative meanings. I relate stories from real life about what has happened when people have tried to separate the two. We go over what John Paul II says about contraception in Article 32 of *Familiaris consortio,* which is the strongest condemnation of contraception that I have ever heard, calling it simply a lie:

> When couples, by means of recourse to contraception, separate these two meanings that God the Creator has inscribed in the being of man and woman and in the dynamism of their sexual communion, they act as "arbiters" of the divine plan and they "manipulate" and degrade human sexuality—and with it themselves and their married partner—by altering its value of "total" self-giving. Thus the innate language that expresses the total reciprocal self-giving of husband and wife is overlaid, through contraception, by an objectively contradictory language, namely, that of not giving oneself totally to the other. This leads not only to a positive refusal to be open to life but also to a falsification of the inner truth of conjugal love, which is called upon to give itself in personal totality.

I point out that *Humanae vitae* is still the norm by which thousands of people live out their sexuality. I also point out, however, what John Paul II himself says at the conclusion of his treatment of *Humanae vitae* in *Familiaris consortio:* "Clerical unity of moral and pastoral judgement is paramount in the area of sexuality." Married couples need to hear the truth from their pastors, and need to be called to live up to that truth.

In describing the role of the family in "serving life", John Paul II follows up his discussion of the transmission of life with a discussion of education. This is perfectly logical, since just as the unitive and procreative meanings are inseparable in the transmission of life, so also is procreation inseparable from education. Sometimes the forces of nature, or death, or some other outside force does disrupt the connection, so that somebody other than the parents has to educate the children. But in the normal course of things, if a husband and wife have children, then they are the first people responsible for the education of these children. Be it education in virtue or in anything else, they are responsible. John Paul II puts it in no uncertain terms in Article 36 of *Familiaris consortio:*

> Hence, parents must be acknowledged as the first and foremost educators of their children. Their role as educators is so decisive that scarcely anything can compensate for their failure in it. . . . The right and duty of parents to give education is essential, since it is connected with the transmission of human life; it is *original* and *primary* with regard to the educational role of others, on account of the uniqueness of the loving relationship between parents and children; and it is *irreplaceable* and *inalienable,* and therefore incapable of being entirely delegated to others or usurped by others.

Then we examine the third role of the family; helping in the development of society. Here we spend a lot of time on the "law of free giving". I try to present useful examples. It is a very important law because no family can exist without it. It is simply the exact opposite of some of the so-called "contract marriages" that we hear about. I let the students read a "contract marriage" that came up in San Francisco many years ago where the couple put down everything that they were going to do. "You are going to do this a certain number of times a week, and I am going to do that." Then it came to the question of having children. They said, "Neither of us wants children. If by chance we become pregnant, there has to be a vote of two in favor of having the child for that child to survive. If there is one vote against, the child is to be aborted." That is the total opposite of the law of free giving here. Of course the students understand that, when it is put in juxtaposition with a contract marriage like the one just described.

Then I bring up something that is very dear to the Holy Father's heart, and that is hospitality. This is the kind of hospitality that opens up the doors to your home. I tell them, for example, about the family that used to invite us over to Thanksgiving dinner every year in my hometown in Minnesota. The husband was a doctor, and so was his wife; she was a doctor at the local state hospital. Every Thanksgiving, she would bring back two mentally ill patients to eat with us. She opened up her doors. That impressed me a lot, especially because she was not Christian; as far as I could tell, she was between agnostic and atheistic.

Finally, we go on to the fourth role of the family, which is to participate in the life and mission of the Church. Here we talk about prayer and the family. and particularly about the importance of starting prayer in the family early, because it is much harder to start it later. Here I tell another story taken from the life of my own family. The older children were about eleven or twelve years old, and the youngest was about three. My wife and I and the two older children had all gathered in the living room for the family rosary; we had our rosaries out, and I was going to read from that little book, *The Scriptural Rosary.* The youngest, Mark, wanted to be a part of this, too, so he came up and took the book away from me, and then he went around and took all the rosaries away form everybody else, put them around his neck, and sat there pretending he was reading, with all the rosaries. In order to get the rosaries and the book back from him without creating a scene, my older son came up with the idea of getting his own First Communion book, which has pictures in it, and of giving it to Mark to keep him occupied. Mark looked at those pictures and became completely engrossed. But when he came upon a picture of the Crucifixion, he became visibly upset. For while we have crucifixes in our home, there is no blood flowing from the wounds, and for the first time Mark saw a picture of the Crucifixion with blood flowing from Christ's hands, feet, and side. When he realized that this is what actually happened to Christ on the Cross, we had to stop everything in order to go and get the iodine from the bathroom, and bring the iodine back and actually dab those wounds with the iodine. I still have that little book, and it still has iodine all over it.

Now I do not tell that story to my students just because it is cute or appealing. There is a lesson in it, too, and that is that not all kinds of family organizations and family outings are going to come out the way they have been planned. I tell the students that they have to be ready for imperfection, because they are going to see a lot of it.

The last thing that we do in the first half of the course is to go through Part Four of *Familiaris consortio,* on the pastoral care of the family. We go into all of the stages of marriage preparation, remote, proximate, and immediate. We talk about the irregular situations, such as "trial marriages." In trial marriages there are no mitigating or extenuating circumstances. It is very plain: there is no case where a trial marriage can be countenanced—none!—because the very definition of a trial marriage is that one party is using the other to find something or to discover something, and that person is using the first party in the same way. As long as one party is using the other, it is against the personalistic norm, which the Pope sets forth in his book, *Love and Responsibility,* with which I am sure you are familiar.

So much for the first half of my course. In the second half, I take what we have learned in language, and look at practical challenges to chastity. We look at the difference between NFP and contraception, at fertility appreciation, at married love, at new ethical questions. We deal with NFP in a marriage relationship. We deal with all those things, but I am not the only one who is speaking to those issues. For example, in the first session of this practical part, session six of the course overall, "Challenges to Chastity," I talk about sexual fear, sexual fantasies, masturbation, pornography, premarital sex, this kind of thing. But for supporting material, I have little articles, such as the one, "Sexual Freedom", by V. Mary Stuart, which shows quite well the application of the law of gradualness, rather than the gradualness of the law, as the Holy Father puts it. I also present the Vatican's *Declaration on Certain Questions Concerning Sexual Ethics.* We use Father John Harvey's "Masturbation: the Sin Against Faithful and Lifegiving Love." The students read these things and then we discuss them.

In session seven, "Fertility Appreciation," my wife and I give a slide presentation on the physiology behind natural family planning, so the students are aware that natural family planning is based on something that is real.

In session eight, "The Difference Between Contraception and NFP", I use Bill May's *Sex, Marriage and Chastity*, paraphrasing some of what he says about the dissenting views of American theologians on this issue. It is very effective. I pass out copies of "Pope John Paul II and *Humanae vitae*," by Janet Smith. This is an excellent article and one of the favorites among the students because it gives a very understandable rendition of the language of the body. I use my own article from a long time ago, "A Transition From Contraception to NFP." As part of this, we try to get across the notion of moral growth, so that a decision in favor of natural family planning reflects a clear rejection of contraception as a matter of principle, refusing to consider its use as a back-up or last resort, and also a willingness to live the virtues of patience, respect, and self-control that NFP requires, without having recourse to oral sex or other means of avoiding the sacrifice inherent in practicing abstinence.

The last item that I use in session eight is an excellent article by Don DeMarco, "The Chief Obstacle in Teaching NFP". With Don's typically droll sense of humor, he says, "What is the moral difference, students will say, between abstaining from sex and using contraception? The intention and the end are identical in both instances: the avoidance of pregnancy. What I find particularly unsettling about this remark is that its absolute predictability brings to mind images of a conspiracy." He goes into the distinction between invitation and disinvitation; it is a brilliant analogy, and something that the students can readily grasp.

In session nine, "Married Love," I hand out another article by Don DeMarco, "A Christian Woman Today, From a Man's Point of View." The first paragraph sets the tone for the entire article:

> In one part of ancient Greece, according to the legend, whenever a man proposed a law in the popular assembly, he stood on a platform with a rope around his neck. If his law passed, they removed the rope. If it

failed, they removed the platform. In any part of today's world, a man who proposes a norm for the Christian woman, stands in the historical shadow of these intrepid Greek legislators. I am no exception.

I have had girls in my class read this over and over again, because they want to discuss the many important points that Don makes, such as the difference between a "male" and a "man". The point that I am trying to make is that this practical part of the course makes use of good material from a variety of other sources.

The last session is a presentation that my wife and I make together, called, "NFP and Its Effect on a Marriage Relationship". This consists simply of our own story, which includes many of the stories from our life together, such as the ones I have given above.

The point of all of this is what I said at the beginning: what I have found in this particular course is that, at least for me, it works well to put *Humanae vitae* within the context of *Familiaris consortio,* rather than to try to work outside of it. If I may put it this way, *Familiaris consortio* seems to add life to *Humanae vitae,* and then *Humanae vitae* adds life to *Familiaris consortio.* Instead of merely a double effect, it seems to produce almost a quadruple effect; it is a strange phenomenon.

Still, I do not think that this is enough. I think that it is then necessary to take that living body of teaching about chastity, and marry it with practical questions. In this way the students can actually get a number of important questions out into the open and deal with them. One final, but vital, point: the students do not have to say a word in class. I never ask them a single question. If they do not want to share anything, then they do not have to, because the cardinal rule that I follow in this very sensitive area, unless we are dealing with a strictly academic point, is that I must respect their reservation. I must be very prudent.

Chapter 20

EDUCATION IN CHASTITY: A SUMMARY DISCUSSION

On Thursday, August 11, 1988, presentations were made regarding three educational programs in human sexuality which promote chastity and respect for life:

(1) *Teen S.T.A.R.—Sexuality Teaching in the Context of Adult Responsibility,* by Hanna Klaus, M.D., Executive Director, Natural Family Planning Center, Bethesda, Maryland;

(2) *Love and Life* and *Sex Respect: The Option of True Sexual Freedom,* by Coleen Kelly Mast, President, Respect Incorporated, Bradley, Illinois;

(3) *The Wonder of Love and Life,* by Mercedes Arzu Wilson, Executive Director, Family of the Americas Foundation, Mandeville, Louisiana.

For several reasons, such as the informal and interactive nature of the presentations or the incorporation of graphical materials, it is not possible to reproduce the presentations in these proceedings in the same way as the formal papers delivered by other participants in the symposium. Nonetheless, the presentations made an invaluable contribution to the symposium, so we have included a descriptive summary of each program, with an indication of how to obtain further information on each one.

—EDITOR

1. HANNA KLAUS

The Teen S.T.A.R. program is premised on the supposition that neither the provision of contraception nor the simple exhortation to preserve chastity serves the needs of adolescents to integrate their biological capacity to procreate into their operational self-concepts. Instead, Teen S.T.A.R. uses experiential learning about fertility to facilitate the integration of biologic maturity with adolescent emotions, cognition, capacity, life goals and behavior.

Contraception dichotomizes sex and procreation, thus facilitating relationships that are fragmented and often solely or largely genital, and which do not lead to growth. While teens are often exposed to exhortations to moral, i.e., chaste, behavior, many have not yet reached a level of personal integration that enables them to implement this teaching, even when they are disposed to do so, because they are immersed in the adolescent personality task of establishing their ego identity. This requires at least a theoretical distancing from the "parental ego" in order to discover which values are their own, and which are passively incorporated from their parents. These youngsters cannot "hear" adults when they say that genital union can have its full meaning only within marriage, because they still need to master the preliminary adolescent personality tasks. A high priority for teens is to understand their sexuality as well as their procreative capacity. Until youth can "own" their fertility more than just intellectually they cannot integrate their sexuality and become mature. Only after coming to terms with the fact that one is now biologically capable of becoming a father or a mother, can a young man or woman integrate awareness of this capacity into choices about present behavior which are consistent with future life goals.

Teen S.T.A.R. approaches the prevention of teen pregnancy by teaching adolescents the biological facts about their capacity to procreate, and the high value that they should attach to that capacity. Instruction in basic reproduction is joined to discussion of the personal, social, intellectual and spiritual implications of sexuality and the exercise of genitality. This makes possible an understanding of the human person as an incarnate spirit, into which the notion of one's body can be integrated, which is radically different from the fragmentation of the genital act into sexual and procreative functions posited by the use of contraception. Those who operate from the notion that response to the human sexual drive is autonomic, on the order of the need to eat or to breathe, embrace a dualistic notion of the human person that in effect denies that our bodies are an integral part of our personhood, and asserts instead that our bodies are beneath our personhood, subject to manipulation.

While the rate of premarital sexual intercourse is over 50 percent beyond age 16 in our general population, the presumption that teens who have become sexually active will continue to be active is not borne out by our experiences in the Teen S.T.A.R. program. Clearly, the freedom of the human person includes sexual freedom; each sexual act is a free choice. There is nothing weird about practicing control in one's sexual activity. Once they are given additional reasons to take into account, many young women and men understand that they cannot enter into a relationship whose fullness is not yet realizable, because they are too immature, or too unschooled to be able to marry and establish a home. In an early study done by the Teen S.T.A.R. program, nearly all of the male participants who were seniors in high school wrote afterwards that the program came much too late in their education. In light of this recommendation the program is now being directed to younger students.

Parental consent and client-teacher confidentiality are required in the Teen S.T.A.R. program, in an attempt to balance the developmental tasks of adolescence with parental responsibility; the early adolescent begins to separate from parents by belonging to a peer group of the same sex and by keeping secrets. In middle adolescence the peer group usually becomes heterosexual, and its values outrank those of the parents. By late adolescence teens begin to make their own decisions, and quite often return to the parental values unless the intervening generational struggles have been so confrontational that they have fixed the teen in an intermediate stage.

Unless parents have begun the sexual education of their children prior to the children's puberty, someone other than the parent needs to shoulder the task initially, because teens are unable to "see" their parents as sexual persons. Once the topic is opened up, parents can express their values and expectations. The Teen S.T.A.R. curriculum is designed to build just such bridges, and has shown that parental involvement which does not violate privacy facilitates growth. On the other hand, the exclusion of parents, as when contraceptives are provided to teens without parental knowledge or consent, may well prolong middle adolescence. The secrecy inherent in such a practice leads to an emotionally-charged relationship between the teens who are the clients of contraceptive clinics and the adults who work in such clinics; this relationship often takes the form of a prolonged dependency of the adolescent clients on the adult workers, which such workers have noted but apparently have not investigated.

None of the instruments used to date to measure emotional growth have reflected the trend toward maturity that the participants in Teen S.T.A.R. have in fact shown: moving away from peer group pressure, making their own decisions, and assuming responsibility for those decisions. The literature is replete with correlations of contraceptive compliance with psychosocial information and high self-image, yet the papers cite as "successes" teen women with a high self-image who, having failed to use their oral contraceptives, abort their babies. Perhaps it is time to look beyond the available scales to explain the reasons for the continuing high teen pregnancy rate, tied into the much higher failure rate of contraceptives in teens which is based partly on inconsistent use and nonuse. Granted that many teens conceive because they wish to, however, the high rate of teen abortions is indisputable evidence that, at least in the area of sexual behavior, a conscious desire to avoid pregnancy does not, of itself, counterbalance youthful romance in all its complexity. The Teen S.T.A.R. program, on the other hand, has helped many adolescents to maintain primary chastity, to reduce previously-begun coital patterns, and to avoid teenage pregnancy in a great many cases. The holistic thrust toward body-person integration appears to be more powerful than the intellectual division between sex and procreation.

* * *

(Adapted in part from *Teen S.T.A.R.: Sexuality Teaching in the Context of Adult Responsibility*, VALUES IN PUBLIC POLICY, G. Reiger, ed. (Washington, D.C.: Family Research Council, 1988), pages 261–271.)

2. COLEEN KELLY MAST

Love and Life and *Sex Respect: The Option for True Sexual Freedom* are two curricula designed to be used in junior and senior high schools to promote chastity and virginity as a vital dimension of sexuality education. Their fundamental message is that human sexuality involves not only the physical dimension of human beings, but also their mental, emotional, and spiritual dimensions as well, and as such, it can secure its true meaning only in the context of marriage. These curricula offer the positive approach of fostering self-control and mature attitudes and values, instead of limiting the discussion of sex to a "value-free" presentation of anatomy and physiology.

Love and Life is a positive, life-affirming presentation of God's plan for life and love. It shows how we learn to live and love within the Church according to God's two greatest commandments and the Beatitudes, which are nurtured in us through our lives in Jesus Christ and which are revealed to us through the love and guidance of the Holy Spirit.

Love and Life focuses on the true meaning of Christian family living. It is through the family that we first experience God's love for us. And it is the family that provides the context for understanding sexual maturity as a life-giving and life-supportive gift from God that respects *all* life and which gives us special powers in God's plan for creation. The sacraments, the liturgy, our prayers, devotions, sacrifices and faithfulness to the commandments, together with the practice of our love for God and neighbor, are presented as the spiritual resources that we need in order to know, love, and serve God as mature, responsible Christians.

Sex Respect is a program similar to *Love and Life,* but it has been carefully developed to reflect a public health perspective, so that it can be used in public schools. It has been approved by the U.S. Department of Health and Human Services, Office of Adolescent Pregnancy Programs, which provided a grant of $300,000 for a three-year pilot study covering several states.

Each curriculum includes three textbooks: a workbook for students, a guidebook for parents, and a manual for teachers. It is important that the schools work with the parents, not against them, on sex education, so that family intimacy will grow. Loving relationships are vital for human beings, especially during the teenage years. Most teenagers involved in premarital sex are searching for love. Merely providing them with contraceptives not only has proven to be ineffective in reducing teenage pregnancies, but also conveys the message that adults do not care about them enough to teach them what love really is.

Both curricula emphasize that human sexuality is not an irresistible urge, as in animals; as intelligent human beings, teenagers have the freedom to choose *not* to have sex before marriage. Thus, each program invites the students to think about the consequences of premarital sex, and shows them that there are, in fact, very good reasons to abstain from premarital sex, since it often does serious physical, emotional, psychological, and spiritual harm to those involved. On the positive side, the programs help the students to understand that sexual self-control can bring freedom, maturity, confidence, and good health in both the physical and spiritual realms.

Both programs have been prepared and tested over several years by professional educators, parents, and teens. Each follows a step-by-step progression that involves the students, parents, and teachers in interactive exercises, discussions, creative writing, and role playing. The materials use a lively, down-to-earth commentary to communicate with teens on their own terms, but with a level of challenge that both motivates and rewards them for good effort. Included are poems, letters, and slogans created by teens for teens. The materials in the *Love and Life* program also draw upon Sacred Scripture, the documents of the Second Vatican Council, and the writings and lives of the saints.

Creative answers are provided for the situations in which the invitation to premarital sex is typically made. The programs also explain the difference between repression and integration, teaching that it is healthy to recognize the sexual drive and how to re-channel that energy into other constructive activities. Understanding and guidance are offered to students who have already had sex, so that they can enjoy a "second virginity," that is, deciding to stop having sex until marriage. Many teenagers who have had sex now regret having made that choice, and wish that they had been told beforehand what the consequences would be.

Although both programs can be used at home, in small groups, or even individually, they have been designed primarily to be taught in junior and senior high schools because teenagers and parents need help in resisting social pressures and in counteracting the distorted view of sexuality presented in the media. The task of educators in either a religious or secular setting is to present virginity in a positive light, despite the cultural promotion of promiscuity. The two curricula do not extend below the junior high school level, on the premise that questions about sex from students below junior high school age should be answered by their parents at home.

* * *

Respect Incorporated
231 East Broadway
P.O. Box 349
Bradley, Illinois 60915

3. MERCEDES ARZU WILSON

Love and Family is a family-centered program of sexuality education that allows the parents to give their children the gift of understanding sexuality as a normal and integral part of their growth and development. The program addresses the critical role of the family unit and the powerful influence of parents in their children's development. Parents participate in helping their children to understand the wonders of sexuality and fertility, and the benefits of family life that come from following moral guidelines.

Love and Family strengthens the family as the first and best source of education in human sexuality for children by:

— involving parents and their children in an educational process based on traditional family values;
— developing and strengthening communication among family members;
— helping parents to identify and communicate their values to their children;
— building and reinforcing the confidence of parents in helping their children through the difficult times of puberty and decision-making;
— providing information about the development of children and adolescents; and
— presenting the latest research about the anatomy and physiology of human fertility, thereby fostering respect for life from the moment of conception.

The program is offered in four sessions:

(1) The importance of the family;
(2) Discovering self-worth and establishing communication;
(3) The normal growth and development of human sexuality;
(4) Respect for human fertility: the wonder of life.

The following is a summary of each of these four sessions.

(1) The Importance of the Family

Early family life and how it is interpreted by the child contributes a great deal to the formation of attitudes, values and behaviors which are likely to endure throughout adult life. While other molding forces, such as schools and friends, also influence attitudes and values, nothing has a greater impact on a child's life than his family experience. When children receive love, affection, and proper training in the home, they will develop the ability to recognize the truth when they see it, and to reject falsehood and propaganda when they encounter it in the outside world.

In educating their children in sexuality, parents must first refute the propaganda that outside "experts" can do the job better than they can. They must establish their authority as the primary educators of their children, by taking an active role in sexuality education. Secondly, they must reject the exploitation and distortion of human sexuality presented in the media, and reaffirm that human sexuality finds its fulfillment only within the enduring commitment of marriage, where love is transformed into children who will carry the family, community, and nation into the future.

Parents will be able to accomplish these goals by providing a daily model of attitudes and values about life and sexuality; by guarding their children from sexually explicit material, which tends to break down children's natural modesty; by being available to their children for support and questions; and by faithfully living out their own commitments as husbands and wives, as fathers and mothers. Children who are taught to love and respect themselves and others, who receive loving discipline from their parents, and who observe and are inspired by the generosity and gentleness of their parents, will have a realistic optimism toward the future. On the other hand, if love is not provided in generous amounts by their parents, children will usually seek it in the first person who gives them any kind of serious attention.

One of the strongest pressures that children, especially adolescents, encounter outside the home is that which is exerted by their peers. In order to be secure enough to resist this pressure, children need to experience strong and loving parental leadership within the family. Even apparently rebellious teenagers respect and trust parents who are not afraid to be strong leaders; they need and want their parents to be in charge. Thus, parental support and reinforcement are vital if their children are to have the courage that is often necessary to act contrary to the sexual mores of their peers.

Above all, the adherence by children to the values of sexual morality that they have been taught by their parents will depend upon the fidelity, respect, and generosity that they observe in their parents' own marriage. Almost always, successful parents are first of all successful spouses.

(2) Discovering Self-worth and Establishing Communication

Every person is born with self-worth, an inherent value and dignity that cannot be forfeited or taken away. Children whose parents are able to help them to discover their inherent dignity as persons are likely to grow into healthy adults who are capable of giving and receiving love in their turn.

The absence of the childhood experience of being loved and cherished frequently shows up in adolescence when young people attempt to find love and acceptance among their peers, often through sexual activity. Often they do not understand that this kind of behavior is motivated by a desire to feel important and needed. Thus, parental love is a strong deterrent to inappropriate sexual behavior during the years of growing and maturing: if children receive love in the home, they are less likely to seek it elsewhere.

Helping a child to discover his or her self-worth does not consist in indulging the child's whims, but in showing forgiveness and reverence, even when the child has failed. Discipline should be loving and directed to the correction of the problem rather than to the destruction of the spirit of hopefulness within the heart of the child. Sometimes parents feel guilty because they have not given their children enough time or attention, and they try to compensate for this with material gifts. This is not done for the children, but to make the parents feel better. Especially when families enjoy material prosperity, the parents will have to discipline themselves by not giving too many things to their children. Instead, parents should concentrate on showing affection, trust, and recognition for good behavior.

(3) The Normal Growth and Development of Human Sexuality

For a young person, the proper understanding of sexuality is not something that occurs because a parent has explained human sexuality well in a one-time discussion. Chastity formation is part of a youngster's identity formation and begins long before the teenage years.

As a young person's sexuality begins to manifest itself in physical and emotional changes, it becomes part of the instinctive desire to achieve an adult identity. Society, too, begins to have different expectations of them. They are capable of more responsibility and better judgment. However, it also takes time for them to assimilate their new feelings and sensations, to name them, to become acquainted with them, and to learn how to live with them. At this time, parents should speak straightforwardly with their children about sexual morality, appropriate behavior, the advantages of chastity, and the catastrophic consequences of premarital sexual activity. It is particularly important to explain how boys and girls differ in the way that they perceive love, sex, and the relationship between the two.

Teenagers should be helped to understand that self-control and self-discipline are an intrinsic part of being an adult, and that their sexual behavior needs to be incorporated into this process just as much as are other aspects of their lives. They need to learn that sexual maturity does not mean removing the barriers to sexual activity, but the ability to control their actions. Such discipline needs to have been taught from early childhood if a young person is going to be able to draw upon it during the turbulent period of adolescence.

It is the task of parents and educators to assure young people that they are capable of leading ordered and responsible sexual lives. The promotion of contraceptives at home or in schools sends precisely the wrong signal: it implicitly says that adults

319

consider adolescents to be weak and incapable of controlling their sexual impulses, like animals. The only thing to be done is to try to minimize the inconvenient consequences to parents and society of adolescents' promiscuous behavior. Parents who were able to contain their sexual desires before marriage should not allow themselves to be deceived into believing that this generation of young people cannot do the same thing. On the other hand, parental lack of confidence in teenagers' ability to control themselves may well reflect a lack of self-control by the parents themselves.

(4) Respect for Human Fertility: the Wonder of Life

"Fertility" refers to the ability to participate in the creation of life. "Human fertility" is the combined power of a man and a woman to participate in the creation of a new human life. Human sexuality is not just a biological function which serves only for reproduction; it serves also as a powerful support and expression of love between the spouses.

Therefore, while some knowledge of the body's reproductive system is necessary in order to appreciate human fertility, it is not sufficient. To fully appreciate human fertility requires an understanding of all the spiritual, physical, intellectual, cultural, and emotional aspects of being masculine and feminine. This becomes especially clear, in a positive way, in the explanation and practice of Natural Family Planning. It also becomes apparent, in a negative way, through an examination of the harmful effects that come from the attacks on human fertility in the form of contraception, sterilization, *in vitro* fertilization, abortion, and pornography. Each of these in its own way tries to isolate or undo the generation of new human life and the expression of love in human sexuality.

A proper understanding of human fertility leads to several important conclusions:

(1) human life must be respected and protected from all destruction or exploitation from the moment of conception;

(2) the harm caused by sexually transmitted diseases will never be eliminated solely by medical research and treatment, but only by adherence to the norms of sexual morality;

(3) new human life deserves the protection of a stable, monogamous marriage; in the case of teenage pregnancy, for example, it is not wise to pressure young teenagers into a marriage that would likely fail.

In conclusion, it is imperative that the family be protected, and that the laws and institutions of society do not offend, but rather support and defend the family's rights and duties. The family is where the wonders of human sexuality and fertility are conveyed to each successive generation, and where a society's future is determined.

* * *

Family of the Americas Foundation, Inc.
P.O. Box 219
Mandeville, Louisiana 70470-0219

Chapter 21

THE CONTRACEPTIVE CULTURE

George Gilder

In *Humanae vitae* Pope Paul VI wrote the great prophetic document of our time. In fact, it might be better called a document against our time, because it flouted the most powerful beliefs of our culture, this "contraceptive culture" as it has been termed. It might also be termed the "abortive culture" because abortions are the unavoidable harvest of a society devoted to contraception as the favored condition of the act of love. It might even be called the "looking for love in all the wrong places culture." But whatever we call it, the Pope exactly identified its

Mr. Gilder's address was adapted from material which subsequently appeared in his book, MICROCOSM: THE QUANTUM REVOLUTION IN ECONOMICS AND TECHNOLOGY, published by Simon and Schuster in 1989.

fundamental problem, and made a number of very specific prophecies about the result of its spread. He said that men would come to objectify women, that they would leave their families, that general immorality would emerge. He exactly identified the set of problems that currently is sweeping through the United States, and that poses the single most serious threat to the future of the nation.

Let me say at the outset that I am no enemy of modernity; I embrace modernity, for I believe that it offers great promise for all human societies. Our science and technology afford incomparable vistas of opportunity. But we may well come a cropper on this most fundamental point, which the Pope expounded in his great prophetic document of 1968.

The fundamental point of the contraceptive culture is hedonism: the sovereignty of pleasure. This is really the religion of the day—the belief that pleasure is the fundamental motive force in all human life. It is at the root of much of the social theory taught in our universities: the idea that the society can be treated as a collection of individuals optimizing for pleasure. Beyond this collective belief is an implicit assumption that pleasure is primarily physiological, that it consists in the gratification of bodily needs and desires.

This belief is heavily manifest in psychiatry, which in general is based on the assumption that mental illness can be overcome by contemplating oneself. This does not mean contemplating oneself in all the dimensions of one's being, as in the sacrament of Confession. It means contemplating oneself with a "contraceptive," a contraceptive against spirit, which means a contraceptive against conscience, against the recognition of sin and guilt and need for God's forgiveness. In the prevailing psychology, we are invited to contemplate a truncated version of self, a self estranged from God. The pursuit of pleasure, therefore, is really a pursuit of a truncated self, estranged from God. This pursuit of a God-forsaken happiness is itself the primary mental illness of our times. When practiced in this way, psychiatry itself is the fundamental mental illness.

This pursuit of pleasure and this vision of human beings has even deeper roots; it is a more far-reaching religion than can be identified in psychiatric terms. The real enemy that the Pope is attacking in *Humanae vitae* is materialism, and materialism embraces far more than just the preoccupation with self in bodily terms. The contraception against spirit implicit in the vision of man as a materialist pleasure-seeker also leads to a numbing suppression of life, which is meaningless without spirit. The selfishness of hedonism fosters a barren amorality that not only severs the pleasure seeker from the sustaining life of new generations but also destroys the moral compass and goal of his own intellectual life. A culture based on the materialist pursuit of pleasure can ultimately support neither science or philosophy.

For all the claims of enlightenment and all the achievements of technology, most scientists and other intellectuals for more than two centuries have been dedicated to the overthrow and suppression of mind itself. Intellectuals have pursued an agenda of self-destruction best described as materialist determinism. This materialism, in fact, is the primary religion of the last three hundred years. Today, for the first time, we have a chance to overcome this religion and to restore real religion in the culture of our time. To do so, however, we must overcome the most deeply entrenched beliefs of the secular intelligentsia that dominates the media, the culture, and the universities.

This belief in materialism, this effort to overthrow mind and spirit and replace it with inert, blind, meaningless matter, originated in the great scientific triumph of the seventeenth century, Newtonian physics. Isaac Newton was himself a deist but he had a vision of the world that was profoundly materialistic and determinist. He believed that at the basis of the universe were solid, immutable, impenetrable, inert, mindless, blind bits of matter, and that the universe is built up from these bits of matter in a great determinist machine, like the workings of a clock. Although he acknowledged the need for a watchmaker-God, this need was readily rejected by those who exulted in the enormous power over nature that Newtonian machines gave them in an immediate way.

This is a world in which choice plays no role. Pierre Laplace followed Newtonian physics to its logical conclusion with his famous assertion that if he knew at one instant the positions and motions of every particle in the universe, he could theoretically compute its entire past and future.

Man subsists not on his practical possibilities but on his ultimate philosophies, which he inexorably transforms into his religions. Materialist determinism became the implicit religion of science and the most profound enemy of all other religion and morality.

What mattered was not the practicality but the teleology and eschatology of determinist science: the goal of a thinking machine, the reduction of the brain to a material paradigm, the apparently continuing march of knowledge toward a fully mechanistic determinism. Even as the scientist promised to prolong life and enrich its pleasures, he seemed resolved to destroy its meaning.

As Nobel Laureate Steven Weinberg puts it, "The more the universe becomes comprehensible, the more it also seems pointless." Many physicists still entertain with interest Ludwig Boltzmann's hypothesis that the visible universe is just an improbable fluctuation—a rare disequilibrium—amid a predetermined whirl down the entropic drain. The scientific revelation believed to underlie all the heroic achievements of modern man, that provides him his addictive wealth and comfort, his sustenance and support and his hope for health and happiness, is a revelation of eternal death.

Contributing to the vision of materialist determinism was the computer. Even human intelligence, the unique special claim of the species on its road to ruin, was seen as likely to succumb to a mechanistic rival. In gaining dominion over the world, we lose control of our own machines.

When switching speeds plummeted into the picosecond range (trillionths of a second), it seemed plausible to many analysts that for all its user friendliness and endearing idiosyncrasies—such as "common sense"—the brain was no longer "merely a computer," but was in fact far inferior to computers in speed and computing power. Theorists estimated that the human brain contains some 10 billion neurons (a number of switching devices within the reach of the supercomputing technology of the next decade) and each neuron switches at only one millionth of the speed of an advanced transistor.

The computer thus lent enormous new authority to the determinist vision. Not only could it be used to achieve enormous new advances across the range of the scientific enterprise but the computer itself constituted a paradigm for comprehending the very fabric of thought in materialist terms. The computer seemed to subordinate thoughts themselves to things, mind to matter, soul to solid state physics. It seemed to unmask the mind and demystify it, and thus to banish sacred and spiritual powers from the world.

Deeply believing—whether at some subconscious level or in a conscious paradigm of research—that human mastery of nature would end by destroying the mystery of human nature, the Western intelligentsia gullibly adopted a medley of materialist determinisms. From Marxism to behavioralism, from routine evolutionism to logical positivism, from deconstructionism to reflex psychology, scientists and scholars produced an unending stream of theories that reduced man to a mechanism.

Artists always tend to follow the prevailing science, often with a lag as long as a century. Converging on the culture from every hall of academe, scientific determinism prompted a bizarre stream of doom-laden or absurdist works of art and literature. The most prestigious novelists—from William Faulkner and George Orwell to John O'Hara and Robert Stone—left man in the twentieth century as arrant a victim of inexorable fate as he was in the great god-ruled tragedies of the ancient Greeks.

The counterpoint of determinism was existentialism. With history a saga of blind fate, heroism emerged chiefly as anarchic revolt by defiant individuals, supermen who leaped onto the stage abandoned by the gods and hurled thunderbolts of rebellion at the clockwork world. But by their very desperation and frenzy—and ultimate futility—the existentialist rebels seemed to vindicate the determinist philosophers.

With science believed to be abandoning man, and the dignity of his soul, men rose up to claim the dignity of science for squalid temporal schemes of the state and to ascribe soul to the new machines. After contributing indispensably to the rise of science, religions began renouncing the great human enterprise of understanding and mastering nature, and thus failed to comprehend the real message of the scientific revelation of God.

Laboring desperately to reassemble the smithereens of a shattered grail of faith, the public clutched at a new pagan polytheism. Materialist intellectuals widely worshiped the god of the machine, artists reveled in the god of the senses, and churches retreated to a preindustrial vision of an ecological Eden. Even the most sophisticated apologists of religion expressed a nostalgia for Newton's cosmos as a causal clockwork and God as a watchmaker. People came to believe in a religion that resembles very closely that of the pygmies in the jungle; in other words, they believe only in things that they can see, and touch, and measure. The pygmies worship the sun, the trees, and the world; the modern intellectuals worship the measurable, palpable, visible, mechanical kinds of phenomena that their senses can present to them, and deny as a matter of principle all dimensions beyond these domains. The people in the jungle, however, have at least this advantage: they believe that the trees are fundamentally alive.

In presenting this idea of materialist determinism, science is playing with a fear afflicting the very heart of modern man. The fear is rarely declared to the world, but its outlines can be clearly descried in the culture of the time. Indeed, it is a fear that suffuses most of the art, literature, and philosophy of the West. The highest purpose of the leading universities, for example, seems to be to reduce philosophy to a mechanical positivism, to reduce history to statistical fluctuations and class exploitations, to deconstruct literature to a flux of words and writers' neuroses, and to banish heroes from human life.

The underlying vision emerges as a fable. Modern science grants us incomparable riches, but only as part of a Faustian pact: a deal with the devil whereby we gain wondrous machines in exchange for our very souls. We give the scientist first our money and then the very meaning of our lives.

Plunging into the world of modern science, from this point of view, we lose first our human dignity and then our free will. The physical world is ultimately a tomb: the death site of both God and man. God dies with the eclipse of the Creator and the end of meaning. With the death of human dignity and uniqueness, man degenerates into a mere intelligent machine that differs from a computer chiefly by thinking more slowly and by more quickly and irremediably wearing out. As the capstone of the nihilist enterprise, science as a creation of free human minds also perishes in the microtomb.

Yet all this anguish and ardor—all the fatalist philosophies of nihilism and existentialism—are mere delusions arising from the great modern superstition of materialism. Refuted by an entire century of modern science and by the findings of computer theory itself, materialist determinism falls of its own weight.

The overthrow of matter reached its climax in the physical sciences when quantum theory capsized the rules that once governed and identified all solid objects. There is good news from modern science, subverting the contraceptive culture of materialism that banishes spirit from the domains of human life. Quantum theory is the basic physics of today; it as a vision is profoundly different from the Newtonian vision. Rather than finding at the foundation of all matter inert, blind, impenetrable, blank particles, physicists now agree that matter derives from waves, fields, and probabilities. To comprehend nature, we have to stop thinking of the world as basically material and begin imagining it as a manifestation of consciousness.

The fundamental entities in quantum theory are wave-particles, a profound paradox that was first launched in 1887 when Albert Michelson and E. W. Morley did their famous experiments that showed that there is no ether in the universe. Until the experiments of Michelson and Morley, the fundamental belief was that the universe is filled with solid matter, which would be needed as the medium through which light waves could propagate. Earlier experiments had demonstrated conclusively that light is a wave; it was assumed, therefore, that there must be a material medium through which the waves of light could travel. By dispelling the notion of ether as the luminiferous medium bearing light, Michelson and Morley effectively banished most of the matter from the universe.

Light thus emerged as an esoteric paradox of waves without substance traveling at a fixed speed in relation to a medium without substance. In 1905, in a Nobel Prize-winning paper, Albert Einstein declared that if there was no ether, light could not be a wave. It had nothing to wave through. Extending the insight of another earlier researcher, Max Planck, Einstein said that light consisted of quanta—packets of energy—that he called photons. Although said to be "particles," photons observed the equations of wave motion developed by James Clerk Maxwell in the 1860's. They seemed to be a cross between a wave and a particle.

In terms both of classical physics and of human observation, this wave-particle cross was an impossible contradiction. Waves ripple infinitely forth through a material medium; particles are single points of matter. At once definite and infinite, a particle that is also a wave defies our sensory experience. Newton's universe, built of solid, hard, impenetrable, movable particles was foundering.

The overthrow of matter afflicted the theory of physics with contradiction and paradox. In successive steps, Niels Bohr, Louis de Broglie, Werner Heisenberg, and others showed that not only light, but also electrons, protons, neutrons, and other atomic "particles" likewise exhibited wave action. Eventually, the paradoxical duality of wave-particles would come to exclude all materialistic logic; in the usual way, quantum physics does not make materialist sense.

Quantum physics can make sense, however, if it is treated in part as a domain of ideas, governed less by the laws of matter than by the laws of mind. The paradoxical stuff of the quantum domain, atomic phenomena seem to represent the still mysterious domain between matter and mind, where matter evanesces into probability fields of information and mind assumes the physical forms of waves and particles. Even paradox, a perplexity for things, is a relatively routine property of thoughts. Conceiving of the quantum world as a domain of ideas, we make it accessible to our minds. The quantum atom is largely an atom of information, a rich domain of information at the foundation of matter.

Thus, the fundamental entity in quantum theory is a cross, a cross between a wave, which is infinite in extent, propagating infinitely through its surrounding medium, and a particle, a point of no extent. All the universe is based on these crosses of waves and particles which are utterly paradoxical, but which accord very deeply with the fundamental paradoxes of the Christian religion: the Word made flesh, the God-Man, the eternal and the temporal, the infinite and the particular. In place of what had been an inert, blind bit of matter at the foundation of the universe, we find a cross.

The second great breakthrough in recent times came in 1975, when neurosurgeon Wilder Penfield reported discoveries that in the historic saga of the downfall of materialism may rival even the experiments of Michelson and Morley nearly a century before. While Michelson and Morley combed the cosmos seeking signs of material ether, Penfield pored through the material brain looking for signs of mind.

Penfield's researches were altogether as unique and unprecedented as the ether tests. He performed surgery on 1,132 epileptics over a thirty-year period. After removing a part of the skull of the patient under anesthesia, he would bring him back to full consciousness. Then Penfield would explore the brain widely with an electronic probe. Since the brain lacks sensitivity, the patient, though fully alert, could feel no physical pain.

With the patient guiding the surgeon's explorations and reporting the results of stimuli at different cerebral sites, the doctor would often find and remove the cause of the epilepsy. In the process of pursuing this procedure with more than a thousand patients, Penfield gained a unique and voluminous body of data on the responses of different parts of the brain to an electrical stimulus. Combining these experimental findings with extensive studies of epileptic effects—also consisting of localized electrical bombardment of regions of the brain—Penfield made many original contributions to the mapping of brain functions. But as in the case of Michelson and Morley's ether tests, more important than all his findings was a momentous absence. Nowhere in the brain did he discover any evidence of mind: the consciously deciding, willing, imagining, and creative force in human thought.

Penfield sums up his conclusion:

> The electrode can present to the patient various crude sensations. It can cause him to turn head and eyes, or to move the limbs, or to vocalize and swallow. It may recall vivid re-experience of the past, or present to him an illusion that present experience is familiar, or that the things he sees are growing large and coming near. But he remains aloof. He passes judgment on it all. He says, "Things are growing larger" but he does not move for

331

fear of being run over. If the electrode moves his right hand, he does not say "I wanted to move it." He may, however, reach over with the left hand and oppose his action.

Penfield found that the content of consciousness could be selectively altered by outside manipulation. But however much he probed, he could not enter consciousness itself. He could not find the mind or invade its autonomy.

Penfield concludes: "The patient's mind, which is considering the situation in such an aloof and critical manner, can only be something quite apart from neuronal reflex action. . . . Although the content of consciousness depends in large measure on neuronal activity, awareness itself does not."

Like Michelson and Morley before him, Penfield began his investigations with the goal of proving the materialist superstition. Like them, he failed utterly. "I like other scientists have struggled to prove that the brain accounts for the mind." Instead, he showed that the critical elements of mind—consciousness, will, commitment, decision, reason—are not locally manifest in the brain.

The intruding scientist could affect contents but not consciousness. The brain's activity always occurred within the dominating and enveloping radiance of an autonomous mind. Some epileptic seizures would break the brain's connection with the mind. As a result, the person would become an automaton. Like a programmed computer, he could proceed with his existing activities—walk down a street or even drive a car. But he could not change his course or adapt to unexpected developments.

While Penfield's electrodes could cause specific events, he could not usurp awareness of them; the patient could always distinguish between authentic mental processes he had willed and processes evoked by the probe. Stampedes of electrons could not cause a conscious whim in the mind, but a whim of the consciousness could cause stampedes of organized electrical and chemical activity in the brain.

Penfield's book is entitled *The Mysteries of the Mind,* but he did not purport to have resolved them before he died about eight years ago. But his conclusion accords with the reports of anguished armies of other investigators throughout the domains of cognitive science, neurophysiology, and artificial intelligence.

Computer pioneer Norbert Weiner made the essential point as early as 1948: "The mechanical brain does not secrete thought 'as the liver does bile,' as the earlier materialists claimed, nor does it put it out in the form of energy as the muscle puts out its activity. Information is information, not matter or energy. No materialism that does not admit this can survive at the present day."

The brain is a kind of computer. But it differs sharply from existing electronic computers. The kind of electrical probe used by Penfield would utterly scramble a microprocessor. Unlike a computer, the brain claimed a level of consciousness transcending local neuronal activity.

If the brain cannot function without a human mind, it should not be surprising that a computer cannot function without a human mind either. The idea of the computer as a mind is an idol of the materialist superstition. The human brain serves the mind. The artificial intelligence vanguard wanted to show that the mind was merely brain in order to support the feasibility of building computer minds. But the industry will now have to give up its goal of usurping mind and focus more effectively on serving it, as the brain does.

In his book, Penfield gave a clearer view of the relationship between mind, brain, and computer: "Because it seems to me certain that it will always be quite impossible to explain the mind on the basis of neuronal action within the brain . . . and because a computer (which the brain is) must be programmed and operated by an agency capable of independent understanding, I am forced to choose the proposition that our being is to be explained on the basis of two fundamental elements." He sums up: "The mind seems to act independently of the brain in the same sense that a programmer acts independently of this computer, however much he may depend upon the action of that computer for certain purposes."

Penfield's researches were compelling and unprecedented. But it is impossible to prove a negative. That his elaborate probes and epileptic bombardments failed to find the mind in neuronal activity does not establish that the mind is not matter. In the long run there is a more powerful reason for rejecting the computer as support for materialism. As we have seen, the same quantum revolution that made possible the computer is destroying other materialist superstitions as well.

In the atomic domain, we do not find Newton's lifeless, opaque, inert, and impenetrable bits of matter. We find a high drama of richly intelligible activity, shaped by mathematical possibilities and probabilities, where electrons combine and disappear without occupying conventional time or space, and things obey the laws of mind rather than the laws of matter. Things combine and collapse, emerge and vanish, like tokens of thought more than like particles of mass. In other words, both at the highest levels of nature where meanings, purposes, structures, functions, and other conceptual entities prevail, so at the fundamental level of physical reality, thought dominates things.

The reverberations of this change sweep through social science as well. Gone is the view of a thermodynamic world economy, dominated by "natural resources" being tuned to entropy and waste by human extraction and use. Once seen as a physical system tending toward exhaustion and decline, the world economy has clearly emerged as an intellectual system driven by knowledge. The key fact of knowledge is that it is anti-entropic: it accumulates and compounds as it is used. Technological and scientific enterprise, so it turns out in the age of the quantum, generates gains in new learning and ideas that dwarf the loss of resources and dissipation of energy. The efforts that ended in writing "$E = mc^2$" or in contriving the formula for a new photovoltaic cell or in inventing a design for a silicon compiler—or in spreading the message of a moral God—are not usefully analyzed in the images of entropy. To see the world primarily in terms of its waste products is possibly the most perverse vision in the history of science. The history of ideas cannot be comprehended as an entropic cycle of the production and disposal of paper products.

The materialist superstition succumbs to an increasing recognition that the means of production in capitalism are not chiefly land, labor, and machines, present in all systems, but emancipated human intelligence. Capitalism—supremely the mind-centered system—finds the driving force of its growth in innovation and discovery. In the age of the quantum, value added shifts rapidly

334

from the extraction, movement, manipulation, and exhaustion of mass to the creative accumulation of information and ideas.

At the heart of this progress is a bold human sacrifice. After centuries of struggle against the elements—human masses pushing and pulling on massive objects at the behest of armed rulers—man stopped hoarding gold and jewels, land and labor. He stopped trusting only the things he could touch and feel. He stopped believing only his eyes and ears. At last relinquishing the sensory world, he gained access to a higher power and truth. And all those other things are being added unto him.

Overthrowing the superstitions of materialism—of anthropomorphic physics, of triumphant entropy, of class conflict and exploitation, of national and tribal bigotry—modern man is injecting the universe with the germ of his intelligence, the spoor of his mind. Sloughing off every layer of macrocosmic apparatus, the computer will ultimately collapse to a pinhead that can respond to the human voice. In this form, human intelligence can be transmitted to any tool or appliance, to any part of our environment. Thus the triumph of the computer does not dehumanize the world; it makes our environment more subject to human will.

Giving up the superficial comforts of a human-scale world, mankind moves to mind scale. In the image of his Creator, he exalts the truly human—and godlike—dimension of his greatest gift from the Creator: his creativity. Giving up the material idols and totems in his ken, he is gaining at last his promised dominion over the world and its creatures.

The key lessons of the era spring from an understanding of hierarchy and freedom rather than of topology and determinism. Just as the large integrated circuits at the heart of computers cannot be designed from the bottom up, just as evolution could not have occurred from the bottom up alone, the human mind cannot be understood without a clear comprehension of the hierarchical structure of the universe.

The key error of materialism is to subordinate a higher level of creative activity to a lower one: the dramas of humanity to the determinations of lifeless and unintelligible monads of matter. Opening the atom to find a world of information, we discover that the inverted hierarchies of materialism are as false empirically as the ancient philosophers found them bankrupt logically.

In the hierarchies of nature, the higher orders cannot be reduced to the sum of their parts. Even the concept of wholes and parts is misleading; every part is also a whole, and every whole is also a part in a higher order of meaning.

The long dream of physicists that by studying the structure of atoms we could comprehend the purpose of nature, or the dream of biologists that the study of evolution would reveal the meaning of life, have both proved false. In the same way, neither the physics nor the chemistry of DNA will explain the code of genetic information any more than the analysis of spectrograms will reveal the meaning of a word or phrase.

Far from a model of human intelligence that might excel its creator, the computer offers a very limited perspective on mind. The usual assumption of materialism is that the brain, the hardware, comes first and mind somehow emerges from it. But the computer offers a contrary example. The computer design itself is a software program and determines the structure of the electronic circuitry that constitutes the computer. Similarly, the brain consists of a rich panoply of neuro-physiological processes that serve as analogs for physical experience and perception. Yet neither system can function as an information tool without a consciousness to interpret the information.

Knowing the location of every electronic charge and connection in either brain or computer gives scarcely a clue of its purpose. It is the human mind that brings meaning or semantic content to the syntax of the machine, whether hardware, software, or wetware. The higher-level languages of software lend significance to the dumb electrons circulating through the system. But the language is still sterile until it is translated by the human consciousness. Neither brain nor computer could think without an embracing presence of mind. The higher-level languages of software do not obviate the need for a controlling intelligence that transcends them.

Any lower level of existence finds meaning only in higher orders outside itself. Physics finds meaning largely in chemistry, biology in man, and man both in knowledge and culture and in that higher level of meaning ordained by God. The study of science is thrilling and rewarding on its own level, and imparts new powers and technologies for action on higher levels. But

336

movement up a hierarchy leads to domains of increasing freedom and dignity and spiritual fulfillment, not into a materialist or determinist trap.

In his efflorescent exposition of *The Age of Intelligent Machines,* Raymond Kurzweil cites the phenomenon of dreams to show how humans might imagine themselves free in a determined world. In dreams, he says, we have an illusion of freedom and choice that vanishes when we awaken. But surely this analogy is wrong. The very essence of a dream—or a nightmare—is a sense of being carried away beyond choice or control. Whether in relief or anguish, we awaken to freedom. In assuming consciousness, we move up the hierarchy from involuntary association and drift, to voluntary action and purpose.

The entire history of technology suggests a similar awakening to new powers and horizons, new freedoms and opportunities. The new age of intelligent machines will enhance and empower humanity, making possible new ventures into outer space and new insights into atomic structure. It will relieve man of much of his most onerous and unsatisfying work. It will extend his lifespan and enrich his perceptual reach. It will enlarge his freedom and his global command. It will diminish despots and exploiters. It may even improve music and philosophy.

Overthrowing matter, humanity also escapes from the traps and compulsions of pleasure into a higher morality of spirit. The pleasure principle is the governing force of a physical determinism, whether in psychology, sociology, or economics. Physiologically defined, pleasure makes the materialist world go round. Optimizing for bodily pleasures, human beings can take their place in a determinist scheme. Believing in determinism, they can escape the burdens of a higher morality.

Pleasure seeking is entropy in social life. It leads to the image of dissipation as the effect of happiness. Moving in the direction of entropic forces—sliding down the gradients of our physiology—we live in a world of Boltzmann's laws rather than of his life and creations.

Overthrowing all forms of materialist determinism, however, the world of the quantum imposes its own more rigorous laws of freedom and responsibility. Requiring long planning and sacrifice and exacting disciplines, this microcosmic world epitomizes the longer horizons and altruistic rules of life in the image of the Creator. The exaltation of mind and spirit leads to a higher order of experience and a richer access of power than any of the forms of physical dominance and exploitation that pervade the precincts of material pleasure. The first victim of the hedonistic vision is the disciplined quest for knowledge and truth.

Far from being a heuristic tool, the materialist assumption stultifies science itself. Any science becomes self-contradictory when it attributes to its object of study a nature that renders the science itself inexplicable or unintelligible. An intellectual theory that materializes or mechanizes theorists is self-defeating. Behavioral psychology, determinist biology, materialist physics and evolution are all mere gibberish because they explain away the scientist himself and his transcendent pursuit of truth.

The entire history of the twentieth century testifies to the bitter fruits of sacrificing the scientist to the science. Nazism, Marxism, and all the other diseases of politics feed on the belief in some final truth, worthy of some final physical enactment, to which all the mere scientists themselves must succumb. But science is meaningless outside of the unending enterprise of search and discovery, in freedom and faith, by the community of explorers themselves. Outside of the living fabric of knowledge in the minds of believers, free to search for God, beliefs themselves become idols of destruction.

Matter is subordinate to mind and spirit and can only be comprehended by free men. As computers master new levels of the hierarchy of knowledge, human beings can rise to new pinnacles of vision and power and discover new continents of higher truth. As Carver Mead declared in his defense of Boltzmann, the universe offers infinite degrees of freedom. The computer will give mankind new vessels to rule the waves of possibility. Its promise can be betrayed only by the abandonment of the freedom and faith that made it possible.

Wielding the power of knowledge, the human mind is the great and growing disequilibrium at the center of the universe. Made in the image of its creator, human mind wields the power of knowledge against the powers of decay. Conquering the world of the quantum, mind transcends every entropic trap and overthrows matter itself. This is the true significance and meaning of the quantum era.

Near the end of his book, Penfield reflects on the further fruits of the overthrow of matter. "What a thrill, then, to discover that the scientist, too, can legitimately believe in the existence of the spirit!" Writing toward the end of his life, he observes that while the brain and body, memory and muscle, deteriorate, the mind suffers "no peculiar or inevitable pathology. Late in life it moves to its own fulfillment. As the mind arrives at clearer understanding and better balanced judgment, the other two are beginning to fail. . . ."

Recently I read Malcolm Muggeridge's latest book, published when he was 86 years old, an exquisitely written, eloquent exposition of his pilgrimage. It shows that there certainly has been no significant deterioration in his mind. A few weeks ago, at a similar age, Peter Drucker wrote one of the best columns of his life. In these and other famous people, we see borne out the proposition that the mind, despite its intimate connection with the brain and its manifestation through the brain, which clearly does in some sense decay, can persist with ever greater clarity and power.

Writing "from the physician's point of view," Penfield suggests, "in conformity with the proposition that the mind has a separate existence, it might even be taken as an argument for the feasibility and possibility of immortality!"

In the beginning was the word, the idea. By crashing into the inner sanctums of the material world, mankind overcame the regnant superstitions of matter and regained contact with the primal powers of mind and spirit. Those new powers have rendered obsolete all the materialist fantasies of the past: the notion that by comprehending things, one could understand thought, and that by controlling things, one could rule the world. We have entered the epoch of free men and women scaling the hierarchies of faith and truth seeking the sources of light.

I realize that the arguments that I have put forth against materialist determinism, and in support of human dignity and freedom and of the spiritual nature of the mind, are essentially secular in nature. These are truths that we know by revelation and faith. It is valid to make the secular arguments because the religious arguments of the Church are all true, and because they are true, they apply everywhere. Anywhere one pursues the truth deeply, be it in science or in any other field, he will discover the same realities that the Church reveals. At the same time, it is useful to present the secular arguments because, while the overthrow of matter by mind continues across a wide range of the sciences, the rebirth of mind must combat some of the deepest superstitions of intellectual culture and society, including the realm of organized religion. Even today we find the widespread adoption by the leadership of certain churches of what amounts to a materialist religion. Thus, it is often necessary to have recourse to arguments that do not depend upon the invocation of religious authority.

In economics, for example, I am often frustrated to find very religious people who again want to clutch to the materialist vision of the economy, appealing to such notions as incentive structures that operate in a mechanical way. It is really the old Newtonian machine as developed by Adam Smith and propounded in economics, and it is just as false. Yet such people do not want to believe that religious truths are absolutely essential to the economic domain, and are indispensable to the operation of the "invisible hand" which Adam Smith describes.

The reasons for the triumph of the pleasure principle, this fatalism in both psychology and physics, this belief that the world is all headed toward an eschatology of lukewarm gas, is being overthrown from the precincts of science itself. This provides us with a great weapon in the natural order to fight the absurdities of current policies that are based on a similar contraception against spirit and against the biblical truths that the Pope has been expounding. It leads to the possibility of asserting with ever greater confidence what *Humanae vitae* asserts: "Marriage is not, then, the effect of chance or the production of evolution of unconscious natural forces; it is the wise institution of the Creator to realize in mankind his design of love." When this contraception is removed, it then becomes possible to achieve the true spiritual pleasures which are the deepest and most important and the essential gratifications of marriage.

At the same time, however, we cannot prevail without the aggressive, persistent, courageous, and implacable leadership of the Church. This is indispensable. The Church has been providing

340

this leadership in recent years to a great extent, and certainly there is no better example of it than *Humanae vitae* itself. Without such leadership, we cannot prevail in the long run; materialism is too powerful and too deeply entrenched.

We are now in the beginning of a new epoch in which these materialist philosophies will collapse at every hand, almost universally. The one point on which I did not agree with Malcolm Muggeridge in his book is the notion that the decay of Western civilization is beyond recovery. On the contrary: this is an immensely hopeful moment in world history. I only hope that we will have the good sense to take advantage of it.

Chapter 22

STRAIGHT TALK ABOUT CONTRACEPTION: THE CHURCH'S "YES" TO THE GIFT OF LIFE

John M. Haas

The truth of the teaching on contraception in *Humanae vitae* is unfortunately not self-evident—not even to sincere Christians. Both my wife and I were raised in devout Protestant households. We went to church at least every Sunday as I was growing up. We frequently read and discussed Scripture together as a family. My father taught adult Sunday School well over twenty years until the day he died.

Published in *Crisis* February, 1989, pp. 32–38. Reprinted here with permission. Crisis Magazine, P.O. Box 1006, Notre Dame, IN.

We tried to be faithful Christians and prayed to God to help us lead a moral life. Part of that moral life for married Christians was, in our opinion, the use of contraceptives to determine the size of the family. We did not simply tolerate the use of contraceptives as a lesser evil to achieve a greater good. There was no ambivalence about it. Contraception was, in our minds, a moral good. I still remember the minister from the pulpit enjoining the married members of his congregation to contracept and limit the size of their families. For the married, contraception was virtually morally obligatory!

Nevertheless, through God's grace, we had come to the decision to become Roman Catholics. I still could not understand the Church's position on contraception. Yet the more I thought about this question, the more it seemed unreasonable that the Catholic Church could be correct with all her other teachings and be wrong in this one small, yet terribly important matter. I was ready and willing to accept Catholic teaching on the seven sacraments, the hierarchical ministry, the immaculate conception and assumption of the Blessed Virgin, papal infallibility, transubstantiation. So in the final analysis it just did not seem reasonable that the Church could be correct about all these matters and wrong about contraception. So initially I accepted the teaching on contraception on the basis of the Church's authority. The Church had been given the divine mandate to teach all nations and to lead them to the truth. I had to trust the Church. As St. Augustine had said, "I would not believe the Gospel were it not for the authority of the Catholic Church."

Accepting Catholic teaching on contraception on the basis of Church authority may have been sufficient for the rest of my life were it not for a development in my career shortly after our conversion. Because I had earned an advanced pontifical degree in moral theology while I was still a Protestant clergyman, I was offered a teaching position in a Catholic seminary. Taking note of my married state, the seminary authorities informed me that I was to teach sexual morality! Suddenly simply accepting the Church's teaching on contraception was not enough; I now had to try to *understand* it.

344

The task of coming to understand the teaching of *Humanae vitae* was ultimately made possible by the truth of another insight of St. Augustine's: "Understanding is the reward of faith. Do not therefore try to understand in order that you may believe; but believe in order that you may understand." I am not so sure that grace made the task of understanding Catholic teaching on contraception any easier in my case, but I do know it did make it possible.

As I struggled through hours in the library on this subject, I found some intellectual attempts to explain the teaching wholly inadequate. Through this experience I came to see clearly that the truth of Church teaching and our obligation to accept it cannot be dependent on the adequacy with which the teaching is presented. However, I also knew it was an article of faith that the moral teaching of the Catholic Church is accessible to the powers of natural reason, even unaided by grace, for, as St. Paul said, God's laws are written in the hearts of all. So I continued to search.

One inadequate explanation of the Church's teaching on contraception, in my opinion, might be called the "perverted faculty" theory. (This does not refer to the professors at the college where I teach!) This theory maintains that God created us with certain faculties ordered toward particular purposes and if we prevent a faculty from achieving its God-given purpose we pervert it and thwart God's will. As the word implies, genitalia are ordered toward the generation of new life and if one prevents them from achieving their purpose one perverts that divinely given faculty. The problem with this approach is that it is easy to think of any number of "perversions" of faculties which could hardly be considered immoral. Factory workers use ear plugs to keep their ears from achieving their purpose. A husband plops a pillow over his face to block out the light of his wife's bedside reading light.

Another poor explanation of the immorality of contraception led to terrible problems for the Church. It was taught that the immorality of contraception could be seen in its unnaturalness, its artificiality. "Artificial" contraception was wrong because it was contrary to the natural order which was created by God.

345

Condoms, diaphragms, and foams interfered with natural marital sexual acts. They were intrusive, distasteful, and unnatural.

Other practices of the Church which had nothing at all to do with morality seemed to underscore this approach. No synthetic or artificial substances were to be used in worship, for example. Altar candles had to be of pure bees wax. There could be no artificial coloring in communion wine. Mass vestments and altar linens could not be made from synthetic fibers. This attitude seems to prefigure the disdain—almost moral revulsion—which young upwardly-mobile professionals now show toward individuals wearing polyester. Only natural fibers will do.

The weaknesses of the approach became apparent, I believe, with the introduction of the birth control pill. Untold confusion then resulted in many Catholic circles. Taking the Pill seemed no more unnatural than taking an aspirin. In fact, it was argued, it remedied "a defect of nature." Furthermore, it did not interfere with the spontaneous love-making of the marital couple unlike other methods of birth control. It seemed the natural—and hence moral—contraceptive had been found. The issuance, then, of *Humanae vitae* came as a terrible blow to Catholics who were using the Pill, and it convinced the secular world that the Catholic Church was thoroughly unreasonable in its sexual teachings.

One of the things *Humanae vitae* taught us, however, was that it is contraception itself which is immoral, not the artificiality of it.

How then, can the immorality of contraception be understood? I must admit that I was helped more by the writings of married Catholic philosophers than by the books of moral theologians. It is, of course, possible that the rationale which I have found convincing will not be helpful to others. However, this would not alter the authenticity and binding character of the Church's teaching.

We can legitimately ask what is natural for the human person so that we can know what will contribute to his self-fulfillment. That which is most natural for the human person is to act rationally. Rationality is the most distinctive characteristic of the human. But how do we know a person is acting rationally? We know a person is acting rationally if he is acting with a purpose, with a goal or an end in mind. The person who acts aimlessly, who wanders about with no purpose, is perceived as acting irrationally. He is usually locked up for his own good and cared for by others.

The rational act is understood as being freely and consciously ordered toward an end, a goal. We understand what a person is doing by virtue of the end he has in mind. We see a young woman standing on a street corner in a light rain on a cold, miserable November day. She just stands there, and we think she must be insane. Even a dog would know enough to seek shelter in such weather! When we ask her what she is doing she replies that she is waiting for a bus. Suddenly what appeared to be irrational behavior becomes eminently reasonable. And the more we inquire of her the more reasonable her behavior appears. She is waiting for a bus to go to the stationery store to buy paper to type her research report for her physiology class in the medical school she is attending in order to become a physician so that she can help and heal others. The act of medical healing becomes the "end" or goal which ultimately explains her actions on the cold November day.

Of course, we do not act simply on behalf of or for ends, but rather for ends perceived as goods. A good is something perfective of our nature which we desire to possess because it will lead to our happiness, as was the case, for example, with the young woman whose goal was to be a physician. In fact, it is ends perceived as goods which make human action possible and which enable us to exercise our freedom. As T. S. Eliot said, "The end is where we begin." The end or goal defines our action and makes it intelligible. Indeed, it makes it possible. One of the beautiful things about life is that we have a virtually endless array of goods spread before us for the choosing. The moral life consists in being open to all the goods which are offered to us and in choosing those which truly perfect our nature.

We are clearly not obliged to act on behalf of all the goods which are arrayed before us. That would be an impossibility. We are finite creatures and can only act on behalf of so many goods. I cannot attend a conference, spend time with my family and read the latest novel on the best seller list all at the same time. It is impossible, and to think we could do so is unreasonable.

However, what we are obliged to do is never to act directly against a good, for to do so would mean not recognizing its properties of goodness and the role it plays as the source of free, rational human action. We may never treat a good as though it were an evil. This would undermine, indeed make impossible, free human action since reasonable human behavior is understood as being ordered toward ends perceived as goods. When I was younger I enjoyed sketching. Now that I am older with family responsibilities I no longer have time for the avocation. However, that does not mean that I regard sketching as a frivolous activity unworthy of a human being. I remain open to it as a good to which I may some day return.

One time a young priest came to give our parish Lenten retreat. In the course of the retreat, he revealed a tremendous hostility against football. Professional football was the most evil of American activities, he maintained. The Soviet Union was a far superior regime than the United States, because there the workers and ordinary citizens went to the ballet rather than football games. I was perplexed by this hostility toward a perfectly (potentially) wholesome game of athletic prowess and team cooperation. Some years later the priest's name came up in conversation, and I learned he had had a rather sad childhood. His father had been a football coach and his older brother a star quarterback. However, as a boy the priest had contracted polio and was never able to play football. Suddenly his aversion to the sport exhibited during the retreat became understandable. There had been a good which he had been incapable of realizing. But instead of maintaining an appropriately open and accepting attitude toward the good, he rejected it as though it were an evil.

At times I may have to choose between playing tennis with one of my children and undertaking a professional task such as writing a paper. I may choose *for* the professional task without choosing *against* friendship with my child, and the child knows it. There will be another opportunity for a game of tennis. However, if I respond with, "Beat it, kid! You make too many demands on me. You're interfering with my professional career!" then, clearly, I have acted against friendship with my child.

348

Again, there is no obligation to act on behalf of all goods of which we are capable, but there is an obligation never to act against a good as though it were an evil, for this would undermine the basis of reasonable human behavior. To misread a good as though it were an evil is to misread reality; it is not to trust and act upon the truth. It is rather to act on the basis of a falsehood.

Now, what makes sense of human sexuality? What makes sense of the fact that we are differentiated as male and female? As the Second Vatican Council teaches us, we can look at the nature of the human person and his acts to find the answer. (*Gaudium et spes*, 51). Reasonable human acts are those directed toward ends perceived as goods. And three fundamental goods or ends can be found to be inherent within our sexuality: sensual pleasure, friendship, and the child. But which of these most adequately and fundamentally explains our sexual natures? Sexual pleasure does not ultimately explain our natures as male and female since it can be achieved to some degree even in isolation. Friendship is a great good of our sexual natures, but we know it does not ultimately explain the differentiation of sexes since even homosexuals seek this end, even though they are never able adequately to realize it. Ultimately what explains the sexual differentiation of our natures as male and female is the child toward which our sexuality is ordered. Clearly this priceless good of human life toward which our sexuality is ordered is not the only end of our sexuality, but it is the one which ultimately and most adequately explains it. This is all that is meant by the traditional formula that the primary (not exclusive) end of marriage is the procreation and education of children.

It seems to me that what is fundamentally wrong with contraception is that it invariably treats the procreative good, the child, as though it were an evil. Contraception always involves opposition to the realization of the procreative good which otherwise might arise from the marital act in which two people have freely chosen to engage. The very name of the practice makes it clear that this is what is happening: contra-ception. Contraception always posits an act against the good of life, whether it is taking a pill or using a condom, an IUD, a spermicidal foam, a diaphragm, or *coitus interruptus*.

Now, the motives of people using contraceptives are often quite moral. They are usually the same ones Pope Paul VI himself used in *Humanae vitae* as justifications for limiting the size of one's family: the physical or emotional health of the mother, or to "secure the harmony and peace of the family, and better conditions for the education of the children already born." (*Humanae vitae*, 16). Indeed, the Church has always encouraged married couples to be as generous as possible with the gift of life, but she never enjoined them to breed as many offspring as they are capable of having physically with no regard to the task of nurturing and educating them. Our family name Haas is Dutch for rabbit, and some people have accused us of trying to live up to our name with our eight children! But human beings are not to breed as animals; they are to raise a family in a reasonable way.

Although the spacing of one's children is a morally legitimate undertaking in the eyes of the Church, the use of contraception to do so is not because, as has been said, contraception always involves the positing of an act against the good of human life. Even if people do not think they are doing this, the reality of their act has a way of manifesting itself even when people are not aware of it. The misreading of the procreative good of a child has insinuated itself insidiously into our culture at all levels. A pregnancy becomes a contraceptive failure or mistake, and failures and mistakes have to be corrected. The attitude has thoroughly worked its way even into our pop culture.

It sometimes seems that the greatest fear of the United States Agency for International Development is the human child. Millions of dollars in economic aid to developing countries are made contingent upon those countries first launching an assault on their children. *People* become the problem. Rather than addressing the real problems, such as an inefficient economic system of maldistribution of goods or an inadequate delivery system for medical care, which would require considerable effort, the easiest solution is sought: eliminate the children already conceived and prevent more from being conceived. The good of human life is seen as an evil.

350

When I grew up it was not unusual to find vending machines which dispensed condoms in the men's rooms of gas stations. The machines always bore the message: "Prophylactics: Sold for the prevention of disease only." A prophylactic, of course, is a treatment or device for the prevention of disease. It is interesting that the machines had to carry that message. Most of the states in the Union at that time had laws *against* the selling of contraceptives because their use was considered immoral and harmful to the common good. The state legislatures at the time these laws were passed were *not* populated primarily by Catholics but by Protestants. One of the things we forget is that until very recently Protestants believed the same thing about contraception as Catholics. In fact, a tremendous propaganda effort was required to change Protestant attitudes on contraception. This effort is chronicled in a book by James Reed entitled *From Private Vice to Public Virtue: The History of the Birth Control Movement and American Society since 1830.*

However, it was not principally disease that my classmates thought of when they used the vending machines. It was unthinkable that one's girlfriend had a disease. The condoms were purchased to prevent babies. But a curious and subtle thing happened. A certain association developed between disease and babies, both of which came to be seen as evils to be avoided.

This attitude was poignantly illustrated at a convention of Planned Parenthood Physicians a number of years ago. A physician representing the federal government came from the Center for Communicable Diseases in Atlanta to talk about the deplorable spread of venereal disease among teenagers. He stated that the most prevalent form of venereal disease in the country was gonorrhea. The second most prevalent form of venereal disease was unwanted pregnancies and the most effective way of dealing with it was abortion! This outrageous statement was made by a highly educated man to a group of highly educated medical professionals and was apparently accepted without protest. The priceless good of human life, a precious child, has come to be viewed as a disease. To this monstrous assault on the good of human life the Church does indeed deliver a resounding "no." The Church says no to the practice of contraception and abortion because she pronounces first a yes to the good of human life.

What I came to see was that the basis of the Church's teaching on contraception was an affirmation of the good of human life. That was really the subject of Paul VI's encyclical. It was not primarily a condemnation of contraception, but rather an affirmation of the good of human life, as the name of the encyclical itself implies: *Humanae vitae,* Of Human Life.

The defense of human life by the Church is obvious throughout her history. From the very beginning the Church had to face threats to this good. There was a very early heresy under the guise of Christianity known as Gnosticism. The Gnostics believed that the material world was not good. It was supposedly created by a fallen demigod and was thought to be evil. The flesh was a prison for the divine spark within us. The goal was to shed the body and release the spark to be reunited with God. They denied that Jesus was actually in the flesh because it was unthinkable that God would have united Himself with the filthy material world. The Gnostics also opposed marriage because it led to children and the entrapment of more divine sparks within the prison of the body.

The Church responded early and forcefully to this threat to the good of human life by insisting that our bodily existence was a divine gift. The sounds of struggle against this early heresy can be heard in Holy Scripture itself. The First Epistle of John stresses in the strongest language that Jesus came in the flesh, and that God thereby gave the strongest affirmation of the essential goodness of this created world. The Church trusted this truth, affirmed the goodness of human life, and finally triumphed over Gnosticism.

However, this dualistic heresy which assaults the goodness of the crown of God's creation, human life, has surfaced again and again throughout history under a number of names: Docetists, Manicheans, Bogomils, Cathars, Albigensians. Time and again the Church has had to launch a defense of human life against these threats. Always these heretical groups claimed the name of Christian and insisted they were morally superior to the Catholic Church since it was carnal and they were spiritual.

352

Cathari, for example, is Greek for the "pure ones." They became dominant in southern France during the twelfth century. The Cathars believed that the material world was created by an evil principle. They rejected marriage because it led to offspring, the greatest evil which could be perpetrated by a human being. They would go through the marriage ceremony and simulate marriage, but went to great lengths to avoid conception.

The Cathars were a rigorous lot and were quite disruptive of the social fabric. The "perfected ones" would undergo a practice known as *"endura,"* which was essentially a fast unto death so that the spirit could escape the body. They became a real menace to society and on one occasion murdered the papal legate sent to deal with them. Eckbert of Schoenau in 1163 likened them to the Manicheans and wrote, "If they indulge in marital intercourse, they nevertheless avoid conception and generation by whatever means they can." The greatest evil for a Cathar was conception, for it brought another "son of the Devil" into the world.

The Cathars had a sacrament necessary for salvation known as the *"consolatum."* After sinning, they could confess to their priest and receive anew this *consolatum.* However, there was one sin which was so horrible it could not be forgiven even if the person were at the point of death—pregnancy.

The Church reacted against this threat to the basic good of human life and family with an intense vigor. When this dangerous heresy had finally been extirpated in southern France the Catholic bishops held a council in Albi, the former seat of the movement, in 1254 to enact measures for the restoration of the faith and to counter any recurrence of Cathar belief. Up to that time all Catholics over the age of seven were required to memorize the Creed and the Our Father. At the Council of Albi another prayer, the Hail Mary, was added which would effectively counter the anti-life beliefs of the Cathars: ". . . and blessed is the Fruit of thy womb, Jesus."

The fruit of the womb is blessed. It is holy. It is not a curse. It is not evil. It is a wondrously beautiful gift from God. Yet the threat against the good of human life has continued through history to rise up, and the Church has continued to fight back in defense of life.

A namesake of the Cathars arose in England centuries after their elimination in France. The Puritans, the new "Pure Ones," had the same uneasiness with the flesh. It was somehow dirty, fallen corrupt. Catholics were denounced as sensual and dissolute and worldly. The modern descendants of the Puritans, Planned Parenthood, continue to see the locus of evil in the world as the flesh, the human child, new life.

Yet as we saw earlier, the child is one of the goods which makes sense of our sexuality. It is one of the goods on behalf of which we act when we engage in the marital embrace. If we treat it as though it were an evil, something on behalf of which we should not act, we render our sexual acts meaning-less. We limit our potential for human action since the source of our actions are ends perceived as goods.

The question might be asked how natural family planning, or abstinence from sexual intercourse during fertile periods to avoid having a child, could be justified in light of this approach. Earlier it was pointed out that we have no moral obligation to realize all the goods of which we are capable. This is true in the area of child-bearing as well. If there is a weighty moral reason to avoid a child at a particular time, the couple merely refrains from engaging in an act which would likely result in the generation of new life. Consequently, one does not have to posit an act, other than the marital act, which is directed against the good of human life. One simply refrains from acting altogether.

Yet the section of the encyclical which judges periodic abstinence to be licit has led to confusion. In section II, Pope Paul VI states that "each and every marriage act *(quilibet matrimonii usus)* must remain open to the transmission of life." This does not mean that procreation must be the specific intent of every marriage act, as the context makes clear. Yet some people have interpreted it to mean that.

The intent of the teaching might have been clearer if it had been expressed in the negative. No marriage act may ever willfully and knowingly be closed to the transmission of life. Contraception is always wrong because it always involves an act against the realization of the procreative good when two people have freely chosen to engage in marital intercourse. Periodic absti-

354

nence from intercourse during fertile periods is in itself morally indifferent but would be immoral if the intention were immoral, or licit and chaste if the intention were good and the circumstances warranted its practice.

Through some considerable reflection, then, I came to see that the Church's teaching on contraception is reasonable because it is based on an understanding of human actions judged reasonably by virtue of their being ordered to ends perceived as goods. I have also been surprised to see some of the unexpected quarters from which the Church receives support for this view. I ran across the following in the writings of Sigmund Freud; the passage could have been lifted from the pages of a Catholic, moral theology text:

> It is a characteristic common to all the [sexual] perversions that in them reproduction as an aim is put aside. This is actually the criterion by which we judge whether a sexual activity is perverse—if it departs from reproduction in its aims and pursues the attainment of gratification independently. [*Introductory Lectures on Psychoanalysis,* Allen and Unwin, 1952, p. 266]

I came, then, to see that the Church's teaching was indeed reasonable and could be supported by rational argument—even by non-theological disciplines. I came to see that the Church's teaching on contraception was not so much a no as a yes. It was a Yes to the gift of human life, the most precious gift God gives us. And through the centuries the Church has consistently and faithfully echoed the Yes which Mary declared when she was overshadowed by the Holy Spirit and ushered in the Lord of Life and our redemption.

Chapter 23

CHILDREN AND VALUES

The Reverend Monsignor Cormac Burke

A FREQUENT GROUNDS of annulment is that marital consent was vitiated through the exclusion of one of the three traditional *bona* or *values* of marriage: the *bonum fidei* (fidelity to one partner; the uniqueness of the marital union), the *bonum sacramenti* (permanence of the marriage bond; the indissolubility of the union), or the *bonum prolis* (offspring; the fruitfulness of the union).

Given the aspect of *obligation* involved in each of these *bona* or values, it is logical and, I suppose, healthy enough that

Published in *International Review,* vol. 12, n. 3, Fall 1988, pp. 181–192. Reprinted here with permission.

ecclesiastical judges like myself center their attention on the question of whether or not this obligation has been truly accepted by the person marrying. I do not think it is so healthy, however, if other people begin thinking of these *bona* mainly or simply in terms of their obligatoriness. If their thinking were to go this way, they could easily come to conclude that, since an obligation is normally something burdensome (and we all tend to avoid burdens), the exclusion of permanence or fidelity or offspring cannot really be thought of as strange or exceptional; one can even begin to find good reasons for maintaining that it is something to be expected.

These are, of course, not merely theoretical considerations. I am afraid that to quite a number of Christians today—and, not least, to many who have a special mission to form and guide others (pastors, teachers, counsellors . . .)—the idea of people excluding one or other of these *bona,* when they marry, no longer tends to seem surprising; it even seems natural.

Exclusion Is Not Natural

Exclusion, however, *is* surprising, precisely because it is *not* natural. It is not natural because one does not logically reject the obligations or responsibilities that necessarily accompany the acquisition of a *good* thing. If the thing is good enough, the goodness more than compensates the responsibilities. The purchase of an automobile involves burdens and responsibilities; but most people regard a car as a good thing and think that, despite the burdens involved, they are enriched by the acquisition of one car, or of two or three cars, if they can afford them.[1]

Thank God for St. Augustine when he hit on the happy idea of describing the essential elements of marriage as *bona:* as *good things.* Thank God for Pope John Paul II when, in *Familiaris consortio,* he speaks of indissolubility in terms of something joyful that Christians should announce to the world. "It is necessary," he says, "to reconfirm the *good news* of the definitive nature of conjugal love."[2]

Fidelity and offspring are good things. Indissolubility is good news! The Bishop of Hippo and the Roman Pontiff are making affirmations that spur us to think: to pursue a line of thought that can lead to discovery or rediscovery. To my mind, it is vital for the future of marriage and the family that we rediscover the something hidden here that is elementary, that should be all too obvious, but has become all too obscured: the simple fact that each of the *bona matrimonialia* is exactly that, a *quid bonum,* a *good* thing. Each is "a good" because each contributes powerfully not only to the good of society, but also to the *bonum coniugum,* to the "good" of the spouses, to their development and maturing as persons who have grown in worth and character and generosity, persons who have learned to love. (And that, of course, is the ultimate good that each of us needs to acquire and develop here on earth: the ability to love.)

It is Natural to Want an Exclusive, Permanent Bond

Only when people recover this way of thinking will they properly understand that since these *bona* are good things, they are *desirable;* and *it is natural to want them.* It is natural, because it corresponds to the nature of human love. Man finds something deeply good in the idea of a love (1) of which he is the privileged and singular object, (2) which will be his for as long as life lasts, (3) and through which, by becoming a co-creator, he can perpetuate himself (and, as we shall see, more than himself). Precisely because of the goodness which he sees in these "goods," what is natural to man is not to fear or exclude them, but to seek and welcome them.

It is natural then to want an exclusive, permanent, and fruitful marital union. It is *unnatural* to exclude any of these three elements. We need to get our thinking back into proper perspective so that we are hit by—and can hit others with—the fact of the natural goodness of these "goods" of marriage.

The good of fidelity or exclusiveness is clear: "You are *unique* to me." It is the first truly personalized affirmation of conjugal love, and it echoes the words God addresses to each one of us in Isaiah: *Meus es tu*—"You are mine."[3]

The good of indissolubility should also be clear: the good of a stable home or haven, of knowing that this "belongingness"—

shared with another—is for keeps. People want that, are made for that, expect that it will require sacrifices, and sense that the sacrifices are worth it. "It is natural for the human heart to accept demands, even difficult ones, in the name of love for an ideal, and above all in the name of love for a person."[4] It is a strange head and heart that rejects the permanence of the marriage relationship.

For the purpose of the present article, however, I will not enlarge on these two aspects but wish rather to limit attention to the *bonum prolis:* the "good" or value of offspring.

Depriving Oneself of Goodness

The contraceptive mentality—probed into so painfully by the healing intent of *Humanae vitae*—is an ailment that could prove fatal to Western society. Debate or disagreement about the specific morality of family planning *techniques* is not the heart of the matter: In itself, in fact, the morality of those techniques is just one aspect of the overall pathological picture. The real sickness here is that practically our whole Western civilization has come to look on family limitation as a good thing and fails to see that it is the *privation* of a good thing.

I am not thinking here of those couples who, for health reasons, economic factors, etc., really need the help of natural family planning (and have recourse to it with regret). I am thinking of those others—the very many others—who could afford to have a larger family and freely choose not to, without apparently realizing the *goodness* of what they are thus *depriving* themselves of. They prefer to have less of the *bona matrimonialia,* less in particular of the "good" of offspring, so as to have more of material goods. And the quality of their life—more and more materialized, less and less humanized—flows inevitably from their choice. Material goods cannot hold a marriage together; matrimonial goods, especially the "good" of offspring, can.

There is, indeed, something profoundly good in that specific aspect of conjugal sexual union in which is to be found its true uniqueness: the sharing together not so much in what may or may not be a unique pleasure as in what *is* a unique *power,* a power—the result of sexual complementarity—to bring about a new life. Man and woman have a deep desire for such a true conjugal sexual union, and that desire is thoroughly rooted in human nature.

It seems particularly important today to underline, in all its fullness, the *personalist* thrust of this natural desire, which goes beyond any desire for either mere self-assertion or mere self-perpetuation.

Self-assertion? Self-perpetuation?

Contraceptive sexual intercourse between spouses can be merely self-assertive: each one seeking himself or herself and failing truly to find or know or give to the other. True marital sexual intercourse, open to life, is—of its very nature—*love*-assertive. It asserts mutual conjugal love and donation, precisely in the uniqueness and greatness of the shared sexual potential of the spouses.

The desire for self-perpetuation is something natural which in itself already has a deep personalist value. (If modern man does not readily grasp or feel this, it is a sign of the extent to which he is humanly devitalized, denaturalized, and depersonalized.) Conjugality, however, takes the procreative sexual urge beyond the natural wish to perpetuate just *oneself*. In the context of conjugal love, this natural desire for self-perpetuation also acquires new scope and meaning. It is no longer a matter of two separate selves, each wishing—perhaps in a selfish way—for self-perpetuation. It is rather the case of two persons in love, who naturally want to perpetuate *the love* that draws them to one another, so that they can have the joy of seeing it take flesh in a new life, fruit of that mutual spiritual and carnal knowledge by which they express their spousal love.[5]

Two persons in love want to do things together: to design or make or buy or furnish together something that will be peculiarly *theirs*, because it is the fruit of their united decision and action. Nothing is more proper to a couple than their child. Other people can have a similar or better house or TV set or car; no couple but they can have *their* children.

The sculptor hews his vision of beauty into lasting stone. Only parents can create *living* works of art, with each child a unique monument to the creative love that inspires and unites them.

A society, through the monuments it builds, evokes the memory of the great things of its past, in order to keep its values alive in the present and for the future. Spousal love needs such monuments. When romance is fading, when perhaps it has died and the spouses are tempted to think that the love between them has died with it, then each child remains as a living testimony to the depth and uniqueness and totality of the conjugal gift of self which they made to each other in the past—when it was easy—and as an urgent call to keep giving now, even when it is hard.

Planned Absences

In my work at the Roman Rota, I not infrequently come across petitions of annulment of what clearly are perfectly genuine marriages of couples who married out of love, but whose marriages collapsed fundamentally because they deliberately delayed having children and thus deprived their married love of its natural support.

If two people remain just looking ecstatically *into* each other's eyes, the defects that little by little they are going to discover there can eventually begin to appear intolerable. If they gradually learn to look *out* together at their children, they will still discover each other's defects, but they will have less time or reason to think them intolerable. They cannot however look out together at what is not there.

A series of *planned absences* is turning the married life of many couples today into a hollowed-out reality, a vacuum that eventually collapses in on itself. A married couple can stare the love out of each other's eyes. If married love is to grow, it has to contemplate, and be contemplated by, other eyes—many pairs of eyes—born of that very love.[6]

Conjugal love, then, needs the support represented by children.[7] Children strengthen the *goodness* of the bond of marriage, so that it does not give way under the strains that follow on the inevitable wane or disappearance of effortless romantic love. The bond of marriage—which God wants no man to break—is then constituted not just by the variables of personal love and sentiment between husband and wife, but more and more by their children, each child being one further strand giving strength to that bond.

In his homily in Washington, D.C., in October 1979, Pope John Paul II reminded parents that "it is certainly less serious to deny their children certain comforts or material advantages than to deprive them of the presence of brothers and sisters, who could help them to grow in humanity and to realize the beauty of life at all its ages and in all its variety."[8] I would suggest to parents, who too easily incline to family limitation, to read the Pope's reminder in the light of the Vatican II teaching that "children are the *supreme* gift of marriage and contribute to the *greatest* extent to the *good of the parents* themselves."[9] It is therefore not only their present children, but also *themselves,* that such parents may be depriving of a singular "good," of a unique experience of human life, the fruit of love.

Educated Choices

One frequently comes across statements to the effect that "family planning or limitation is more easily accepted by people as they get better educated." Whether we realize it or not, to admit such statements unquestioningly is to concede a whole philosophy of life. A very particular type of education, thoroughly imbued with a very particular kind of values (or rather of anti-values), is necessary before people are brought to the point of easily accepting family limitation. Can such education be regarded as Christian education? Can it be regarded as *true* education at all? It is worth recalling the judgment that John Henry Newman, some 130 years ago, passed on the education of his time. Modern man, he said, is instructed, but not educated. He is taught to do things, and to think enough so as to do them; but he is not taught to think more. . . .[10]

This whole issue is one of values and choices, of goods and options. Few people can have all the goods of this world. But most people have a certain choice. I can choose *good* A or *good* B, though possibly not both. Then I have to choose between them. The wise and properly human choice takes the *better* good, and knows it is richer in choosing so; that is the educated choice. The less human or less wise choice opts for the inferior good and probably does not know it is duping and impoverishing itself. There is a forceful passage in the Bible which is not altogether without relevance here: "I have set before you life and death, blessing and curse; therefore choose life, that you and your descendants may live."[11] There is no half-way choice between life and death. What, one may ask, is the real term of the choices the Western world is making?

In Kenya a couple of years ago, an African who had learned that the Western fertility rate averages about 1.7, remarked to me: "Western couples must be *very poor* if they can't afford to have more than 2 children. . . ." He was not a qualified "expert" in the Western sense; yet his words may be worth pondering. They could be complemented with another bit of "non-expert" wisdom, this time from the West itself. Some time ago, back in England, I knew a recently-married, normal couple who wanted children. One child was born, but then there was an unwanted delay of three or four years. At last the mother became expectant again. Their first-born too was filled with expectations. But a miscarriage occurred. The father had to tell the child that he was not going to have that little brother or sister he wanted. "Look, Mom's not going to have that baby after all"; and, bowing before God's inscrutable ways, he added, "It's better that way. . . ." The kid, however, did not bow so easily: "But Daddy, is there *any*thing *better* than a baby?" Computerized programs never anticipate the things that children come up with. The wisdom of children is part of the *bonum prolis*.

Sense of Values

The child in that episode had a true *sense of values* which, according to *Humanae vitae,* is precisely the first thing a married couple need to possess if they are to approach family planning correctly.[12] A true sense of values is not shown by the couple who fail to see that a child is the best "acquisition" they can make, and the one that enriches them most.

Many married couples in the West no longer seem to realize the simple truth that children are the most personalized fruit of their own conjugal love and are, therefore, the greatest gift they can make to one another, being at the same time God's gift to both of them.

"But, if we have an extra child, our children and we, ourselves, will be less well-off." You will hardly say that the extra child will be less well off, unless you wish to rank yourself among those who wonder whether life itself is a good thing, or whether non-existence may not, after all, be preferable to existence.

"But our other children—those we have already—will be worse off." Will they? The pope suggests that, in terms of truly human values, they will not.

"But we, ourselves, will be less well-off. We will have a tougher time." You may have to work harder, that is true (many people work very hard today so as to have material "goods"), but will what you are working for make you less happy?

In seminars, when this matter comes up, I have at times asked my students to consider a small matter of comparative analysis. It goes something like this:

	CHILDREN	CARS	TV/VCR	EDUCATION OF CHILDREN	HOLIDAY ABROAD
Family A:	2	2	2/2	Good or best schools	Yes
Family B:	5	1	1/0	Second-rate schools	Never

After putting this on the board, my first question to the students is: Which family has the higher standard of living? They all answer: Family A, of course. So I repeat the question: Which family has the higher standard of living? There may be the slightest hesitation, but they repeat the same answer. So I repeat the same question again, and a third, and perhaps a fourth time. Perplexity sets in, hesitations grow, until in the end someone "concedes": "Well, of course, if you start considering children as *part* of your standard of life. . . ."

"If you start. . . ." It is time, indeed, that we started putting children on the assets side and not on the liabilities side. On *both,* you say? OK, on both: like your motor car. A car is an asset *and* a liability. It costs money and effort and attention to acquire and to maintain, just as a child does. Your choice should begin by considering which is worth more, because to choose the other is to lower one's own standard of living.[13]

"Which will give me more satisfaction?" is no doubt a utilitarian rather than an idealistic viewpoint. Yet, even if a person wishes to apply that view to our subject, he or she would do well to consider the money and time and effort that people nowadays put into gold or computers or creative gardening, *working* at them, *reading* all about them, in search of a satisfaction they do not always get.

How come they do not think parenthood worth working at? How is it they do not study books (there are plenty available) on how to enjoy caring for one's children, on the satisfactions of being a parent? And how is it (our horizons broaden again) they do not sense the call of an utterly unique creativity, the adventure of being co-creators?

Somewhere deep in their hearts, couples probably do sense the truth of the fact that a child is a good and a great gift. The trouble is that they have been conditioned not to *trust* that truth. They have to be helped to trust it; and clearly (at least to my mind), it is only couples who have chosen the "good" of offspring—in all the fullness with which God wished to bless their marriage—who can teach them. Pope Paul VI, in *Humanae vitae,* took good care to mention such parents *first,* among those who live up to God's expectations for responsible parenthood and exercise it "by the deliberate and generous decision to raise a numerous family."[14]

So many marriages today are suffering from *self*-privation, a voluntarily induced impoverishment brought about by a refusal of the gift of life and a rejection of the fruitfulness of love. Our modern well-off Western society may go down in history as "the *deprived* society"; where people—entire peoples—ailed to death by having a sense of true human values gradually sucked out of their lives.

366

The Loss of Sexuality

A final word on this concept of privation. At times a privation may be wise and necessary, for instance when health reasons demand that a person abstain from solid food. But it is nonetheless a privation. And, if it is not to end in death, it must be a temporary measure, so that the patient can get back to being nourished by a normal and healthy appetite. The Western appetite for sex today is not normal; nor is it healthy; nor, as I have suggested elsewhere,[15] is it really sexual.

The proponents of contraception maintain that it is perfectly all right "to separate sex from procreation." But that is *not* at all what is actually being done. The Church maintains that the procreative and unitive aspects of conjugal sex are inseparable. Now, what contraception does is not really to separate these aspects (with the implication that it annuls one, the procreative, and respects the other, the unitive). It destroys *both*. Contraceptive sex is not procreative; that is clear to everyone. What is not so clear to people is that it is not unitive, in any conjugal sense. The ultimate analysis, however, tells us that it is not *sex*, in any real human sense, at all.

What is being separated is not sex from some element extraneous to sex or even from some element peculiarly connected to sex by an unfortunate accident of biological design. What is being separated is the action of sex—the *apparent* action of sex—from the *meaning* of sex. The reality of sex is being totally put aside; and people are being left with a mere pantomine of sex.[16]

What is being separated is the very "body" of sex from the "soul" of sex; and what is being left is the corpse of sex. What contraception gives people is *apparent* "body-sex," that is actually soul-less sex. It is mummified sexuality; dead sex. Our modern world is busy in the process of killing sex and sexuality.

Many modern marriages are lacking a true sexual appetite. The sexuality marking them is not a truly human sexuality. A maimed masculinity and a maimed femininity are meeting in no authentic conjugal encounter. Such marriages, denied the essential humanizing and personalizing qualities of true conjugal sex, denied the true *bonum sexualitatis*—the true "good" of sexuality—are in danger of death by conjugal-sexual starvation. A

367

self-imposed barrenness is denying their love the fruit which love itself is designed to produce, and which it needs for its own nourishment and survival.

NOTES

1. I know an African family with 18 children and no car, and an American "family" (if it can be called that) with 18 cars and no children. And I honestly think that the African family is much happier: about 18 times as much.

2. *Familiaris consortio,* no. 2.

3. Is 43, 1.

4. Pope John Paul II, *General Audience,* April 28, 1982; cf. *Insegnamenti di Giovanni Paolo II,* V, 1 (1982), p. 1344.

5. Cf. Gen. 4, 1.

6. The love of naturally barren couples, to whom God does not give children, should of course also grow; but it too needs dedication to others, if it is to do so.

7. By one or two children, perhaps, or maybe by five or six. It is only God who knows the measure of support each marriage requires. Hence the vital need for spouses, if they are to resolve the matter successfully and happily, to approach it prayerfully.

8. Homily, October 7, 1979; cf. *Insegnamenti di Giovanni Paolo II,* II, 2 (1979), p. 702.

9. *Gaudium et spes,* no. 50.

10. Cf. *On the Scope and Nature of University Education,* Discourse IV.

11. Deut 30, 19.

12. Cf. *Humanae vitae,* no. 21.

13. An African footnote. Disconcerted by Planned Parenthood arguments, a Kenyan remarked: "Traditionally if the neighbor's cow gave birth to a calf, one congratulated the family, because their standard of life had increased. Nowadays if the wife gives birth to a child, one is apparently supposed to sympathize with them, because their standard of life has gone down. . . . I have to figure that one out."

14. *Humanae vitae,* no. 10

15. "Marriage and Contraception," in *L'Osservatore Romano* (English Edition), October 10, 1988, p. 7.

16. *L'Osservatore Romano,* October 10, 1988, pp. 7–8.

Chapter 24

Postscript

MAN BETWEEN REPRODUCTION AND CREATION: THEOLOGICAL QUESTIONS ON THE ORIGIN OF HUMAN LIFE

A written contribution by His Eminence, Joseph Cardinal Ratzinger Prefect, Congregation for the Doctrine of the Faith

1. Reproduction and Procreation: The Philosophical Problem of Two Terminologies

What is a human being? This perhaps all too philosophical sounding question has entered a new phase since it has become

---

This article was originally an address given by Cardinal Ratzinger in connection with the 900th anniversary celebration of the University of Bologna (April 30, 1988), and, with slight modifications, on the occasion of the conferral of an honorary doctorate on Cardinal Ratzinger at the University of Lublin (October 23, 1988). This translation was first published in *Communio: International Catholic Review*, vol. 16, Summer, 1989. Reprinted here with permission.

possible to "make" a human being, or, as the technical terminology has it, to reproduce one *in vitro*. This new ability man has acquired has also brought forth a new language. Up to now the origin of a human being has been expressed in terms of begetting and conception; in the romance languages there is also the word *procreation*, with its reference to the creator, to whom ultimately each human owes his or her being. But now it seems that instead of these the word "reproduction" describes the handing on of humanness most precisely. The two terminologies are not necessarily exclusive; each represents a different mode of consideration and thus a different aspect of reality. But the language has in each case the totality in mind; it is hard to deny that deeper problems show up than just the words: two differing views of mankind can be heard, two differing ways of explaining reality altogether.

Let us attempt first to understand the new language in its inner scientific origins, in order then to touch upon the more far-reaching problems carefully. The word "reproduction" means the process of originating a new human through biological knowledge of the properties of living organisms, which can, in contradistinction to artifacts, "reproduce" themselves. J. Monod, e.g., speaks of three determining characteristics of a living thing: its proper teleonomy, autonomous morphogenesis, and invariant reproduction.[1] There is a special emphasis on the invariance: the distinctive genetic code is "reproduced" unchanged each time; each new individual is an exact repetition of the same "message."[2] So "reproduction" expresses on the one hand the genetic identity: the individual "reproduces" anew only the same thing; on the other hand the word refers to the mechanical way in which this imitation occurs. This process can be exactly described. J. Léjeune has formulated the essentials of human "reproduction" as follows: "Children are always united with their parents by a material bond, the long DNA molecule, on which the complete genetic information can be found in an unchangeable miniature language. In the head of a spermatozoon is the master DNA in twenty-three parts. . . . As soon as the twenty-three chromosomes of the father, which are introduced in the spermatozoon, are united with the twenty-three of the mother, which are carried in the ovum, all the information is collected which is

370

necessary and sufficient to determine the genetic constitution of the new human being."[3]

We could also say in a rough shorthand that the "reproduction" of the human species occurs through the uniting of two information strings. The accuracy of the description is undoubted, but is it also complete? Two questions force themselves upon us immediately: Is the being thus reproduced merely another individual, another copy of the species man, or is it more: a person, that is, a being which, on the one hand represents invariantly the species man, and on the other is something new, one of a kind, not reproducible, with a uniqueness that goes beyond the simple individuation of its common type? If the latter, whence the uniqueness? And the second question is related to this: How do the two information strings come together? This apparently too simple question has become today the locus of the real decision, on which not only theories about man split, but where praxis becomes the incarnation of theories and gives them their whole pointedness. The answer seems, as we said, to be at first the most obvious thing in the world: the two complementary strings of information come together in the union of man and woman, through their "becoming one flesh" as the Bible has it. The biological process of "reproduction" is enveloped in a personal process of the body-soul self-giving of two humans.

Since the biochemical part of this totality, so to speak, has been successfully isolated in the laboratory, another question arises: How necessary is this connection? Is it essential to the event as such, should and must it be so, or have we here a case of what Hegel calls a trick of nature, which uses human instinct toward one another as it uses the wind, or the bees and the like, as a means to transport seed in the plant world? Can one claim that an isolated cell process is the really and only important element distinct from purely factual modes of union, and can one accordingly replace the natural process with other rationally directed methods? Various counter questions arise here: Can one designate the coming together of man and woman as a mere natural process, whereby the psychic turning to each other of the two would be also merely a trick of nature which deceives them, that they are not acting as persons but merely as individuals in a species? Or must we say exactly the opposite? With the love of two people and the spiritual freedom from which it comes, a new dimension of reality comes into being which corresponds to it, that the child too is not simply a repetition of invariant information, but a person, in the newness and freedom of an I, forming a new center in the world? And is not one blind who would deny this newness and reduce all this to the mechanical, but in order to do so must invent a tricky nature, which is an irrational and cruel myth?

A further question arises in this context from an observation: obviously one can isolate the biochemical process in a laboratory today, and thus bring the two information strings together. The connection with the psychic-personal event is then not to be defined with that kind of "necessity" which is valid in the physical sphere; it can also be done another way. But the question is whether there is not another kind of "must" than the purely physical. Even if the personal and the biological are separable, is there not a deeper kind of inseparability, a higher kind of "must" for the union of the two? Has one not in reality denied humanity if one acknowledges only the "must" of physical laws as must, and denies the ethical "must" which bears the obligation of freedom? In other words, if I consider solely the "reproduction" as real, and everything beyond that which leads to the notion of "procreation" as inexact and scientifically irrelevant verbiage, have I not then denied the human as human? But then who is discussing with whom, and what should then be said of the reasonableness of the laboratory or of science itself?

From these considerations we can fashion the question we want to take up precisely: how is it that the origin of a new human being is more than "reproduction?" What is this *more?* The question has acquired a new urgency as already indicated, from the fact that it is possible to "reproduce" a human being in a laboratory without any personal self-giving, without any union of man and woman. Today one can in practice separate the natural, personal event of the union of man and woman from the purely biological process. Against this practical separability, in the conviction of the morality grounded in Scripture and mediated by the Church, stands an ethical inseparability.[4] On both sides decisions of principle come into play: the activity in a laboratory does not follow purely mechanical premises, but is the result of a basic view of the world and of man. Therefore before we proceed purely argumentatively, a twofold historical review will be helpful. First we will attempt to lay out the philosophical background of the idea of the artificial "reproduction" of man. The second historical overview will look at the biblical witness regarding our question.

2. A Dialogue With History

2.1 "Homunculus" in the history of thought

The thought of being able to "make" a human being most likely has its first form in Jewish Kabbalism with the idea of the Golem.[5] At the basis of this notion lies the idea recorded in the Book of Jezira (c. 500 A.D.) that numbers have creative power. Through the proper recitation of all possible creative combinations of letters the *homunculus,* the Golem, will come into being. Already in the thirteenth century the notion of the death of God arises in conjunction with this: the *homunculus* when he finally appears will tear away the first letter, aleph, from the word *emeth* (truth). Thus there will be on his forehead, instead of the inscription "Yahweh God is Truth" the new motto, "God is Dead." The Golem explains the new saying with a comparison which ends, in brief, "When you, like God, can make men, people will say, 'There is no God in the world but this one.' " Making is brought into conjunction with power. Power belongs to the one who can produce humans, and with such power, they have done away with God; he no longer appears upon the human horizon.[6] The question remains whether the newly powerful, who have found the key to the language of creation and can combine its building blocks themselves, will remember that their activity is only possible because the numbers and letters which they know how to combine already exist.

The best known variation of the homunculus idea is in the second part of Goethe's *Faust.* Wagner, the science-fanatic disciple of the great Dr. Faust, succeeds with the masterpiece in his

373

absence. So the "Father" of this new art is not the all-questioning spirit reaching out toward greatness, but rather the positivist of knowing and doing, as one might well characterize Wagner. Nonetheless the little test-tube man recognizes Mephistopheles immediately as his cousin. Thus Goethe establishes an inner relationship between the artificial, self-made world of positivism and the spirit of denial. For Wagner and his kind of rationalism this is, of course, the moment of greatest triumph:

> God forbid! As formerly begetting was the custom,
> We declare it as an empty farce.
> . . .
> If still the beast himself therein delight,
> Still man must, with his so much greater gifts,
> In future have a more exalted source.

And a little later:

> So 'tis our wish in future chance to scorn,
> And so a brain which ought to think
>   aright,
> Will also in the future thinkers fashion.
> . . .
> What do we wish? What does the world
>   want more?
> The mystery lies open to the day.

Goethe exhibits clearly in these verses two driving forces in the search for the artificial production of man, and wants thereby to criticize a form of natural science which he rejects, as something he would consider "Wagnerian." First there is the desire to unveil mysteries, to see through the world and reduce it to a flat rationalism, which attempts to prove itself through its capacity to make something. Besides this, Goethe sees operative here a despising of "nature" and its mysterious, higher reasonableness, in favor of a planning, goal-determined rationalism. The symbol for the narrowness, falsity and inferiority of this kind of reason and its creations is the glass; homunculus lives *in vitro:*

374

Here a peculiarity of things:
The universe suffices nature not,
What's artificial needs a closed-in space.

Goethe's prognosis is that the glass, the wall of the artificial, will at last smash against reality. Since homunculus is artificial even though taken from nature, he will slip out of the hands of his maker; he stands in the tension between an anxious fear for his protective glass ("The taste of glass and flame are not alike") and his impatience to split the glass in search of real becoming. Geothe sees a conciliatory ending: homunculus returns in flame to the elements, in the Hymn to the Universe in its creative power, to "Eros who began all." The flame in which he disappears becomes a fiery wonder. But even though Goethe both here and at the end of his Faust's road replaces judgment with reconciliation, still the flaming smashing of the glass is a judgment on the arrogance of the making, which puts itself in place of becoming, and after a journey full of contradictions must end in fire and billow.

On the very threshhold of its realization Aldous Huxley wrote his negative utopia, *Brave New World* (1932).[7] In this definitively and fully scientific world it is clear that men should now only be generated in laboratories. Man has now emancipated himself from his nature; he wants no longer to be a natural thing. Each one will, as needed, be purposively concocted in the laboratory according to his task. Sexuality has by far nothing further to do with propagation; the very memory of it is felt an insult to planned man. Instead it has become part of the anesthetizing by which life is made endurable, a positivistic hedge around human consciousness by which man is protected, and the questions arising from the depth of his being are eliminated. And so naturally sexuality may no longer have anything to do with personal commitment, with fidelity and love—that would lead man back to the same old domain of his personal existence. In this world there is no more pain, no care, only rationality and enjoyment; everything is planned for everyone. The question is only, who is the bearer of this planning intelligence? It is the World Controllers; the rule of reason simultaneously makes its basic lunacy apparent.

Huxley had written his book, as he remarked in 1946, as a sceptical aesthete, who saw mankind living between the alternatives of insanity and lunacy, of scientific utopia and barbarian superstition.[8] In the Forward of 1946 and again in *Brave New World Revisted* he makes it clear that his work is to be understood as a brief for freedom, as a challenge to mankind to seek out the narrow space between insanity and lunacy: existence in freedom.[9] Huxley is understandably more precise and cogent in his critique than in the more generalizing positive images that he develops. On one thing he is certainly clear: the world of rational planning, of the scientifically directed "reproduction" of mankind, is not a world of freedom. The fact that it reduces the origin of humans to reproduction is, on the contrary, an expression of the denial of personal freedom: reproduction is a montage of necessities; its world is the reality pictured in the Kabbalah, a combination of letters and numbers. Whoever knows the code has power over the universe. Is it a coincidence that up to now there is no positive poetic vision of a future in which mankind will be produced *in vitro?* Or is there in such an enterprise an inner denial and ultimate elimination of that dimension of humanity which poetry brings to light?

2.2 The Origin of Mankind According to the Bible

After this glance at the best known historical sketch of reproduction ideology, let us turn to that work which is the decisive source for the idea of human procreation, the Bible. Here too there can of course be no question of an exhaustive analysis, but merely a first glance at some of its characteristic statements on our subject. We may restrict ourselves in this essentially to the first chapters of Genesis, where the biblical picture of mankind and of creation is established. A first, essential point is formulated very precisely in the Genesis homilies of St. Gregory of Nyssa:

> But man, how is he created? God does not say "Let there be man!" . . . The creation of man is higher than all. "The Lord took. . . ." He wishes to form our own bodies with his own hands.[10]

376

We shall have to return to this text when we are no longer speaking of the first man, but of every man. It will become apparent that the Bible shows in the person of the first man what its conviction is about every man. Parallel to the picture of man's coming from the hands of God which form him from the earth is the statement in the later, so-called Priestly document, "Let us make man after our image and likeness" (Gen. 1:26). In both cases the aim is to present man in a specific way as God's creation; in both cases the aim is not to have him appear merely as one specimen in a class of beings, but as a new being in each case, in whom more appears than reproduction: a new beginning, which reaches beyond all present combinations of information, who presupposes another—*the* other—and thus teaches us to think "God." It is even more important that in the creative act itself he created them man and woman. Differently from the animals and plants, where the charge to multiply is simply imposed, fruitfulness is here expressly bound up with being man and woman. The emphasis on God's being creator does not make human orientation to one another superfluous, but rather gives it its quality: indeed because God is engaged in this action, man cannot configure the "transporting" of the chromosomes at will; indeed the mode of such creation must therefore be worthy. This worthy mode is according to the Bible only one: the becoming one of husband and wife, who "become one flesh."

We have touched upon two important formulations of biblical language here, about which we must think more closely. The description of Paradise ends with a saying that seems to be a prophetic oracle on the being of mankind: "Therefore a man leaves father and mother and cleaves to his wife, and they become one flesh" (Gen. 1:24). What is the meaning of "they become one flesh"? There has been much argument on this. Some say it means sexual intercourse, others that it refers to the child in which the two combine into one flesh. Certitude is not to be found, but probably Delitzsch comes closest when he says that it expresses "psychic unity, all-embracing personal community."[11] In any case such a profound unity of man and wife is looked upon as characteristic of mankind, and as the locus in which the creation-mandate to man is fulfilled, because it corresponds in freedom to the call of his being.

Another term of biblical anthropology points in the same direction: the sexual union of man and woman is referred to with the verb "to know." The beginning of the history of human begetting reads "Adam knew his wife Eve" (Gen 4:1). It may be correct that one cannot read too much philosophy into this way of speaking. To begin with, we have here simply a case of what Gerhard von Rad rightly calls a "modesty of speech," which reverentially covers the inmost human togetherness with mystery.[12] But then it is important that the Hebrew word *yada^c* means *know* also in the sense of experiencing, of being acquainted with. Claus Westermann believes he can go a step further when he says *yada^c* means "not really knowing and understanding in the sense of objective knowing, as to know *something* or understand *something,* but the knowing in an encounter." The use of the word for the sex act then shows "that here the corporal relationship of man and woman is thought of not primarily as physiological, but primarily personal."[13] There appears again an inseparability of all the dimensions of being human, which precisely in their being combined comprise the specialness of this being "man," which is falsified when one begins to isolate individual parts.

How does the Bible concretely represent the becoming of man? I would like to present only three places which provide us with a good, clear answer. "Thy hands have made and fashioned me" says the petitioner to his God (Ps. 119:73). "Thou didst form my inmost parts, thou didst knit me together in my mother's womb. . . . My frame was not hidden from thee, when I was being made in secret, intricately wrought in the depths of the earth" (Ps. 139:13,15). "Thy hands fashioned me and made me. . . . Remember that thou has made me of clay. . . . Didst thou not pour me out like milk and curdle me like cheese?" (Job 10:8–10). Something important shows up in these texts. For one thing, the biblical writer knows very well that man is "knit together" in the mother's womb, that there, he is "curdled like cheese." But the mother's womb is also identified with the depths of the earth, and so each biblical worshipper can say of himself, Your hands have fashioned me, like clay you have formed me. The picture which describes the origin of Adam is valid for each human in the same way. Each human is Adam, a new beginning; Adam is each human being. The physiological event is more than a physiological event. Each human is more than a new combination of information; the origin of each human being is a creation. Its wonder is that it happens not next to but precisely *in* the processes of a living being and its "invariant reproduction."

Let us add a last, puzzling word to this to round out the picture. At the very first birth of a human being, according to the biblical narrative, Eve breaks out into a joyous cry, "I have gotten a man with the help of the Lord" (Gen. 4:1). The word "gotten" here is rare and much debated, but one could say with good grounds that it is rare because it has a unique content to express. The word means, as in other ancient Near Eastern languages, "creation through begetting or birth."[14] In other words, the joyous cry expresses the entire pride, the whole happiness of the woman become a mother; but it also expresses the knowledge that each human begetting and birth stands under a special presence of God, is a self-transcending of man, in which there is more than he has and is: through the human action of begetting and birth, there occurs creation.

3. The Unique Element in Human Origin

The current importance of this biblical statement is obvious. Certainly the question forces itself upon men of today, for whom the positivistic hemming in of thought seems a kind of obligation of honesty: Must God really be involved here? Is not that a mythologizing, which explains nothing, and impedes human freedom in dealing with the data of nature? Is not nature thus made taboo, and conversely, spirit made natural, in that one ties its freedom of movement to a law of nature as a supposed expression of the will of God?

Whoever enters into such a dispute must be clear on one thing: what is said about God and about man as person, as a new beginning, cannot be taken as the same kind of positively verifiable knowledge as that which can be ascertained with equipment about the mechanics of reproduction. The statements about God and man intend precisely to point toward this, that man denies himself, and so denies incontrovertible reality, if he refuses to go beyond the laboratory in his thinking. So one can best "prove" the correctness of the biblical synthesis by making apparent the impasse of its denial. Goethe has predicted that the glass world of homunculus, the one who reduces himself to reproduction, will someday necessarily shatter against reality. In the ecological crisis of today something of the tinkle of glass can be heard. Marx had already been able to call with enthusiasm for the battle of man for the subjection of nature. "Battle against Nature" and "Freeing of Mankind" are for him almost synonyms.[15] Today this freeing begins to be alarming. The use of nature turns into using it up, and the notion that now technical understanding will bring about the reasonable assembling of unreasonable reality has long proven itself to be a romantic myth. The inner reasonableness of creation is greater than that of man the maker, who does not possess it as pure reason anyway, but as an interest group with the whole short-sightedness of a party-determined goal, which pays the bill of today with the life of tomorrow.

And there we touch upon deeper levels of the impasse. The notion that an ethics coming to us from the very nature of things is in reality but a myth replaces the idea of freedom with the assemblage of necessity. But this is in reality the denial of any freedom. The reducing of reality that is bound up with such a viewpoint means first and foremost the denial of man as man. Of course the danger arises here that the glass of homunculus will not only strike its inhabitant, but will fall upon all of mankind and destroy that too. The logical connection, and that is what we are concerned with here, is unavoidable. It seems harmless to remove the taboo from the personal uniting of man and woman as a mythic divinizing of nature. It seems to be progress to isolate the biological cell process and to imitate it in the laboratory. It is logical then that becoming human is merely reproduction. It is unavoidable then to consider all that goes beyond reproduction as mythical-seeming; demythologized man is only a combination of information, and so one can, guided by evolution, go in search of new combinations. The freedom which emancipates man and his research from ethics presupposes at its inception the denial of freedom. What remains is the power of the "World Controllers Council," a technical rationality, which itself stands only in service to necessity, but wants to replace the accidental occurrences of its combinations with the logic of planning.[16] Here Huxley is simply correct. This rationality and its freedom is a contradiction in itself, an absurd arrogance. The impasse of reproduction logic is man; it is on him that the glass shatters, and proves itself the shell of the artificial. "Nature," for which the faith of the Church demands respect in the begetting of a human being, is therefore not a falsely sacralized biological or physiological process; this "nature" is rather the dignity of the person itself, or of the Three Persons who are involved. This dignity reveals itself also precisely in bodiliness; to this bodiliness must correspond the logic of self-giving which stands written in creation and in the hearts of men, in accordance with the great statement of St. Thomas Aquinas, "Love is by its nature the primary gift, from which all other gifts follow of themselves."[17] Such considerations make clear where God's creative activity can enter into what seems merely a physiological, natural process: the natural process is borne and made possible by the personal action of love, in which human beings give to one another nothing less than themselves. This giving is the inner locus, where God's giving, where creative love, is at work as a new beginning.

The alternative before which we stand today can now be formulated very precisely: One can on the one hand regard only the mechanical, nature's laws, as real, and consider all that is personal, loving, giving, as pretty appearance, which, though psychologically useful, is ultimately unreal and untenable. I find for this position no other designation than the denial of humanity. If one follows out this logic, then the notion of God becomes of course mythological verbiage with no reality content. Next to this, according to the other alternative, things are just the opposite: One can consider the personal as the real, the stronger and higher form of reality, which does not reduce the other realities, the biological and mechanical, to mere appearance, but absorbs them into itself, and thus opens to them a new dimension. Then not only does the notion of God retain sense and meaning, but the notion of nature appears in a new light, since nature is then not just a coincidentally sensibly functioning ordering of letters and numbers, but carries within it a moral message, which precedes it and appeals to mankind to find answers within it. The nature of the matter is such that the rightness of the one or the other basic decision cannot be decided in the laboratory. In the dispute about man only man can decide, in deciding to accept or to deny himself.

Is it still necessary to defend this vision of reality against the charge that it is inimical to science and progress? I think it has become adequately apparent that a view of mankind which does not allow reducing its origin to reproduction, but understands it as creation, in no way denies or hinders any level of reality. The case for the personal is also a case for freedom, for only when there is such a thing as a person and when it is the central locus of all human reality, is there such a thing as freedom at all. Bracketing out man, bracketing out ethics, does not increase freedom, but tears it from its roots. Therefore the notion of God is not an opposite of human freedom, but its presupposition and its basis. We no longer say enough about man, about his dignity and his rights, if we banish speech about God as unscientific from our language of thought into an area of the subjective and the edifying. Language about God belongs in language about man, and it therefore also belongs in a university. It is no accident that the phenomenon of a university arose where each day the sentence sounded out: In the beginning was the *Logos*—meaning, reason, the intelligent word. The *Logos* brought forth *logos,* and gave it space. Only under the presupposition of the basic, original and internal intelligibility of the world, and its origin from intelligence, could human intelligence engage in questioning the intelligibility of the world in detail and as a whole. But where intelligibility is accepted only in the details, but in the overall and as basis is denied, the university dissolves into juxtaposed individual disciplines. It follows very quickly from this that for the entire life and activity of mankind reason, intelligence, is valid only for partial areas of our existence, but that reality as a whole is unreasonable. The consequences are evident. Thus it is a false impasse if one, in the name of progress and freedom declares the law of power, of success, of ability to make, the only law of science, and in its name then wishes to fend off a supposed tendency to make nature taboo. In place of such false alternatives a new synthesis of science and wisdom must step forward, in which questions about details do not suppress the view of the whole, and the concern for the whole does not undo carefulness about detail. This new synthesis is the great intellectual challenge that stands before us today. It will decide whether there will be a human future, a future worthy of man, or whether we are heading for chaos and the self-destruction of man and of creation.— *Translated by Thomas A. Caldwell, S. J.*

NOTES

1. Jacques Monod, *Chance and Necessity: An Essay on the Natural Philosophy of Modern Biology* (New York, 1971), p. 13.

2. Ibid., pp. 14f. and especially, chap. 6, "Invariance and Perturbations," pp. 99–117.

3. J. Léjeune, "Intervention au Synode des Evèques," printed in *Résurrection,* Nouvelle Série 14 (1988), pp. 15–12; citation p. 16. Cf. also the informative article of A. Lizotte, "Réflexions philosophiques sur l'âme et al personne de l'embryon," in *Anthropotes* 3, no. 2 (1987): 155–95.

4. Cf. *On the Inviolability of Human Life. On Ethical Questions of Biomedicine,* Instruction of the Congregation for the Doctrine of the Faith, published with a commentary by R. Spaemann (Freiburg, 1987). From the extensive literature on the question, note: M. Schooyans, *Maîtrise de la vie, domination des hommes* (Paris/Namur, 1986); R. Löw, *Leben aus dem Labor. Gentechnologie und Verantwortung: Biologie und Moral* (Munich, 1985); D. Tettamanzi, *Bambini fabbricati. Fertilizzazione in vitro, embryo transfer* (Casale Monferrato, 1985); R. Flöhl, ed., *Genforschung: Fluch oder Segen? Interdisziplinäre Stellungnahmen* (Munich, 1985).

5. Cf. K. Schubert, "Golem," in *Lexikon für Theologie und Kirche* IV, p. 1046 (bibliogr.).

6. Cf. G. Thielcke, *Der evangelische Glaube. Grundzüge der Dogmatik* I (Tübingen, 1968), pp. 328–31; G. Scholem, *On the Kabbalah and its Symbolism* (New York, 1965).

7. A. Huxley, *Brave New World* and *Brave New World Revisited* (London, 1984).

8. "Pyrrhonic aesthete" in the Forward of 1946, p. 6; "insanity . . . and lunacy." ibid.

9. Ibid. See especially the Foreword and the chapter, "Education for Freedom," pp. 361–73.

10. Gregory of Nyssa, *Second Homily on Genesis 1:26, PG* 44: 277ff.

11. Claus Westermann, *Genesis,* I, Chapters 1–11 (Neukirchen, 1974), p. 318. [The English edition is a condensation—Trans.]

12. Gerhard von Rad, *Genesis, A Commentary* (Philadelphia, 1961), p. 100.

13. Westermann, *Genesis,* p. 393. Valuable clarifications can be found in the extensive article "jada" by J. Bergmann and G. J. Botterweck in *Theologisches Wörterbuch zum Alten Testament,* ed. Botterweck-Ringgren, vol. 3 (1982), pp. 479–512.

14. Westermann, *Genesis,* p. 395.

15. R. Spaeman refers to this in the commentary in *On the Inviolability of Human Life,* p. 81.

16. Current positions under discussion concerning dealings with humans can be seen, e.g., in S. Z. Leiman, "Therapeutic Homicide" in *Journal of Medicine and Philos-*

ophy 8 (1983): 257–67; see also: R. Löw, "Die moralische Dimension von Organtransplantationen" in *Scheidewege* 17 (1987/88): 16–48.

17. *Summa theologiae* I, q. 38, a.2, Response.